CRONIES

CRONIES

A BURLESQUE

Adventures with
KEN KESEY, NEAL CASSADY,
THE MERRY PRANKSTERS,
and **THE GRATEFUL DEAD**

KEN BABBS

TSUNAMI PRESS
EUGENE, OREGON

CRONIES is a work of creative nonfiction. The events described in this book represent the recollections of the author as he experienced them. Dialogue is not intended to represent a word-for-word transcription, but it reflects the author's memory and fairly reconstructs the meaning and substance of what was said.

Some of the material in this book was previously published in *We Were Arrested*, a chapbook published by Tsunami Books Press.

Published by Tsunami Press
2585 Willamette Street
Eugene, Oregon 97405

www.tsunamibooks.org

Cover photo, copyright by John Bauguess. Used by kind permission of his estate.

Lines of Grateful Dead lyrics, copyright by Ice Nine Publishing Company. Used by permission of Warner Chappell.

Excerpt from *Hey Rube*, copyright by Hunter S. Thompson. Used by permission of his literary executor, Douglas Brinkley.

Lines from "Manifesto: The Mad Farmer Liberation Front," copyright by Wendell Berry. Used by gracious permission of its author.

ISBN 978-0-9894462-9-7 (hardcover)
ISBN 978-0-9894462-8-0 (ebook)

Library of Congress Control Number: 2021915332

Book design by S. G. Ellerhoff

Printed in the United States of America

10 9 8 7 6 5 4 3 2
Second printing before publication

For the Keseys, the Pranksters and friends.
Long may you endure.

BURLESQUE — an historical accounting with additions, exaggerations, embellishments and inventions. See *Diedrich Knickerbocker's History of New York City*, by Washington Irving.

"It's the truth, even if it didn't happen."
 — Chief Bromden Stamper in the great American novel,
  Sometimes a Great Cuckoo

"If you can remember it, then you weren't there."
 — Timothy Leary

"We don't need facts, we need stories."
 — Ken Kesey

PROLOGUE

In 1953, when two high school senior boys were graduating two thousand miles apart, a craggy-faced, black-haired, casually dressed man was being shown into the conference room of New York literary agent Sterling Lord's office. The man carried a cylindrical package wrapped in butcher paper.

He walked to the far end of the table and sat down. He rose to his feet when Sterling entered the room, pulled a roll of teletype paper out of the cylinder and said, "Here's the book."

He gave the roll a push. It unrolled the length of the long executive table, onto the floor, over the top of Sterling Lord's shined shoes, out the door, down the hall, past secretaries, typists, editors peering out of offices with hands over their mouths, *what hath God wrought?*

A literary bombshell, a fusion of jazz and free-form writing which combined real-life experiences with made-up embellishments that blew the lid off staid, ordinary prose.

Four years later, as the two younger men were graduating from college—and still separated from one another by two thousand miles—the roll, now known as the Scroll, was published. The book was *On the Road* and its author was Jack Kerouac, fictionalized in the book as Sal Paradise. His soul brother and fellow protagonist was Neal Cassady, aka Dean Moriarty.

The two younger men, one from Oregon, the other from Ohio, were Ken Kesey—a great author in his own write, and bigger-than-life protagonist of his own myth—and Ken Babbs, best friend and second lead in their almost-huge hit movie, *Intrepid Traveler and His Merry Band of Pranksters Look for a Kool Place.*

When I was a little kid my brother Chuck and I
explored a ditch and found an old accordion. We
took it apart and hidden amongst the valves and
bellows we found a piece of paper that said,
WHAT THE HELL ARE YOU LOOKING IN HERE FOR,
DAISY MAE?
— Ken Kesey

1

A Culmination of Peculiar Circumstances

A jaybird yacketed in the branches of an oak tree. The late sun lit up the deck of a sprawling single-story house. Centered in the light, a man stood erect, balanced, hands at his side, slight smile on his lips, balding head a golden dome. His glinting blue eyes drew me to him like metal filings to a magnet. We sized one another up. He was five-ten, 190 pounds, a compact frame, thick forearms and a wrestler's body. He didn't slouch, his hands weren't in his pockets, his arms weren't crossed in front of his chest, and he wasn't leaning against the railing.

In contrast: my lanky, six-foot-two, basketball-player's 190-pound frame topped by dark hair, green-flecked eyes and a five-o'clock shadow.

He stuck out his hand. Neither of us smashed the other's in a bone-crushing grip. A good start.

"Ken Babbs?" he said. "I've heard of you. Aren't you the guy who was up in the city on Blabbermouth Night at the Place, railing at the audience, telling them to get a bath, get a haircut, shave their armpits, wear decent clothes, get a job, get a car, get a house, take on big debt and start participating in the American

Way of Life?"

"Come on," I said. "I was just kidding."

"Then why did they boo you off the stage and throw you out the door?"

"They didn't know it was satire. And aren't you the guy who's already written a novel before the writing class has even started, all about the denizens of Grant Street who don't give a shit about making money?"

"That book's over and done with and I don't ever want it published. I thought about some author who told his family and heirs he didn't want them published, and what happened? It wasn't ten years after he was dead than those books were on the market, garnishing big bucks."

"Interesting notion. Let's get a drink."

We touched glasses.

"You seem to have a handle on this writing thing right from the get-go," I said.

"Yeah, a culmination of the peculiar circumstances that began with my birth, a Depression baby born in the dust bowl of Colorado. My mother jammed towels and rags under the doors and in the edges of windows, and left the plates upside down on the table until it was time to eat, but it didn't do any good. The dust was everywhere, even in the hospital room where my birth dragged out way too long.

"'Forceps,' the doctor ordered.

"'No, Doctor, not the forceps,' the nurses cried.

"'Yes, time is of the essence.'

"He checked his watch.

"'I have a golf date in an hour.'

"When he yanked me out, I was so ugly the doctor slapped my mother. She had to shape my head with her hands every day, until she got it straightened out."

"Nice to know you became a healthy kid."

"Not entirely. When I was a little feller, I rolled on the floor in a fit. I frothed at the mouth and my eyes rolled back in my head and I began gibbering."

Kesey's eyes got big, he raised his splayed hands, widened his nostrils, his face broke out in a sheen and he began speaking in a high, thrumbling voice: "*Fire,* and he used words and shadows and monsters and poetry and music, robes and masks and dance and drums; beautiful were the maidens, powerful and manly the knights, but the heckler stoppered the smoke-filled bottle, a sighing admission of wisdom: the shaman was right on."

He grinned and dropped his hands.

"Didn't impress my parents much. When the neighbors heard about it, they nodded knowingly. '*Teched,*' they said and they didn't mean in the divine sense of *touched by God,* but in the mortal sense of *being loony.* Turned out there was a medical reason. I was mildly epileptic, but pills cured me and now I'm strictly normal."

"It's important to keep up appearances. As for me, I was flying high, riding the kindergarten playground swing, a bigger kid pushing me."

My hand described the swoop of the swing.

"When I went over backwards, in free-fall ecstasy, the back of my head smashed onto a rock, sent my eyeballs spinning, stars and bars flashing 'Stars-and-Stripes-Forever'—and when I opened my eyes, everyone was staring at me, wanting to know, *you okay?* And all I could say was, 'I had a title once but the king banned T-shirts in the hall, hooray for soldier toys, and let's bomb them for Christ's sake, never say you are throwing like a girl in the den of commerce.' I've still got the flat spot on the back of my head. Want to feel it?"

"I'll pass. You know where that name, *Ken,* comes from? Old Celtic word; means, 'to know,' like in the song, 'Do ye ken John Peel?'"

"'With his coat so grey.'"

"The very same. And what does a man know most about himself?"

"His name."

"No. His nuts. So when someone says to you, 'Ken, you're nuts,' he's not talking about your head, he's talking about your balls."

"Ha ha, very clever. I'll write that down."

Kesey gulped down his drink, set the glass on the rail and we headed across the deck into the party being thrown by Wallace Stegner, the Western fiction writer who headed the Stanford Graduate Writing Program. It was a chance for the members of the class to meet one another before school began.

That note. The note that sprung from the frail-looking blind man. The note that screamed, "I live to play, I live to do this music." I live, and we all live, to breathe our own special note into this world."
— *Ken Kesey*

2

No One Knew
What to Make of That

Kesey played football in high school, a guard in the line. His team was the Springfield Millers, their archrivals the Eugene Axemen. Springfield was losing to Eugene in the final minute, by a single point; seventy yards away from a touchdown but they had the ball. Their coach, a World-War-Two grizzled groot, called the plays, every one a line plunge, to the left or to the right. When he called for the usual line plunge, Kesey said in the huddle, "Wait a minute. That's not going to work. They know what we're doing every time. Let's fake the line plunge and throw a pass."

The players were shocked shitless. "Are you kidding, the coach will kill us."

"There's worse things than dying," Kesey said.

"Like what?"

"Losing to Eugene High School."

The coach leaned over, hands on knees—*that's it, line plunge, wha?* He straightened up, alarmed—*what the fuck you doing, a pass? You goddamn...* TOUCHDOWN! He jumped in the air, both hands over his head—*way to go, way to go!* Next year Kesey called all the plays in the huddle.

Kesey was also into dramatics. At play practice he looked up at the top of a ladder and saw a girl painting the backdrop. She smiled down at him and they became friends. His future wife, Faye.

He was an amateur magician and a ventriloquist, had a little dummy named Blinky, performing between features at the Saturday afternoon movies at the McDonald Theatre in downtown Eugene. His dad was manager of the Darigold creamery, and ran contests on the milk cartons. You tore off the side of the carton, filled out the answers and sent it in. On Saturdays Kesey awarded the prizes, having Blinky doing the talking. When the winner came onstage, Kesey pulled a half dollar out of the kid's ear, then made the coin vanish, only to find it again in his other ear.

He played on the freshman football team at the University of Oregon, but the coach told him he was too small for college ball. Instead, he wrestled, winning a Pac-8 Championship, until he tore his shoulder and had to give up the sport.

He joined Beta Theta Pi fraternity. Kesey and his frat brother, Boyd Harris, put a gigantic slingshot on the back of Boyd's jeep and drove around campus firing water balloons. They spotted ROTC cadets marching on the infield of the track and let fly.

"Fix bayonets!" the cadet commander ordered. They charged the jeep. Boyd ripped around the corner and headed down Sorority Row where the girls, standing in rows on the porches, were singing. The jeep had blundered into the annual Best Sorority Song Contest.

"We are the best," the girls were belting from the porch. "We are the best. Those Tri Delt floozies act like doozies when they're all total loozies and their boyfriends are all dumb boozies."

Kesey let fly, *blap*, right into the middle of the first row. The girls shrieked, hairdos awry and blouses clinging to their chests, when, from behind the jeep, came the fast-clopping of hard-soled boots—cadets with bayonets to the fore.

"Pedal to the metal," Kesey shouted.

The jeep careened around a corner and down an alley. They beat it back to the fraternity and hid the jeep in the garage.

Kesey told me he had an awakening when he was at the U of O. "A flash," he said. "My short story teacher was J.B. Hall, a real controversial character because the man wore white shoes. He pointed out to me a part in a Hemingway story called 'Soldier's Home,' in which this guy Krebs has come home from the war and is sitting at the breakfast table wondering what to do with the day. Whether to watch his sister play indoor baseball or just exactly what. His mother wants him to get a job: 'God has some work for everyone to do.' She gets on her knees. 'I pray for you all day long.'

"Krebs looks at the bacon fat hardening on his plate.'

"And J.B. Hall says, 'See, there's where it happens; right there.' And I saw it. A door opened up to me and it's never been closed. I thank this man from the bottom of my heart. It's a turn-on and has nothing to do with intelligence. It has to do with somebody grabbing you and saying, 'I know something that's good. I'll give it to you for nothing. You'll have it all your life.'"

Kesey wasn't an English major. He was a Performing Arts major. For his graduation recital he did a Lord Buckley bit.

I had one of his records. A Chicago-based hipster stand-up comedian, dressed to the nines, Buckley looked like some guy from London dappery, but was born in California's Sierra Nevada mountains. He did long monologues using a deep voice and hip jargon.

The bit Kesey did for his recital was the one where Nero and his bevy of beautiful chicks are bopping over to the Colosseum to catch the rumble between the Christians and the Lions. They stroll down the steps to their seats in the front row just as a wide-eyed Christian cat comes scuffling lickety-split across the dirt, raising a bodacious cloud of dust; out of the cloud right behind him, a flowing-maned, jaw-gaping lion bolts straight to the wall where the Christian cat makes a leap and grabs the rail in front of Nero, watching with imperious majesty as the hand slips and the Christian slides into oblivion.

Nero rises to his feet, the crowd hushing. He looks regally around, then slaps the railing.

"Mark a golden spike where that cat blew."

"No one knew what to make of that," Kesey told me, "but they gave me a passing grade and I got my diploma."

The one thing obvious in watching and
taking part in social gatherings is that ninety
per cent of what anyone says is just to convince
others not to be suspicious of his rap. Just seeing
if we can agree to agree.
— Ken Kesey

3

That Instant When He Is Confused

The real character in the graduate writing class at Stanford was Mitch Strucinksi, a Pole from Chicago with a weathered face and battered body. He wrote a frightening story about a hog that died. The farmer and his sons cut the hog into pieces and shoved the bloody hunks down an old dry well. It had great gory detail, a wonderful contrast to the normal highfalutin literary story.

Mitch was at Stanford on one of the prestigious writing program's Stegner Fellowships. He was an ex-con and had submitted his application from prison. Wallace Stegner took a chance, doing something to help out a man gone bad, but a man with promise, a man who could find a literary life, rise above the criminal element.

Kesey threw a party at his Perry Lane house in Menlo Park across the street from the Stanford Golf Course. The house was one of a group of cabins connected by winding paths and narrow driveways. He spent the night before and the morning of the party roasting a whole pig over an open fire.

I was at the gym playing basketball with some frat-rats and invited them to the party. When I arrived, Kesey was carving big hunks of meat and putting them on a platter. As fast as he filled the platter, hands grabbed the slices and added them to the piles of baked beans and salad on their paper plates.

At dark we moved inside, leaving what was left of the pig on what was left of the fire. The fraternity guys had shown up and they prowled the house in a pack, eyeballing everything. They stood in a bunch in the living room and Kesey overheard one of them say, "I hate the guy who asked us to this party. Let's trash the place."

Kesey jumped into the guy's face and said, "What are you talking about? This is *my* house. See that picture on the wall. That's my wife." In a swift wrestler takedown move, he grabbed the guy by his shirtfront, fell over backward, pulled the guy with him and slammed the frat-rat's face against the floor. Blood shot out of the guy's nose. The other frat-rats stepped forward. There was a crash of glass against the brick fireplace. Mitch Strucinski stepped in, holding a jagged-edged beer bottle. I grabbed a broom and stuck it in front of me like a lance.

Kesey was wearing a lumberjack outfit: black jeans, lace-up boots, striped logger's shirt and bright red suspenders. Mitch was in his usual dark slacks, Florsheim shoes and tweed sports coat. Me, in my mesh, see-through tank top, green Bermuda shorts, penny loafers without socks. We were an imposing trio. The three musketeers: Artist, Arnold and Pathetic. Before an all-out brawl, the guy on the floor staggered to his feet and went out the door, leaving a bloody trail. The others followed.

Kesey looked at me. "Just what did you think you were going to do with that?"

I looked at the broom.

"I was planning to discombobulate them long enough so you could throw one down and hold him on the floor while Mitch carved K K on his chest with that broken beer bottle."

Mitch chortled. Kesey shook his head. A startled look came on his face. He rushed to the open door.

"What the hell..."

A big mongrel dog ran past the house, dragging the pig into the night.

"Party's over, men," Kesey said. "Time to go home."

An intramural wrestling tournament was coming up. We both entered, but Kesey's name was stricken from the list because he had been a varsity letterman at Oregon, therefore ineligible for an intramural event.

In order to win the intramural championship by proxy, he coached me. When the brackets came out, we found our hopes dashed. I drew the number one seed: a big redhead, strong, quick and nimble, well-versed in all the moves. He was going to be a tough nut to grapple, let alone crack.

"You only have one chance," Kesey told me. "You'll have to take him in the first few seconds."

Easily said, but Kesey had a plan: The Telephone Takedown.

"Soon as the ref blows the whistle and you square off, you go *Brrrinnnngggg*, like a telephone ringing. Stick out your hand, hold it a sec and say, 'I have to take this call.' With your other hand you hold an imaginary phone to your ear and in that instant when he is confused you dive for his ankles, pull him off his feet, pounce on his chest and pin him."

"Yeah, right."

"No, you can do it," he said, and we practiced the maneuver.

I was also playing in the intramural basketball league for the English department team. Just after a tough game, when I was wheezing, drying off, Kesey came running in and said, "Come on, what are you doing, your wrestling match is in five minutes."

"Forget it," I said, "I'm too beat."

"Here, take this." He handed me a white pill with an X etched on one side.

I eyed it warily. "What's that?"

"It's an energy boost. It will get you through the match."

What the hell.

I faced off against the redhead. The ref blew his whistle. I did the telephone fakeout, the redhead hesitated, I dived for his ankles. He stepped back, shoved my head into the mat, flipped me over, and pinned me. Two seconds flat.

Kesey leaned over me. "Good try," he said. I didn't move. "What's the matter?"

I turned my head and spit out a chunk of tooth. "Motherfucker broke my tooth. Thanks a lot."

I was pretty surly but the crosstop was kicking in, and that, plus a painkiller and a few pitchers of beer, elevated my mood considerably. We spent the night listening to classical music on my record player: Richard Strauss's *Till Eulenspiegel's Merry Pranks*. We were too wired to sleep so we lay on the floor and let the music sweep over us as we envisioned Till's prank, the one that had top rank: speaking of a smell that stank up Lady Stuckup's shank to her dark dank, after Till plugged up the sewer pipe and milady, holding her nose, took flight, her bedclothes all aflutter, exposing her ample derriere; my, how Eulenspeigel did howl at the sight, then gave the lady a deep bow and strode off, proud to have pranked the stuck-up sow. Kesey and I rolled on the floor cracking up over our imagined medieval lore.

Ever see the birdie trilling in the tree?
She's got a song that always thrills me,
But she never shuts up and there's the rub
When I'm taking a bath, I sink my head in the tub.
  — Donovan

4

The Beneficial Effects
of Chaos Theory

W hen they were in high school, Kesey and his brother
Chuck would drive to Eastern Oregon with their dad,
hunting or going to the Pendleton Roundup. They often stopped
at Celilo Falls on the Columbia River. The mile-wide river narrowed to 140 feet at Celilo Falls and dropped precipitously over
large round rocks.

Indians stood on shaky wooden platforms and speared salmon as the fish leaped from the water. Sometimes, fishermen
flinging their spears in the bad weather were swept off the slip-
pery platforms. In 1930, the Bureau of Indian Affairs required
the fishermen to tie themselves to the platforms or to the shore.

Wooden racks on the riverbank held rows of cleaned and
gutted salmon, being preserved by the sun for winter food.
Tribes from the Pacific Northwest came to Celilo Falls, as they
had for thousands of years; the river, the fish, the sun, the season of plenty providing for the season of want. A tradition soon
to be dammed by the demand for electricity.

In 1952, Kesey's junior year in high school, construction
began. Five years later, when Kesey was a senior in college, he
drove to Celilo Falls, parked on the side of the road and joined

the crowd gathered on the riverbank. Drums pounded and chanting filled the air. Kesey brought a gallon of burgundy wine and passed it around. He was pretty well lit when the lower falls went under water, then the middle falls, and finally the fishing platforms and the rocks of the upper falls. Everything under water. A howl rose from the people. Kesey saw salmon flashing past below the surface. Suddenly, a bare-chested Indian man, long black hair flinging beads of water, rose out of the river and raced past Kesey onto the open road, where a fully-loaded cement truck swallowed him in its massive grille.

Kesey ran to look. Nothing there, not even a wet spot on the pavement. Kesey flung the wine bottle into the bushes.

T he draft was still on, a leftover from World War Two. Everyone aged eighteen had to sign up. I decided if I was going in, I was going in as an officer. I was awarded an NROTC scholarship that paid my tuition and books, plus fifty dollars a month spending money. Since Kesey had screwed up his shoulder wrestling at the University of Oregon, he received a 4F deferment and never went into the military.

At the end of our year at Stanford, in May 1959, I received my commission in the Marine Corps and spent a year at the Officer's Basic School in Quantico, Virginia, learning the rudiments of pooping and snooping.

Kesey stayed at Stanford another year. His Perry Lane neighbor and friend, future psychologist Vik Lovell, turned him on to a job at the Menlo Park VA Mental Hospital, testing certain chemicals to see what would work on soldiers to make them better at the war game: steroids of the mind.

Eight o'clock every Tuesday morning, the doctor gave Kesey pills or a shot in the arm or a glass of bitter juice, went out and came back later, asked Kesey how he felt, took his blood pressure and temperature, asked him a bunch of questions, then left him alone. Occasionally a nurse peered in, to see how he was doing. Sometimes the pill was a placebo, other times he experienced mild euphoria or stimulation; every once in a while, it was a wowsy-dowsy, all-out, fly-you-clear-to-the-moon-and-throw-away-the-wings, mind-blowing high. Kesey and the other subjects compared notes and came up with a plan: *When they give us the good stuff, we'll pretend nothing is happening. They'll cut us loose and we'll be out on the streets happy and high.*

Six months after completing the drug experiments, Kesey was hired as an aide at the VA Hospital, working on the same ward where the experiments took place.

Once, drunk on smuggled-in vodka and orange juice, Kesey was working the night shift. He was too sleepy, tired, funked and sapped to do anything but get through his shift, looking through a little window into the room at the people who were the regular patients, not students going through experiments. They had serious problems, he realized. People hallucinating, people in bad shape. *Being crazy is painful,* he thought, *crazy is hell whether from taking a drug or trying to lead the normal American way of life. It's hell and there's nothing fun about it.* He felt like he was seeing it through a lens, but it was hard on the eyes.

The vodka smooths the edges. *What's this?* Some guy shuffles into the room where he's sitting. *A manic depressive up outta bed,* Kesey thinks, *musta just come in from washing his rectum in the can, using the dust mop no doubt.* Wants to know if he can please mop something. *Fine.* Kesey puts him to work mopping the floor.

Kesey's eyes drift to the door of the doctor's office, the same doctor who gave him the experimental pills. He fingers the ring of keys on his belt, moves to the door. One of the keys opens the lock. He walks across the room, opens a desk drawer, surveys the bottles inside. His eyes widen, his mouth opens in a soundless laugh. He takes out a bottle, his hair sticks out, his ears flap forward, his aura smashes against the ceiling, bounces around the room and paints the walls red, orange and green in psychedelic hues.

He pockets the bottle, closes the drawer, leaves the room, locks the door, goes back to his station. The old guy *slop-slops* with the mop. Kesey, wide awake, stone sober, aura back into its calm halo, counts the minutes till the end of his shift, and out he goes, great God almighty, free at last. Two hundred hits of one-hundred-percent-pure Sandoz Laboratory LSD, stashed in his pocket.

Those first LSD highs were innocent fun, groups of six or seven at Kesey's, up all night, laughing and grooving, no mystical experience or time traveling or probing inner regions of the psyche. A group grope, nothing sex-driven, everyone fully-clothed, crawling over and climbing out from under one another in a mixed-up pile on the floor, unable to tell whose body was whose, even your own. Up, laughing and drinking wine, listen to and play along with and sing to music on the record player; sit yakking, take a downer, stagger off to bed.

Powerful medicine, not to be taken lightly. We came from solid homes, backgrounds that gave us reliable launching pads to blast off from on our psychedelic trips. We had benchmarks, touchstones. No matter how far out we went, we had something solid to come back to. We were astronauts of inner space and, like astronauts, had to be in good shape for the trips—physically, spiritually, mentally, even morally.

Kesey was working another night shift. The peyote tea he drank before he left home tied his stomach in knots. He sat at the window and watched the patients prowling, scratching and muttering, leaning catatonic against the wall. Kesey squeezed his gut to stop the churning. A bolt of blue light shot into his eyes. A man stood on the other side of the window and looked in. He had a broad face, a flat nose and long black hair.

Thick-muscled and bare-chested. His face shimmered and his hair radiated in concentric waves. He opened his mouth and words came out circled by colored bubbles: *FOG FINS CARDS BOAT BROOM.* The bubbles popped and the words fragmented. The man's eyes widened and salmon swam in the viscous orbs. Water shot from his ears and rose up the window, to his chest, over his head. He turned and swam away, the sinuous movement of a salmon, tail whipping back and forth, then he vanished, just like on the road at Celilo Falls.

Kesey grabbed his notebook and pen and began writing: "They're out there. Black boys in white suits up before me to commit sex acts in the hall and get it mopped up before I can catch them..."

Two days later, Kesey was on duty in the dayroom. The patients hung out, played cards, watched TV, read books, sat and stared at the blank spot that obstructed their minds. Kesey looked out the window at the lush lawn stretching from the building. Blades of grass rippled in the wind. A bell clanged and a large, metal overhead door opened. A gaggle of patients rushed out, each one pushing a lawn mower. They fanned across the grass, wheeling and turning in circles, heading straight to the fence and careening off, crisscrossing one another, never stopping for a second, some tearing along like mad, others plodding. It made Kesey dizzy. They went at it for an hour, until the bell rang. They headed for the door, disappeared inside and the door clanked shut.

Kesey looked at the lawn, ran his gaze from the building to the fence, around the perimeter, across the entire expanse and saw that every single blade of grass had been cut. It was the first time that he gained an appreciation of the beneficial effects of chaos theory.

The Saturday afternoon Perry Lane croquet tournament was in full swing. The course started in the front yard, crossed the driveway, went down the side of the house and across the deck in back. The washing machine and dryer were on the deck and the washer was running a load. The washer was out of balance and the machine jumped and hopped around. The croquet players had to judge when to whack the ball to get it through the machine's gyrations as it lurched from side to side. Then they played through the backyard, into the yard next door, and circled back around to Kesey's front yard.

Miles Davis's song "Out of the Blue" blared over the speakers. The thwack of the croquet balls was a rhythmic counterpoint while the laughs and comments of the players trilled amongst the noise. A car roared up the lane and turned into Kesey's drive. It skidded to a stop just as a croquet ball zoomed past the grille. The driver hopped out.

"Made it in the nick. I could hear the back bearings going but luckily had my bearings from the directions they gave me at Kepler's."

He loosened a pack of Camels from the sleeve of his T-shirt and shook out a cigarette, his head moving from side to side, craggy face acknowledging the croquet players with a raise of eyebrows and quick grin. He lit the Camel and took a big drag. Kesey's dachshunds yipped around his ankles.

Neal Cassady had arrived on the lane. Recently out of prison, he had swung by to meet Kesey. After they shook hands, Cassady said, "I was at a party over in Oakland and needed a ride to my brakeman's job on the railroad and announced I'd give two joints to anyone who could help me out. Two dapper gents obliged, only to find out they weren't such gents at all, for when I got out of the car and thanked them for the ride, they asked for the joints. I most happily complied, then they announced, 'You are under arrest.' Two years for two joints in Quentin, but no sniveling, as you well know, even though it cost me my job on the railroad and a divorce ensued while I was incapacitated or incarcerated, however you spell it; what it amounts to is I need to borrow some tools, inasmuch as the rear end of my Jeepster has succumbed to what appears to be a lack of the greasiations..."

When Kesey produced the tools, Cassady disappeared under the back end of the Jeepster. Everyone knew who Cassady was: Jack Kerouac's best friend and his fictional partner in *On the Road*, as well as a prominent character in other works of fiction, poetry and prose. They didn't get a chance to have a conversation with him though. He was under the car, talking all the time, the croquet players pausing occasionally to listen.

"We're fourth-dimensional beings inhabiting a three-dimensional body living in a two-dimensional world, black and white, good and evil, with a touch of grey ... our fingers, ya know, are ... the claw, and as for me ... three inches the bigger thumb ... lost the tip of the other one, took a swing at Looo Ann and hit the wall instead, osteomyelitis set in and Doctor Butcher had to amputate the tip; the bandage hid my thumb and gave me a chance to reveal my Greek torso ... the only writing I ever did was a laudatory letter ... but on marijuana, *oooooooooh* ..."

"Are you alright under there, Mr. Cassady?" someone asked.

"I'm having these insights you see ... I knew I should've worn more paisley ... I'm serious about America ... speed or endurance. Six days it was. Finally she grabbed the Vick's Vapo Rub instead of the Vaseline and that was what ended it. The only three-way I ever had. Kerouac's not queer and he was always looking for a willing cohort ... Keroassady ... he found her in Bedford-Stuyvesant. There wasn't nothin' he wouldn't do for me and nothin' I wouldn't do for him, so we sat around all the time doing nothin'. Don't eat when you're angry. Who was ever happy angry? I played short-short ... outfield, no glove ... I learned an illegal pitch and caught Satch Paige barehanded after the 303-pound guard had done me in 'cause the coach thought

I was chicken. *Why bother* was my vein. But see here, Hard Dick. My medical secretary works for Stiff Dr. Peck ... on the left he wears these rings. A sensitive, we're all sensitives ... President Cleveland had certain proclivities, and canines may have been one ... remarkable your dog has kept it a secret all these years. I'm gone, not to reappear until lamentations from the Holy See are no longer sought, all for naught."

And more of the same, *all day long*. Clunk of mallets hitting balls, screeches of triumphant scores, Pretzels the dachshund poking her nose in to check on his progress. Cassady not emerging until dark, when he wiped his hands with a rag, put it on the ground, laid Kesey's tools neatly on top, then drove off, not to be seen again until that fateful day in June 1964.

She was mad,
mad as a madwoman
scattering her manure.
He was riding a wave
that rolled in
like a tsunami.
She ate his egg roll
and called him
a baby doll.
A turn in the barrel
is part of the job.
It's the revolution test
with better Kool-Aid
than all the rest.
  — Ken Babbs

5

Snuffling Like a Vacuum

When I was in the Marine Corps, stationed in Santa Ana, California, I flew the chopper up to Moffett Field near San Jose to visit Kesey on Perry Lane. I took a cab to his house and when I got there, Kesey and Faye were leaving to go see Jane Burton. A pal from the first days we were at Stanford grad school, Jane had since moved and resettled in Oakland. She invited the Keseys over for dinner, for it was her birthday and an opportunity to meet her new boyfriend.

Jane was tall, and she was from Texas, so she was Texas-tall, and had a mind to match. Philosophy was her major and she loved to ask philosophical questions, usually involving numbers. I was never good with word problems in school—like, if two trains leave Chicago and New York at the same time and one is traveling 38 mph and the other 63 mph, what time will they get to Cleveland? I could never solve Jane's problems either—like, how many pounds of coconuts dropped from a tree by a monkey would it take to tip over a basket of clothes carried on the head of a woman walking beneath the tree if the clothes weigh twelve pounds and each coconut weighs a pound and a half? Forget it.

Kesey told me to come to Jane's house with them. He held a scruffy dog in his arms.

"What's this?" I asked.

"A present for Jane. He's homeless, been hanging around the lane for weeks. Ain't he cute?"

Curly coat like an unsheared sheep, pointy ears with raggedy tips, dark, beady eyes, toenails broken, stub of a tail.

"Hi there, Scruffy." I reached out to pet him.

He bristled, laid his ears back, showed his yellow teeth and gave me a low growl.

"His name's Fluffy," Kesey said. "Don't insult him. He's a sensitive dog."

"Good boy, *Fluffy*," I said, emphasizing the *fluff*.

His eyes brightened, his ears pricked forward, he stuck out his tongue and panted happily, stub of a tail wagging.

"See, it's all in the name," Kesey said.

"A dog by any other name would piss as sweet," I said.

We piled into the car and headed for Oakland.

Jane was glum when she met us at the door. The house was tidy and neat, the table lit and spread with candles. Flowery painted plates set for four. She wasn't expecting me, but as it turned out she didn't need to set another place.

Breaking into tears, she gave us the bad news. Her boyfriend hadn't shown up. He was supposed to be there an hour ago for pre-dinner wine. The bottle sat open on the coffee table in front of the couch, two empty glasses waiting.

"Oh hell," she said. "We might as well drink it. He's not coming."

She went to get two more glasses. Kesey set the dog down and Fluffy ran around the room, sniffing everything. We quickly emptied the wine, then sat down at the table. Jane carved roast beef into tough chunks, served up mashed potatoes and green beans, all cold. Kesey and I tried to initiate a lively conversation but we couldn't cut through the gloom.

"When things look the darkest, there's always something to light the way," Kesey said.

He reached into his pocket and pulled out two thin marijuana joints.

"Pot," Jane exclaimed. "You've got pot? Oh boy, just what the doctor ordered. Light that fucker up."

This was a new one on me. My LSD cherry had already been popped, but acid wasn't against the law. Mary Jane could put you in jail. Furtherest thing from Jane Burton's mind. She took a big hit, held it, let it out her nose and sucked it back into her mouth. Grinning wickedly, she held it to me.

"Don't be such an uptight Marine," she said. "There ain't nobody here but us chickens."

I took a big puff, sucked it in, and all hell broke loose. Smoke alarms screamed, I couldn't breathe. I coughed so hard I thought my esophagus would blow out my mouth. Kesey whacked me on the back and poured a glass of water over my head. I tilted back to let the water quench the burning fire.

"Easy does it," Kesey said. "Start slow, little bit at a time till you get used to it."

The joint went around. Faye declined. She'd drive home. I was able to keep the smoke down, but I didn't notice anything happening, although Kesey and Jane were having a good time laughing and talking. Seemed to me the whole thing wasn't what it was talked up to be. Except for the coughing fit, I didn't feel any effects. After we finished the second joint it was time to head home.

We left Jane in a good mood. The table looked like a band of raging Mongols had ridden across on their horses. I stumbled over the empty wine bottle. Fluffy scarfed up every scrap he could find, first standing on a chair, his front paws on the table, then down on the floor, snuffling like a vacuum. Now he lay sprawled on the couch, belly extended like an old uncle satiated from a Thanksgiving feast. We left him there. A birthday present for Jane.

Kesey and I fell into the back seat, Faye at the wheel. We wound through Oakland and climbed onto the Bay Bridge. The radio was playing. Kesey said, "Turn it up."

The music boomed in my ears. The lights of Oakland grew from pinpoints to large beacons that blistered my eyeballs. Cars tore past.

"Slow down," I yelled at Faye. "You're going way too fast, you'll get us all killed."

Kesey laughed. "Yeah," he said, "what do you think, we're on a raceway to the Lane?"

"I'm only going forty-five," Faye said in a calm voice.

Kesey and I cracked up, rolled around on the seat and floor, slapped one another on the back.

"Here," I said, "have some Dentyne."

I tore a stick from a pack and handed it to him. I stuck a piece in my mouth. It exploded, tart-hot and sweet, shot up my nose—*wham-bang*—taste receptors sent telegrams of deliciousness to my brain.

I looked at Kesey. His eyes were big.

"We have to capitalize on this," he said. "The world needs to know."

The disc jockey on the radio was asking if anyone had anything interesting to pass on to his listeners, some pertinent or important piece of information. He was opening the phone line.

"Get that number," Kesey yelled.

Faye looked around at us, exasperated.

"Phone booth on the left," Kesey said. "Phone booth on the left!"

"Over there, over there," I answered.

Faye pulled over to the curb. Kesey and I leaped out and ran for the booth.

"The number, the number," I cried.

Kesey ran back to the car. Wrote on his hand with a pen. He hustled back, holding out his hand for me to read.

I popped in a dime and dialed.

"KBFR," the disc jockey said. "You're on the air. What you got?"

"Only the biggest thing to hit America since Pearl Harbor," I said.

"Except this is an explosion that will blow your mind, not your battleship," Kesey said, our mouths tight together against the phone.

"Lay it on me, cousins, I'm all ears."

"Dentyne chewing gum," we yelled, and broke into song:

"My Bonnie has tuberculosis.

My Bonnie has one rotten lung.

My Bonnie spits blood in a bucket

And pops in a stick of Dentyne gum."

There was a short pause. The disc jockey asked, "What have you two idiots been smoking?" and hung up.

Kesey and I grabbed one another.

"He dug it, he dug it, he double-dug it," Kesey said.

I yelled back, "And then he dug it some more."

Faye patiently drove us home. I stumbled to the guest room and collapsed on the bed. My shoes clunked on the floor and I stretched out in my clothes. Next thing I knew, Pretzels, Kesey's dachshund, was licking my face. *Get up get up sun is out let's play.*

Oh glorious drug now pulsing, permeating around
and thru my being—how are you called—dabs
of chemicals, relaxing and liberating my very being.
No matter that fools call it a spasmodic, muscle
tightening, frightening, contracting agent. Here I go
knowing that my now condition is to be alive in this
world, in the beginning, and at both ends.
  — Ken Kesey

6

Interrupted in the Berry Patch

I n 1961, after his second year in the Stanford Graduate School Writing Program, and with *One Flew Over the Cuckoo's Nest* under his belt, Kesey moved back to Oregon and rented a cabin at the coast, where he worked in isolation on *Sometimes a Great Notion.*

When he finished the book, Kesey rented a house on the Mc-Kenzie River in Springfield, Oregon. The house was a two-story affair with gabled upstairs windows and a porch that ran across the front. The backyard sloped down toward the river.

That summer I finished flight school at Pensacola, Florida, and had orders to report to a Marine helicopter squadron in Santa Ana, California. I took two weeks leave and, after visiting my parents in Ohio, drove with my brother John—I was the elder by fifty-three weeks—to Oregon, where we stopped and visited the Keseys.

"You want to take some IT-290?" Kesey asked us.

We'd never heard of it.

"Superbly mellow," he said. "You've got the perfect day for it, hot and sunny, and the river is calling."

J ohn and I stood in the river, cool, clear water swirling around our legs. An osprey glided overhead, hit the water with a splash, struggled, wings beating furiously, picked up enough speed to rise, a trout struggling in its talons.

A noise from behind brought us whirling around. Mike Hagen stood on the riverbank. He held up a watermelon. A brown, heavy-haired dog stood panting alongside. Long, floppy ears and gobs of drool. Big loving eyes.

"He's not mine," Mike said. "He followed me here."

Mike gave us the melon and left, shaking his head. *Leave these loonies to themselves, they can keep the dog.*

"No closer," I yelled. The slobbering beast sat and watched as we felt the melon all over, rubbed our faces on its smooth, cool surface, passing it back and forth.

"Time to get into this thing," I said and karate chopped it. A dull thump split the melon into two geysering pieces. Black seeds shot out like bullets. I squished a big chunk and squeezed it into pulp. John smashed his foot on the other half on the ground. He toed the red mass, then stepped in it, ecstasy to the extreme. He wiggled his toes in the goo spreading on his feet.

"What are you two sons of seacooks doing? You're supposed to be eating that melon, not desecrating it," Kesey said, walking toward us, an inner tube slung over his shoulder.

"This is a squishing melon, not an eating melon," John said.

"I can see that. Where'd you get the dog?"

"He just appeared, like the osprey," I said. "Want to join in?"

"Not now, time's a-wasting," Kesey said.

The sun beamed low in the western sky, casting shadows across the rocks and sand.

"I'm going to float down the river to the bridge," Kesey told us. "You guys tell Faye to come pick me up in the car."

Busily squishing, we nodded. The dog nodded too, drool flying.

"Remember, tell Faye to pick me up at the bridge," Kesey said, and walked down to the river, where he settled in the inner tube and floated away.

"Why does he keep repeating himself?" John said.

"Why are you asking me?"

"Who else am I supposed to ask?"

"Oh, forget it."

"That's just it, we're not supposed to forget it."

"Put it in your subconscious and we'll call it up when we need it."

The sun dipped behind the trees. We put on our pants and shirts and headed toward the house. A bright reflection near the tree line caught our eyes. We veered to it like a dog to a bone. The dog perked up. *Bone?*

The sun shone on a four-foot-diameter circular saw blade sitting in a wooden frame. The reflecting sun sparkled off our teeth shining in big shit-eating grins and off the drool hanging from the dog's mouth. A wooden handle turned the blade. I gave it a crank and started the blade turning, making a roar that rose in pitch and volume until it was singing like a choir in church. The dog raised his muzzle high to the sky and howled along. John whanged the saw with a rock and the blade rang like the bell in a steeple. John played the saw like a demented musician, composing and performing a symphony from—if you were in the vestry—*heaven*, or—if in the basement—*hell*.

A shirtless balding apparition dashed past and vanished in the bushes, darting in and out of my peripheral vision. I paid it no attention. Apparitions had been flashing past my peripheral vision all day.

The pickup truck that pulled up and shined its headlights on us wasn't an apparition, nor was the scowling man in a logger's striped shirt, suspenders, black pants and thick boots.

We let the saw slow to a crawl.

"Just what in the ever-loving, blue-eyed hell you two idiots think you're doing?" he asked, glowering like a bear interrupted in the berry patch.

"Uhhh," I stammered, "we were walking. Down along the river..."

"This is private property," he interrupted. "And Jesus fucking Christ, I could hear that racket all the way up to the house. Now skedaddle your asses on out of here and don't come back. And you, Brutus," he said to the dog who was slouching with a hang-dog look, shoulders hunched, muzzle close to the ground, drool a straight line, mouth to dirt, "you dumb fucker, what you doing consorting with these nincompoops? Get in the truck."

The dog slunk away and we did the same, back to the river path.

"Man, I'm beat," I said, as we walked along.

"Me too. Say did you happen to see Kesey back there?"

"I thought so. Damn, here he is again."

Kesey popped out from behind a bush. He breathed hard.

"I tried to warn you," he said, "but I couldn't outrun the damned truck."

"Hey, we found a great saw," John said. "We played it like a church organ."

"Sounded more like a freight train derailing. Everyone could hear it, all the way downtown probably. What happened? You were supposed to go back to the house and tell Faye to pick me up at the bridge."

"Absolutely," I said, "and we didn't forget. We were on our way. How did you get home so fast?"

"Fast? I waited at the bridge for two hours, then hitchhiked home. Come on, snap it up, Faye's got supper waiting."

What is this foolishness
we call fooling around
instead of God-fearing
legitimate money-making
moral-lifting endeavors
of a productive kind,
like wiping the condensation
from the windshield of memory?
He swipes the rag
across his forehead
and has a revelation.
He's got a screw loose.
He always has
but sometimes
it is looser
than other times
and this seems to be
one of those times.
    — Ken Babbs

7

On a Plummet to Hellsville

Kesey and Faye and Kesey's brother Chuck, and Chuck's wife Sue, and my brother John and I drove to Seattle to take in the 1962 World's Fair. A gamine of indeterminate age, anywhere from fifteen to thirty-five, had stopped by Chuck's creamery, when she heard we were going to the World's Fair, and said she had a place where we could stay.

The place was an old, beat-up, eight-story office building that had DANGER – BUILDING CONDEMNED – NO TRESPASSING signs plastered across the outside walls.

"She told me to go around back and there'd be a door open,"

Chuck said.

It opened into a dark hallway. Chuck had a flashlight and he led us down the hall to an elevator. The elevator was a cage, open on all sides, with a big metal dial and a handle you turned to the number of the floor you wanted. Chuck spun the handle to four. The elevator lurched and groaned, cables whined, and the cage started up, each floor bleak, dark, cavernous, trash in the halls. The elevator jolted to a stop. Chuck slid open the metal door and we walked out.

A big sheep dog with long floppy ears, hair hanging over its eyes, bushy tail flailing, rushed forward and stuck its nose into Chuck's crotch. Chuck jumped back. The dog barked and aimed for Kesey. Kesey dropped to one knee, took the dog's head in both hands and rubbed him briskly.

"That's a good dog, good dog."

A girl's voice called out: "Sit, Bluto." The dog plonked down.

She introduced herself. Chuck's friend, Periwinkle. Short, black hair tugged tight on her head. Bright green eyes. Black-and-white-striped, long-sleeved T-shirt. Black miniskirt over mesh panty hose. Red high-top sneakers. Bright smile and even brighter teeth. She led us down the hall.

"We've taken over this whole floor. The owners know but they don't mind; better us than destructive morons. Here's a room I've saved for you."

The room was huge and totally empty. Tall windows let in the light. We dropped our sleeping bags and flashlights and bags of food: yogurt and granola and trail mix.

"We're still working on patching in electricity from the pole outside, but we do have water, cold only," Periwinkle said. "The bathroom is down the hall. Unisex of course. We're all family here."

The dog bounded in and sniffed around the room. When Sue bent over to straighten her stuff, he homed in and hit the mark. She shrieked and jumped and, while still in the air, turned and whacked the dog with her shoulder bag. "Stop that!"

Bluto whimpered and slunk away.

The next morning, we ate psilocybin mushrooms and set out for the Fair to take a gawk at the Space Needle, ride to the top, sway in the wind, binocularize the city and fairgrounds, ride the Monorail, swoosh downtown and back, wandering the pavilions representing other countries.

I'm wearing my white cotton pants and white shirt and white sneakers and a white eyeshade, so official-looking no one notices when I jump on the front seat of an empty pedicab, a three-wheeled bicycle with a back seat big enough for two adults. Brother John plops down on the passenger seat and I pedal around the fairgrounds, pointing out places of interest.

"Off to the right there, a miniature Eiffel Tower atop the French Pavilion and, on our left, an exact replica of the Taj Mahal. Look out!"

I'm riding up the ass of a miniskirted woman—I swerve and brush her bare leg with the back wheel, skid to a stop, jump down, whip out my hanky and swipe at the black mark on her leg, assuring her, "The Fair will cover all damages. Can I give you a ride to the first aid tent?"

"Get away from me, you cretin," she says.

"Of course, ma'am, but here, take my number."

I pick up a scrap of paper, dig out my pen, write down the number that's painted on the side of the pedicab.

"Will you please hurry it up," my brother yells. "I'm paying by the hour."

"Yes sir, right away, sir."

I hop on the seat and pump fast as I can before the heat comes down—*whoops, didn't count on this incline*—can't keep up the pace, the pedicab is pushing me faster.

"Whoa up there!" John hollers.

We're on a plummet to Hellsville, skidding too fast, can't

swerve away from a brightly colored information tent, crash through the unmanned tent and smash it to the ground, maps and brochures flying in the air. The pedicab comes to a wet, sloppy stop in a small pond, where it sits immersed to the hubs.

My brother, wild-eyed and blurbering, helps me out of the wreck.

"Let's get out of here before we cause a scene," he says.

"Certainly can't have that. Give me a hand. No, not me. The pedicab. We can't leave the fucker there."

We pull the pedicab out of the water and park it next to the crumpled tent. Passersby give us a curious look but walk on, unalarmed, just some workers cleaning up the place. Come on, my brother implores. I hold up my hand.

"Check this out."

The bottom of the pond is covered with coins.

"This looks like a definite water hazard to me," I say. "Someone should clean this mess up."

John agrees, greedy glint in his eye. A worker nearby sweeps up trash with a broom and a long-handled dustpan.

"Say, can I borrow that for a minute?" I ask him. "A spot of dreck over here."

He gives it up and walks away, lighting a cigarette. I wade into the pool and start sweeping the coins into the pan. Pour the contents into John's T-shirt held in front of him. Pretty soon it's sagging to his knees.

"What the jumping Jesus, standing-in-the-water, shit-grinning-like-idiots are you two fools up to now?" Kesey yells from the edge of the pond.

"Jes' cleaning up this mess, boss," I answer.

"You better bail on that and get out of here. There's heat on the way."

At the top of the incline, I could see the green garb of security.

"This way," Kesey said.

We cut around a pavilion and up a ramp leading to a big domed building, John clutching his shirt with both hands. Slipped into a semi-dark theater, finding seats in the back. The lights dimmed and a star show brightened the top of the dome.

We sat back and roamed through the galaxies, the sound of tinkling coins a byzantine counterpoint to the soaring music of Holst, *The Planets.* Hours later we staggered out, eyes big as the brightest stars in the heavens, our pockets bulging with coins.

We wandered along an elevated walkway. Stations along the way displayed wares from the future. We stopped in front of an electric typewriter, one we had never seen before. No typebars to rise and strike the paper; instead, an aluminum ball ridged with letters spun and hit the page as fast as you could type—and I could type as fast as any mofo, except maybe Jack Kerouac, who could go 120-words-a-minute on a manual typewriter. Kesey and I were fired up. We had to get one of these machines, an IBM Selectric, and we did, a year later, when it came out in the stores.

Walking toward the exit, we stopped at a coin-stamping machine. Put in a quarter, pull down a big handle, one letter at a time, and the machine prints your words around the edge of a souvenir Seattle World's Fair coin. We stood and looked, thinking what to put on the coin.

"Something to keep us grounded when we get too far out," Kesey said, talking about the rickshaw and pond, no doubt.

"I've got one," I said.

I set the pointer on a letter, pulled the handle and stamped it onto the coin. I repeated the process until done. The machine clattered, banged and wheezed, spat out the first choice of great words to live by: DON'T BREAK THE COOL.

Kesey had another phrase for the ages. He started another coin. Again the stamping, the clanging and banging and spitting: DON'T BUG THE FUZZ.

Chuck was next. The machine spat out the third coin: DON'T CARRY.

There was a pause before Sue grabbed the handle, stamping out number four: STASH.

We passed the four coins around, rubbing and reading. I unbuttoned my shirt pocket, dropped them in and buttoned up again. Didn't want to lose them, for those four coins were the first Prankster credos—and still pertinent today, even though the coins are long gone.

We went back to the squatter's hovel, crashed, arose the next morning and packed our gear. Periwinkle waved goodbye. Bluto sat alongside, his nose angled toward her crotch, tail wagging. The ancient elevator wheezed and shuddered.

"This is a rough way to come down," I said, steadying myself against the cage.

"Just like always," Kesey said. "But it's better to be coming down than to have never been high at all."

No argument there. We headed for the car and the long ride home.

You try to leave
your illusions behind,
for to see sideways
is to know
more about the
higher side of things
than the coming
down of things.
    — Ken Babbs

8

An Eerie Dreamy Light

K irk Douglas was a great movie hero to us. Dimpled chin and toothy grin, walking across the oars in *The Vikings*, slaying the Cyclops in *Ulysses*, playing the trumpet in *Young Man with a Horn*, cutting off his ear in *Lust For Life*, shooting it out with the Clanton gang in *Gunfight at the O.K. Corral*, drowning his trainer in a pot of boiling soup in *Spartacus*.

When Kirk Douglas first read *One Flew Over the Cuckoo's Nest*, he liked the book so much he bought the movie and stage rights. Both he and Kesey were undefeated wrestlers in their college days. "I don't know how I would have handled Ken on the mat," Douglas wrote in a 2002 article for *Entertainment Weekly*. "It would have been tough."

Kirk's first attempts to make a movie of the book met with no success, so he decided to transform it into a play. He hired Dale Wasserman to write the script. William Daniels and Gene Wilder had major parts. Kirk Douglas played McMurphy.

Douglas wrote a letter to Kesey about the play: "We tried it out in Boston, with much success. During a week there, I received a letter from Timothy Leary. He invited me to join his group in a 'mind expansion program.' It sounded very exciting to me, although I knew nothing about LSD or all the other so-called mind-expanding drugs. I was very interested in being a participant, but my schedule did not permit me to join the group. I always wondered how Dr. Leary came to invite me. Later I learned that Ken Kesey brought it about. He thought I would be a good candidate for the group."

Kirk talked Kesey into coming to New York to watch the play, free front row seats.

"Kirk Douglas was so good it was like I had written it for him," Kesey told me later.

They had sat in Schrafft's together after the show waiting for the newspaper reviews, which turned out to be more bad than good. Kesey and Douglas said their goodbyes and Kesey headed for home, deciding he'd come back with some friends the next summer for the publication party of *Sometimes a Great Notion*, and also to take in the 1964 World's Fair.

I was in southern California then, home from Vietnam, and finishing up my five-year stint in the Marine Corps. I had been assigned a week of search-and-rescue duty at the Marine air base in Yuma, Arizona, which consisted mostly of hanging around the line shack at the airstrip, watching TV and reading books while firing up the chopper twice a day and roaming around the desert. I had to keep the skill levels sharp in case I had to pick up a jet pilot who ejected after a flameout or mid-air collision.

At the same time I was at Yuma, Kesey, George Walker and a newcomer, Sandy Lehmann-Haupt, were driving in George's station wagon from New York City to Oregon after attending the *Cuckoo's Nest* play. Sandy, a string-bean sound technician and drummer, was the brother of a friend of the Keseys.

Kesey wrote me a letter about the cross-country trip: "Early in the turnpike dawn, looking forward to one of those long drives where everybody tells all the secrets of their sinful childhood ... listening to teenage radio stations across rock and roll America while zooming across one of those faceless states between New York and Chicago, watching for a Howard Johnson's for coffee and pie ... there was an eerie dreamy light sweeping ahead of us, sifting through a thin ground mist that fell from the cold sun like pollen from an alien flower ... the radio was advising that big girls don't *cry-yi-yi* ... when the Hotline interrupted with a bulletin: *Dallas. President Kennedy was shot today just as his motorcade left downtown Dallas...*"

At the same time he was hearing it on the radio, I was watching TV in the line shack. A special report came on giving me the same news, riveting and shocking.

"I kept driving," Kesey said in his letter. "George and Sandy were silent. The turnpike rolled away into the mist. No other cars, no road signs or billboards. That dim otherworld blossom overhead ... *streets were lined by crowds. The President had landed only a short time before at Dallas' Love Field* ... the car warm, steady, fields drifting by with grey cutouts of animals supposed to resemble cows ... *blood was seen splattered over the limousine which had been flown in specially to carry the President* ... *Secret Service agents thought the gunfire probably came from the grassy knoll to which motorcycle policemen raced* ... Buy some cough drops too, if one of these goddamned places ever ... What? ... *given blood transfusions at Parkland Hospital in an effort* ... It's been a good hour now since ... What? ... *Mrs. Kennedy was heard to cry* ... What? ... But this is nuts. This is insane ... *John Conally of Texas also* ... But what! ... *two priests stepped out of Parkland's* ... But wait. What? ... *first priest announced to the crowd of newsmen* ...

"Dead?

"My God..."

In Yuma, I had the same reaction. All over the country there was the same reaction. Anger. Disbelief. Revulsion. Sympathy.

A pall of sadness. Millions of disparate individuals united in the same feelings, drawn together into a tight knot.

"I could only respond to George and Sandy's comments at the time," Kesey wrote, "by adding hoarsely, 'The pricks, the dirty pricks, the dirty goddamned *pricks!*'"

In Yuma, Arizona, I stayed glued to the TV, watching the arrest of Oswald, knowing this wasn't over yet, and later, on live TV, Jack Ruby putting a bullet into Oswald's gut.

I turned off the TV.

*Cassady was the real link. Kesey and I fell into the
crack between the Beats and the psychedelic generation.
The movement was much more than hallucinogens.
It covered the gamut of the arts, a way of viewing life and
relationships with others, a merciful attitude, plus a
questioning of the government. Let the kids apply their
greater brainpower and understanding. So, as Cassady said,
"Went through life a balanced man at last."*
—Ken Babbs

9

In the Reverse Direction
of the Settlers

Kesey had two novels under his belt, one already published, the other in the works. I had finished a novel and sent it off to our agent, Sterling Lord. The typing burned us out. Not the initial writing and drafting, but the editing: make a mistake or do a change, have to retype the page. The whole process was too slow, too time-consuming; we were moving forward, moving faster, tape-recording our stories, making them up as we went along, staying up all night yakking into the microphone, others joining in, an entire novel in one session, descriptions, dialogue, characters, the works.

Bob Stone, one of the Stegner Fellows in the Stanford grad school writing class, was the best. He would assume a character—say, a New Jersey gangster—and be that character, with the accent, the mobster turns of phrase, a mean cigar-chewing, blow-'em-away guy, done to the nines in a very serious manner. But Bob was a tremendous comic with a great sense of humor he couldn't keep bottled up. It rose like a shaken Coca-Cola can erupting in a laughing spurt of diabolical madness the rest of us had to hustle our asses to catch up with.

Next day we would listen to the tape, ascertain whether it was any good or not, or if we were wasting our time and nothing would ever come of it. We realized we had something going, something unique. We were able, talking off the top of our heads, to come up with interesting creative stories. In order to make anything commercially worthwhile out of the material, someone would have to go into the tape and do some manicuring and weeding, and who had time for that? We moved forward in another mode.

George Walker showed up with a 16 mm movie camera and we were up off the floor, donning costumes, acting out the parts in a cinematic drama, even providing the music: Kesey on the clarinet, me on the trombone, others on drums or guitars. Book-writing languished, for now we were *moviemakers*. The stars were lining up and the future was an open-ended, big-screen extravaganza, along the lines of *The Rungs of the Underlings*. Art at its highest. Hop-pop-opera, with costumes, settings, music, story, plot, action, conflict, love interest, the climactic final re-solution—and none of your staid talking in ancient-style badinage; instead, exciting movement and appropriate dialogue, witty and intelligent, moving the plot along, with the addition of the killer nouveau innovation: *all made up on the spot*. And, if needed, the ability to shoot even more footage, adding to the scenes.

We decided to take a break. Someone noticed there were four James Bond movies playing in Palo Alto and the neighboring town, Menlo Park, spaced just right timewise. If we were clever and on the ball, we could make them all, one after the other. Two carloads headed out. One car hit three drug-stores, the other car hit three others, and we rendezvoused at four o'clock in the afternoon at the first theater. Each of us washed down two bennies with a bottle of Romilar, a cough syrup loaded with codeine, then went into the movie.

Moving as swiftly as our mellowed bodies allowed, at the end of the first movie we piled into the cars and drove to movie number two at six o'clock, followed by movie number three at eight, and the final, number four, at ten. Then, eyes bleary and minds numbed, we returned to Kesey's house at midnight, a memorable outing, barely remembered.

I n 1964, Kesey and his family were living in La Honda in the redwoods on the ridge separating San Francisco Bay from the ocean. Friends were gathering every weekend, some from the writing class. Ed McClanahan, Kentucky-bred and born, who came west to teach English at Oregon State University— and had Gidget in his class—left OSU for the writing class at Stanford. Another Kentuckian, Gurney Norman, who had been in the writing class and was now a lieutenant in the Army, stationed at Fort Ord, came to La Honda on the weekends. He brought along another lieutenant, Ron Bevirt, a Polish buzzcut from St. Louis. George Walker, Kesey's old University of Oregon chum, who was born in Eugene and went to Eugene High School, and also Mike Hagen, originally from Pendleton and meeting Kesey at the U of O, were often in attendance. I was still in the Marine Corps but was in and out of La Honda, flying up from my base in Santa Ana, south of LA.

One night when the whole gang was sitting around a campfire under the redwoods, Kesey revealed he knew a place on the coast we ought to see. He and George Walker and I drove to the spot, the LSD we had dropped just beginning to come on. We parked and Kesey led us to a hole in the ground.

"Goes all the way to the ocean, looks over the water from high up in a cliff."

We crawled through a tunnel. Blacker than the blackest you can't see with your eyes closed on a dark moonless night. We stopped and rested. I leaned against the dirt wall and looked at the nothing I couldn't see. Thought about the others back in La Honda. I rose up through the dirt overhead, flew in the air above Kesey's house, and looked down at our friends sitting around the fire, talking, calm and comfortable. I was satisfied everything was okay and returned to the tunnel. Out of body, out of mind.

We crawled to the end of the cave and looked out over the ocean. The waves broke below, white lines glittering in the dark.

"It's a World-War-Two lookout spot," Kesey said. "They kept an eye out for submarines, come to shell the artichoke fields, ruin the local economy. Never saw any subs though. The Japanese interpreter had trouble with A words, thought the map said avocado, not artichoke, and they blasted an orchard down in Santa Barbara... What the hell?"

A huge wave approached, high as a skyscraper, boiling like a steam locomotive, coming right at us. What we didn't know was that there had been an earthquake in Alaska and it set a tsunami racing up and down the California coast. What we did know was we better get the shit out of there and fast. You never saw three guys scurrying on hands and knees in any Olympic games, but if you had, this would have been the gold medal team.

We broke out of the hole. The small stream we had stepped across was a raging torrent.

"What now?" George asked.

"Never fear," I said, "the Intrepid Traveler is here and will lead us to safety."

I stepped confidently into the stream. My legs went out from under me. I was on my way to the ocean when Kesey grabbed my shirt collar and hauled me out.

"Let's wait a few minutes," he said. Soon the creek was shallow enough we waded across and drove back to La Honda.

We approached the campfire, our forms murky in the dark.

Mike Hagen yelled, "Who goes there?"

I stepped into the firelight, the music from *Till Eulenspiegel's Merry Pranks* playing in my head.

"'Tis I, the Intrepid Traveler, come to lead his Merry Band of Pranksters across America, backwards, in the reverse direction of the settlers, our goal the obliteration of the entire nation, not in the physical sense of course, but spiritually. Blow their minds, not their buildings."

They welcomed us into the circle with resounding cheers and exclamations over our adventure in the cave and, with everyone jacked-up, we laid the groundwork for the intrepid trip to New York City for the publication party of *Sometimes a Great Notion*, plus a visit to the 1964 World's Fair, filming and taping the whole thing. Our moviemaking careers were officially under-way.

The bus was an experience machine. That was what
you had when you went on it: an experience. Every
time you got near it, you started experiencing, hotly.
— *Roy Sebern*

10

A Greater Pontificator
of the Trip

"Ready, Maëstro?" the director said. "Lights up on Number 3. Camera rolling. Action."

The director sat down in his chair. A tall man, in black tux and tails, top hat on his head, smiled and looked into the camera.

"The pump don't work 'cause the vandal stole the handle, but it doesn't matter because papa's got a brand new bag. Reworking the old '60s beat. What *were* Mom and Dad doing when the kids went to bed, Mister Jones? Not working on Maggie's Farm, that's for sure. Things you wouldn't believe. Better than two-hundred mikes of sunshine-daydream mental-flossing you ear-to-ear with easy listening."

He pulled a red bandanna from his pants pocket and patted his forehead.

"Return with me now to America emerging from the Eisenhower years, when the car took over as the major inroad on social behavior. Nothing had a greater impact on the American experience. It gave us the drive-in movies and darkened lanes, the unhooked bra, the upturned skirt, the reckless plunge. They were banging like rabbits, drinking like fish, partying like the bomb was going to go off before they did. The arms race in full swing. Brain-drain think tanks invented new deodorant and the ads to go with it. Split-level homes, color TV and a gas-hog freeway cruiser."

He took a big breath and shook his head.

"Contrast that with the growing involvement in Vietnam, the Cuban Missile Crisis, JFK's brains blood-splattered across Jackie O's pantsuit, freedom marchers murdered in Mississippi, plus a new generation of kicks-seeking freaks wanting to know *the meaning of life*. In 1964 a cauldron steamed and, no matter how heavy the forces of repression, the lid was about to blow. Came the heat of summer, it happened—*Blastoff!*"

He raised his hands in the air and jumped a foot off the floor.

"Would you believe the vehicle that loosened the bonds of gravity, freed earth passengers from the restraints of Aristotelian logic, and flung the minds and human consciousness into the wide-open spaces of quantum physics was *a bus?*"

His eyes got big.

"Gaze at its simple yellow and black lines. Look deeper into its metallic sides. Once a school bus carrying 1939, end-of-Depression, scrubbed-fresh, schoolyard kids, the bus was discharged from duty and took up life as a vacation home for a Catholic family. Good Papists, they were copulating diligently and popping out a kid annually."

He made an O with his thumb and finger, stuck the finger from his other hand in and out of the O.

"Three tiers of bunks in the back afforded sleeping space for the little tykes. The middle held a dining suite bolted to the floor. Next to it, a kitchen replete with freezer, fridge, sink, stove, oven and pantry. The navigation compartment was in front with map rack, two-way radio, CB and shortwave. The cockpit and driver's console filled the space behind the dash."

He paused, put hand to chin in momentary thought.

"There was room for all the rug rats, Mom riding herd, Pop driving, oldest boy vectoring on the map board, and the next-oldest, with earphones and microphone, dutifully keeping tabs on Smokey the Bears and Convoy Joes up and down the West Coast. Forays ventured into the Sierras, the Nevada desert, the high plains and the Rockies, until the nightly banging-and-frothing gave birth to too big a tribe even for this behemoth of a bus, and it was time to start anew."

He took off his top hat, wiped the sweatband with his finger, held the hat alongside his leg.

"A FOR SALE sign sat in the windshield but, because of the gigantic size of the bus and the complicated equipment filling its interior, there was no mortal who felt up to the challenge. Until Ken Kesey drove past."

"Cut," said Kesey, rising from his chair. "That's a wrap."

I smiled and walked toward the bathroom to change clothes.

S hot of empty highway, *William Tell* Overture playing, *deedee dum, deedee dum, deedee dum-dum-dum.* The music lowers and an announcer's gravelly voice booms out from the speakers:

"Board! All aboard." A wildly painted bus with speakers blaring, a lurch forward, a low engine growl and the amplified cry, "*Bo-ard!*" Neal Cassady, the garrulous and muscular driver, grips the wheel and mashes the gears, searching for the Kool Place in 1964 America. Nowhere in the celluloid film strips of archival footage can one find a greater Pontificater of the Trip. Return with us now to those Fluorescent Days of Lasteryear. From out of the Tire Tracks of Mythic Conveyance comes the Powerful Rumble of the Great Bus *Further* approaching a movie camera in the middle of the road. The bus passes over the camera and emerges, driving away, fading in the distance.

Roll the title:

INTREPID TRAVELER AND HIS MERRY BAND OF

PRANKSTERS LOOK FOR A KOOL PLACE

When I first heard Kesey say we were going to
paint it, the idea didn't appeal to me at all. I thought
it looked fine the way it was. I didn't see any
reason to obliterate it. I'd been paying attention to
abstract expressionism, in other words, "having at"
whatever you were painting. This bus was a canvas
that you could keep "having at" all the way to New York.
The longest painting in painting history.
  — Roy Sebern

11

We're Nothing but Vibrations

C alifornia State Highway 84, a two-lane blacktop, runs west from Redwood City, up over Skyline Ridge, then curves through La Honda, and straightens out in front of Ken Kesey's house. A steep cliff abuts the shoulder north of the road. La Honda Creek parallels the road on the south.

A bridge crossed the creek into Kesey's place. I walked across the bridge into the yard where 300-foot-tall redwoods circled the drive and home. A porch with couches and chairs extended across the front of the house; a big river-rock chimney covered one end.

The yard was a madhouse of activity. Kesey, *El Jefe*, the Chief, stood in the middle, orchestrating the confusion. He wore black pants, an unbuttoned long-sleeved shirt over a red T-shirt. A black sleep mask, held on with an elastic band, perched on top of his head.

"Here," he said, handing me a small glass vial.

I eyed it warily. Unscrewed the lid and sniffed the contents. The vapors set my nose hairs curling. Root hog or die. I took a sip. My lips puckered, my tongue curled, my throat constricted, my stomach made a fist, blood cells sent Code-Red messages racing through the system: *Wake up, wake up, there's a new world a-rising and it's gonna reshuffle the deck.*

Kesey tucked the vial away.

"The painting has been going on for two days," he said. "We started kind of slow, then someone took a broom on top, spilled paint and wiped it around with the broom, making patterns. We took the bus for a drive when it was still wet so it would streak back and give it a flame-hooded appearance."

"What's that on top?" I asked.

"Hagen had this fantasy I couldn't understand. He talked and talked about putting something up there. Every time he gets a wild fantasy I don't understand, my natural inclination is to say no. The thing that holds me back is I always think, God, I'd never do something like that. Or, I'd do it, but I sure as hell wouldn't do it that way."

He pointed to a laundromat dryer drum welded to a hole cut in the roof—a hatch with a ladder going down inside, for climbing up to the roof while traveling down the road. A platform with railings was added to the back of the bus, extending the length another six feet. A bench seat leaned against the back window. A gas-powered generator was bolted to one corner of the platform, a motorcycle rack fixed to the other. The motorcycle sat off to the side of the bus, leaning on its kickstand. A 1963 Triumph Daytona, 500 cc, twin-cylinder, painted purple and silver, everything factory stock except for an elk-hide-covered seat and the front fender removed.

Cans of paint spread out on the ground, their lids off, paintbrushes stuck inside. Kesey picked up a brush and stood back, contemplating the bus.

"What this bus needs," Kesey said, "is some brighter colors; gussy her up a bit. What do you say, Roy?"

Roy Sebern, wearing jeans and a short-sleeved white shirt, black-frame glasses covering his eyes, stroked his beard and pondered. He was a neighbor of Kesey's when Kesey was in the Stanford graduate writing class, and they'd been friends ever since. He loved big canvasses, the bigger the better, and had come down to La Honda from San Francisco, where he spent the prior two weeks painting the side of a warehouse.

"I don't know," he said. "Now that Janet's feet have ruined the purity of the original paint job, I reckon my hand won't hurt."

Fifteen-year-old Janet, from up the road, had been drawn to the activity by the sound of John Coltrane blasting out of speakers. She stuck her bare feet in a tray of green paint and walked across the roof, leaving jungle footprints. Then she dipped her hands in red paint and rubbed them over the tops of the headlights.

"What this old bus needs is a good luck name," Roy said. "It should be a poem too, only short. A haiku is fewer words than most poems, and one word is even fewer words, so this one lucky word is what she'll have for a name."

He climbed on the hood and painted FURTHER in big, yellow, capital letters on the black destination sign fastened to the roof.

Jane Burton had a quizzical look on her face. "Why *Further?*"

"I had this very strong feeling that having a name like *Further* would give the bus the impetus to keep it going when it might get stuck or broken down; the word would have power, like *Shazam.*"

"That makes sense," Jane said. "I guess."

"Way to go, Roy," Kesey said. "You know, there's all kinds of other places that I'm interested in enough to get some paint on too. The sides, for instance."

He dipped a brush in a can of blue paint, pulled the sleep mask over his eyes and painted blue looping arcs of brain cells with tails, hoping while blindfolded to connect meaning out of abstract blobs. He pulled the mask down, stepped back, and looked over his work.

"Not bad for a blind man."

A crow cackled overhead. A camp robber jay shrieked and the crow lifted off. Flapping wings battered the shimmering vibrations enveloping the giant redwoods, in turn sending pulsating waves crashing into my upturned face. *What the hell?* Everything vibrated. The trees, the sky, the sun, the house, the people, the bus—all vibrating—some fast, others slower, some solid, others effervescent—but all vibrating. *That's it, we're nothing but vibrations.* I shook my head. *Tumble, you tumble weeds. Enough.*

Kesey's eight-year-old son, Zane, wearing a long-sleeved red shirt, an American flag stuck in the crook of his arm, reached out a tentative finger and smeared a wet blue line his dad had just painted. A looping arc of a brain cell lost its clean-cut edge.

George Walker, active and determined, loped up, wearing heavy black motorcycle boots, leaving heel marks in his tracks. He had brought along the motorcycle as an emergency vehicle; also as something anyone stressed from riding in the claustrophobic bus could bug out on.

"I think I see something here," George said. "You have any black tape, Sandy?"

Wearing earphones, Sandy Lehmann-Haupt, shirtless, barefooted, black shorts, adjusted the dials of a Sony four-track, reel-to-reel tape recorder.

"Why don't I put on the tape of *Africa/Brass*?" Sandy said.

"That's black, but still no cigar," Kesey said.

Sandy looked at Kesey. "Why cigar?"

"Don't you know that thing? *Pah-ching*! Close, kid, but no cee-gar. Oh my God, look what just arrived."

Kesey's fiddle-playing cousin, Dale, stood inside the gate, his arms extended, a big grin on his face. He wore a raggedy straw hat on his head. A green vest covered a green, short-sleeved shirt.

"I'm coming along. You'll need my fiddle. Add a professional air to your feeble attempts at making music."

Of a religious bent, he had a calling for this kind of shenani-gan. The Lord's Will Be Done, best that Dale can see it, if only it weren't so dad-gummed murky.

"Just drove down from Redding," he said. "Looks like most of the gang's already here. There's Steve, for instance."

"How's it going, man?" said Steve Lambrecht.

Slim and trim, dressed in jeans and T-shirt, with light-brown beard and mustache, a recent graduate at San Jose State, Steve Lambrecht couldn't make up his mind if he wanted to come on this trip or not. His girlfriend was working as an intern in Manhattan at *Cosmopolitan Magazine* and it would be a chance to go see her. But, on the other hand, this looked pretty iffy.

"It's busy from the looks of things," Dale said. "Everyone working and getting ready."

A camera-fied apparition, carrying a professional Arriflex 16 mm camera mounted on a shoulder-pod, aimed in on Kesey. Two hotlights glared from stalks stuck on the pod's sides.

"Remember our black tape song?" Kesey asked.

Mike Hagen looked up from the eyepiece.

"No, what's our black tape song?" Mike asks.

"*Black tape, black tape,*" Kesey began singing.

Mike remembered.

"*Black tape, black tape,*" Hagen joined, and they sang in unison: "*With black tape and chewing gum we set about to change the course of ti-i-i-ime.*"

"There was nothing there but rocks before something began to grow," Kesey intoned in a deep voice. "Nothing there but ice and that bull sat right there in the ice, butt first, front feet waving and him a-bellerin', and the heifer looking on and him just a-grievin' its cattle's grief. We had to chop him out with an axe, and if you don't think that was one irritated animal by the time he got loose..."

Sandy looked up, big grin on his face. He squeezed his earphones tight, made sure the tape recorder needles were in the black.

"Listen," I said, hand cupped to my ear. "The falls. Our search for the bull has brought us near the falls. What's that?"

A high shrill laugh erupted across the yard, raising the hairs on the back of my neck.

"*Run you fools,*" Kesey yelled.

A crow shrieked from the top of a redwood and flew away. The camp robber screamed at its leaving. *Yack-Yack, coward-coward.*

"This is it," Kesey cried. "Run you sons of bitches or we're all doomed by morning. The falls are closer, we'll never outrun them. We're going to trip over the side of bristling straits, down in the grievling doom. I've been predicting it all along. Let me lay down and rest for Christ's sake, I've been toting this heavy bag of worry for so long I think I'll swim some."

Sandy circled the air with his finger, keep it coming. The words, captured by shotgun microphones, transported into the tape recorder and blared out over the yard through big speakers, were then picked up once again by the microphones, and looped through the tape recorder with a slight delay—giving everything an echo that fed back on itself.

"There he goes, breaststroking his way away," I said, sadly. "Just when we need him the most, off into the goddamn water like a fish."

"Let's just hope by that time it's not too late," Kesey said, resignedly. "The instant it runs backwards it explodes in negative time."

"Hey mon, *no problemo,*" I said, reassuringly. "You can move from the dark to the light, from the positive to the negative in a reverberating sort of fashion and never move off the same piece of time."

"That's it, podnar. Time, it can't go nowhere without you. And if you get caught in that slot of complete horizont, time just gotta sit there and twiddle its thumbs."

"He's out of his jurisdiction."

"He can't touch you in that land."

"No, suh."

We bowed to one another, then locked eyes. *Who's doing that crazy laugh? Creepy.*

Sandy patted the tape recorder. This is what he came west to discover, to snatch out of the very air, seal the deal on acetate. And to think, this is only the beginning. He cackled. *Hours to go before I sleep and miles to go with sounds to keep.*

S chnapps and Pretzels, the two dachshunds, prowled the yard, sniffing the gear and rucksacks. Jane Burton pondered her opened suitcase, wondered if she should bring along any warm clothes. She looked up. A red MG sports car drove across the bridge and parked in the yard. My brother John—a shorter, more academic Babbs—jumped out, carrying a duffel bag and baritone horn. Having just finished an English-teaching stint at Southern Oregon College, he was ready for a summer romp to the Big Apple, clear the cobwebs.

Page Browning wandered past. Ex-swabbie and ex-Marine with close-cropped hair and a raspy voice, after leaving the service he hung around Michael's Alley, the coffee house in Palo Alto, where he discovered Kesey and the Pranksters. He hitch-hiked to La Honda, wanting to do something, and had been bugging Kesey for orders.

"Oh, alright for Christ's sake," Kesey told him. "Take this can of white paint and go paint the porch out back."

Page glowered and mumbled, picked up the paint and brush and walked around the side of the house.

"*EEIIII!*" George Walker screamed from inside the bus. "This goddarn wire, I tell you, I've stuck my thumb with that enough times I'm hearing echoes. By the way, the horn doesn't work."

Kesey shook his head. "I'm back here checking this bitch for piles and you're wanting me to come up and look at her adenoids?"

"For a horn you could mount that trombone on the fender," Roy said.

"Good idea," Kesey said. "Okay, George, turn everything off. A sharp driver should be able to figure out what's happening if he's following us."

"A sharp driver should have more sense than to follow us," George replied.

A gangly, long-haired man wearing glasses and talking to Jane, drawling the words out slowly in a southern accent, caught my attention.

"Meet Ed McClanahan," Jane said. "He lived off Homer Lane when we were all on Perry Lane."

"I knew Kesey before that," Ed said. "I moved from Kentucky to teach English at Oregon State University and my Kentucky friends told me I should take a trip down to Springfield and meet the guy who wrote *Cuckoo's Nest* and so I did. Met him in a bar. The next year I was in California and got to know him again."

"Oh, don't be so modest," Jane said. "Ed also was one of the coveted Writing Fellows at Stanford."

Ed laughed.

"I haven't been shy about it. Kesey let me read his first fifty pages of *Notion* and I told him I didn't understand that business about the severed arm hanging from a pole above the river. 'What's that all about?' I asked him. 'How should I know?' Kesey said. 'That's why I'm writing the book—to find out whose arm it is!'"

Kesey's kids ran screaming onto the porch. The sun sunk lower, the shadows grew longer. Bags and suitcases and musical instruments were tied on top of the bus. Page Browning was back, prowling. Kesey asked him if he finished painting the porch and Page said, "Yes, and I had some paint left over so I painted the Mercedes, too."

When people ask what my best work is, it's the bus.
Those books made it possible for the bus to become.
I thought you ought to be living your art, rather than
stepping back and describing it. The bus is a metaphor
that's instantly comprehensible. Every kid understands it.
It's like John Ford's Stagecoach, *with John Wayne in the*
driver's seat just like Cowboy Neal.
   — Ken Kesey

12

Just The Beginning of It

A car screamed around the corner. Pretzels barked and ran across the yard. Schnapps joined in. A low-slung Olds missing its muffler, shooting sparks out of its dragging tailpipe, bounced across the bridge.

"Oh no, you can't fit through there!" Jane Burton yelled.

Brakes squealed. Birds screamed.

"He's jockeying through an enormously tiny space."

Feathers floated from the sky. Kids hid behind the couch. The Buick skidded to a stop between two parked cars, its radio blaring something about kissing a cop on 34th and Vine.

"It was eight to five on your getting through there," Kesey hollered.

Neal Cassady jumped out of the car, blowing smoke out of his nose. He skipped across the dirt, eyes bright blue, hair perfectly in place, skin taut on his face, deep crevasses from nose to mouth, close-cut hair receding from his forehead.

"*Pshaw*, nothing to it."

He took a drag on the Camel, tilted and drained a can of Hamm's Beer, ground the cigarette under his foot, reached with a sinewy arm and bulge-veined hand, daintily picked up the crushed butt, stuck it in the Hamm's, and pitched the can into the back seat of the car.

He had been dropping by Kesey's place regularly, a participant in our psychedelic adventures. We put microphones on our stomachs and recorded the sounds. His stomach surged and splurged at twice the speed of anyone else, formed words we couldn't make out, on the edge of clarity.

"So, it's Sunday morning then," Cassady said. "You want me in a movie, is that right? Be gone a couple weeks?"

The work on the bus stopped. Everyone inched in closer to hear.

"Y'know, it's funny, every summer I go on a trip with a car. Seems like I've done that every year all my life. And this is the first time I realized it."

"But as far as right now goes," Kesey said, "you have to, what?"

"I'm not doing anything except going home to paint the house tomorrow."

"Well, in a while we may take off in this thing."

"Tonight you mean? Gee, you're so much more reckless than I am. Honestly, I've never gone anywhere in my life without a destination."

"Oh, your destination is already made. But let me finish with my inclination about the trip."

"Trip. There you go. Intrepid Trips. The corporation that's going to make the movie. Is it really likely I'm going to be a movie star in my declining years?"

"There is nothing I would rather do for you."

Cassady shuffled his feet.

"Well color me dead—no, no, no—but that would relieve me of painting the house. Such courtesy, oh stop it, will you. My inclination is...?"

"My inclination is that this is available and if you would like to hang around, we have, ah, various things."

"Hmm, he knows my nature. It is a temptation. Yes, I'm sure you'd perhaps rather skid around these wet roads all by yourselves? No, no, you've already got an investment, why fuck it up? Do you mean to say you'll make movies all day? Talk and soundtracks and all, and you'll cut it all up and edit it?"

"And spend a year or so putting it together."

"I see, it's a project. And that would be the end of it."

"No, if it worked right, it would be just the beginning of it."

"Doctor, I'm feeling better."

"Then why don't you stay up here and take some of this LSD and spend the rest of the day with the people who will probably be present on this bus trip?"

"I understand. And orient vibration-wise."

"That's exactly right. We have to keep in mind the purpose of this trip is just to have fun."

"I thought the purpose of the trip was just to get to New York," Steve Lambrecht said.

"I thought the purpose of the trip was just to go to the New York World's Fair," George Walker said.

"I thought the purpose of the trip was to shoot a full-length movie about our life on the road," Mike Hagen said.

"I thought the purpose of the trip was to take LSD and intermingle with the American people," Sandy said.

"I thought the purpose of the trip was to go to the publishing party for your book," I said.

"Have we whittled it down to a ten, nine, eight, liftoff time?" Dale asked.

"Just about," Kesey said. "Sandy, are you plugged into the extension cord we ran from the house? If you are, you better unplug it right away because it's starting to smoke."

Sandy ran to unplug the tape recorder. The group around Kesey and Cassady broke apart and everyone scurried back to work.

A rogue white cloud drifted through the redwoods, enveloped the bus in a filmy mist, licking the metal before it wafted away, leaving a sheening wet coat. The energy field in the yard crackled. Blue atmospheric lights sparkled, vibrations jangled, yells and orders fractured and loud. The camp robber jaybird dive-bombed the bus, leaving a streak of white across the hood.

"A good luck shit-blob from the gods," Kesey said. "Cover that glob with a coat of fixative."

Faye Kesey, wearing a pink, long-sleeved shirt with a red collar, moseyed over to see how things were going. She smiled at the sight of Kesey's rear end sticking out of the luggage compartment, one hand holding the overhead door open, the other feeling around to make sure the hydraulic jack, the four-way tire wrench, spare tire, and the emergency flares were stowed inside.

"All right, then," he said, crawling out. "I feel like I've been stuck here in the asshole of this bus for what seems like a good four years, and I'm grittin' and I'm groanin' and I'm getting awful tired of it. I think we can go ahead and batten down these hatches."

Jane stood up from her chair on the porch.

"Looks like they're not going to provide safety pins or Kotexes or anything like that. Looks like it's every woman for herself. Luckily, we do have a spatula. Wonder if we'll be able to turn the refrigerator on so the milk won't go sour."

"I've got a few spare keys, if that will help," Cassady said. "There's one missing so I'm down to four. I've got four of everything. Four socks. Four hankies. Four incarnations. Four photos of four wives, and I'm having no difficulty in the hammer department, carrying the four-pounder, which is standard."

"Speaking of four," Sandy said. "Whose mad laugh is that I'm picking up on the tape recorder? It sounds like four of her."

"That's Cathy Casamo," Hagen said. "She's got the earphones on and is listening to a long echo. What do you think about her coming along?"

Dark black hair, deep dark eyes hiding beneath black bangs, olive Mediterranean skin, dressed in a black tank top and black leotards, she looked the part of a drama ingenue, except for the darting eyes and nervous laugh that betrayed her worried mind.

"I don't even know her," Kesey said.

There was some concern. These astronauts of inner space had trained for a long time, so the thought of bringing someone along we didn't know was trepidatious.

"She's a good actress," Hagen said. "I think we ought to take her."

"We'll wait and see," Kesey said. "Let's start wrapping it up and gathering our stuff together, bolting everything on and getting ready to go. Did you ever get the fuse in, Dale?"

"Yes, but it looked like a dome light fuse."

"Gentlemen," Cassady said, "the secret of the fuse is to think of the soul and not the ego. It took the Chinese years to discover swallowing tadpoles by the dozens does not make for effective contraceptives."

He pounded the front tire with his hammer.

"What's this? Oh no, don't paint the tires. Not even that piece of glitter there. Someone is trying to undermine us."

"Forget the tires. Get in and start her up."

"Just check the oil, first, sir. It would probably stand a half a quart."

"We can get it at the first gas stop. And here's the rest of our crew, just in time."

"Howdy," Kesey's brother Chuck said. Chuck ran the Springfield Creamery, shot the longbow, pulled a sixty-pounder without a hitch, and wouldn't miss this trip for the world.

"Well, what do you think of it?" he asked the young woman who came in with him.

"Great," Paula Sundsten said.

Paula was a nineteen-year-old college student from Oregon, came to catch a ride to her summer job in Manhattan working at Jack Dempsey's restaurant.

"What's that platform for in back?" she asked.

"That's where we'll carry the motorcycle, like a dinghy on a boat," explained fresh arrival Ron Bevirt. Ron was organized, energetic, just out of the Army. When Kesey found out he was a photographer, he invited Ron to come along and shoot stills for the movie.

"Hey," Ron said, "Neal's cranking her up, we better hustle aboard."

Cassady settled into the driver's seat. Clutch stiff but not sticking, brakes firm, solid pedal, ignition on, a start button—*how quaint*—choke out, two taps on the gas. He hit the starter.

The engine ground and coughed.

"Stay with it, bus," Hagen said. "Come on, old-timer."

"Hit it again," George said.

Blue smoke poured out of the exhaust.

"It sounds more like a Model A than an International," Dale said.

"All aboard," Cassady yelled. *"Bo-ard!"*

Hagen grabbed Cathy by the arm.

"Come on, get in there."

She shrieked, laughed, and disappeared into the bus.

"Start counting, back in the back," Kesey yelled, "so we'll know how many we are."

"Three!" Sandy yelled.

"Seven and nine are fifteen," Paula responded.

"Are you sixteen?" Hagen yelled.

"Sixteen-and-three-quarters and never been kissed," Ron Bevirt yelled back.

"Come on, you guys, do it right," Jane said. "Start at the beginning."

"Forget it," Kesey said. "We're going."

"We're on our way," Chuck said. "Aren't you coming, Roy?"

"No, I can't leave my painting job in the lurch. I'll see you when you get back."

Ed McClanahan stood and watched. Shirtless, wearing cutoff jeans and a red bandana around his head, Page Browning, who knew all along he wasn't on the bus, took a hit from a bong and handed the hubble-bubble to Ed.

Kesey sat down next to Cassady on the box that held the four-hundred-foot camera magazine. Steve Lambrecht hovered at the back of the bus. *Should I or not? Oh, what the hell.* He slipped under the railing and onto the back platform.

"A drink, a drink, my kingdom for a drink," Kesey called over his shoulder. "A drink is needed. Ah, thank you, Bevirt."

He poured the contents of the little glass vial into the drink and raised it high.

"And now, ladies and gentlemen, with this drink we will christen this bus so it takes us far beyond any known realms. Here you go, Bevirt. Pass it around."

Kesey stood, leaned out the open door, pointed ahead with a fire extinguisher and shot out a blast. The bus inched through the white cloud, climbed onto the bridge, hiccupped and died. A stunned silence, followed by flummoxed eruptions.

Dale jumped to his feet. "Let me check that coil."

George shouldered him aside. "One of those wires shorted out."

Steve yelled from the back platform, "Would this be of any help?" He waved a can of gasoline and ran to the front of the bus.

"You know," Kesey said, rubbing his chin, "he might just have something there."

Jane sank back into her seat with a groan. "Didn't even get across the bridge and we're already out of gas."

Get that goddammed ex-Riviera freak off my rear.
So, rearward, then, girls. I hope you'll let me call
you girls. We have competition. Any one of you
may scream as I return to the right lane with all
due fear. We are in a very peculiar predicament
of third gear. He's behind us again, the one who
almost saw the faux pas of me being on the wrong
side of the road. Stay left, you phony. Second time
he tempted me. If we only had a passing gear, no,
no, let's find fourth gear instead.
    — Neal Cassady

13

Desperately Need Food

The mid-morning sun sent heat waves rippling across the flat landscape, empty except for isolated, haggard bushes and occasional signs: GAS AHEAD LAST CHANCE FOR 100 MILES. The bus was a mess. Clothes scattered everywhere. Musical instruments crowded the seats and table. Empty film cans littered the aisle. Heads hung out the windows, sucking up the moving air. Sweat coursed down Cassady's back as he tensed over the steering wheel, squeezing it like a health-spa isometric tension machine.

I sprawled on the big rear seat, trying to figure out if Neal Cassady was a total goof, ready to wreck everything and everyone around him for the fun of getting kicks, or a savant able to communicate something profound and important.

"Only two things I wanted out of life when I was a kid," he yelled above the engine's roar. "To run the mile in the Olympics and play left-half so I could throw seventy-yard touchdown passes left-handed on the run at Nurtured Dam, rather than be a Ken-Blabbs, ambidextrous javelin thrower for His Lady of the Locks School, the tips covered with tennis balls so he didn't injure the bystanders he speared all the time."

He had been ragging on me since, surrounded by jaw-hanging admirers, he described the four-wheel drift in a racing car while deftly—so he thought—putting the bus through the maneuver, throwing us from side to side, and I yelled, "That's all very well and good in a race car, Neal, but in a bus full of passengers, you need an expert driver at the wheel so—it doesn't matter if the bus is going around steep curves or up and down hills or around potholes—the passengers never notice a thing, they are as comfortable as if they were in their living rooms."

He was annoyed, but I could put up with that because he became an impeccably smooth driver, even though the generator on the back of the bus jitterated a vibration that went down to the very bone. Still, we needed it to supply juice to the sound system blaring Ray Charles, "What'd I Say," over two speakers inside and two others on the roof, where you could lie on a double mattress tucked comfortably out of the wind behind a windshield bolted to the front rail. Only the hardiest could withstand the sun burning them into what they thought a great tan until they were so fried they climbed down the ladder and cried for lotion, *lotion.*

A microphone hung from an elastic cord above Cassady's head. He pulled it down to his mouth.

"I found out I was color-blind when I was out there, as youngsters will do, on the grass and all, and to me it looked red. Charley Wooster, my Cole Junior High School friend, said, 'The grass red? You're nuts!' I was so mad at that grass I learned cars. *Pashoom...*"

Cassady dropped smoothly into fourth, waved the gloved hand he used to manhandle the gearshift knob, then slapped the steering wheel with his bare hand.

"Dig that car going by. Just like my old Buick, my first car.

At that time you know I couldn't get the stamp, the certificate, so—I think I was only thirteen—I hitchhiked into—ah, '39, that's right—Kansas and stole a pair of plates. Hitchhiking back, hot day and all, the sheriff, a local guy, says, 'Whatcha got under your vest there boy?' 'Why, that's just my chest there.' The vest and the chest weren't right. No. Eight days! *Hah!* So. Buick's gone."

Kesey said someone should always be riding shotgun alongside Neal when he drove all night and provide him a listening ear, otherwise an edge of fear might enter his voice and force the words with desperation, like the flame of a candle sucks melted wax up the wick in fear of sputtering out. Another person close by could forestall it.

During the day, Cassady was sharp and alert, clean-shaven, dressed in a pullover referee's shirt with vertical black and white stripes and a white collar, eyes flashing from the rearview mirrors to the road in front.

Earlier, we had stopped at a big box store and bought fifteen striped shirts, some vertical stripes, some horizontal, and various colors in order for everyone to wear the same shirt during the trip, giving, as Kesey explained, a continuity to the filming. Once we started editing, we could use takes from different scenes and different times and no one would notice the difference because we were always wearing the same shirts.

Sandy switched the sound system to the radio. Martin Luther King intoned: "All the armies that ever marched. All the navies ever afloat. All the parliaments that ever passed. All the kings that ruleth that ever lived, have not had the effect on the lives of mankind as has this one personality... He was wounded for our transgressions."

"*He was wounded for our transgressions!*" Dale screamed, his religious fervor pricked. "Did you hear that?"

Sandy switched the station, Lambert, Hendricks and Ross singing along, asking Daddy for dat big elephant over dere.

We joined in, beat on pans, played the clarinet, sax, fiddle, trombone, standup bass. The music rose to a crescendo, died down and petered out. Dale wanted to know why we didn't put this music on the film as a background soundtrack.

"We're not doing this music for the movie," Kesey said. "Just for us now. It may never be done again. We can do music for the movie later. We have film, so we can load the cameras. We bought eight-hundred dollars worth, so we're into this thing up to our wallets. Which reminds me, the way we'll pay expenses, we have a thousand dollars in singles in a plastic sack that Babbs is holding. When we run out, we'll wire for more."

"If you spend your own money for anything," George said, "get a receipt and put it in this shoebox and you'll get paid back."

"What we'll do now is have a brief laying of cards on the table," Kesey said. "Straightening out anything anyone has to say which will be said to the whole group at once. We'll start up here with the driver."

"Touch and glow," Cassady said. "Touch and glow cannot hold a candle to my new blue Barbie Doll. It changes, of course, chameleon-like."

"The man seems to be having a brief trouble," Kesey interrupted. "There's a barber trying to cut his hair while he's traveling down the freeway at four-hundred-words-a-minute while we're passing the microphone around making brief statements, each to all."

"Well then," Cassady said, "is it true the exit known as Riverside Freeway is on the right *eemeedgitally*? What? Still three miles ahead? I wasted your time. That's why I'm not ready for the tape, thank you. Anyhow, we have other visitors."

"Okay," Hassler said, "I'll take over."

Hassler, the ex-Army lieutenant formerly known as Ron Bevirt, first one up in the morning, started his day off rummaging through the equipment drawer, banging and clanging pliers and screwdrivers and electric cords and batteries and other odds and ends when Jane, sick of being awakened by the noise, yelled, "What are you doing making all that racket?"

"Just hassling this gear in the equipment drawer, putting it in some kind of order."

It gave him his bus name: The Equipment Hassler.

"I want to carry on with the thing that I've been doing and that's hassling people to get stuff picked up," he said. "Don't throw stuff down. Put it back where it belongs."

"I hope the thing that is already happening will continue to happen," Kesey said, "and that is that all of us are beginning to do what we are ordinarily doing anyway, and we are doing it openly—"

"*Bullshit!*" Jane yelled.

"Yes, we are," Kesey said. "Listen, Jane said, 'Bullshit,' and if that wasn't Jane being Jane, I don't know what is. And that's okay, for none of us are going to deny what the other people are doing and what the other people are being, and none of us are going to make apologies for it. If you're stepping on my toes, I'm going to knock you off my toes but that has nothing to do with you as a person who steps on people's toes. It's like when we were driving on the freeway and Babbs was saying you don't have to really put someone down to criticize; you can apologize for a misdeed by saying, 'Excuse me, ma'am, for kicking you in the ass. I'm sorry I did that. But I'm not sorry I'm an ass-kicker.' That's the way we're going to play it."

"Right," John Babbs said. "I like the sound of that. Sitting here in the back, I can see we're working together as a unit, playing like a team. We're gonna go all the way and we're gonna score. We can take 'em, the whole city of New York. Unity above everything; fighting for a common cause. So, remember those fine words: *Sacrifice. Glorious.* And *In Vain.* I'll sign off now with everybody working, fighting, loving and playing together."

"So much for the bullshit," Hagen said. "I think we ought to get some grub in the icebox. Lots of milk and lots of good things to eat."

"Plenty of time for that," Kesey said. "We've finally begun the move east."

"Yes," I chimed in. "We're now embarked on the intrepid, tricky, bus-trek trip."

"Out of the rainy country and into the flatlands," Kesey said. "What's the report from the driver's seat?"

Cassady grabbed the overhead mic: "From the rearward then, we have the passing of a black car necessitating that I prevent touching the brakes and avoid hitting the Chrysler New Yorker, woman-driven obstacle. Good Lord! What's that?"

"I'm going to light your cigarette," Hassler said, appearing alongside.

"Well, *light it! Light it!* Oh gosh, what a terrible voice I have. We need it though, to obtain some reassurance on the right."

"All clear," Kesey said, checking to make sure. "Go over. Go over."

"Good work," I said, "to be heading east with unity in the front, and reassurance on the right."

"*Yas*, especially in the faster lane," Cassady said, "I'm holding my speed, gentlemen. This is not for the ladies. After all, they're built more for endurance, as we've gone into earlier, talking about the World-War-Two Bill Mauldin cartoon when Willie says to Joe—what did he say? They're so tired before Cassino, you may recall, and what happened, the Major's jeep, the left front tire went flat and the Major was sadly but of necessity shooting it, as one does the horse for want of a shoe. He wasn't shooting the left front tire, he was shooting the fender. My point of contention then was, by having the Major shooting the left front fender rather than the tire itself—for the object was already flat—the Major showed the folly of Cassino. So, Willie turned to Joe and said—'Was this, may I ask, for the boys or for the girls?' The punch line changes and I wouldn't say anything

more about it except that we're now approaching the point of—
IIIiiEEeee! It's burning me!"

The engine screamed—the gearbox shrieked.

"Mayday! Mayday!" Kesey yelled. "Emergency in the driver's seat!"

The bus lurched. I ran forward.

"My God!" I recoiled backwards.

"What is it? What's the matter?" Jane screamed. "Are we going to crash?"

"Remain calm," I said. "It's merely a hung butt. A cigarette butt is glommed to Cassady's lips. I may have to operate. Get a wrench, I'll wrench it off. Ah, a match. That's better, except the butt is blended so nicely with his lip, I don't know which to light."

"Get it!" Cassady hollered. "Shut up and get it!"

"Fire in the hole!" Kesey yelled.

"It worked," I said. "I applied the match to the cigarette butt and burned it off. Just like a leech."

"A fine operation from a man who professes not to be a doctor," Kesey said.

The engine settled to a steady roar and the gearbox hummed.

"Never did hear what Willie said to Joe," I said, "but we survived chaos and another third-gear mania."

"And a small war," Kesey added.

"And it was that war that was hideous and black," Dale said. "Where dead and green moldy limbs hung on trees, the sinews of the wind."

"That's a pretty sick-sounding now-trip," Kesey said.

"What's the now-trip, if I dare ask?" Jane said.

"It's verbalizing the now that you're in," Kesey said. "You do it by saying, 'Now I am that boxcar. Now I am hard and scaly on the outside. Now I've got stuff all over the inside of me and my bottom is rusty and my hole is bolted shut,' and you just keep going, passing the microphone around."

"I'm orange and I have black letters that say SP1775," said
Zonk, the prankster formerly known as Steve Lambrecht. The
previous night, after the exhilaration and frenzy of the daylong
bus-painting high faded, we broke out the pot. Steve cupped his
hand into a fist and, holding four joints between his fingers,
drew in long deep lungfuls that burned the joints down to nubs.
He slumped in his seat and closed his eyes, out to the world.

"Look at Steve," John Babbs said. "He's zonked."

From then on, Steve was known as Zonk.

"I'm one of the roller bearings," Zonk said. "I am a caster. Engine whine in my mind. I see a big face and my ears are coming
back into me when I look at John Babbs."

"Don't bug me with that shit," John said. "We're checking
out routes. Looks like we're heading south now, going as far as
the next gas station. We hope to make it under the polar ice cap.
When we surface, we're going to fire our first missile, loaded
with an acid warhead. We're talking obliteration of the entire
nation."

"Railroad crossing coming up," Chuck said. "Gate down,
must be a train but I don't see one. False alarm. What's that
light? Is it a cop?"

"No cop," Sandy said, "Everything's cool."

"Then," Kesey said, "since everything's working so good,
let's record the first rendition of our jazz piece: *Cassady's Condition.*"

"Thank you, thank you," Cassady said. "Remember when I
said the first twelve? The time? Twelve-twelve. I was wrong-
fully hoarse. Realizing then I wanted, yes, success, I reached for
the next syllable, a third twelve for the sake of the sound but,
no, stopped, because it was false. You caught it there, Chief, in
its falsity. There's your clue. Your loss-of-voice idea. You can't
go any faster than you can go, but still, you want to get more.
Keep a step ahead, keep your mind ahead. Don't butt your dumb
head against those fink walls. Look for doors and then *Go.* Leave

them snarled up in their worries, their motives. It's their kick, their dreary high. But listen, *never knock the way the other cat swings.* What's that freak Dale doing, leaning out up on the roof? Is he going to fall off?"

"*Who's afraid Dale's going to fall off?*" Jane sang. "Mister Babbs, you'd be in position to know, up there on top with Dale. Are we just booming out across the countryside?"

"Yes, nothing but scrabbly dirt as far as the eye can see and a cloudless sky from horizon to horizon."

"There's a person leaning out from the top of the bus, ladies and gentlemen," Chuck said, looking out the window. "It's Dale, whiskering along, whiskering along. I would like to have an instrument, a trombone I can go *holler-holler-holler* through."

"Do you have a knife?" Dale asked while leaning down from the top of the bus. "I need a knife."

"The situation has been given to the back of the bus," Chuck said, "that I am to furnish Dale with a knife and he in exchange will furnish me with a trombone to go *ooh, anhhh* through. Somebody up there's got that trombone. Who is it? Dale almost threw a guitar halfway across the bus. The wind pushed it back. Now he's trying to jab a violin down the turret. What are we going to do?"

Chuck looked around, hoping for inspiration or at least an intelligent answer and, I being, so I thought, the intelligence officer of this operation, said, "We have to stop for food. We have run out of grub and grog at the same time. The grogs all ran overboard. They deserted us like sinking ships off a rat. We desperately need food."

"Gas station to the fore," Cassady said, "replete with sustenance market."

"Engines all slow," Kesey replied. "Prepare for docking at foresaid gas station festooned with plastic and bugs."

"A bug condition on turquoise rug, *pshshaw, spfllt.*" Cassady mimicked the engine sound as he geared down. "*I vant to go left,*

I see. Thank you."

"Be sure we get filled on the card, if we've got any credit cards that will cover this," Kesey told me.

"Roger Dodger on the card," I said, fishing out my wallet. "Saving the cash for the food."

Cathy Casamo came forward—as shy and demure as a young lass approaching her stern mathematics teacher—with what she hoped would help her earn, if not a passing grade, then at least the teacher's good graces.

"Let me buy the food," she said. "I haven't been any help so far."

"You?" I said. "Why not? But make it snappy. We'll be gassed up and out of here in a few minutes."

I counted twenty dollars from the plastic sack.

"That ought to cover it."

"Good for you, Babbs," Hagen said, giving me a fist bump to my upper arm.

"Aw, shucks," I said. "Us gyrenes ain't all bulldog breath and leathered neck. Mine's sweaty. It's hot out here in this desert."

"Must be a Kool Place somewhere," Hassler said, slathering and lathering in sweat. "Even desert rats need food and water."

"Navigator, Navigator," Kesey bellowed, having heard quite enough of our palaver. "Report to the conn."

John Babbs's eyes popped open. He sat up from his nap, grabbed the map and ran to the front of the bus.

"Navigator, aye," he said, giving Kesey the Prankster salute, pinky extended like giving the finger.

Kesey scowled. "What have we got for a Kool Place? The crew's getting salty. Let's see that map." He circled his finger in the air and plunked it down on the map. "Aha, what about there?"

"According to your finger destination, the Big Sandy River isn't too far away," John Babbs said. "Place called Wikieup."

"We'll head for there, once we're gassed up," Kesey said. "A swim is in store."

The gas gauge didn't work. We measured the gas in the tank with a yard stick. Fifteen inches was a full tank. We figured we got ten miles to the inch. The odometer worked and if we kept track, we'd remember to gas up before we ran out.

When the gas tank was full, I paid and we were ready to go. Cathy scurried in with the change and the food: one little lobster tail and a small box of oyster crackers.

"*Boar-ord!*" Cassady yelled. "All-l-l aboard! Clear to the rear, dear? Here we go, then."

Looking both ways, he pulled onto the highway.

"Reminds me of the Model A. Mine didn't have brake one on it. You know what I did? Over the floorboard I nailed a pedal. I used to hit curbs like when I was on my first job with bicycles, bouncing off because my bike was a single, no brakes on it. I'd hit cars, bounce between them, throw my feet out, just like you'd throw out the feet to guide yourself on the rocks. And I tell you, sliding right through, real straight, just like the Model A."

He hit the gearshift and dropped into fourth.

"Ha! Didn't clink a clog on that change."

Sizzles and boils, word-sticks pop bubbles,
stir the mess with swizzles. Whoa, slow down.
Always good to remind myself, if you know
you're high, you're okay. Okay? Then let's go.
Time is lineal laid end to end, and time is
quantum happening all at once; a psychedelic
adventure is time.
    — Ken Babbs

14

Take Us Straight to the River

"Cassady's very sharp today," Hassler said, watching Neal work through the gears.

"Goaded by his belly, I believe," George said.

"I heard that, George," Cassady said. "I want to get rid of my garbage mantle. I disapprove of degenerate appetite. Oyster crackers get stale very fast in the humidity. Oh, sorely. So, we'll swallow it. Let it melt in the heat."

We downed the oyster crackers immediately. The lobster tail sat untouched in the sink. Tormented by his appetite, Cassady spit out words like stale grub.

"It's the mind, working all the time, though it's not a question of work. Wrong connotation. It's a pleasure, a quirk, a schematic misunderstanding. Its negativity is sticking out, the same thing as oysters—oyster *crackers* of course. Well there you are, turning the bad into good. Just imagine what they're named *after* and not the horrible sadistic thing done to them alive."

"Hey," Hagen yelled at Cassady. "Lighten up."

Mike turned to Cathy.

"It's okay, they don't mean anything. Just yakking, you know how they are."

"I don't know anything. I've been kicking myself in the ass for coming on this trip. I can't do anything right."

"Well, you have to admit, one limp lobster tail and a box of stale oyster crackers doesn't really cut it for this crew."

"I noticed how they gulped down those crackers fast enough. Then dumped the lobster tail in that filthy sink. No wonder no one will touch it. Ratburgers! That's all we eat. Cheapest hamburger you can buy. Anything under twenty-four cents. Hideous."

She sat hunched in a ball, staring out the window. Brooding. Worried. Her giggle gone. She left her three-year-old kid to go off on an adventure with Mike Hagen. She had invited Hagen to a party, was flattered by his attention to her good looks and him telling her she would star in a full-length movie. Hours later she accepted his invitation to ride to New York on the bus. Cassady's voice grated on her nerves like steel rubbing steel.

"Twelve-twelve, and all's well," Cassady yelled.

The desert lay bleak and silent, telephone poles zipping past the only evidence of our passing. Neal bounced in his seat. He yanked a blue bandana out of his pocket and mopped his brow.

"Well, I tried to be a town crier and made myself a liar."

"I know what I want," Kesey interrupted. "Don't let anyone take my seat."

He swayed to the galley and rummaged through the equipment drawer. The bus hit a slight rise and Cassady geared down. He missed the shift and ground it in, wincing at every growl of the cogs.

"So, the voice is as official as a third-gear interference, yet as soon as I start feeling strain or want to be serious, I lose it. I lose it *all*. The throat. The voice. The third gear. And *all*. No. Wrong again. But somehow that's an art. I've forgotten the rule but poetic license will have to subdue, as it were, in *lieu*."

Kesey appeared at Neal's side with a handful of colored jelly beans.

"What are *these* things? Candy! I see."

He flipped the jelly beans in the air and caught them in his mouth. Hassler came alongside Cassady, grabbed a jelly bean out of the air, popped it in his mouth and sat shotgun.

"Thank you," Neal said, "for the interruption. The Chief would've seen my panic there if he'd heard me say I'm under a strain. Good thing he's eavesdropping on the secretaries at the moment. You know, I think I've told you this before," he munched a jelly bean, "but this is the only thing I've had since those oyster crackers in..." His words were drowned out by the Pranksters shouting for a Kool Place—*have to get out of this bus and into some water.*

"Hard right, Cassady! Hard right!" Kesey hollered. "Onto this dirt road. My instinct tells me it'll take us straight to the river."

"Water!" Zonk yelled. "Cool, clear water. My body is aching to wallow in water."

"Anything to take my mind off food," Hassler said.

Cassady drove onto a rutted dirt lane that wound through desiccated flora and withered fauna, eviscerated by the heat.

"Riverbank ahead," Cassady cried. "Dead ahead, sir."

"Go right to it," Kesey said. "Close as we can get."

"Mighty sandy," Cassady warned.

"That's its name, the Big Sandy. Go right up to the edge. We want to have the bus near the water when we start shooting."

"Edge it is, sir, right here. Pushing the edge till there's no edge left. How's this?"

"Great. Now back around so we're parallel."

"All-l-l to the rear, sir. *Pashoom!* Emergency, emergency! No traction, sinking fast, sir! Condition: spinning right rear duals..."

The engine whined. The wheels spun.

"Rock it! Rock it!" Kesey ordered.

"Exactly my point. Sand, you see, not having the solidity of the aforesaid rock, and without the rock of which you so nimbly speak, on hand to replace the—"

Cassady jammed the gear in reverse.

"Hold it, hold it!" George yelled. "You're going in deeper."

Cassady goosed the bus forward and back, and though he kept backing and filling, while talking and gesturing, we were genuinely stuck.

"I'll get out of this fucking hole by God or we'll be here for as long as it takes."

To no avail.

"Shut her down," Kesey said. "Okay, Pranksters, muster up. We'll have a brief briefing before we alight. I'm going to take some LSD. Babbs will take some. Cassady, you want to take some?"

"I would, yes, I would," Cassady whispered from the driver's seat.

"Pass the orange juice around while I describe what we'll do," Kesey said. "Hagen will be on the Arriflex. George on the Bolex. Hassler on the still camera. Sandy, run the microphones out as far as they will go. You four guys go easy on the acid. John and Dale and Chuck and Paula and Cathy and Jane will get high, be the loaded loonies, out for a Kool Place lark."

"I'll pass on dropping acid," Jane said. "I'll be the assistant, or whatever it's called in the big-time movie business."

"This is the big time," Kesey said. "It doesn't get any bigger than this. Let's start loading the film magazines here and—Hey! Whoa up there, Cathy! I said only a slug, not half the bottle."

"Half the bottle, hell," George said. "She drank the whole damn thing."

"Good thing she was last in line," John said, "or the rest of us would be screwed."

"Well she wasn't last in line, I was," Jane said, "but I didn't want any anyways, so there."

"Okay, everybody out," Kesey ordered.

"Yeah, go on," Jane said, remaining seated. "You have all the fun and we'll do all the work. Hagen, you ready to start filming?

What do you want me to do?"

Hagen grinned, a loopy grin, and walked away.

"Oh crap, he's already reached the stage of incomprehensible imbecility. This is starting to get depressing. Stop berating yourself, Jane. I did read where pregnancy is fraught with rapid mood swings, but be damned if I'll tell these guys what's going on. I'd never hear the end."

Kesey stood at the bus door, looking out.

"Hold it right there," he said. "Cathy brought us a lobster."

He dangled it between his finger and thumb.

"What did you expect?" Hagen said, pointing the camera at him. "You've got a stone in her mouth and a whip in her face."

"Oh, for the love of Jesus and all His Holy Family," Hassler said. "What are you doing, Kesey?"

"Have you forgotten we are making a movie?" Kesey answered. "What the hell are *you* doing? And *this* is supposed to feed us all? Where is the loaf of bread? Who do you think I am, for Christ's sake?"

"Genghis Khan?" Dale Kesey said.

"A combination of a penis and potato?" John Babbs said. "A dicktater?"

"Julius Caesar?" Paula Sundsten said.

Kesey shook his head, *what's the use*. Up in front of the bus, Cassady was shaving. Dry shaving—no water, no soap—looking in the big side mirror. He scrunched his cheek with his hand and peered at his reflection.

"It's funny, I don't feel a thing, except maybe irritation at the realities. Oh, here's Jane, healthy enough. All woman to me. The idea of woman as what? Lighter rather than darker. Spiritually speaking, of course. The symbolism and all. Perfection perfected. I've tried, you know, to make a form of saying we're being handled by a higher power. You have to use the same body you begin the symphony with, y'see? But that's the thing: group experience. What is there but One Force? That is, of the soul? And with judicious application of that One Force, can't one go to the higher, mmm, fourth-plane riches? Mmmm?"

Jane shook her head. "I'm not interested, Cassady."

Jane was irritated. Irritated as all shit, as she would put it. Everybody else seemed to think it was Sunday driving, apart from the few thousand dollars of film gear. Last night, she'd gone to sleep in one of the upper bunks and her purse fell out the window and she lost all her traveler's checks, her money and her driver's license; everything that she didn't want to lose, she'd put in her purse. She could have lost her suitcase easily. Here she was, penniless, riding with a band of maniacs.

Trapped, she felt horrible, just wanting to brush her teeth— but her toothbrush was in her purse on the road somewhere. There was no getting through to anybody—they were all high. She hung her head, disconsolate.

Cassady patted her on the shoulder.

"You need the blindness to have the light," he said. "That's how the angels fly together at four-thousand-plus. They're not screwing around when they're a fraction of an inch wingtip-to-tip. Chance is chance, and chance is chance, but how many *fahlooking* chances do you have to have thrown in your face to find out it's all four-hundred percent chance? Mmmm?"

Jane gamely tried to smile.

Cassady preened and flashed his pure-white pearlies.

"I don't mind if you want to use my toothbrush," he said.

"Really, Neal? Can I borrow your toothbrush?"

"Well, certainly, ma'am. You certainly can and here it is."

He reached into his shirt pocket and produced a toothbrush, sheathed in a clean, white hanky.

"I'd be very proud to loan it to you," he said. "And it's never been used."

"Neal, that's wonderful. I'm going right down to the river to brush my teeth. Maybe even splash out my crotch."

Dale Kesey muscled the motorcycle off of the platform at the back of the bus. Kesey had told him to find someone with a piece of equipment big enough to tow the bus out of the sand. Dale kick-started the Triumph, popped the clutch, roared around the curve and disappeared.

Chuck Kesey stood in the river shallows and poured different colors of enamel paint on top of the water. He dipped Zonk's white T-shirt in the paint and the cloth picked up the patterns. Swirling, vivid colors. The world's first dip-painting, done in the wild.

"The great America," Hassler said. "We're painting the face of the nation."

"I'll never drink downstream from the Merry Pranksters' campsite," I said.

Zonk put on the shirt and spun around, arms outflung. He stopped, stood forlorn, the shirt clinging to his gaunt frame, paint stuck to his skin.

Sandy Lehmann-Haupt, wearing baggy, low-slung BVDs, his balls sagging, wandered around with the shotgun mic on a long cord. Mike Hagen filmed with the Arriflex camera. Kesey poked a broken fishing pole in the water, his prod-rod he called it. He swung at cattails, cutting off their heads. I picked up a tree branch. We crossed swords and parried.

"Take that, Swashbuckler, you pirate chief," I said, our play-acting giving Kesey his bus name.

Paula Sundsten floated in the water on her stomach and paddled downstream.

"It's all opened up to me," she said, holding her head out of the water, green slime hanging from her in wisps. "The water, the weeds, the murk."

"Looks kinda scary," Zonk said, splashing behind.

"Yes. You might go in and never come back. I'm curious about it. What's this? Green lights dividing and dividing and dividing. What bliss."

"Merely algae," Chuck observed. "Basic of basics. Gotta start somewhere, I guess."

"Ick," John said, face close to the water. "Too murky."

"Super clean," Paula cried out. "Crystalline. It's a green star, a swirling emerald sun, bigger than heaven."

"Makes a nice hat," Chuck said. "Think I'll wear it to the fair."

"*Look at Gretchen, she's mighty fetchin',*" Zonk sang, and from then on she was Gretchen Fetchen.

Cathy Casamo ran dripping out of the river, sweater sleeves soaked with sand. Water hung from her arms like flowery tentacles. She pirouetted in grinning joy, then spun slower and wilted, sleeves sagging and dragging on the ground. She pitched forward, fell face down in the sand. Lay motionless. Then raised her face. Tears coursed through the sand stuck to her cheeks.

Cassady walked toward her. His shirt was off and he was barefooted, beltless jeans hanging below his belly.

"Popeye, you dumbass. What are you doing running around? How can any man be so mean?"

Neal shook a cigarette out of a pack.

"This Eye-talian—or was it E—opened a pack of Camels upside down, impressed even me."

He pulled a mandolin from behind his back and handed it to Cathy. She covered her chest with the instrument, strumming and singing:

"*Com-pro-mise ... while the rain comes down*
and kills a spider in the groin."

Neal sat down and leaned his back against hers.

"Well, that's *not* a compromise, my dear."

Cathy sang and twanged:

"*With frogs hopping, hopping,*
and the bees that are kept
in the bee-keeper's hive,
must not go without stopping."

Neal put his face alongside hers. "I've really found matches, by God, by the score."

"Yes, oh yes, oh sweet spon-ta-nee-ous earth.
How often have the fingers of prurient philosophers
pinched and poked thee?"

Cathy tugged at her wet sweater. Cassady pulled it over her head with a quick jerk, her skin pallid white against her black bra.

"Slime. Sentimental drama."

She cupped her breasts in her hands. "Plus my dear tits. Pop-eye, you dumbass. How can you be so mean?"

"You know, I think we can make you a real hit. You do everything I say and we'll give that producer a year and a half. What's this?"

A white stallion, head cocked, peered at them from across the river. Hagen zoomed in with the camera.

"He's liable to shoot it," Cathy wailed. "A little black death."

"Hmm, I see you are held in violence," Cassady said.

"And Jean-Paul Sartre is dead. Oh yes."

"What a savior. Oh, help me. Oh fart."

A mare stepped out of the bushes and joined the stallion. The two drank from the river. The stallion bit the mare on the neck.

"Men are always ugly," Cathy said.

The mare threw her head in the air. Droplets shimmered in the afternoon sun.

"This headache is killing me," Cathy said.

"I'll get you a few aspirins," Cassady said. "The last girl took fifty. It wasn't quite enough. I decided a hundred would be more like it."

Cathy sniffed in disdain. "I have no time to dance and sing. I must play the fool for this errant king."

The horses snorted and wheeled, their hooves flinging sand as they galloped away.

"*Eee-haw!*" I yelled, running up out of the river. "Looky there. Dale's brought us a savior."

"How embaraskin,"
said Popeye the sailor man,
but that's what I get
for smoking my sox:
a real no-high,
and that is the pox.
I can't eat bagels and lox.
Instead I'll hide them in a box.
I do not like them Sam what I Am.
I do not like those eggs and that ham.
What I likes is me spinach, not yam,
and that is why I yam what I yam.
— Neal Cassady

15

As Real as It Gets

A Case tractor with a vertical flapping muffler followed Dale across the river. The driver backed the tractor to the tail end of the bus and climbed down, leaving the engine running. He was stocky, round-faced, grease-stained baseball cap on his head, stomach bulging in a dirty T-shirt. He fastened a chain to the back of the tractor and hooked it to the axle of the bus.

"Come on, Cassady," Kesey said. "Get in and start it up."

"Okay, we're ready," I said, swinging my tree branch. "We'll take it out of the sand and keep her on dry land this time."

"Back it up, Neal!" Kesey yelled, then gave the farmer the go-ahead. The tractor roared, straining, pulling. The bus's engine spewed smoke, the tires spun.

"Stop, stop," Kesey yelled. "You're working against yourselves. Tail-to-tail pulling in a chained-up tug-of-war. Put it in reverse, Neal!"

Once again, the engines roared, the chain tightened and, with the tractor and bus now going the same direction, the bus rolled out of the sand, onto hard ground, past Cathy lying face down. Hagen crouched and pointed the camera at her.

"Atta boy, Hagen," I yelled. "Get a close-up and then point at the bus. Now back on her, Hagen. Atta boy, back on the bus now."

"Yeah, c'mon, Hagen," Kesey said, drily. "Get a picture with dispatch. That's her bag. That's the horn she plays."

Kesey looked at Cathy's swirled hair, eyes bottomless pools, mouth bubbling.

"I know what you're thinking," Kesey said.

"Oh, really?" she answered, and laughed madly.

"What do you think, Hagen?" Kesey asked. "Is the comedown from this high going to be too rough on the gal?"

Hagen shrugged and looked at Cathy grinning at him. "She can handle it."

"In the general realm," Kesey said.

The tractor man walked up.

"That was no great strain. I've got ten speeds forward. Look, there's a little tadpole."

"There's some pretty good-sized tadpoles in there," Kesey said. "I grabbed hold of one, it felt like a salmon."

"You can't hardly tell what kind of a frog they will be," the tractor man said. "Hard to say until they hatch. I mean, until they shape up."

"They ain't gonna be very big," Dale said, joining them at the water's edge. "You know, sometimes it actually rains toads."

"Huh?" The tractor man looked at Dale. "Who the hell ever told you that?"

"Yes," Dale insisted. "The water sucks them up out of their roosts."

"Taunts them to come out of hiding, I suppose," the tractor

man said.

"I never went very deep into it why it sometimes rains toads," Dale said. "Old Pharaoh story I suppose."

The farmer spit a gob of tobacco and peered at the sky. "I never heard such a load of bullshit in all my life."

I dug out the plastic sack and counted thirty-five one-dollar bills. He looked at the wad, shook his head, stuck it in his pocket and headed for the tractor. He passed John Babbs sprawled out on the ground, an arm flung across his eyes.

"You seem to have an interesting part in this movie," the tractor man said. "You playing a corpse? Nope, saw yer eyelids flutter. What do you do in real life, son?"

John opened one eye. "This is about as real as it gets."

The tractor man stalked off, saddled up and skedaddled.

"Let me tell you," Hassler said. "We're just like gypsies."

"We might as well take a rest upriver," Kesey said. "Looks like George is starting a fire."

Dale began playing his violin, copying the sound of the water gurgling past.

"Dale Stravinsky," Hassler noted. "We is highbrow white trash."

"Like Rubenstein," Cassady said. "Anything but Ira Stein. But by God, I don't know why not. Isaac Stern certainly has the tone, of course, but we're not concerned. He doesn't stand in the mud."

"Would you possibly have any interest in issuing any statements whether we stay or depart?" Hassler asked Kesey.

"We've arrived at the fire. That's about the only statement I can make."

The sun descended below the trees and a hard day's high nibbled the lips of a long night's hot, thirsting for a cool. Birds whistled in the willows. An egret shifted from one foot to the other. Red-flecked, fleecy clouds bounced across the sky. Water bugs zipped across the river's inlets. Busy critters and curious creatures hopped and buzzed and sang.

"Looks to me like a good place to spend the night," Dale said, noodling on the fiddle.

"Has everybody else got sixty-two-million-thousand bugs on them?" Chuck said.

"You're moving and you're hot and you don't have a shirt on," Hassler said. "Get cool, put on a shirt and sit down."

"This swarm will leave as soon as we get some smoke on them," Kesey said. "One time when Chuck and I were camping with Daddy and the mosquitoes were thick, I noticed they didn't bother Daddy and I asked him why and he said, 'I don't let them get on me.'"

"You kinda sense that's how it works," Cassady said. "That's exactly the position I foretell. Like here we are and what are we about? The refinement, of course. Which we're uncertain of, and loose right now."

"We're trying to tighten it up," Kesey said.

"I know. I believe it," Cassady said. "All trembling to it. I knew I must be high because happily I looked in the rearview mirror and, my God, I looked so—it was all golden glow. But I didn't feel a thing. If I hadn't looked, I wouldn't have known. I shudder to think of the many possibilities of handling the discipline and necessities to move this mic here, that camera there. It's like tightening a belt and then you wear it. And go thirty-six hours without sleep."

"This is the way I think you accomplish something," Kesey said. "You sleep a long time and then you go at it like a son of a bitch."

"Can't you freaks see it," Cassady asked. "What did we drive out here for? To get mosquito-bitten?"

"Might be," Kesey said. "I'm not deciding."

"That's for the year of editing," Cassady said. "And another year of—"

"To scratch when we itch," Dale said.

"That's what I mean," Cassady said. "I believe in every man here. And you know that I know that."

I swished at the fire with my tree branch. "Looks like we're nesting here."

Dale played his violin. Kesey joined in on the flute. Cathy plucked at her lute, Cassady mumbling along: "You don't win prizes like thirty-four and four or whatever it was. Trivial idea. Curiosity is going to complete—I mean, you just can't go into anything with just anybody. I never thought I'd be in the woods with a Jim Bob or a Bob Boy. I don't know a damn thing about it."

The sun dipped below the horizon, shrouding the river in dark shadows. The bonfire blazed. John Babbs held up a limp blob.

"The lobster tail," he cried. "Supper for all."

He threw it in the fire. It sizzled, popped.

"Hey, don't waste that," Hassler said.

He picked up a stick and pulled the lobster tail out, rubbed away the dirt and charred grit with his shirttail, and held out the tasty crustacean. An offering. Everyone recoiled from the ghastly morsel.

"Alright, you had your chance, now you can savor the pangs of hunger."

He threw it back in the fire. The mandolin twanged. A sour flute joined in. Sunset's scarlet streak morphed into the shrouding dark of night.

Summer's in the city and the back of my neck's feeling
mighty gritty. The latest tabulation is in. No one wants
that easy listening crap. More bus tapes, they're saying.
Quit playing those fucking insipid love songs. It's okay
in liberated America to use the F-word, but it is station
policy never to mention the dreaded M-word. The one
everyone sells out for. Makes the world go round. The
one the Pranksters never laid down on their backs for.
You can believe trusty old Kay Bee on that.
    — Ken Babbs

16

A Situation in Phoenix

Tangled Path. Arizona Route 93, radio blasting:
   "Jesus, lover of my soul, lead me to the sugar bowl
   If the sugar bowl is empty, lead me to my baby's pantry.
   Zeek! Zeek!"
   "Isn't that interesting," Cassady shouted over the radio. "Not only are we given the grace of, ah, like say, an *aesthetic*, but we can go twenty times faster. Like exceeding seven times the speed limit. Wrong line. Spin again out. Hike Pike's Peak climb. I've climbed that mountain many a time. Mostly sixty-three percent of outside hairpin curves are over the shelf, if you know what I mean. But you can't make your time cutting off them corners without making a straighter line. So, going wrong this curve, set up for that."
   Wickenburg. Beardsley. El Mirage.
   "Zeek! Bless the meat, damn the skin,
   open your mouth and cram it in.
   If you don't like my apples
   then don't shake my tree."

"I'd always have to stop going into something—bouncing off curbs, nothing to it—but you know what it really amounted to? I found out that you could throw into reverse anything under ten-miles-an-hour. But roadblocks now, that's something else!"

"This is an election year," Kesey said. "And we're in a candidate's home state. Whaddadya think of that?"

"I think, don't go on the wrong side of the bridge railing," Cassady said. "That is, of course, unless you is, I mean, really wailing. At that point all you can do is blast. So you see right then it don't matter much whether you're choosing this side of the curve or that side of the curve—you got to go on the other side of that railing, or else now, I mean to tell you the truth, *smash!* And *blasta-smashus. Begorgeous* and *be-gashus.*"

"Precisely," Kesey said. "Choosing this side or that side. What I think we oughta do is come out on his side."

"You mean support Barry Goldwater for president?" Hassler asked. "He's the antithesis of everything we represent. Running on a fervent Vietnam War platform, nuke the fucking gooks, a *macho-serioso* effort on his part, but over-the-top ridiculous and deserving of a prank that would puncture a hot air balloon."

"Aye, that's the rub," I said. "What've we got to lose? We're not running for anything and, so far, not running *from* anything."

"Unless," Cassady said, "you go on the wrong side of the railing of the bridge. When that time comes, at least in that day, whatever's in the way is going to join you. They ain't fighting against you. All they can do is make you look sheepish. Unless of course you feel a little something else kind of creepish. Like they say on the railroad, *you can always tell by the fear in dah belly how limited you are.*"

"Absolute to the true degree," Kesey agreed. "Attention all hands. Approaching Phoenix city limits. Break out the paints and flags."

"*Zeek! Life is short, death will come*

Let's go after it while we're young
Ain't no food on the table
and no pork up in the pan.
But you better not complain boy,
you get in trouble with the man."

"There's a place we can pull over," I said. "Let's get to work, Pranksters."

"Tsh, tsh," Cassady said, easing to the curb. "What I'm concerned with, will he beat my time down the hill? Talk about a bum's tour! A limited concept. Don't mess with the previous form any more than you have to. On the other hand, don't say the same thing twice. Not until the second time around."

We got out of the bus and spray-painted big letters on the side: A VOTE FOR BARRY IS A VOTE FOR FUN.

"Looking good, Pranksters," I shouted. "Let's not overdo it. Everybody in, we're going cruising."

Cassady fired up the engine. The outside speakers blared "The Stars and Stripes Forever." Dale and Zonk ran back and forth on the roof, waving big American flags.

"Bring her back," Kesey said. "It's all clear to the rear."

"Clear to the rear, dear," Cassady sang out. "Clear as far as the eye can see, but then you realize the eye can't see all that far."

He backed into traffic—and kept backing—past the stores, the bank. Pedestrians stopped in their tracks, women clutched their purses, men felt for their wallets, boys hooted and pointed, girls stuck noses in the air and turned faces away, babies cooed, waggled tiny fingers, a dog raised its leg and peed on a lamppost.

Sitting in their squad car on the corner, officers Callahan and Murphy, two of Phoenix's finest, balefully eyed the spectacle. They knew an insult when they saw one. Officer Callahan reached for the microphone.

"Hey, Kesey," Sandy yelled. "I'm picking something up on the scanner."

"Put it out on the speakers."

"Uh, Senator Goldwater, we have a situation in Phoenix. There's a big crazy bus with A VOTE FOR BARRY IS A VOTE FOR FUN painted on the side and it's driving backwards down Main Street with a bunch of people in striped shirts on top waving American flags and they're blasting, uh..."

He looked at Murphy.

"'Stars and Stripes Forever.'"

"Right. Over loudspeakers. You can hear them four blocks away. You want I should run them in?"

Awk! "Har, har, that's a good one, Callahan," Senator Goldwater answered. "I suspect those are some good old boys from up in Prescott funning with me. Certainly can't hurt the campaign any, long's they're not causing any trouble."

Squawk! "None so far."

"I think we've gone far enough," Kesey said. "Turn off the loudspeakers. Full speed forward, Cassady. Let's get while the getting's good."

"Timing perfect, as usual," Cassady said. "Escape lane open. Right turn, *harch*. City limit sign dead ahead."

"*Zeek! Floor to let, inquire within.*

Lady put out for drinking gin.

If she promise to drink no more,

Here's the key to her back door."

"*Desert escape! Desert escape!*" I yelled over the sound system. "Well-pranked, Pranksters. Secure from pranking quarters. Resume normal travel mode. All bunks well-snored. Full grog rations and meritorious conduct ribbons awarded."

Sometimes the load gets heavy,
other times it is a feather
blowing in the happy wind.
Look, here we are
laughing and giggling
and pissing all over ourselves.
Give it all you got, me hearties,
or as Cassady said,
"Don't eat when you're angry;
no one was ever happy, angry."
   — Ken Babbs

17

Three-Pronged Stickers

The radio in the bus was blaring Creedence Clearwater Revival and Dale stood at the bus door, jumping from one foot to the other. "What about a piss stop? Gotta go real bad."

"Piss stop, aye," Cassady said. "First cactus of concealment, bound to be one soon."

"How about behind that billboard?" Hassler said.

"Looks good to me," Kesey said. "Someone poke Cathy and see if she wants to stretch her legs. She's crashed since we left Wikieup."

"She's up," Hagen said. "No poking needed. It's peeing time for her, too."

"Okay. Men to the right, women to the left," Hassler ordered, assuming his military mantle. "No, not there. Go to the other side of the billboard, Cathy. The other side."

Ignoring Hassler, Cathy, still in her bra and panties, ran past the billboard and dived headfirst into a clump of flowers.

"No, Cathy!" Hassler yelled. "Don't roll around in there. Oh great Mary, Mother of Jesus, and all His sibling rivals!"

"Such beauties. Just like little babies," she cried, rolling in the clump. Then she began to scream. She hadn't come all the way down from her LSD high and wasn't conversive with the natural order of things.

"S-O-S! S-O-S!" Hassler yelled. "Give me a hand. Help pull her out."

Barefooted, I walked into the flowers.

"Son of a bitch! They're pointed as nails and twice as sharp."

"Let me in there," Kesey said. "I've got shoes on."

"Yow! Wish I did," I said. "What are those things anyway?"

"Goatheads. Three-pronged stickers hiding on the stems beneath the flowers. She's covered with them."

Kesey reached down for her.

"You beast," she snarled, pulling away. "I can see what you want. You're not fooling me."

Kesey and Hassler lifted her up.

"Take it off, take it off," Cathy shrieked, pulling at her bra. Kesey reached out with one hand and deftly sprung it loose.

"Pretty smooth move, Ex-Lax," I said.

"Years of back-seat experience. Look at that. The goathead lumps are turning purple. They match her areolas."

"Oh for Christ's sakes, Kesey," Jane said. "You're disgusting. But what would you expect from a man? Here, Cathy, let me help you."

She put a blanket around Cathy.

"Yeah, get her aboard before we get busted for indecent exposure," I said. "If the cops see her in this state of mind, we'll all be in the soup. Someone find the tweezers. I've got a thousand stickers in my feet."

"*Bo-ard!*" Cassady yelled. "All aboard for Houston. Next stop, Houston."

"*If you're ever in Houston, you better do right.*
You better not gamble, you better not fight.

Or the sheriff will grab ya and the boys will bring you down.
And the next thing you know, gal, you're prison bound."

"What are we going to do, drive all night?" George asked.

"Have to," Kesey said, "if we're going to get to McMurtry's tomorrow like I told him. Everybody settle in for a long haul. Keep an eye on Cathy. Where is she now?"

"Sitting out back on the platform, staying cool," George said.

"Keep her that way," I said. "We don't want to be trolling with cop bait."

"Come on, Babbs, lighten up," Hagen said. "Get off her case."

"Yes, *case*. That's what I'm worried about, that she goes from being a case to becoming some DA's caseload, and we're all dragged in with her."

"No sweat," Hagen said. "She's cool."

"Oh yeah, cool is as cool does. I say keep an eye on her. She still doesn't have any clothes on."

"*Zeek!*
Burning rubber in a hot rod Chevy,
Heading for a make-out down at the levy,
They be girls on blankets girls on the sand.
Yabba dabba, yabba dabba doo!"

With the coming of night, we cooled off. Jane sang quietly into the microphone, her voice oozing on through the speakers over the low-rumble roar of the bus:

"*Is there anyone up above us?*
If so, would they please sing a lullaby to us?"

I was in a bunk in the back trying to sleep when, just at the sweet edge of slipping off, I heard a truck roaring up behind—*AAAAAAAGGGGHHHHH*—gearing down, Jake Brakes blatting. Cathy had shed her blanket and was staring into the headlights of the truck's big orbs.

"Hey, John, John, wake up," Zonk said.

"Hunh? Whatsamatter?"

"Those trucks. They're acting weird."

"Get Sandy to turn on the CB."

"Good idea. Hey, Sandy, wake up."

"Yeah, yeah, I heard you."

He put the CB on the speakers.

Awk! "That's a ten-four, Big Chrome Dome, I've got her in my peeps now. What I don't get is how she can stare into the glare like that without blinking."

"Watch," Zonk said. "He passes us, and there's another one catching up."

"Not too hard to figure," John said. "A naked woman on the back seat. We better get her inside. Come on, Zonk. Help me."

"No!" she screamed. "Don't touch me, you cretins! I can do it myself."

She climbed through the rear window.

"Get her, Sandy!" Zonk yelled. "She's racing toward the front door."

He grabbed at her as she went past but her skin was too slick with sweat. He shook his head.

SCHBONK!

"You'da thought she'd stop before she reached the windshield."

"Head-on," Zonk said. "Let's assess the damage."

"None the worse for wear," Cassady said, steering with one hand, the other helping the dazed Cathy to the shotgun seat.

"Oh yeah?" Zonk said. "What about that windshield?"

"An excellent pattern," Cassady replied.

Cracks radiated from the center of the glass like a spiderweb where Cathy's head had smashed into it. Jane wrapped the blanket around Cathy.

"Zeek! I'm gwine away to leave you, an' my time ain't long.
The man is gonna call me an' I'm a-goin' home.
Then I'll be done all my grievin', whoopin', holl'in', and a-
* cryin'.*
I'll be done all my studyin' 'bout my great long time."

*What I'm doing is always more interesting than
what I've done. I don't know much, and what I
do know I often doubt. But as time goes by, I do
know there is a bunch more to know, and I find that
thrilling. It isn't by getting out of the world that
we become enlightened, but by getting into the world.*
— Ken Kesey

18
Pretty Straight Folks
Around Here

Houston. Rice University. Quenby Street. Shady oaks. Manicured lawns. Respectable homes. A curtain pulled back from a front window and a bespectacled eye peered out.

"See anything yet?" a female voice asked from the kitchen.

"They called from Flatonia, so it should be a few minutes yet," Larry McMurtry told his wife.

He stood looking out the window, his three-year-old son, Jamie, in his arms.

"Oh, God!" he said, dropping the curtain.

"What is it, dear?"

"It's them. But what a *them.*"

"What do you mean?"

"You'll have to see for yourself."

We parked the bus under oak canopies. Birds chirped in the quiet Houston neighborhood. A shrill laugh came from inside the bus. Carrying Jamie, Larry walked to the curb. Cassady opened the door.

Without a whisper of a warning, Cathy shucked her blanket

and hurtled clear out the door. Crying, "Oh, Frankie, Frankie!" she plucked Jamie from Larry's arms and cuddled him to her bare bosom.

"Ma'am," Larry said in his soft drawl, reaching for the boy. "Ma'am, would you please let go? The boy is crying."

Ron Bevirt, The Equipment Hassler, stood with eye locked to his still camera. Larry tugged Jamie. Cathy held fast. Jamie bawled.

Cassady popped out of the bus and draped the blanket over Cathy's shoulders. "We all have children back home, m'dear, and even our hardened hearts are suffused with longing; but you must admit, this is not the one."

She turned her dark eyes on Neal and loosened her grip. Larry held Jamie to his chest and walked back to the house, Pranksters trailing after.

Hassler stood staring, camera in hand.

"Did you get it?" I asked him. "Did you get that shot of Cathy and Larry and his son?"

Hassler shook his head no.

"She was naked. Stark Naked."

"And so she will always be known," I said, patting him on the shoulder. "Come on, let's go in."

"That naked woman going to be alright?" Larry asked Kesey.

"I hope so. Strung out is all. If she can make it through the next day or so it ought to wear off."

"Better keep an eye on her. They're pretty straight folks around here, you know."

"Hey!" I said. "Straight is as straight does. Like an arrow, *va-room*. Not to worry, we got it under control."

"Hmm," Larry murmured, looking at me over the top of his glasses.

"Okay, listen up, everyone," Hassler called out in his hefty Army voice, big grin on his face, *can't take this military shit too seriously.* "Let's get the laundry together, the brooms out, clean sweep fore and aft on the bus, then a good relaxing rest before we hit the open road."

Brooms. Trash cans. Laundry. Baths and showers. The outside light faded and sleeping bags were spread across the living room floor. Kesey made sure Stark Naked was in the middle, surrounded by Pranksters. To be on the safe side he told Dale to stay up all night and keep an eye on her.

Cicadas cackled in chorus from the trees. Snores answered from the house. A dark shape rose, slipped out the door and walked down the sidewalk. A dog barked. Clouds covered the moon. A thin band of light appeared in the eastern sky.

"**W**ake up!" Hassler shouted. "Wake up, you guys. She's gone."

"Nice going, Dale," Jane said. "You were supposed to be watching."

"I was right next to her. She was sound asleep. No way she could have gotten up and I didn't hear her."

"Well, she's gone now. Good thing she was dressed. Someone wake up Kesey and Babbs."

"Huh? Whazzat?" I mumbled, rubbing my eyes. "What's the plan?"

"Either go and search or wait it out here," Kesey said. "Let's check with Larry." He walked to the foot of the stairs. "Hey Larry, better get down here, something's come up."

Larry came down, tucking in his shirt. Kesey told him what happened and asked him what he thought we should do.

"Oh my," Larry said. "I think we should at least look around."

"Roger Dodger, old codger, that's a ten-four for shore," I said. "I'll roust up two volunteers. This is a touch-and-glow mission, fraught all the way."

"No, just you and me," Kesey said. "Larry drives. Rest of you get the bus ready to roll. We may have to beat a hasty retreat."

"Retreat, hell," I said. "We haven't even spotted the red of her eyes. Damn her torpedoes!"

"Right, full speed ahead," Kesey said.

We cruised the neighborhood, our eyes peering at eyes peering from porches and windows. We peered at bushes and lawns, behind oaks and maples and trees smelling of magnolia blossoms, no sign of Stark Naked.

"This is about the extent of the houses," Larry said. "From here on in it gets into the business area. I don't think she'd be out there in the open very long before she got picked up."

"Better return to home base," Kesey said, "see if there's been any report."

"Has there ever?" Hagen said when we got back. "Larry Hankin, her boyfriend from San Francisco, called. She phoned him from jail. Hankin is arriving in Houston on flight Four-Oh-Three United, gives us just enough time to meet him at the gate."

"Let's go," Kesey said. "We'll take the bus and pick him up on the roll. A moving target is hard to hit."

"Board!" Cassady yelled, hitting the starter. "*Bo-oard!*"

"Preparing to mount the flying deck," Kesey said. "I need liquid. I got trapped up here last time without liquid."

"Blast off," Dale said. "With one melon gone, they're counting them now in even rows."

"Six-four, six-four-nine," Chuck said, doing a mic check.

"Oodle-bee-bug smeared on the window," Dale answered. "That's paranoia for sure. Liberation yet to come. Ah, to hear the old harmonics, that train heading down the rusty trail. Another day gone and another sun rising and another five thousand galaxies spun into being. My cells feel the hard hat beating against the constant wind of time even as the wavelengths add scientific ratio to the stars."

"Did Dale take a little swiggle out of that reloaded orange juice jar?" Chuck said.

"Trying to work off his nighttime blunder, no doubt," Hassler said. "Letting Stark Naked wander off..."

"Navigator's report," Kesey requested from on top.

"Parkway dead ahead," I said. "Follow signs straight to air-port. Notice the airplane on the sign."

"Instrument corrections not needed," Cassady said. "Yellow light. Automatic second, sir. We go left and we're in the right lane."

"Liquid, must have liquid," Kesey said.

"Go, cars, go!" Cassady shouted. "Easing forward."

"Liquid going to the top. Airport dead ahead," I said. "What's the recognition signal?"

"I have him in sight," Kesey said. "Blue shirt. Black pants. Slicked-back hair and a patrician nose, bedecking a serious, six-foot frame looking wildly around for a plain, nondescript bus. He's spotted us and is cringing. Don't let him escape."

"Prepare for landing," I said.

"All stop," Cassady said.

"Landing party out." I opened the door and jumped down.

"Target is crouched behind a baggage cart." Kesey said. "I'm activating the outdoor speakers. *Hankin! We have you spotted. Do not be alarmed. This man is here to help you.*"

I took Hankin by the arm—"Right this way, sir, you are in safe hands."—and eased him through the door.

"Our guest is aboard," I told Kesey.

"Got it. All ahead full, Cassady. Beat feet out of here."

"Full ahead, sirrah. Clear to the rear. Merging traffic."

"Send our guest aloft," Kesey said. "I'll brief him on the situation."

"This way, please," I said, escorting Larry Hankin—still not speaking a word, not even a hello to Hagen—to the ladder and up through the turret.

Everything's still basically the same as it used to be.
Fire hurts when it burns you. If you fall in water,
you can drown. Rocks bruise. Wolves bite.
You go through a certain bunch of things that are the
same. The job of the shaman mystic is to pull away
from the Freudian mind. Let's quit examining ourselves
and trying to make ourselves psychologically perfect.
We aren't and never will be.
   — Ken Kesey

19

A Winning Hand in This Thing

Larry the writer and Larry the actor put their heads together and decided to call the police, find out what they knew about a woman named Cathy Casamo.

Larry McMurtry made the call and handed the phone to Larry Hankin.

"Hello, we're looking for a lost person," Hankin said. "She's about five-six, black hair, shoulder-length. She's wearing a black skirt, no shoes, no identification. I don't think she has a purse, even. Cathy Casamo. It's Spanish origin. She's twenty-five. She has one child. Me? I'm Larry Hankin. I'm from San Francisco and so is she. She came to Houston on a job, to work on a movie. I stayed in San Francisco. I got a call from her yesterday and she sounded like she was in trouble so I flew in and, when I got here, she had disappeared. The people who live here where she was staying say they last saw her about three in the morning, before everyone went to bed."

He turned to Hagen, covered the mouthpiece with his hand.

"Where was the last place you saw her?"

"Right here," Hagen said.

"She wandered outside and we thought she went onto the bus," Kesey added.

"In the house, in the living room," Hankin spoke into the phone. "How long have I known her? Six months. I'm really worried about her. What? Childhood diseases? I don't know. She had her baby in the hospital. Why? *Really?* Is she blacked out? No. Thank God. Where is the police station? Capital Avenue? Fourth floor. Okay. Thank you very much, sir."

He put the phone down. "Can one of you drive me?"

"You do it, Hagen," Kesey said.

"The jail will be on your left," McMurtry said. "The library and then a bunch of parking lots, and then the jail."

"It's all my fault," Hagen said. "She was perfectly straight in San Francisco before all this. And then she flipped out."

"You know, when we took that LSD," Kesey said, sticking his head in the car window, "she didn't take any. I watched her and she maybe took a sip but she didn't swallow it."

Hagen nodded. He could run with that.

"You got to be very cool with that stuff," Hankin told Hagen as they drove off. "It's not your fault. Kesey's in charge of this fucking mess. I don't blame him for letting her come along though. She's got a great face. Great for photographing."

"I was sitting outside last night and I knew where she was and I thought she was alright and suddenly she was gone," Mike said.

"When somebody's in trouble, you help them," Hankin said. "But to just let somebody go... To see them crack up... On the phone she told me she was kidnapped... I didn't sense it... She made a joke of it... Said, perhaps her condescending airs would turn them off... Like when she was starting acting classes at the university."

He leaned his head out the window. "Sir. Do you know where the police station is? Right ahead? Thank you, sir."

B ack at the house, Larry McMurtry was talking to his lawyer.

"Hello, Larry. Larry Golden? A situation has come up where I might need an attorney. Let me advise you as briefly as possible. Some friends of mine came in from California yesterday and they had a girl with them who was pretty disturbed; she was disturbed when she got here and got more and more disturbed during the day. During the night she got away from us and the police picked her up and put her under psychiatric surveillance. Is there any way that can be voided? I have a psychiatrist here, Larry Schwartz, and perhaps I could talk to him and have her put under his care. Alright, let's see what we can do. Much obliged."

He hung up and turned to us.

"I think we've got a winning hand in this thing. With me and Larry Hankin and Larry the lawyer and Larry the psychiatrist, we should be able to get her released in our care. As for the rest of you, it would probably be best if the bus were no longer around for any fingers to point at."

"Exactamente to the utmost," I said. "That is, I totally concur. What you think, Keez?"

"I think the quicker we get everybody aboard and get out of Dodge, the better for everything all around."

"*Bo-ard*, board," Cassady called, leading the way out. Kesey and I lingered to thank the two Larrys for covering for us with Stark Naked, and for putting up with our cockamamie intrusion. Handshakes all around, then we hit the highway and headed east.

Jane was looking morose.

"Whassamatter, Jane, you got the hongries?" I asked. "Or are you upset we left Stark Naked behind?"

"Neither. It's my suitcase."

She sat on it in the middle of the aisle.

"I don't have the nerve to carry it up the ladder and tie it on top while we're moving."

"Hells bells and cocker shells, I can do that for you."

"You'd do that for me?"

"Certainly. T-N-T, T'ain't Nothing To it. Move your butt and I'll do it right now."

I hefted the suitcase topside and lashed it to the rails along with the other bags and musical instruments. Something ahead caught my eye and I raced down the ladder.

"Pull over. Pull over," I yelled and, as soon as the bus pulled to the curb, I ran across the sidewalk into a small office, emerging ten minutes later waving a piece of paper.

"I did it, we are now free of all moral outrage and guilt trips baying at our behinds."

"What is that fool talking about now?" Jane asked.

"It was the Western Union office, so it must be about a telegram. But to whom and concerning what?" Dale said.

"What else but a note of succor to our dearly departed fellow traveler?"

I read the telegram aloud:

"*To Cathy aka Stark Naked stop congrats on fine performance stop captured on film and tape stop future stardom assured stop pressing demands of shooting schedule forces departure stop continued success and well wishes from the Merry Band end.*"

With the bus gone, a four-of-a-kind winning hand, Larry the writer, Larry the actor, Larry the lawyer, and Larry the shrink, worked together to get Stark Naked out of jail. Larry the writer picked her up at the police station. She was quiet and he didn't press her, except to ask if she wanted something to eat. She nodded and they stopped at a restaurant. As she packed away a large breakfast, he realized she hadn't eaten at the hospital, probably refused food. A full stomach loosened her tongue and she filled Larry in on what happened.

"I began to feel alienated. They were artists and actors and filmmakers and this made me feel even more apart... I mean if there was any group of people in this world that would be mine, where I would belong and feel like *this-is-it*, as far as a lot of things go for me, it should have been them... But it wasn't, and I was starting to withdraw. I didn't get in trouble until I went for that walk. I saw this police car pull up and someone said, 'Hey, sister, come over here.' The next thing I knew, I was on the ground handcuffed. They kept asking me for my name and address and slapping me around because I wouldn't answer. The only address I knew in Houston was yours, and I didn't want to give it to the police. Not the way the Pranksters were acting, with all that pot and stuff on the bus. I decided not to say anything. They thought I was a Mexican, maybe an illegal alien. The police put me in a hospital in a cell next to a woman in restraints. She never stopped screaming or crying. All the time there, she never stopped and nobody ever came to see her."

Sitting and listening to her gave Larry a chance to figure out what to do. He drove Stark to the airport and bought two tickets to San Francisco. He'd go with her. While sitting at the gate, they were surprised to see Larry the actor walk past. He was going to San Francisco, too. Larry the writer asked him if he'd be willing to take Cathy off his hands. He agreed, so Larry the writer said goodbye, had the money refunded on his ticket and went home.

We found out later that what Stark Naked did with the police and the hospital psychiatrist—keeping mum about where she was staying, not mentioning being with any other people—she had done deliberately, to keep the heat off of us. She bought us enough time to slip away—and for her heroic actions we awarded her, in absentia, her lifetime Prankster stripes.

I can believe anything. Let's look for some plot,
read a book at eight o'clock Sunday morning
down the middle of Canal Street or back of the
L & N Depot on the mouth of the Mississippi.
We could even manuscript a dandy circulating eye
around a steamboat fueled by the coal.
— *Neal Cassady*

20

Whatever the Trip Permits

"What's that godawful smell?" Kesey asked.

"All the stuff ground into the rug," Jane said. "When are we going to clean this place up?"

"New Orleans," Kesey said.

"*I don't want no corn bread, peas, and black molasses,*" Dale sang. "*At supper time.*"

"*The grizzly, the grizzly, the grizzly bear. Nobody scared of the grizzly bear,*" Kesey joined in. "*Cap'n come-a down, he says come along with me and I'm-a lock down and I'm-a freak but I'm a lost man, and I don't know where I'm a-wandering around.*"

"*To the store and to the bank,*" I sang, "*and don't forget the dirty shirts need washed, come on hit me, switch me, britch me in back room Looeasyeeanna.*"

"*And when you're all alone,*" Cassady added in an old crooner's cadence, "*with no regrets. Little coquette, I love you. Just a gigolo. Everywhere I go.*"

Neal's head was full of World-War-Two love songs and jazz crooners, bits of old lyrics burbled up from memory, mixed with fluttery blap of lips and deep croaks from his gravelly throat.

"The bridge," Dale yelled. "Crossing the Mississippi."

"Drink to your neighbor," Cassady said. "We turn south on

Bay Cruise. I'd like to put the bus on the ferry to Algiers, go to Burroughs' home. He lived there for a time; it's quite a ways in, after you get off the ferry, four or five miles."

"Did you try to read those last things by Burroughs?" Kesey asked.

"*The Soft Machine*, yes, but I don't think it's as good as you do."

"I liked *Naked Lunch* very much," Kesey said.

Dale played a plaintive tune on his violin, a sad plantation refrain, redolent with moss and ground fog.

"We're coming into New Orleans," he said. "In honor of New Orleans, we ought to play 'When the Saints Go Marching In.'"

We did, but not like any "Saints Marching" they ever heard on Bourbon Street.

"Looking at God," Dale said, "face like a lantern, but for the world of mind and pattern, he left his heart in a furnace, saints marching, marching in..."

"I'll be crawling on my belly," Cassady cut in. "Crawling all the way to New Orleans. We will make it to the store and buy groceries. Don't forget the lurchy-church where we'll perch with the sisters and wrestle with the brothers. There will be kids and billy goats running from their mama in the flannel dress coming at me with her hand paddle to switch me—Oh, how she britches me, in New Awleens, *Looeyseeanna*."

We pulled over, shut it down and went to bed.

The sultry night gave way to a sweaty day. The bus was parked on a dock overlooking the Mississippi River. Water lapped against the piers. Sea birds perched on pilings. A banging on the door rousted Hassler.

A hefty cop wanted to know what we were doing there.

"We were looking for a place to sleep and this seemed like a good one," Hassler said.

The rest of us spilled out of the bus and milled around. The cop didn't look any older than we were in his black shades, khaki shirt with a white T-shirt underneath.

"What seems to be the problem?" I asked him.

"We got a call from downtown. The dispatcher said, 'There's a bunch of people down on the dock come here on a bus, freedom riders from what we hear. All dressed up in flags. They're a nuisance and I want you to go down there and stomp the living shit out of them, can you understand that?'"

Seemed clear to me why he was here. I backed off and the cop wrote our names on his clipboard. Another cop stood by their car and watched with an expression on his face that looked to me like he was thinking where's the best place to get a box of doughnuts.

Satisfied that we were no threat to the city and its denizens, they drove away.

We trooped back on the bus and slumped down on the seats.

"Walked away from another one, Chief," Cassady said.

Kesey grunted. He took a bowl out of the sink and mixed up an LSD-loaded drink we took turns drinking from, down to the last bitter drop.

"Crank her up, Cassady," Kesey said.

Neal wheeled around in the driver's seat and hit the starter.

We drove past stately houses fronted with porticoes and moss into the commercial district, where we found a place to park. Kesey wore his broad-striped, red-and-white T-shirt, a tape recorder hung from his shoulder. Chuck was clad in a vertical-striped, red-and-white shirt. I wore my red-white-and-blue-striped T.

I stopped at a recruiting sign that said, THIS IS A MARINE TALKING. I crouched next to it so Hassler could take a photo. Hagen shot with the Arriflex. I hammed it up.

"You might have thought that for a man to be a real man, he had to be a Marine," I said.

I pointed to the picture of the Marine in his dress blues on the front of the sign.

"This guy has it all wrong, dressed like that. Let me tell you how it really is. You have to put on your fatigues and work with the least amount of equipment the government will give you in order to obtain the best results."

I made a fist and flexed my muscle.

"The strength you know, you have to get it from within."

I banged on the door of the recruiting station. Shook my head—not open, too early—Sunday morning.

"I'm trying to get back in, and they're locking me out. I can solve their problems. They should let me take over."

I gave it up and we walked on.

An old, bearded man wearing a crushed fedora took a bite out of a candy bar and threw the wrapper on the sidewalk. Hassler picked it up and looked for a trash can. A Black guy approached us, a sign over his shoulder: AFL-CIO WAITERS AND HOTEL WORKERS ON STRIKE.

"Nobody pays any attention to a strike," Kesey told him. "Don't you have any dynamite?"

"Yeah, as a matter of fact, I do."

"Whoa," I said. "Destruction is not the name of the game."

We continued walking, hotter and stickier, to the Old Absinthe Bar where we heard a song and the tinkling of a piano oozing out the open door.

We made out the tune: "Moonlight Sonata." Peered into the gloom and saw a man slouched at a piano, hat over his eyes. A woman in a striped dress stood next to him, the Popsicle Queen of New Orleans, her stripes melting around the edges. She made an attempt to sing but her words trailed off. She gave it up and flowed into the other room.

Flies struggled on fly paper. Ice clinked in glasses, everything moved slower, like in a molasses mind warp.

"*I wandered around this country*," the man sang in a low and throaty voice.

"It's Moonlight Sinatra," Zonk said.

We took that morning jolt of acid with us into that room and sat on chairs, raising dust that floated in the air.

"Whatever the trip permits, we'll do," Kesey instructed. "Whatever's in front of us, we'll dig. Whatever is going on, we'll accept."

"I've been from town to town,

  seems to me it was always the same."

We stared at him with big oily eyes. He flashed that we saw something in him he never before realized he had.

"Some folks call me bad news.

You know I've got the blues.

I've wandered around this country.

Been from town to town."

He banged on the piano.

"Every time I see one of those big tall cameras, you know it makes me nervous."

"Only one thing to do at this point," I said. "Have a drink."

He lifted a glass from the piano top and downed the contents. Began playing and singing again.

"Hey bartender, give me one time,

The same time you gave me

One time before."

Kesey broke out his flute and played along, trying to find some kind of compatible clue. Moonlight Sinatra had no idea whether Kesey could play the flute or not. Kesey wasn't sure if Moonlight could play the piano. But he figured if they kept at it, they would communicate, they would harmonize. Otherwise, the people in the other room would come in and kick the living shit out of us.

Moonlight Sinatra took a break and told us his story. He was a welder in his dad's shop in Bayou Gauche and was hauling ass from the job. He had a gimp leg and other problematic sorrows. He motioned to a mangy mongrel with a stub of a tail, short yellow hair, misformed back leg.

"That's little Lame. He was a stray hanging around the welding shop and one day knocked a piece of steel off a pile. That damned dad of mine kicked the dog across the floor. 'Git rid of him, he's dead,' the sumbitch said. I couldn't hardly see I was so teared-up. When I reached to pick him up, his brown eyes fluttered, his tail wagged, he shivered all over and tried to crawl. Lame lived. I picked him up and left for New Orleans and we been here ever since on a three-day drunk."

Kesey never did discover what key he was playing in. Laughter came from the other room, air thick with dust motes swirling, and when Kesey asked Moonlight if he'd like to come with us to New York City, he said yes and followed us out the door to the bus and got in.

Dressed in his city-going clothes, pork pie hat, wrinkled, blue serge suit, threadbare white shirt open at the sweat-stained collar, Moonlight Sinatra heaved a drunk sigh and sat down on the couch. When he spread his legs, a gagging funk rose from the miasma of his three-day, punk-junk drunk. We realized we better tip this guy in the water before he went off.

"Where's the nearest pond?" Kesey asked him.

"Go to Lake Pontchartrain."

He didn't know where it was, somewhere up north toward Tuscaloosa, near his dad's welding shop.

Little Lame jumped on the bus, scooted past Kesey, gimped up to Moonlight Sinatra and climbed up on the couch.

"Gonna need gas, Chief," Cassady said.

He drove to a station. Regular, 28 cents a gallon. Two small boys, shirtless, stood gaping. Two ladies, one in a white dress, the other wearing red, walked past without a glance. The gas attendant, short-sleeved, round hat with the brim turned up, stuck the hose in the tank.

Kesey emerged from the bus with a flourish of a bright red cape. He was dressed as a matador, round, flat top hat with a strap under his chin, the kind a movie bellhop wears, except the hat was covered with plastic flowers that concealed earphones and a two-way radio.

I felt my way down the door steps. I had the same earphone and radio setup in an aviator's helmet. A black, plastic visor covered my face. Small bull horns were glued to the top of the helmet. Sandy gave me directions over the radio.

"*Now*," he cried and, head down, I charged forward to where I hoped Kesey waited. Kesey flourished his cape and twirled around. I shot past and, under Sandy's orders, skidded to a stop, turned around and charged Kesey again, back and forth while Kesey swung and twirled, making appropriate "*oles*" with me snorting and bellowing to roars and applause from the crowd that had grown, bullfight music from Bizet's "Carmen Suite" piped out of the speakers on top of the bus. "*Toreadora don't spit on the floora, use the cuspidora, that's what it's fora.*"

"Board, *bo-ard*," Cassady roared and we stumbled into the bus. Moonlight Sinatra sat on the couch with his arm around the dog and sang in his ear:
"*Yesterday's love, tomorrow's memories,*
but there will be no tomorrow for me.
And my love will last through all time to be.
Yesterday's love come back to me."

We drove out of town. Two Black men sat on upturned crates beneath an open-sided machine shed, the lot overgrown with weeds. At the end of the shed, a wooden-slatted trailer and a black sedan sat in the grass. Behind them, a yellow tractor with an umbrella leaning over the seat.

We pulled into the parking lot at Lake Pontchartrain. The place was layered with time. Large trees overhung the graveled lot. Blue sky streaked through the branches. A reality folded in like a cake.

We walked through people sitting on blankets and standing

on the grass. John Babbs took the plunge and the rest of us followed. Sandy stood in the water and held up his hand, spray-painted red. Hassler played mournful notes on the trombone, one of his rare trombone solos. We floated on tubes, tootled on our instruments. A studly man in a tight, red swimming suit, a key hanging around his neck, strode by. John Babbs slapped the water with a deflated inner tube. Zonk, beating the water with sticks, said, "Just like at the river Styx."

Chuck said, "Looks to me like we've got it stirred enough."

"And we better get the Hades out," Kesey said.

"Yes, I'm getting the feeling we're not entirely welcome here," Jane said.

Hassler looked around. He couldn't put his finger on it, but something wasn't right.

"Let's get in the bus," he said.

We gathered our gear and walked away from the lake. Two boys watched us go by. We heard them talking behind us.

"Man, you see them cats floating on inner tubes and playing those horns?"

"Yeah, but didn't sound like no music to me."

"No. What that tall cat say—'Form of nonverbal communication?'"

"Yeah, but communication with what?"

"Some kinda angel, else they'd been busted for swimmin' in our mudhole, and that's a beatdown no-no out here."

The sound system on the bus blared James Brown, "Please Please Please." Barefoot teenagers gyrated on the hot asphalt. We clambered aboard. The music abruptly stopped. The starter ground. The engine caught. Cassady eased onto the highway and hit the gas.

The sudden acceleration set Lame the dog a'barking and Moonlight rousting from his nap. He sat up, looked around wildly, struggled to his feet and grabbed the dog. We were out on the highway, picking up speed.

"Let me out, I have to get back to the welding shop. Let me out right now. Right here."

Neal pulled over and Moonlight staggered off the bus, carrying the dog. Neal drove away, leaving the bewildered duo behind, two forlorn silhouettes receding in the dust.

"You, know, we did some kind of reverse integration back there," Hassler said. "A wonder nobody called the cops."

"What's that, officer?" Cassady yelled from the driver's seat. "Freedom riders? No siree, sir, we don't know from no freedom riders. We're making a movie, right, J.B.?"

We may be sleazy and we may be hot, but we're
all we've got. Ritual is necessary for us to know
anything. You've got to get out and pray to the
sky to appreciate the sunshine; otherwise you're
just a lizard standing there with the sun shining
on you.
— Ken Kesey

21

That's What Comes from Reading *Tom Sawyer* in the Third Grade

We were tired, hungry, broke and sweaty-hot when at last we came to a small town in the Florida Panhandle. We pulled in and stopped to regroup, restore our supplies, restock our sagging energies.

"Where's the money sack?" I asked, poking around in the seats. "Ah," I held it up. "What's this, down to the last bit? Time to get more."

We called on Faye to wire us another grand. The phone rang twenty times, looking like it would be the longest standing-around-not-doing-anything phone call in the history of the phone booth. We left George Walker on the line and went back to the bus and bagged up our clothes, hiked to a laundromat, stripped down to our undies, filled machines with our grungy outfits, jammed quarters into the slots and, to kill time, chanted and sang and beat out *whang-bang* rhythms to the *shoosh, whir, glurp* of the washing machines and the *thud-thock* of the dryers until they wheezed to a stop. We put on clean clothes, folded the rest and turned to leave just as two cops came in.

"We got a report saying some crazies are tearing up the place and making an awful racket. You see anything like that?"

We looked at one another, shook our heads.

"Not while we were here, officers."

We paraded out the door while they poked around the washers and dryers, looking for clues we presumed. We met George on the sidewalk.

"I finally got through to Faye. The money's on its way."

Kesey and I hustled to the Western Union, then to the bank to cash the money order and—money bag full of one-dollar bills, stomachs full of ratburgers, duffel bags full of clean clothes, gas tank full of gas—on we rolled. Cassady burbled, "We're living in the moment. Emerson and the transcendentalists taught that if you get totally into the mundane tasks, you transcend your normal woes and cares and worrisome thoughts, and find real glee. Like me, doing the dishes; Carolyn loved me for that."

We drove across the Panhandle, lolling and dozing in the Deep-South heat until early evening, when we pulled over at a state park next to a refreshing lake. Jumped in and cooled off. Spread blankets on the grass. Cut up a watermelon. Savored welcoming, wet relief.

A police car pulled up behind the bus. The officer emerged from the car, his wide-brimmed campaign hat with a twisted cord around the top of the brim tied neatly in a square knot with the ends dangling.

Kesey picked up two slices of watermelon, walked over and offered one to the policeman, who shook his head, mouth a stern line. Shiny, bright sunglasses reflected the black watermelon seeds Kesey spit toward the ground.

The rest of us sat watching. Everything from the bus was strewn on the grass, for we had emptied the interior to clean it. Cassady paced the perimeter, smoking a cigarette and muttering.

"We're not out for kicks alone; we have a genuine mission, forces of chance at work and all."

"Y'all's going to be mistook for freedom riders," the cop told Kesey, "unless you get some Confederate flags up there on that vehicle. And y'all better put that-there motorbike on the back where it belongs."

"We can be trusted to drive an enormous bus all the way around the nation," Kesey told him, "but not a Mustang around the Bay Area. This is the fear thing, you know. It doesn't matter how much security and credit and community goodwill and social prestige that you build up, there always exists in the framework of our rules in society the fact that all you have to do is push the right button and it's blown. That's our great talent. We're unerring in searching out those buttons."

"I don't know ary-thang 'bout that," the cop says, "but if I was you I'd push the button that starts that bus and takes you all the hell out of my county."

"Only too happy to comply," Kesey said and, after putting everything back in the bus, we hit the road, continuing our hot summer search for the Kool Place.

Searching for the Kool Place had a double meaning. We were looking for a place to cool off, like a swimming pool or a lake or river, but searching for the Kool Place also meant finding the Kool Place inside yourself where you would be happy, or at least content. One of the ways we learned to find the Kool Place was to do the now-trip, because when you're totally in the now that is a Kool Place, free of hang-ups and old, tired, rehashed frets and worries. Someone once asked me, "Can you write a good explanation of finding the Kool Spot in people's souls?".

"I doubt it very much," I told him, "unless you include sitting quietly in lotus obsession unraveling the knots in your belly-button. Divine revelation can't be beat up or knocked down in a ten-round fight or seven-minute brawl when arguing the finer points of angels gathered on the heads of pins deciding what to wear to the prom."

"Let's rig the sound up," Kesey said. "I think we should give it a whirl. I think sometimes, we don't need to record right now; if we don't get it this time, we can get it later. But that's not necessarily true, because each time is totally individual; resolve is put into it by various individuals. We'll get everything working and do the now-trip."

"Didn't we already do that?" Dale said.

"Yes, but this time we're recording it. We can include it on a record."

"Oh boy," Hassler said. "A movie and a record both—hot shit."

Sandy turned on the tape recorder. Zonk took the microphone and started it off.

"Dale's in front of me with his crossbow and Cassady has a horn in his hand. Chuck is in front of the amplifier, there's the speaker, the tape recorder, a paper cup, the joints, lights going past outside, my fingers touch the top of my head."

Chuck took the microphone.

"Top of my head, hair's all mussed up, I see lights, headlights, bright lights, green lights, joint rolled, need a match. We could light it with a bug, real hot bug, loose-rolled joint drops sparks, ashes glow."

Dale took the mic next.

"I've got the lights in front of me, cars coming at us, shifting gears, the horn *oooooh ahhh,* things on the floor wiggling toes, the vibration coming up, up my legs, into my rear, up my back, down my arms, and out my fingers and I slump into a cigar."

He passed the microphone to Kesey.

"I'm feeling the sweat on my forehead and the slight pain that's about to go away underneath it, hearing the bus thinking about trying to be honest, feeling the *jar-jar-jar* of the bus and hearing that little *tweet-tweet* of feedback."

"I see John Babbs gawking at me," Gretch said, next in line. "The back of Cassady's head is bobbing and weaving like a prizefighter's. Sandy is listening in the earphones and laughing. A diesel truck going by is blaring his horn and I'm passing the microphone to Hassler."

Hassler said, "It shattered my head. I'm seeing lines. Chuck with his hand on his ear. Ken a watch in his hand. Neal, arms tensed, contemplating, while I hand him the microphone."

"We have a choice of slicky-time grill, heh heh, oh the truth. More like, 'I've been a lulu in a cake, oh, the ghost of you clings, these foolish things remind me of...' Where's Babbs?" he sang.

"Dale stands in front of me with his crossbow," I said. "Chuck leans on the amplifier, the light from the tape recorder flashes like the lights coming in from the road. Kesey rubs a newspaper on top of my head."

"*I'm back in the saddle again,*" I sang.
"*Back where a friend is a friend.*
Where the cowboys howl
and screw the old man's cow
back in the saddle again."
"*And when you're all alone, with only regrets,*" Cassady sang:
"*Lonely to love you, little coquette.*"

Then added, "Who's doing that melody line? Has anybody seen my comb?"

There were no longhairs on the bus. We were trying to get to the right place, the space between the now and the plow so we could get the ground turned into something worthwhile. Long hair was a pain in the ass. Short hair meant you didn't have to do anything but run a washcloth through it. All that garbage of makeup and deodorant and cologne, who needed it? Taking up your precious time and sapping your ever-depleting energy. We're working against gravity and friction. Path of least resistance is the secret.

Cassady barely needed a comb but running it through his

hair gave him something to do and, as for the oils, his tongue ran on a natural mental grease that slicked words out of his mouth before he had a chance to think about them.

Hassler pulled a long string of dental floss out of its packet and yanked the floss in and out, specks of food shot out, ending in one final swipe as he pulled the floss all the way through. He wound it in a ball and pitched it in the trash.

"What about that guck you just spit on the floor?" Jane asked.

"No sweat. It will get ground into the carpet with the rest of the crud."

"Wonderful," Jane muttered. "My kingdom for a vacuum."

"Supervisors are the mouthpiece like the FBI-boy tickling the neck of every male clue or two," Cassady said. "Thank God the second cousin used Sunkist in the adjournment. Forty moves down he reached morbidity, mother's lost, starving boy."

"Locked away in Bellevue," Kesey said.

"Oh, thank you, that was the clue I couldn't find anew. First I knew, in Denver in '42, was psychosis with the girls."

"We can't think back a lot because I never made a whole lot," Kesey said. "Everybody has to customize me. There's a note on the tree that says *here is what I believe myself to be, because this thing I thought up here is me.* So what kind of grade do I get? Not quite as high as Carnation but a little bit louder than Spam. What grade did you get?"

"An A comes first," Cassady said.

"All these little things that run through our graveled minds," Kesey said.

"Like the boy who said he was going to get away from his small town, he always had it in him but never let it out," I said.

"Unhappily he was second in the soapbox derby that year," Neal added.

"He left behind his twenty-first birthday and last pair of argyle socks," I replied.

"His sack of marbles," Kesey said.

"And set out for California riding his little racing car."

"He got to Indiana," Neal said. "At first he didn't know just how many rubber tires he would need, so he put only a few in his bag. It wasn't as though I didn't know until I joined Woody Guthrie that Kansas would be the name when I first hit forty. Kansas City Kitty had two big ones leaned out the window and said, 'Give me a pint of gin, son.' I said, 'I'm only fourteen,' and she said, 'Alright,' and yelled at the cab to stop here, and looked for some gin at the Joe Lewis Hotel, L-E-W-I-S. Not Joe L-O-U-I-S, who's doing all the letters on this mess. But that's what comes from reading *Tom Sawyer* in the third grade."

We plowed through the Deep South, fought the heat, squashed and sprayed the bugs. Gretchen Fetchen, down to her underwear, slapped at a mosquito on her back.

John Babbs, watching, said, "Here, let me."

She swatted his hand away.

"Eyeball kicks are among the world's greatest," Cassady yelled from the driver's seat. "Second-to-none in terms of abstract thought. The way you handle these kicks is what determines your particular conclusion to each moment's outlook. Remembrances of your life and your eyeball-view are the only two immediate firsthand things your mind can carry instantly."

We drove through the night to the top of the Blue Ridge Parkway, stars ice-bright diamonds, Pranksters crashed in the bunks, sprawled on the couch, stretched out on the floor, cuddled on the mattress up on top.

Down off the mountain, road winding along switchbacks, picking up speed, Cassady's voice following along: "We wallow on the side and top of the ditch, but there ain't no way one of us gonna get down in that muck, no matter how desperate we be. Turds and garbage float past on the slime-covered surface of our salvation. Total miscegenation. Let the kids apply their greater brainpower and understanding."

George, sitting on the film case next to Cassady, looked at

him.

"Neal is there something wrong?"

"Seems the brakes are not cooperating at this juncture in earth-time and the universe is buckling and heaving, trying to compensate, which entails a need to downshift quickly."

He double clutched, gave it the gas when hitting neutral, slipped from fourth to third gear, engine and tranny slowing us down—but we still hurtled along too fast.

"*Pashoom*, the juice is flowing, the wheels are turning, and here we go again..." Double clutched and downshifted. The engine howled. Bodies stirred and eyes opened—something was wrong.

Cassady slipped the tranny into first. The engine roared, headlights piercing the night. Everyone crowded to the front, "Come on, come on, Neal, keep her on the road."

He cut corners on the curves, the grade lessened and, to cheers and hugs and claps on Neal's back, we hit level road, where Cassady dropped into granny gear. We lugged to a stop and parked next to a grassy sward. The sun rimmed the eastern horizon. Kesey said to me, "Get your cap, cape and sword."

I rummaged in the bus for my green cape and hung it over my shoulders. Stuck a jaunty feather into the band of my Robin Hood hat. Grabbed my wooden sword with the red-painted crosspiece and marched out to the grass where Kesey had gathered the troops in a circle with Cassady in the middle.

"Verily we are joined here for the most auspicious ceremony in Pranksterdom," Kesey said, "whereupon we bestow upon Speed Limit the highest recognition of valour, strength and fortitude ever known in the annals of lasteryear. Please kneel."

Cassady looked around, flustered. "Well, never, I mean, once when Carolyn clunked me with her silver spoon, that was a high mark."

He wiped the grass with his hand and knelt.

Kesey pointed the sword waist high.

"With this sword I bestow the title of knighthood upon your personage as testimony to your great deed."

He tapped one shoulder with the blade, then the other.

"Rise, Sir Speed Limit, and take your rightful place in the pantheon of those already sirred, like Sir Lance-a-Lot, Sir Axe-a-Plenty, Sir Sword-a-Thrust, Sir Cudgel-a-Bop, Sir Knife-a-Stick and the multi*dudes* of lesser, Sir Fist-a-Cuffs."

Cassady stood and preened, eyelashes batting, "Reminds me of my first car, a model A. I couldn't reach the brake pedal so I nailed a block of wood on it and found out I could throw the car into reverse anytime under ten miles an hour..."

Interrupted by Jane: "Oh, come on, Neal, don't be so modest."

Then Hassler: "Neal you know this was your top-notch maneuver, all the way down without brake one."

George: "And I sat alongside you every frightening minute and you never flinched, nor blanched."

More of the same until Kesey said, "Let's put a lid on it and put Cassady to bed. He deserves a good sleep."

Neal crashed in the back of the bus. Hassler put a pot of water on the stove to make oatmeal. I skimmed off a cup and went outside to shave in the side mirror. The sun warmed the grass and steam rose into a cloudless sky, boding a good day of driving. Madhattan was a straight shot north.

The only big mistake we ever made, as a force,
was thinking for a while that we were going to win.
We're meant to lose, every time. You make these forays,
you write these books and you perform this music
and make these movies, but the big juggernaut of
civilization continues and you get brushed to the side.
I think all through history there's been these kind of
divine losers that just take a deep breath and go ahead,
knowing that society's not going to understand it, not
even caring. 'Cause everyone's too busy having a good time.
— Ken Kesey

22

The Elementals
Were Getting Through

Flat farm country. White barn in the middle of a plowed field. Sign along road, KEEP AWAKE, followed by another, FOR SAFETY. A car pulling a camper trailer passed on the left. Cassady bounced in his seat. The microphone, hanging from the ceiling by its cord, swung back and forth over Neal's head. Mike Hagen pointed the Arriflex 16 mm camera, loaded with a 400-foot magazine, over Cassady's shoulder, aimed in on the road ahead, then switched to Cassady's face reflected in the driver's rearview mirror.

Sandy sat in front of the Sony reel-to-reel tape recorder, the reels turning. The generator—we called it the jitterator because the vibration made us jitter around to its beat—ran smoothly on the back platform. Cassady's words boomed out of the speakers inside the bus and on top.

"Welcome to New Jersey, speed fifty. New Jersey Turnpike.

New York, one hundred. There's a woman driver, goddamnit, that's why I passed her the first time. Come on around here, black car. Shit, see what I mean? She doesn't have any concept, her ass is full of beans. Git up there, or I'll run right over you. That woman had her dress above her knees—I think it was her knees..."

The bus tooled along a steady fifty in the right lane, a semi passed in the middle lane, cars ripped by in the outer lane. The windows were open, hot wind blew through, curtains flapped in the breeze. Cassady flapped his voice in unison.

"Here's a movie, a suggested screenplay written by Cassady. *Everything*. Returning then, to the rural French town, where our lead, Pierre Levay, obsessed with racing, but who can't race worth a damn, he's the poorest of the bunch, it runs in his family. Right, J.B.?"

Why does Cassady call Kesey, J.B.? we wondered. Something to do with movies.

"Pierre is emotionally and physically tied up with auto racing," Cassady continued, "and he vows like a sick cat, *I'll beat this track*. He builds a car and runs it in the Le Mans, twenty-three hours of auto racing with this cat fulfilling the obsession of his life. He reached for fourth gear and through some freak, some accident of brake, some accident of corner, some accident of everything, *he hit second and BLEW IT*—transmission, rear end, everything, and loses the race. Didn't even finish, ha ha ha. That's his main thought. Not finishing is an obsession with him."

Gretch and Chuck sat on the mattress on top of the bus and listened to Cassady's voice booming out of the speakers.

"Only one race a year," Chuck chortled.

"No wonder he's obsessed," Gretch said.

"So, the next year, Neuberger, this German guy, hires him as a driver in the Le Mans, and he's behind Lance Macklin, driving a Triumph, going about eighty, ninety, wide open. Then behind

Macklin comes Mike Hawthorne driving a Jag. Approaching the
pit, Hawthorne should've gone behind the Triumph, hit the
brakes and slammed into the pit, but instead he chose to pass
Macklin driving the Triumph, then Hawthorne hit the brakes,
and turned into the pits. Macklin, to avoid him, hit his brakes
too, and at the same time turned like a freak toward the stands,
when here comes Pierre Levay barreling down on Macklin in
the Triumph. At a hundred and forty Pierre turns away and bar-
rels into the crowd, nothing he could do, he couldn't change his
position. A hundred-forty-three dead. A hundred-forty-four including Pierre.

"There you go, a typical Hollywood nowhere idea, ha ha. I
did it that way because how else can I think? You know the biggest sport in the United States? It's auto racing. Check that thing
out, off to the left."

A low-slung building sat in a brown grass field. A big white
round balloon, with the words USA'S SPACETEAD painted across
the front, was tied to the roof of the building.

"Secret government space facility," Hassler said. "Don't look
at it."

"Fuck that," John Babbs said. "We're supposed to look at it."

"That's it," Sandy said. "That way they can capture us, not
our physical selves, but our essences of image and sound and
thought."

"Then they are way ahead of any space aliens," Jane Burton
said, "who have to gobble you up in their saucers to figure out
what makes us tick."

"We're trying to catch up," Dale Kesey said. "Like a frog going up the stairs, climbs two and falls back three."

"You're all crazy," Zonk said, rousing from his nap.

"Dig this semi passing," Cassady said. "It forces me behind
the other semi, but the lane widens permanently to three lanes.
An Oldsmobile nemesis to our left, it seems like it always has to
be an Oldsmobile, I don't know why. The first car I ever stole,

an Oldsmobile. Remember this song?

"*Never to be seen in a T-Bird,*

never to be seen in a Merc.

Never to be seen in a T-Bird.

If you're in a Merc you're a jerk.

You're a JERK."

He paused, eyed the dashboard.

"I understand this ethics gauge doesn't move anymore. It might be the only thing that I should know about, like we always know something about batteries. If the battery isn't good, sometimes you'll catch it making a good charge, like batteries will do if they're low, but the last thing I want to mention about this bus is that temperature gauge was not working when we stopped at the White Kitchen, where George Walker sat on the goddamn table on the patio, wailing away on the goddamn saxophone—the best part, the major portion, being George Walker himself sitting with that saxophone, not some phony baloney idea George Walker has of George Walker blowing... *Pashoom...* Ease throttle, that's better, got to keep it under, overdrive on the way out, underdrive on the way back—*OH SHIT*, pull over, pull over... Now as far as the smoking..."

"We've been stopped," George said. "We've been stopped."

"Turn the generator off," Kesey said. "Take the portable tape recorder out."

A cop car pulled to a stop in front of the bus. The officer was young, dressed in a light-blue, long-sleeve shirt, dark-blue tie, leather strap from his left shoulder down to his belt. Dark-blue pants, revolver on his hip, hat with a badge in the middle.

"Get off the top of the bus," the cop said.

Gretch and Chuck clambered down the hole into the bus.

"License and registration," the cop said to Cassady, who had come out to meet him.

"Of course, officer."

Neal stuck a cigarette in his mouth and dug out the paperwork.

"Where are you heading?" the cop asked.

"To a party on Madison Avenue; I think it's Madison Avenue, or one of those places. It's a private party, of course. Our last stop was Gainesville, Georgia, not last night but the night before."

Kesey set the Bolex camera on a tripod and zeroed in on Cassady handing his license to the trooper. The cop looked at Kesey. Sandy, portable tape recorder on a strap over his shoulder, pointed a shotgun microphone at the officer, who then ordered everyone back on the bus. Everyone but Cassady.

The two stood in animated talk, then the trooper walked to his car and drove away. Cassady clumped into the bus, fell in the driver's seat, turned and filled us in.

"We talked, even intimate, and we shook hands, did you notice? There's one thing, and this is serious, not a leg, not a foot, you can't even sleep on the back seat with your feet out the window—the toe can't even stick out. In Texas and the South, you fear for your life just because you are there; up here they fear for your life if your ass is hanging out, or your head under bridges that I pass close by, but not too close—that's why I don't take your head off."

Cassady pulled out onto the Turnpike. Jane asked if the cop was being tough.

"No, he eased off soon as I set him straight. 'Course I realized, the best thing in these short time bits, especially under my present mood, is running commentary. So while he's fiddling and thinking, covering by writing and so on, you're changing his judgment at one-thirtieth of a second, and in that changing of judgment, there's no imposition, he's still the boss.

"'As a railroad man,' I told him, 'I myself, from personal fear, have never put my foot, as you described, officer, never put my foot out the rear window sleeping, and I understand the severity. We come from San Francisco, go up and down the same kind of four-lane highway—bloody Bayshore, perhaps you've heard of it. No? Well, pleasure to shake your hand, and know I'm talking to a man, I'm not talking to someone who could seriously conceive of running over a guy's foot in a driveway.'

"He said, 'What do you mean, are you a mixed crowd?' 'No, no, no, not even political.' His eyes came right with me, all the way and he talked to me like a brother. Nothing personal, he was officious all the way, but his eyes softened.

"He started to write my name and I felt it. Up my spine came the kundalini—not the kundalini as purified, not the real kundalini as transcendence, of course not. We are living by the four lower centers of the endocrine gland, the center of force: the ductless gland, the sex gland, the gonads, the adrenals, and the thymus, the thyroid, yes, then the pineal pituitary—in the head the feel is fossilized, that's why we're not prime soul.

"Anyhow, so what happened, the elementals were getting through, up the spine, and I felt it. I had the intensity, I had the emotion, I had the power and I knew I had him, right there. I saw him write N-E-A of my first name... The tone, the resignation as the fire went up me—of loss, that's what it was—it was the reaction of loss that sent this chill up the spine.

"He still had not written the letter L in the name Neal, and I said, 'I'm no virgin, I'm forty years old driving a '39 International Harvester and it's not as if I haven't been stopped before for driving, and the irony, the matching *ludicrousy*, the only trouble we've had on the trip is here in New Jersey, innocent victims of these young boys' desires. First time in New York, they're a bit out of their minds, a couple of them, those guys on the back.'

"He said, 'I understand, this is a warning, but if you get one again...'

"He had to finish. He did his duty. Gave me his warning words: 'There's nobody on the outside, is there, *no*, and there's *no breaking of the law.*'"

"No breaking of the rhythm either," Dale said. "Let us celebrate with cymbals, harps and lyres."

"Would a mouth harp do?" John Babbs asked. "I've got a harmonica here someplace."

"Oh God," Jane said. "Here we go again with the malapropic Biblical inanities, and on top of that the noise Pranksters call music?"

"Ever and forsooth," Hassler said. "The beat must go on."

"What was it? What's the word for hurling insults at?" Cassady asked. "You know, vindictive? Invective? Invectives were hurled in Pascaloosa, but I didn't mean the town. I told him we had invectives hurled, prejudgment and false judgment, just a strange vehicle, that's all that it is.

"I did time for guilty knowledge of stolen goods, but we know the Nazis stole the art treasures and were guilty. All right, that's enough, and speaking of enough, we don't have gas enough for the final run in, and there's a station just ahead."

"Do it," Kesey said. "There's an extra turn-off lane."

"All clear to the rear, dear? Coming over if that old woman in the Chrysler will let me. Generator is full, so we won't use the pumps on that side. Diesel, we don't want diesel. Buses! That's us."

"They pump our gas," George said.

"They will of course, thank you, what a brain. George, if you do that one more time, you'll have to be a disciple."

Cassady pulled to a stop. Everyone bailed out and headed for the restaurant and restrooms. I hung back and fished the credit card out of my wallet.

"Fill her with regular," I told the towheaded attendant, and headed for the restaurant.

*When Shakespeare was writing, he wasn't
writing for stuff to lie on the page; it was
supposed to get up and move around.
Storytellers told a story. The better
they were at telling it, the more famous
it became. Chopes were writers that
moved from castle to castle. The word,
"Chope," means "see, to see, and be seen."
Chopes went from castle to castle and
told about the castle they just came from,
how beautiful the maidens were and how
powerful and manly the knights were.
They helped prop up a young civilization.*
　— *Ken Kesey*

23

Going in with
Everything Working

"**B**oard!" Cassady yelled, "I want J.B. to know any ordinary
man would have at least taken a piss or washed the fog
out of his eyes after a cup of coffee, but not me. We'll be in the
city in an hour, less than an hour. What's the hang-up? Oh, I
see, they're counting to make sure everyone is aboard. The first
three are solid. Two or three gathered together, twelve is still a
mighty group. Christ, that's all he could handle. Remember the
argument over accepting the gentiles? That was the board's decision, I surmise. Everything is original—first time, for example,
that I've ever done this approach to New York. I don't care if
I've done a million approaches, that's why you're allowed to
freely summarize. Surmise. Come on, car. Thaaat's better. Wo-

man. Perfectly sound, still got her left blinker on."

"She might turn some time," Kesey said. "She might even turn left."

"No, impossible, J.B."

"I wouldn't rule it out," George said.

"I wouldn't rule it out either. She knows this condition, getting ready for it a mile ahead because she drives this road every day... C'mon here, Plymouth, you bitch, come on. *Pashooom!*"— *shifts gears*—"Oh stop that there. See he almost got me; I knew what was coming."

"I was watching," George said.

"If anybody else had been there, I'd have made the mistake. Alright, let's gear back down, I'm trying to go into a guard position. That is, first guard. We'll baby this hill, let her lug down quite a ways, even easing off.

"Well anyhow, then, for my own motive of talking here, at the moment, I'll keep up commentary with a running descripttion of the woman who killed herself. She used to rub my right nut while we drove, a few months later it blew up to twice its size, low grade infection."

Hassler leaned over Cassady's shoulder and handed him a plastic kid's recorder, five finger holes in a fat, white body with a blue, bell-shaped outer end. Neal waved it in the air.

"*Concerto New Jersey Turnpike.* Written, spoken and instantaneously conducted and composed backwards."

He twirled the flute, held it close to his lips, pretended like he was ready to blow.

"The reason this part is so messed up, the flute is backwards."

He blew, *taweet-taweet.*

"No variations on that one—no one was there but I waved at the car anyhow, just in case. He was fucking her with his eyes, just above the dashboard"—*taweet-tadoodle*—"speeders lose licenses"—*toodleee-toodle*—"concerto passing diesel"—*whee-wee-wheela-la-la*—"and a red-hot red Galaxy"—*weet-weet-blurbibly-*

woop—"oh, he's behind me, he didn't pass. I have someone to stay ahead of. New York, fifty miles. Alright, here we go, one-handed delight, no-no-no, that's masturbating"—*tweedle-ta-woot-tweet.*

A tall, thin Black man ambled along the road on the right-hand shoulder. He stared at the bus. He wore a dark suit coat over a white shirt atop dark pants and black shoes. A white T-shirt dangled from his hand. Neal gave him a quick wave with the flute. The man nodded his head.

"I never finished ninth grade because father came home from work at the same time I headed for school. I'd go to bed with his girlfriend and get up in time to greet him returning. She was a woman, thirty-eight, a bit of a redhead. The old man knew I was screwing her and when he'd get drunk, he'd cuss me out. When he needed a drink, I'd say, 'Okay Pa'—he was always sitting there with a hangover and not a sip—'if you want a four-bit bottle of wine, go get it.' I'd give him four bits and he'd run, that fat little old fella, run like hell, while I'd fuck her in the chair, looking out the window so I could watch him coming back, and here he'd come and perfect, just to the last second, the last stroke, just as his hand's on the door, and *plop-bang*, we're sitting there when he gets in, and he knows."

A yellow building crane sat like a huge bird, beak angled over an airport flight tower, the runway parallel to the Turnpike. A small plane took off and flew alongside the bus before pulling up and whisking away.

"Anybody got any liquid? Have you got some? And maybe one bennie. I've only had one and a half bennies. I know you're out. I don't really need another one. A tribute to the last thirty miles is in order"—*taweet-tatootle*—"and this is the last compliment to J.B.: he's got the funniest pot I've ever smoked and I burnt my last pair of pants saying it. Now that just shows you, J.B. Watch this lane shift possibility—hurry up, pickup, c'mon—thank you, pickup. So it happened, in Massachusetts, one of the thirteen colonies, that we first saw the possibility of the white brotherhood, yes, and the black magic... You got to have the voodoo, you got to have the witches' tale and the cockroach juice and all that... There's strict, like in the truck passing, and there is strict, like strict discipline, and there is strict like stricken, but more like arsenic and old lace, strychnine, nine lives, like a cat, Exit Nine, next exit, nine miles."

He gestured with his flute at the Exit Nine sign.

"The Romans of course, had the furlong, ha ha ha, like horses still retain, one-eighth mile, two-hundred-and-twenty yards... Calling attention to himself, unnecessarily, Mr. Cassady proceeded north... Exit Nine, love potion number nine."

He sang, "*I lost my little bottle of...* Love Exit number Nine, then deployed dah power of dah black magic. You got to have all them kidney intros for the black voodoo, why not go for the white? Now applications are taken, you know, some sort of an avatar thing but who wants to do that, that's been done; that savior idea was overdone the first thousand people I told Casey to..."

"Who's Casey?" Hassler asked.

"Who's Casey? Who's J.B.?" Jane said. "Who's Miss Carson? Who's supposed to remember all this?"

"All being recorded," Cassady answered, "to be pored over by generations henceforth and well-meaning. I used to pick up girls on the train, in the caboose, practically daily, by telling them about Casey. I wanted to screw but I'd be so obsessed with Casey that I'd hang over his coffin and bawl for five hours. From that point on I began to miss certain pieces of ass. For the first time in my life, I even turned down one or two. I knew then I was getting old."

"Now we know," Zonk mumbled. "Did you get that on the tape recorder, Sandy?"

"I'm getting it all, even what everyone's thinking."

Outside, the landscape was filled with industrial spires pointing toward the low-lying clouds, farmers' fields falling behind.

"This is for the record, gentlemen, because I understand we are taping, I'll give the hearers of this tape the chance to show the proof that was necessary of J.B.'s true tolerance was to continually keep silent while I, at this precise point twenty miles away, was to do this to his gearbox."—*clash of gears*—"Well, I almost did it, ha ha ha. I usually flatter-batter, flatter-chatter. He's been a prince that boy."

A sign read TRUCK WEIGH STATION—TWO MILES—TRUCKS ONLY.

"This is not a truck," Cassady said. "It is a bus, therefore it should pass, and passenger trains have precedence over freight trains. Easing off, sir. Do the camera work son," he said to Mike Hagen.

Hagen stood in the door stairwell and aimed the camera at Cassady.

"You want these curves, you want these cars from behind, two cars, you got them? Here he comes now, abreast, with a child, a girl reading, J.B., her little report from school, the lunch hour, homeward bound with Daddy."

Cassady pulled his right-hand gearshifting glove tight over his wrist.

"Here comes a Buick. You gotta watch the traffic, that's the main thing. Listen, take scenes of the traffic, this is what you want, dammit. We're coming in, get the camera over my shoulder here. I still want to go right but I can't see a thing because he's got my right eye."

"He's lost his right eye," Zonk yelled.

"There it goes, out the window, rolling alongside the bus," Kesey said.

"Now he'll never be able to see out the side mirror," George said.

"You want this lane over here?" Mike asked.

"No, no, no, but you are in my vision. When I need it, I'll yell. Right-hand lane acceptable after this car, sir. Oh, that semi, let the semi go, oh the convertible, the fucking convertible. Look what it did to my semi. Just for that I'll hit them both in the ass. Look at that son of a bitch, see how he drives, see that move? Get that on camera. We've stuck together for miles, it's like group karma, once you pick your bike you're stuck with it. Come on, you prick, I'm going to punch you in the lips."

"I thought Cassady was a peacenik," George said.

"I heard that, George. What I said was there's no excuse for violence except while making love. I'm going to do it in fourth gear, ha ha.

"That's a foreign car, you know, a Studebaker—never ride in a Thunderbird, you turd—well, a Studebaker is the last to go. Remember S-T-R-I-C-K at the beginning of the tape? Now as we return to the bottom of the stick, stricken, strychnine, arsenic and old lace, that's like the multiple of the problem proving the mathematics, like you prove multiplication by fractions or vice versa. I skipped that grade, too."

The Madhattan skyline formed grey shapes in a blurring mist, hills between the turnpike and city covered with houses climbing over one another.

"Approaching Jersey City on right, entering from here on nothing but city, it's the outskirts of everything. There's Manhattan on the right. New York, ten miles. There's the Empire State Building dead ahead. There's the Woolworth Building, with the sun glinting on it and, of course, the Radio City Music Hall, the bulk on the far left. Get the camera on the left, horse trailer up from Aqueducts. I could watch footage like that all day, guys weaving around, cutting in. I love that shit.

"Last joint before bridge, entering New York loaded, *mmmfff mmmmfff,* George Washington Bridge, four miles, end of turnpike. Now this is the true approach—and if anyone wants to call, incidentally, this is the last phone before the bridge."

Traffic thickened nearing the approach to the bridge, semis in the left lanes, a line of buses entering on the right, cars dutifully falling in order, one behind the other. Good manners reigned. No one wanted the family sedan dinged.

"Get the flag out," Kesey said.

"Yes, flag out, we're identifying this bus. We'll be inundated with thousands of Puerto Rican young ladies grabbing our huaraches. It's about a mile uphill now... Second gear, goddamn... Let's clean up all that pot and those two bennies, for safety's sake; there's only a couple, but pass them around, that way there's none loose. That's the idea. If we get stopped, let me tell you how to treat New York cops. You will know, just to look at them, they are all men... Now entering the bridge proper, Fort Lee, yes, here's where they hung Leona, Nathan Hale's girlfriend. Oh shut up, you're about as funny as Lenny Brooks."

"Who's Lenny Brooks?" Jane asked.

"One of the Brooks Brothers," Chuck Kesey said. "Left the clothing line to take up comedy."

"Ha ha, a well flung arrow. As soon as we go through the toll plaza, gentlemen, stop the music. I don't know what it will cost. Four bits, I believe."

"I have a dollar bill," George said. "Where'd it go? Anyone seen my wallet?"

"Not since Lake Pontchartrain," John Babbs said.

"As a form of strength, sir," Cassady said, "when entering New York, we have to be independently our best."

"Putting everybody on," Kesey said.

"Put everybody on, that's it, sir, I understand. Forget everything, the sincerity, we're tourists now. No explosives, inflammables, radioactive materials."

The toll taker was a Black woman in a snappy blue, toll-taker uniform, a blue cap with a white stripe on her head, a blue jacket with white shirt collar turned, large, dark sunglasses covering her eyes, a single pearl in each earlobe.

"Here's a dollar, ma'am," Cassady said. "It's all in change, I'm sorry to say."

She sorted through the coins.

"It's all there," Kesey said, over Cassady's shoulder.

"I have to count it," the toll taker said.

"Oh, she does," Neal said. "A vote for Barry is a vote for fun at the George Washington Bridge."

"That's okay, she's got it now," I said.

"Clearance overhead accepted," Cassady said. "Forward right retention count, we saved them in Georgia and we saved them in Arizona."

"She'll find there is a dollar one," I said.

She dropped a penny into Cassady's outstretched hand and turned back to the till.

"One penny over, you are right. Thank you for the correct change, ma'am, thank you."

"That's an honest toll taker," Kesey said. "Good to know."

"She said if you want to take shots of the bridge, do it from the back and not from the top," I said.

"Alright, sir, from the back, thank you."

"Once we get over in Central Park, over in Manhattan, it's okay."

"Yes, do anything, right? Why, officer, I've had them hanging out of the door, sir, while under the influence, alcoholic consumption and the like. I've saved them by the ears, yes, I've held all the girls by the wrist, the men by the belt buckle, yes sir."

"Oh man, we're bringing it in," Hassler said.

"We're going to do it," Kesey added.

"A salute to J.B. and the intrepidity of International Harvester, of Betsy's cousin George, the Commander's indefatigability, Army-style..."

"Army-style," I shouted.

"Ken Labbs—I still can't call a man by a woman's name—Ken Labbs, indomitable as a baseball, basketball—in other words, the guy on the team. He'll do it, the balanced man in the abnormal condition handling himself better than most, and fourth gear on that—*bawhoosh*—all ahead, sir. We're at the end of the George Washington Bridge, so much for George Washington, red light, sir. I never want to beat a red light, never, not on the red, never. George Washington, all mine. Want to buy it?"

You have to laugh at the things
that hurt you, just to keep yourself
in balance, just to keep the world
from running you plumb crazy.
     — Ken Kesey

24

A Curio from
the Twentieth Century

The bus roared through the New York streets, speakers blaring. Cassady's growl bounced off buildings: "A vote for Barry is a vote for fun. Here we are at last, in the upper Bronx."

The sidewalk teemed with pedestrians. A stern-faced dude, silver clip holding a thin, black tie to his shirt, scowled beneath a cream-colored Panama hat. An intense young man in a long white jacket feverishly pedaled an ice cream cart through the traffic.

"Here come the people," I said through the microphone on top, my words booming through the speakers.

Black kids in jeans and white shirts waved their arms and shouted at us to stop, darted into the street and sprinted after the bus like hot-footed racers.

"Moving on now," Kesey said into his microphone. "I'm beginning to see the whole scene as a random movie shoot of metropolis characters, like, for instance, that old guy with the bushy eyebrows standing in the middle of the street."

"*Yaarrghhhhh!*" the old guy yelled. He shook his fist at the bus.

"That's the best reaction so far, sir," Cassady said.

"Give that old man a solid salute for the trip of the day," Kesey said. "That man, I say, is responsible."

Sweeping the air with one hand, other hand holding a portable radio blaring foreign language diatribe, the old guy gave another mad shout, "*Arrghaggaglag!*"

"He's the first sanity case since that Prescott, Arizona, fellow," Cassady said. "Upset, no doubt, because we painted '*A Vote For Barry Is a Vote For Fun*' on the side of the bus."

Startled by Cassady's voice booming out of the speaker, a respectable businessman stopped sharp and stared through horn-rimmed glasses, lips pursed in an *mmmmphhh* snort of indignation.

I waved my red-fluorescent-painted hand at him.

"There he sees me. Hi."

Stern mouth gave way to an upturned smile.

"You know, Ken," Cassady said, "I think you stopped him because he's your type. You're a regular Steve Allen, Ken."

"Thank you, Neal, I'm flattered."

"One of these theaters here is where my play starred," Kesey said. "The Cort Theatre. Where's the Cort Theatre?"

"Thirty-fourth Street I believe," Cassady said. "Coming up on the right."

A banner hung on a pole from a second story window: World Premier: What a Way to Go!

"*Grease it out and pull it in, that's the way you'll find your skin,*" I sang. "*This is America, you oughta know, this is the land we're living in. Grease it out and pull it in, that's the way we'll start again.*"

A newspaper truck passed, racing along like it had a deadline. The sign on its side read: The New Moral Climate. Chasing Sex on the A Train. New Series in *New York Post*.

"Catch that one on color film, thank you," Cassady said. "Here's the boundary line, sir; from here on it is true Harlem. I lived anywhere from here south many times."

People packed the sidewalks from storefronts to the street.

"It could all set, suddenly, *click*, like that," Kesey said, "and we could sell it to a pawn shop two thousand years from now as a curio from the twentieth century."

Bakers in white caps and white shirts leaned out of a second-story window.

"What do you make up there?" Kesey yelled.

"Bread," one of them yelled back. "Got any dough?"

"Throw them some money," Cassady answered.

A round-mouthed man blew smoke rings out of a Camel cigarette billboard. Fluffy circles floated over the bus, dissipated in swirling tendrils.

"I need a cigarette," Cassady said. "Cigarette for pilot. You wanted the Viking Press building, Chief? Well, here we are. 625 Madison Avenue, Viking Press. Is it illegal to double-park in front? When in Rome..."

He stopped in the street, engine idling.

A Viking secretary, wearing a green sheath dress, dark sunglasses covering her eyes, black hair pulled back, ran up to the bus.

"No, no, no, this is totally wrong. Are all these people your guests?"

"We're the Merry Band of Pranksters," Kesey said. "We're on our way to the Kool Place."

"Ken, there's a photographer here from the *Tribune*."

She pointed to a short, brown-haired, mustachioed man in a brown corduroy sports coat. Fiddling with a small camera, he scooted along the sidewalk.

"This way, Ken," he yelled. "Ken, give me vision. Ken Kesey. Give me vision, Ken. No. Not just the hand."

"Where's that bag of caramel popcorn you promised?" Cassady said through his microphone.

Popcorn a euphemism for crosstops, slang for bennies, short for Benzedrine 5 mg tablets.

"I sent down a request," Kesey answered from on top. "Put the pressure on someone down there."

"Pressure on, aye, sir, keep it below the window line," he said. "There's tourists on the right."

A middle-aged woman in a brown dress with a thick, beaded necklace and frowsy hair, purse dangling from her finger. A bald-headed man leaning against a pole, bare arm pressing the wood. He smiled, showing teeth.

"We forgot to write '*tourists*' on the side," Cassady said. "But *A Vote For Barry Is A Vote For Fun.*"

The movie camera lingered on the faces of the onlookers: A woman, dark-red lips pursed, eyes shadowed under a black pile of hair, mantilla over her shoulders like moth's wings. A bald-domed man with a five-o'clock shadow, unlit cigarette in the side of his mouth. A young businessman, thick eyebrows, his mouth slightly open, serious but wondering.

"Earth calling," I said over the loudspeakers. "This is Stevenson on Venus relaying flash communications through a third sub-orbital satellite. Can you hear me, Earth people?"

No one reacted. Magazine covers on a newsstand provided a colorful background. The bald, gap-toothed owner gave us a knowing smile. He's seen it all come by, this merely another episode in a long-running show.

"There went a man," Kesey said, "with his hair twisted so tight, if he ever lifted his feet off the ground he would fly like a goddamned kite."

"Hey, you guys," John Babbs yelled from the back platform. "Here come the cops."

Cassady double parked in the right lane. We held up traffic as two policemen approached the bus.

Kesey and I talked to the officers, relegating Cassady to a back position, much to his disgust.

"You still have everyone you started out with?" one of them asked Kesey.

"We've lost some, one sent to the nuthouse."

Neal stood to the side, bounced on his feet, waved his cigarette, watched the interaction and commented *sotto voce*: "The Chief saw the intelligence in the officer's eyes as he appraised the situation, and gave me a purposeful, quizzical look, and I answered his quizzicality with a wave."

The conclave suddenly broke up, thanks to a load of legal blarney laid on by our sometimes lawyer, Paul Robertson, who had flown in from California to join us on the Madhattan adventure. Grinning, Paul led the way back into the bus. Cassady revved up the engine and we drove away.

"I think we did as well there as we did in New Orleans," Neal said.

"I think we're doing a great deal better than we did in New Orleans," Kesey said.

Neal chuckled. "That's a matter of subjective ideas."

He pulled into a parking spot across the street from the New York Tribune Building where two more women secretaries joined up with us, along with a writer from the *Herald Tribune*, a round-faced, smiling gent wearing the mandatory Madhattan black suit, his bright, yellow tie a sign of non-conformity.

Kesey stepped out to meet him. Foreman was his name and, after introductions, Kesey motioned for him and the secretaries to get aboard for a trip around town. Kesey then jumped onto the front fender, stepped on the hood and bounded to the roof, where he sat down behind the windscreen.

This was the quasi-official part of the trip, publicity for the publication of *Sometimes a Great Notion*, and Kesey was primed to give Madhattan and the press a full-on, no-holding-back, bus, Prankster and Cassady experience.

"I've finally got a feel what we're trying to do, Cassady," Kesey said, his words picked up and broadcast through the speakers, recorded on the Sony reel-to-reel, while both cameras rolled, the big Arriflex on top, the smaller Bolex inside the bus.

"I think we should pass around the popcorn and all take a little hit," Kesey said.

"*Yas,*" Neal agreed. "It will prime me for my latest Broadway show: *Kirk Douglas's Dimple, Cassady's Pimple. Bo-ard!*"

"Let's go," Kesey said. "Head on out."

Hassler was still in the street, shooting with the still camera. I threw a blue rubber ball at him. He missed the catch and scooted down the alley after it. A red ball was thrown at him. This was our ongoing Prankster bit, sharpening our mental and physical reflexes, to throw and catch without seeming to pay attention, senses expanding in 360 degrees.

Hassler scooped up the balls and fired them at the bus. I swung my arms like hitting with a baseball bat. The balls flew past. Kesey snagged both, flung them over his head to the Pranksters behind, giving Hassler a snappy salute.

"*Everybody calls me jelly bean,*" Cassady sang and, with Hassler aboard, the bus pulled away from the curb.

After two successful novels and ten times
two successful fantasies I did find myself
wondering, "What to prove next?" I've shown
I can write, then shown I can repeat and better
the first showing. Now, "What do I prove?"
The answer seems to be, "Prove nothing."
I try to be a warrior, like my heroes, and
writing is just one blade on my Swiss Army
samurai sword.
— Ken Kesey

25

Three Blocks from the Park

"Listen," Kesey said into a microphone, voice resounding through the speakers inside and on top of the bus, "the thing that's just occurred to me—you know the fantasy we had about what we're going do when we get here—we were going to cut away a side of the bus, rent a theater and do the things we do? Well, what we really meant is that we'd do what we are actually doing right now."

"So close," Cassady said. "And we have plenty of layers left."

A young, pompadoured man in a light blue, short-sleeved shirt played air guitar. He made a pouty, what-the-hell face, looked at the bus, smiled and snapped his fingers.

"We didn't want to take in any cash money," Kesey said. "We wanted to make a performance and we're doing it, on a moveable stage that is driving around to the audience. We may make money later. Who knows? These people don't even know they bought a ticket."

A young man, attired in white sport coat, a briefcase in one hand, straw hat in the other, turned and stared.

"When people are knocked off their bearings and disorientated, if hit with a sudden blast of goodwill, it melts them like butter."

A young lady with thick, black hair bundling down the sides of her head, raised both hands to her shoulders, then waved.

"Stay with them as long as they stay with us, Cassady," Kesey said. "We've got the largest audience in the world, including not a few compatriots. For instance, there's a man so handsome he's liable to melt, confident the sale he's about to make will be worth the down on a Ford Mustang convertible."

"Liquor store on the right," I yelled. "Liquid for the crew! Can we stop here?"

"A quickie," Cassady said.

Dale Kesey ran into the store—cars honked—out he came, clutching a paper sack. A messenger bike swerved, just missing Dale.

"Listen, if that thing stings you, you die in eight seconds," Kesey yelled. "Keep going by it and don't look at it. Don't let it know that you're skeered of it either."

The *Time Magazine* photographer jumped out the door, cut across the street, metal camera case swinging as he wove between a big-finned Caddy and a boxy Nash Rambler. Safe on the corner, he turned and waved goodbye. Red-painted hands waved back, tootles on the flootles.

"We need liquid to go with that booze," John Babbs said.

A convenience store tucked below an overhead train line had a parking place big enough for the bus. A large billboard overhead announced in huge multi-painted words: RCA IS COLOR TV.

"Dismount is out, Dismount still out," Cassady announced, bestowing upon Sandy his bus name.

"Three blocks from the park and we have to stop," Kesey said. A phrase he used every time we stopped before we came to our destination.

Appropriate, in this case, for we happened to be three blocks from Tavern on the Green in Central Park, where, once we found a parking spot, Kesey did the interview with Foreman, the *Herald Tribune* reporter, while the rest of us cavorted around the bus, throwing rubber balls, tootling flutes. Cassady regaled the Viking secretaries with outlandish tales, toyed with a straw boater he picked up somewhere, set it atop his head, twirled it in his hand, flipped it in the air, twisted and turned his body so as to keep all three women in his sight, verbal gyrations, relentless to the nines.

"Tell me, Ken," Foreman asked him, "what was the genesis of this bus trip?"

"For a lot of us it started when we first read *On the Road*. The book opened our minds to new possibilities. Babbs and I were talking about coming east and it snowballed into what it is now."

"This seems to be a journey without ulterior motives. On the other hand, you're making tape recordings, you're photographing, is this for possible future worth?"

"It's like my dad used to say, you have to take a fishing pole into the woods or other people will think you're crazy for walking up and down the creek. The tape recorder and those cameras have gone a long way toward making us responsible. Able to respond. We had this scene in Wikieup. We'd been traveling a long time and it was hot and we'd been looking for the Kool Place. We found a bog with water, Cassady drove toward it and stuck the bus in the sand. A farmer pulled us out with his tractor. I looked around and saw the two cameras weren't being used. Everyone was interested in what was going on, so they were watching. And I kind of flipped.

"I jumped up on the motorcycle on the back of the bus and shouted, 'This right here is where it's happening, not over there. Get in here and film what's going on.' When you do this to them, you make them aware of what's going on. You're not making a judgment out of it, you're just telling them to record

it as best they can so their apertures can take it in, seeing whatever it is.

"We are trying to pretend that we are not pretending. We go
someplace, we put on a show, play our roles. We do our thing
and the camaraderie builds up. But between people there are
always sparks and friction. George will rag on Neal's driving
when Neal goes into what he calls third gear mania—can't get
the transmission into the right gear. Then Neal fumes at somebody else."

"Is there ever any taking of sides on the part of the others
when this happens? On such a long trip, were there envies
building, jealousies and so forth?"

"We work it in so it's just part of the show. Babbs will storm
forth and say, 'Come now, come now, do my Merry Band of
Pranksters fall apart in this fashion?' We fume and sputter, but
it's hard to know if what we're doing is real or if it's acting. I
don't even think it's necessary we should know because we are
all playing our roles. Like me talking to you like this, it's one of
the roles I play, as crazy an experience for me as I've ever had."

"I know this relates—to use that awful word—to your work,
to your writing."

"In this way: after doing two books, the second not nearly so
much as the first, I realized they are lengthy and clever and en-
tertaining and I still have faith in them as being right, but I
thought I would try to do something else; going around and
gathering sights and sounds, then begin to put these together.
We'll come out of this. I've blown all the money I have into this
thing. If it doesn't, I'll be back working in the creamery for my
brother."

"How many people on this bus are writers?"

"One. Ken Babbs."

"Cassady said he wrote, that he's a writer."

"He isn't a writer, he's a talker. You saw him do it. That's
what he does. It's a less popular art form than writing or paint-

ing, but he still does it and he does it well. It's inner confusing. My brother, sparse of speech, owns a creamery in Springfield, Oregon. Equipment Hassler is a former lieutenant from Fort Ord. Gretch, the Slime Queen, is a tomboy from Oregon. We went through a fever period down in New Orleans, were hot, drunk, wasted. Stopped at the first water we saw, Lake Pontchartrain. It was the colored section but we didn't know it and dived into the water. We were completely accepted, but I began to feel terrible anxieties so we left. The whites who saw us heading out looked at us in a bad way."

"They probably thought you wanted the Negroes to vote."

"They constantly tried to connect us to some kind of racial scene."

"In general, the attitude of the public has been friendly or hostile?"

"Completely friendly."

"The children seem to accept you immediately."

"Children understand. You can see it in their faces when a brightly colored bus with a bunch of brightly, clowny people making a lot of noise comes by, it's just a reaction."

"How much longer will you be in New York?"

"A couple more days. Tomorrow is our last day as a group because Equipment Hassler has to be back to Fort Ord and Neal has to be back changing tires. When we came into New York, going full tilt with sound on top and the bottom of the bus, I was thinking, maybe this is it, this is all it's ever to be. I really felt like we were operating at peak efficiency, playing to an enormous audience, briefly to each person, then moving on to the next one. We've got all this film that I have hopes about. I think if we have anything at all with the film, it should be a pretty accurate report of a learning process."

"It would be interesting to find out what this does to you; even more interesting, I think, to find out what it has done to your audience. A minute, two minutes, could be a focal point..."

A uniformed semi-demi cop with a seen-it-all look on his face, who had been listening, stepped forward and interrupted the interview.

"My name is Shashoon, I'm a former superintendent of the Parks Department."

"This is Foreman," Kesey said, looking Shashoon over. Shined-black shoes, dark-rumpled pants, solid, big belly. "Foreman is the editorial supervisor at the *Herald Tribune.*"

"Well, I'm very surprised at you," Shashoon said to Foreman. "Not at these gentlemen. They are foreigners."

"You mean as Californians?" Kesey said.

"You can't enter the park without a permit," Shashoon said.

"Can't enter the park?" said Foreman, surprised to hear that.

"That's right. Without a permit."

"Why is that?" Kesey asked.

"Why is that? Because of our rules and regulations."

"You mean a bus cannot enter, is that the end of it?" Foreman, the dapper New Yorker in perfect suit and tie, asked with citizenry outrage.

"Any bus, *any* bus, cannot enter this park without a permit from the Parks Department and I must see it before they come in."

"Even as a New Yorker I have not heard of this."

"I'll be patient with you persons," Shashoon said, unperturbed. "It's an organized group. That's number two."

"Have you seen very much organization going on here?" Kesey said.

"Well, they are sitting on walls. If I get out my book of rules and regulations and show it to you, sitting on a wall is prohibited, but I close my eyes to that. Playing football and whatnot. Basketball, rubber ball, whatever they may have."

"I suppose my taking down notes is against regulations too," Foreman said.

"No, no, no, let's keep this on a man-to-man level."

"I do this often..."

"I have no doubt you'll write me up in the paper tomorrow..."

"I'll get a picture," Sandy said.

"No, I don't want any pictures. Even a school group, whatever we have come in here, they must have a permit. They come in to visit the places."

"So did we," Kesey said. "We came to visit the places but the man at the entrance said we had to move quickly..."

"Yes, near five o'clock, that's right. What's the fooling about? I mean, off the record."

"Off the record," Shashoon said, "this is a friendly town and a good place to see the World's Fair."

"We're making a movie of our travels," I said, getting in on the action, "and New York was our destination."

"We wanted a green place to go to where we could talk," Kesey said.

"You people I'll forgive," Shashoon said, then turning to Foreman, "but you I won't."

"Forgive?" Kesey said. "You ought to thank the man. We asked him, 'Where's the nicest coolest spot in town?' and he said this was a nice park. Well, we can take a hint and tell when we're not wanted."

Kesey circled the air with his finger and called in a loud voice, "*Eeehaw*, Pranksters mount up."

Everyone ran for the bus and jammed through the door. Cassady hit the starter. Kesey hustled Foreman inside, yelling at Shashoon, "We're leaving the park, thanks for the *horse*pitality."

Cassady wheeled the bus out of the parking lot, onto the park road and back into Madhattan.

*Fiction must justify itself in every line. Yes.
I'm beginning to frame one—and along rather Conradian
lines. Prose fiction must first of all perform the traditional
functions of storytelling. We need stories. We can't
identify ourselves without them. We're always telling
ourselves stories about who we are: that's what history
is, what the idea of a nation or an individual is. The
purpose of fiction is to help us answer the question
we must constantly be asking ourselves: Who do we
think we are and what do we think we're doing?*
    — *Robert Stone*

26

Don't Spit in the Swamp

The hot summer sun burned across the western spires of Madhattan. Below in the canyons, the shadows crept across the sidewalks and streets. *Further*'s brightly painted sides flashed and dappled in the light after a long day of tootling whistles while Cassady's voice bamboozled amused pedestrians who gawked at my red-painted hand blasting their eyeballs.

Commercial buildings gave way to grey-stoned domiciles, concrete steps leading to heavy glassed-in doors.

The bus pulled to the curb. With a cacophony of raucous chortles and calls, we had arrived at the doorstep of a high-rise apartment building to attend the publication party for *Sometimes a Great Notion*.

We stepped out of the elevator into a penthouse party in full swing. An affable gent in one corner of the room dispensed wines and mixed concoctions. Next to him was a table laden with artisan breads, cheese, meat and fish spreads, cherry tomatoes speared on toothpicks, conglomerations of dips.

Elegantly dressed damsels and gents of literary persuasions—book reviewers, bookstore owners, publishing house gurus—milled about in groups of twos and threes.

The host, a literary arts connoisseur, Marlin Spikes—slight and fit, dapper in a lightweight blue suit with corresponding tie, dark-rimmed glasses, short-trimmed hair—greeted Kesey with a big smile and warm handshake.

"Ken," Marlin Spikes said. "I'd like you to meet my friend, Ira Bloom, the main writer for the *Independent Review*, which as you know, is the top book review paper in the city."

"I thought that was the *New York Times*," Kesey said.

"Well, we run neck-and-neck," Ira Bloom said.

"What did you think of Ken's new book?" Marlin Spikes asked Ira.

"Hmm, putting me on the spot here," Ira Bloom said. "My first impression was that it was confusing, the way multiple characters spoke in the first person without letting us know when somebody different was talking."

"Lost you there, did he?" I asked.

Ira Bloom eyed me over his spectacles.

"Not entirely. Kesey provided clues that allowed him to work with a multiple number of characters, all of whom were very well drawn with a lot of depth. It's a big, big book."

He turned to Kesey.

"What do you think, Ken? Will you be able to do something as hefty again?"

Kesey shook his head.

"Won't happen. I can't keep all that in my head at once anymore. I used to work thirty hours at a stretch."

A plump, scholarly-looking man in tweeds brandished his pipe at Kesey.

"I made it to about one hundred pages and put it down. I had no idea what was happening. Is the way you kept wandering off course due to your being influenced by the Beat writers?"

"You mean that bit they said about Kerouac? 'That's not writing, that's typing.' I liked Kerouac's answer: 'Woe to those who spit on the Beat Generation. The wind will blow it back in their faces.'"

A lady with her hair pulled back so tight her eyes were slits, or maybe it was nearsightedness that gave her that no-nonsense appearance, asked Kesey, "Did you intend to create an audience for your book when you brought that bus to New York?"

"When we drove past a theater, the crowd was coming out so we had an audience already made. On the bus, we try to permit, all the time, for everyone to be what they really are, and act like what they really are. The closer we got to New York, the more people began to play themselves instead of being played by themselves. Like Cassady is Speed Limit. He seems to be going at a great rate all the time."

"Until he goes slow," Zonker interrupted.

"Then he goes so slow you can hardly stand it," Hassler said.

"Anyway, it's still working, it's still happening," Kesey said. "And I don't know where it's going."

"Are you being deliberately enigmatic?" the lady asked.

Kesey studied her. "Well, as my granddaddy said, 'If you're going to eat watermelons, then eat watermelons.'"

"He does tend to be a bit elliptical," Hassler said, grinning.

"Here's an example," Kesey said. "When we parked the bus out front, here came a big, red-headed, virile, tough-looking guy, carrying a mallet, and he's waving it around and he had a bunch of people with him and he's playing golf with it and he's being wacky so I said, 'Dale, get our guns.'

"Dale stood up, the guy pushed him out of the way and the redhead and his friends walked right on past. What Dale didn't know, the big brute threatened him from behind with the mallet. Here's the thing though: we knew something that guy didn't know. We didn't make the scene, we just saw something already going on and added our little bit to it.

"So, here comes Dale with an armload of toy guns he passed out and we went to shooting. I had a little machine gun and I would go, *prrfffft, prrfft.* The redhead walked towards me and said, 'Yeah, but what you guys don't know, *this* is real,' brandishing the mallet. I stood there going, *prrfft, prrfft,* and he started backing off. He was looking right at me, and I was continuing, *brrfft, brrfft,* until he finally tapped his buddy and said, 'Hey, watch this,' and raised his mallet—but all of a sudden it struck him he wasn't dealing with a bunch of sane people. He lowered the mallet and they went on down the street."

"What was it you knew that he didn't?" asked the lady with the pulled-back hair.

"Just 'cause something's little, doesn't mean it can't hurt you. Consider the bee. When one stung me, I felt strangely giddy and lightheaded, like a combination of barbiturate and amphetamine had made me both feverish and incendiary, as though one was putting me to sleep and the other was turning my sleep into a freewheeling, highly charged dream: 'The pasteurizing chart is all the way up to one-hundred-and-seventy-five, Martha. My God, the kid's milk has gone wild.'"

Kesey had been bombarded with questions all day long and it was starting to get to him. On the road, tripping from coast to coast, we were like a sailing vessel on the endless ocean, stopping occasionally to restock the larder and take on fuel and water; an anonymous, unknown vehicle, despite wild coloring and a booming sound system, traveling through a media vacuum—no newspapers, TV, or radio—filling the hours creating our own reality, hooked to our creative juices, improvisational dramas and the ever-present engine roar, which occasionally brought our talk and playacting to a worried halt when a clatter, bang or hiccup from the motor turned everyone's attention to a possible breakdown.

Now we found ourselves in a media spotlight—particularly Kesey—and in a pause between questions, he looked at me for some assistance. I handed him my gin and tonic.

Someone in the back yelled, "Do you think LSD has any debilitating effects?"

"Not in our capacity to get drunk," one of the Pranksters yelled back. It sounded like my brother, John. I searched him out and hustled him out of the line of fire.

Cassady sat in an easy chair, holding court and watching TV, undergoing attention from people he neither sought nor welcomed, their expectation being that he be Dean Moriarty, the character based on Neal in Kerouac's novel, *On the Road*.

"You were great," said an earnest young man, hovering over Cassady. "That time when Sal Paradise was driving and Dean was with the girl in the back seat, her bare legs kicking in the air."

"It's your idea, whatever it is, I don't know," Cassady said, waving his cigarette at him. "I'll give you thirty seconds, count to three, one, two. It's essentially a romance."

"Yeah, we wanted some romance," the guy said. "That's what I was talking about."

"It was the long-term effect of narcotics," an older man said, listening in.

"In the chambers," the young guy said, "two judges were talking things over and one says, 'Well, Horace, don't you think they'd put us in jail if they bloody well had the nerve—caught us in something—and they had the chance?'"

"They would, fascist thinking," Cassady said. "Can't you see? You have to do it to them first. Ha, ha, ha. That's the next step in that logic."

"Can't take things personally around here," the guy said.

On the TV, Godzilla was rampaging through the city. Sirens wailed in the background.

"They've got their guns out," Cassady said. "Oops, watch out, here we go, Godzilla's getting zapped."

Tail thrashing, Godzilla knocked cars into buildings.

"Now he's worked up, fighting 'em off. Notice his chin whiskers; he's adolescent, his whiskers will grow another two or three feet."

Hassler walked over, followed by a slim, brown-haired girl wearing a white blouse and black skirt.

"Hi," Cassady said. "Ask her if she's got a friend."

On the TV, a frantic Army officer yelled into the mouthpiece of his field phone, "*This is Colonel Pauley, get me General Landen.*"

"I knew he wasn't the general," Cassady said. "Who the fuck are you, buddy—the guy who goes back home every day?"

The general's voice crackled over the radio: "*Colonel, the Towers of Justice are right across the bridge from where you are. We're moving up with other units, over on the other side of the bridge.*"

"Oh-oh, too late," Cassady said. "There goes the bridge, the monster crushed it with his foot. He did that quicker than Superman could get out of the phone booth."

A missile zipped past Godzilla's head and demolished a movie theater. The sign, NOW SHOWING: END OF WORLD, crashed to the sidewalk.

Cassady laughed. He stuck his cigarette in his mouth and blew into it. Flames and smoke shot out and hit the TV screen. The girl standing next to Hassler gasped and made a break for the bar.

Hassler stomped the sparks on the carpet.

"Jesus, Neal, watch it. You'll set the place on fire."

Neal tapped the ashes into the palm of his hand.

"Don't spit in the swamp," he said, rubbing the ashes down the front of his pant leg.

A black shape filled the TV screen. A huge bird, screeching a high-pitched cry, landed on Godzilla's back and drove its beak into Godzilla's head, knocking his face into the river. Godzilla rolled over and pinned the bird beneath him. They flailed out of the river, onto the street, smashed buildings, debris rained over their bodies.

Cassady bounced in his seat. "The tide of battle has turned. Mothra has prevailed."

Out on the balcony, Hagen and I unwound a four-hundred-foot roll of ruined overexposed film and let it flutter in the breeze. I grabbed chunks of film and cut them with my pocket knife. The wind blew the pieces onto the street.

"It's the Prankster version of a ticker tape parade," I said.

"Yeah, and at night, who's to see?" Mike asked.

"It will be a surprise for the people on their way to work to-morrow."

Hassler stuck his head out the door.

"Time to mount up, Pranksters. We're going to boogie."

We jammed into the elevator, plummeted to the street, bounded onto the bus and headed for our home away from home.

Nice and clean. But almost anything's better'n
being judged by Roy Bean. You can hang from
any tree but right now you're hanging on this one
with me. Climb that tree faster'n you can skin a
cat fer. Well, now wait a minute, when you get
a catskinner named Disaster, Missy Lou don't
know just quite what to do. When he took off
there on the sands of Daytona, Seagrave lost
his life, wind put him into the surf but, you
know, tide came in!
— *Neal Cassady*

27

A Poetic Shout of Freedom

A brownstone ground-floor apartment on Madison Avenue between 89th and 90th Streets, across the street from a pharmacy. Stone steps led up to a large door that opened into a hallway. To the left, a large living room, then the kitchen with a utility room. Behind that, two bedrooms and baths. The apartment was on loan to us by Chloe Scott's cousin, who was vacationing in Europe—Chloe an old friend from the Perry Lane days in California.

We lugged in personal gear, added it to the camera equipment and musical instruments stacked on the living room floor.

Cassady had gone out and hooked up with Allen Ginsberg and Peter Orlovsky. They picked up Jack Kerouac in Orlovsky's car and drove him to the apartment. Julius Orlovsky, Peter's brother, was with them, his first day out after fourteen years in a mental institution.

Julius was a sad-looking sight, totally inside himself, his face downcast and glum, feet shuffling like an old man's, his body hunched forward. We were working at going right at people and finding a place where we fit, and were able to connect with Julius in a way that others couldn't.

Kesey walked over to Julius and said, "Where are you going?"

"I want to go on the bus."

Kesey led him inside. He sat on the floor and for the first time there was a smile on his face.

We were honored to meet Ginsberg and Orlovsky, and particularly Kerouac. When we read *On the Road,* we recognized right away that he was a major American writer with a style that connected instantaneously with our generation. Plus, Cassady and Kerouac were spiritual brothers, Ginsie forming the third of a triumvirate, Orlovsky lapping at the triangle.

Holy moly, we were consorting with the Beats.

Ginsberg wore a Prankster striped shirt with wide horizontal red-and-white stripes. Too big for him, it hung loosely on his slight body. His beard was stubbled. He peered intently through black, horn-rimmed glasses.

Jack, wearing a button-up white, short-sleeved shirt, collar open, pack of cigarettes in the breast pocket, sat at the end of the couch, his elbow on the couch arm, head resting in his open hand, eyes closed. He looked at me and smiled, face soft in the dim light.

We broke out our musical instruments, donned our colorful regalia, turned on the cameras and tape recorder and broke into spontaneous musical, verbal, and make-believe shenanigans. Madcap, acidhead Pranksters cavorting around the living room, tootling and banging and blatting on instruments, making up songs and dialogue, a conscious performance put on to entertain our honored audience. At the top of our game, we wanted to show off our stuff.

A microphone was taped to the top of a floor lamp. George Walker, wearing a buttoned-up, short-sleeved white shirt with the untucked bottom sticking out of his pants, his hair un-combed, the ends wild, mouth intense, filmed with the big Arriflex camera, balancing it on his shoulder with his right hand while working the zoom and on-off buttons with his left.

Kesey wore a striped, red-white-and-blue T-shirt. Dark sun-glasses covered his eyes, an American flag bandana wrapped around his head, and another around his neck. Red bloomer shorts, bare legs.

Dale Kesey, in a red-and-white shirt, sat in a chair and sawed on his fiddle. Kesey fluttered into his flute. Carl Lehmann-Haupt, Sandy's brother, perched on a chair and played a guitar. Chuck Kesey and John Babbs sat on the couch facing Kerouac, a coffee table between them. Chuck dangled a stuffed red lizard hanging on a string between his legs. I wore my usual red-white-and-blue horizontal tee and, standing up, strummed the upright bass. Paul Robertson, attired in a buttoned-up, thin-striped shirt, sat in a straight chair and sipped a tall cool one.

Kesey, his flute at port arms, raised his hand to his head in a British soldier salute, then sat down on the couch next to Jenni-fer Scott, Chloe Scott's teenage daughter who had bought a pullover red-and-white striped dress for the occasion. It hung over her legs, her feet on the coffee table.

Kesey turned to her and said, "Did you recognize my ren-dition from the opera, *The Magic Flute?*"

Jennifer guffawed and pulled her dress over her knees.

Cassady, sitting in a chair on the other side of the room, sat forward and looked over.

"What's she been doing today? Double approval, hip-hip, hip-hip. Right down my gullet. Hear that? J.B. blew another round for the house."

Bob Stone thrummed and shook a tambourine. Dale sawed on his fiddle, alternating wild improvised screeching with com-plicated Appalachian intricacies.

Cassady said, "This is the climactic scene, J.B., when it all comes together in one meeting."

"J.B. again," Hassler said. "Why is he always calling Kesey
J.B.?"

Bob Stone stopped thrumming on the tambourine. "J.B. was
a famous movie mogul in Hollywood," he said. "A tyrant, rich
as Rockefeller. He dictated every aspect of the film, from the
initial idea through the writing, casting, filming and editing, all
the way to distribution. Everybody hated him, but I'm sure
that's no reflection on you, Kesey."

On the couch, Jack talked in a low voice: "Saw a muttering
bum in a brown-beat suit, obviously twins coming in here, melt-
down, Equanil, and you know, in the ocean there's a very sad
turtle."

Jack was tired—been through too much with the constant
beatdown on him from the media and fans—and hungover. This
was not his scene, and although quiet and demure, even respect-
ful, he was in no shape to be interested in joining our tootle-
flootle fun. We put earphones on him and yakked into the microphones. He listened for a few minutes and took the earphones off. This was old hat to him. He and Neal had made
hours of tapes. Hassler draped an American flag around Jack's
shoulders. He took it off, folded it and laid it on a table.

Gretch, wearing a zip-up, vertically red-and-white sleeveless
shirt, pointed a plastic machine gun and pulled the trigger,
vrrrrrrrpppppp. Kerouac popped a sixteen-ounce Budweiser,
sipped it slowly and set the can on the couch arm.

The Merry Band of Pranksters were on their feet, playing
instruments, showing off the Prankster style of non-verbal
communication. George fingered the licorice stick. Zonk blew
through a hose into a round tube. Dale eschewed the fiddle and
chewed on the mouthpiece of a saxophone. We were passing
ourselves off as serious musicians but we couldn't maintain the
fantasy for long. We took the lampshades off the lights, filling
the room with a garish bright white, overexposing the film. Bo-

dies blurred, undulating until Hagen closed down the lens in time to focus on Kesey, fluorescent, red-painted earphones on his head, a long cord trailing. With Chuck's stuffed lizard in my mouth, I rushed across the room and pointed the toy at Kerouac, who leaned to the side, raised his finger and gestured at me:

"Inches of a hard evening, and one with the force like all life is doomed to be tragic, un-nameable, to make you speechless and sad-faced forever."

He shook his finger at me, dropped his hand to his lap. Kesey grabbed the lizard's tail in his teeth, we locked arms, and circled in a do-si-do around Chuck, who was adding more junk to a six-foot-tall humanoid construction formed around a floor lamp: fedora on top, binoculars around its neck, pajamas for a shirt, a purple skirt.

Jack stood, ready to leave.

At the time, the historical importance of the evening wasn't apparent. Neal had used Kesey as the reason to get Jack to go out late at night. Ginsberg told Jack it was a chance to meet and spend time with a terrific new writer who was a big fan of Kerouac's and had absorbed many of Kerouac's techniques and methods.

It didn't turn out to be a literary evening or a total Prankster dustup, but one in which something more meaningful went down. After the Beats' post-World-War-Two emergence on the literary, art, dance, performance and real-life scenes—an exultant raising of the human spirit that was reeling from the carnage of the war—their heyday was now ending. In its place a direct offspring of the Beat Movement was taking shape: the Psychedelic Revolution.

Kesey and I fell in the crack between the two generations. Too young for one and too old for the other. But we were part of the long line of American spiritual rebels in the tradition of the Transcendentalists, Bohemians, and other artists of print, paint, dance, music and theater: those who keep the freedom spirit of America alive. Neal Cassady was the connecting link between the Beats and the Psychedelic movement with a foot in each, his mind and voice guiding the way.

Everyone went outside and milled around the bus. The Beat luminaries were ready to take Jack home but first Peter Orlovsky had to get his brother off the bus. Julius would not leave. This was his new home. He took off his boots and shit in them and lay down on the floor feigning sleep.

"Oh my, oh my," Peter said softly and took the boots outside. Hassler hustled up a pan of water and a rag; Peter meticulously cleaned the boots and dumped the water in the gutter. He went inside the bus, crouched down next to Julius and talked quietly in his ear. Patted his shoulder and encouraged him to get up. Julius rose to a sitting position. Peter helped him on with his boots, then pulled him upright. We stood and watched, impressed with Peter's loving care, something of the night that stayed with us, long after it was over.

Peter gently helped Julius off the bus.

"Goodbye, Julius, goodbye," we cried.

Head down, Julius shuffled to the car and they drove away.

I had stolen a car. It was left unlocked because
they knew nobody could get it out. So, I backed it,
at a pretty good speed too, like ten miles an hour,
between a telephone pole and another car, and then
I heard a scrape. Next day I happened to notice
both fenders—not even dented hardly, no—but
the paint scraped, and equally on both sides.
An equal pass at twenty miles an hour.
    — Neal Cassady

28

A Thirtieth-of-a-Second Thing

Psychedelics and quantum physics describe a universe in which events are happening all at the same time. Time is merely a convenient way of separating events. One-thirtieth of a second is the fastest human reaction time between seeing something and reacting to it in a straight Aristotelian chronological sequence. Race car drivers, traveling at high speed, Cassady said, could leap across the one-thirtieth. He called the one-thirtieth the lag, the time it takes for a thought to make it from the brain to the mouth. Cassady, by relentlessly driving his rap, could shorten the lag.

He had the rap rep, but along with the rep came the baggage. He had to live up to it. Ran him ragged, but he kept at it, and when he drove his Jeep station wagon into Kesey's front yard and spent a long afternoon repairing the car and never repeating himself once, the man and the rep were one.

When Cassady was into his rhythm, and the right word didn't pop out instantly, he didn't stop talking to try and think of the word; he used numbers and counting to maintain the rhythm until the word popped up.

L ong shadows slid down the sides of the buildings as the sun rose over the rooftops of Madhattan, precursor of another hot day.

Banging and muttering and shuffling of feet and splashes and gurgles from the bathroom announced reveille in the apartment. Preparing to vacate, we rolled up sleeping bags, cooked oatmeal, cleaned up the living room and hauled our movie gear out to the bus.

Ginsberg pitched in on the cleaning while Peter Orlovsky and Cassady and Hassler stood talking in front of the big window looking out on the street.

"Everything he does is a book," Cassady said. "Never stops to correct or anything; just wails right on through, he's so good."

"Is that the way he did *On the Road*?" Hassler asked.

"Yes, that's the way he wrote it."

"*On the Road*, to me," Peter Orlovsky said, "was like taking a good portion of what is made up of life and plastering it on billboards on an endless railroad track, watching the billboards from the train flying by."

"Let me tell you," Cassady said, "about these two young guys I was screwing around with, wailing around at two or three in the morning. I'm spinning out, correcting, double U to avoid the whiplash, and from the back seat comes this voice, 'Hey man, cool it and take us over to this cat's apartment. And we got the guns and all, too.'

"Suddenly it hit me I'm with a bunch of gunsels. Hardass, strongarm, macho males, out-for-a-caper guys. I'm right with them, 'Yeah, that's right, let's cool it, men. I'll get out and walk; I'll see you, men.' That's what I wanted to do, but I drove them to the party where one of these gunsels, one of these strongarm freaks, got me aside and said, 'You know, that Dean Moriarty, you know what he was, all the way through the book? I'll tell you what he was: a flatbed trailer. An eight-wheeler flatbed on fifteen-inch twelve-plies that moves houses and all, this Moriarty, he's a long trailer, a flatbed.'

"So, Peter says I'm a billboard, but the gunsel says I'm an eight-wheeler flatbed. I love it."

Cassady slapped his leg. There was a roar from behind. Dale Kesey ripped across the room, pushing a vacuum cleaner. The cord catching the base of a floor lamp, Chuck Kesey grabbed the lamp and set it upright.

"There was a psychic strength there," Cassady explained. "My weakest point was when I was defending myself last night in the terms of how they were judging me, saying, 'Cassady can't turn off talking, can't complete his pattern of thought.' Of course, Ginsberg, he never says that because he knows.

"Ain't that right, Allen?" he said to Ginsberg. "You never seem to lose control."

"That's right," Ginsberg said.

"I'm about to throw up," Cassady said, "but still ready to jump out of the way of it. That is to say I've got this toothache and I never get a toothache. I'm moaning, suffering my ass off... What's that, I hear a footstep in the hall but, look, nobody's eavesdropping, I know now the realization of when you're alone, you're not bothering anybody, so go ahead and fart."

"You know," said Hassler, "for those of us who had the background like I did—conservative, middle-class scene, St. Louis, Polish-German, smell of smoked kielbasa—*On the Road* was the most tremendous trip because we found out about this gassy, groovy stuff going on. It was the first word that we got, the basic sheer scream that tore along our backs, the first thing that opened us up, let us dig these messages from you guys. Our whole meeting here was predestined. Calling in the flock. The gathering of the troops."

"That's right," Cassady said. "Like the FM beacon. Now I'm equating with things that have moved me in my life. Not like Francis Bacon, who some say really wrote Shakespeare's plays; a personal thing, a form, like Celine's *Journey to the End of the*

Night, a precursor Beat-coming-on novel, but your description sounds more valid, Hassler. In other words, despite himself, Kerouac wrote, and despite myself, I play Dean Moriarty, but if I go into that I'd be living a Moonlight Sinatra."

"Stick to being yourself," George Walker said. He pointed a screwdriver at Neal. "As for me, I'm going to adjust the carburetor. It's running a little lean."

"Lean and mean. Kesey asked me the other day, 'How does it feel, Neal, to have a girl walk up to you and go all goo-goo?' I told him I don't know, I can't answer, not because of the directness of the question, but rather because I can't be your idea of me. I was compulsive, being Moriarty, because I didn't have the sensitives. I'd wail on out just to spite, you see, awkwardly battling through to the end. It's not for everyone, but the intentions and the vibrations just a thirtieth-of-a-second thing in conversations and all.

"When you see yourself doing it, you say, 'Ah, fuck, I don't care about that,' and then, 'Aw shuddap, aw shuddap, Cassady.' That's why I've gotten hooked on this never-the-same-rap stuff. But if we go on this trip, pretty soon it's a counterpoint thing, like those Spanish guitar players, the Flatulent Foursome from Farango, mid-Fifties wily flamencos, they get half notes apart and pretty soon that *pompa-da-pompa-da* is just a beat off and they're wailing their asses off. At least I'm with you guys so I'm of some value, and the point is to make a value, find the good. Peter is worse than I am. He's more into the big gluttony department. I'm pulling Orlovsky's leg. He's reaching for my dick all the time."

Orlovsky laughed and waved goodbye. He had to leave and make sure Julius was okay.

Kesey, bleary-eyed, slurping a cup of coffee, shuffled into the living room.

"Get everyone who's outside in here, we'll have a briefing before we leave. Then we'll finish getting everything stowed on the bus and shipshape. Allen, didn't you have something in mind for us today?"

"You can unwind here or you can keep the thing going," Ginsberg said.

"How can we unwind at this beautiful point?" I asked.

"Before you leave for home, you should definitely go up to Millbrook and check out Leary's scene."

"Oh, the IFIFs," Cassady said. "With the seances and the highs and the group revelations, a chance to make the interconnection in order to cement the eastern and western confluences."

"IFIF," Hassler sounded out. "What kind of a mystical consortium is that?"

"International Federation for Internal Freedom," Kesey said.

"Ah, perfect," I chimed in. "IFIF meets ISIS."

"Now what the dad-blame-dingdong is ISIS?" Hassler asked.

"Intrepid Search for Inner Space."

"Hagen will be shooting," Kesey said. "That's what we'll be doing a good part of the time. Getting the arrival at the mansion. We should have the bus working at peak intrepid chaos."

"We can do it," I said. "General Melee will lead the charge."

"Didn't you command as a major?" Cassady said. "No, *captain*, that's it."

"Who's got a pad," Kesey asked, "and would like to make notes about this thing? We'll start giving suggestions. There's a bunch of things I've been thinking about."

"That's good," Cassady said. "Here's a pad and pencil. Write down, 'girls on the bus,' *mmmfff mmmmfff.*"

"Flutes, whistles," Kesey said. "That smoke bomb we stashed somewhere. Striped shirts and painted hands. We're going to see Timothy Leary, Dick Alpert, Ralph Metzner and Peggy Hitchcock. We were supposed to meet them in Mexico at Zihuatanejo but they got busted and had to come back to the States, so this is where we'll have the historic meeting."

"Looking forward to this with anxious trepidation," I muttered.

"*Bo-ard!*" Cassady called, and we headed north out of the city, speakers blaring Ray Charles:

"Make tracks, Jack!
You're gone and that's a fact.
Oh no, say it's not so,
I'm a'gonna make good and treat you right,
Give you my loving all day and all night.
That's a laugh I've heard it before
Now get your ass outta that door."

G insberg sat on the film case next to Cassady, giving directions out of the city. Hassler, crouched next to Ginsberg, leaned over to yell at Cassady, keep the questions going, a continuation of the talk they were having at the apartment.

"Is Orlovsky putting you on when he's doing that? Reaching for your dick?" Hassler asked.

"He's definitely serious, and the put-on and the seriousness are so close to reality he's perfected that technique. It's an exact mimicry of Ginsberg twenty years ago, ha ha, right, Allen?"

"A matter of subjective reasoning, always up for adjustment," Ginsberg said.

"Allen used to be wild, huh? He's so cool now," Hassler said.

"Running over Columbia rooftops waving genitals and manuscript. That's why he was kicked out, for that, somewhere around '45, but as for Peter, he has grown. Going around feeling the balls of presidents, because he goes right to the top, like in India: 'I was at the Salami School the other day and I told Nehru...' He's learned that from you, Allen. He doesn't fuck around. Steps right in there. So they have to accept him, more or less, but he's a sex freak, a put-on freak, just like us when we're flirting with girls, he gets right in there. So he's part put-on and that's why there's strength of the insight in that situation, a very insecure position in certain areas. To have nothing to do with sex, I guess, I don't know. He's an adviser, you know, for the League for Sexual Freedom."

"There's other healths beside sexual freedom," Ginsberg said.

"Yes. Not only the health of the stream of consciousness understanding, there's the specific of the insights, like with the seagulls in San Quentin. While there, I never was hit once; many near misses, even a shoe-top or two, and I was never looking up either. So if I can go through the big yard for over two years without a hit by five-hundred to thousands of birds, all in a few seconds' time—but they do have sheds that I very artfully used, as a halfback will—the same way I can walk through the Lower East Side streets and never get hit by pigeons, it's a form of work that becomes a construct and there you are."

"That's as insightful as saying, 'Wherever you go, there you are'—and I say that as a compliment, no sarcasm intended," Ginsberg said.

"I know that, Allen, like saying, 'Guys that are hung know they are hung.' But the point is, that doesn't satisfy, just being hung. That's like being some kind of a simple guy who does thousands of things; ask him to do something else, he'll do that too, but a cat who doesn't do anything, he can't even do one thing."

"We've just heard a report from Poughkeepsie over the radio," Kesey said. "The sports fans there needn't worry, Poughkeepsie doesn't touch us. We're going to take this ball club all the way to the top, not all the way to the bottom."

"The father finally gets a dime," Cassady said. "Alcoholic hangover. He pours salt in his beer and of course we had to call Morton to get that, so I put sugar in the beer. I thought that would be cute."

"Remember folks," I said, "after an earlier zonk, the Pranksters are just getting into their own."

"A possum, a possum, a possum in the road," Chuck Kesey

yelled.

"And should he be run over," I said, "he would get the MDT award: the Most Disgusting Trip Award."

"Twenty-year rest stop," Cassady said.

"Who needs to stop?" said Kesey.

"No one," Cassady said. "I'm going to blow that light there."

"Why not?" I said. "Blow it out. Leave us in the dark, you usually do, ha ha, that's a joke, keep talking..."

*I get weary of people who use pessimism to
avoid being responsible for all the problems in
our culture. A man who says "we're on the road
to disaster" is seldom trying to wrench the wheel
away from the driver.*
— *Ken Kesey*

29

In Search of
the Inner Freedomites

"This is Frederickson on Mars," Kesey said from on top of
the bus, his voice booming through the speakers.
"We've just had a bad meteorite shower up here. I tipped the
goddamned liquid overboard, jar and my ginseng and green tea
is spilled all over the road. Broken glass is everywhere."

Cassady slowed, looked right and left.

"Heads down, heads down," Kesey said. "We're approaching
some kind of troll scene. I don't want you running over any
dwarfs."

"It's not that we don't want to pick up the glass," I said. "It's
just that the trolls might be here."

"They can be nasty things," Kesey said, "ready to leap in and
snatch one of us and drag him or her—they prefer female flesh
you know, more tender and all—down to their lair."

Cassady braked to a stop.

"Troll patrol out," Hassler yelled, flinging open the door.

"Troll patrol, how droll," I muttered.

The Pransksters split into two groups, one on each side of
the road, beat the bushes with sticks, picked up rocks, threw

them into the woods, and yelled: "Get out of here you sneaky trolls, back to the darkest part of the forest where you belong. Leave us humans be, us being humans, not ugly denizens of the lower realms."

"Everything looks groovy from up here," Kesey said. "How's everything down below?"

"All clear," Hassler yelled, leading the troops back on the bus.

"Where's Ginsberg?" Kesey asked.

I looked out the window.

"Oh, God, he's picking up pieces of glass. I better help him."

I grabbed the broom and dustpan and went out, nudged Ginsberg, bent over, peering nearsighted at tiny pieces of glass, bigger ones clutched in his hand.

"Allen, here, let me."

He raised his head.

"Babbs, how thoughtful."

"T-N-T, T'ain't Nothing To it," I said and swept the pieces into the dustpan.

"Kesey tells me you're a writer, Ken."

"Like an ass-backward moron, in that I'm more off than on."

"'Write with blood and you will experience that blood is spirit.'"

"Thus, spoke Zorro-Thustra, if I'm not mistaken," I said, hoisting the dustpan and broom.

"Close enough. How did you know that?"

"At Stanford in grad school, Nietzsche was all the rage; philosophy majors spouted his shit right and left. I found a book of his quotes and threw one around now and then to fake what a smart feller I was, not the fart smeller that was the real me."

Ginsberg rose on tiptoes, lips puckered to give me a kiss. I turned my head, he grazed my cheek.

"Back to the bus, Allen, no time for hanky-panky now."

"'Brave, unconcerned, mocking, violent,'" Ginsberg said. "'Thus, wisdom wants us; she is a woman and always loves only a warrior.'"

"Thus, the Marine Corps unlearnt me. We are one blood, no matter our external colors, for we all bleed red."

We climbed aboard the bus.

"Ready, J.B.?" Cassady asked.

"Wait a minute, my hat's been lost too," Kesey said.

"Picked up glass, lost a hat," I said.

"We've lost a Prankster cap back there for Christ's sake," Kesey said. "Goddamnit. Back up and get that sucker."

"Get another run on this capper," I said.

"I like the idea," Kesey said.

"What's the idea?"

"We send a runner after it."

"Left rudder," I said.

"It would put us in the ditch. We need the resistance of a joint up here."

"Yes, I saved it for you," said Neal. "I thought it was in a stash but no, it's the dear little present you gave me and I'm afraid I lost that joint."

Hassler held out another joint.

"You got a match?" I said. "Get it going, get it going."

Hassler lit and passed it through the turret to Kesey. George came aboard with the missing hat and we moved down the road. Neal picked up his rap where he left off:

"Showing intelligence, like it was in the eyes. I was thinking of a woman you don't know, L.C. Seechrist, who was the top girl in Edgar Cayce's thing. She's an open channel, and dig it, L.C. Seechrist. See Christ. And by God, she makes you see Him. She's the finest, swingingest, looks just like a big old man, ha ha ha. That's the open channel I'm talking about. We're trusting that our motives will continue to purify; in other words, who the hell wants to go and clean up after a Julius? You've got other things to do. My weakness isn't yours. But as a form of holding, like the bus holds us together—but still being divergent—we see now the failings because of self."

"Entrance ahead," Ginsberg said. "The way into the Hitch-cock estate."

Cassady pulled to a stop facing a huge gate enclosed by two giant pillars and topped by a stone house. He blasted the horn, *beep beep-a-toot wahhhh.*

The upstairs window opened, a trumpet stuck out and blew a resounding fanfare of rising notes, then reveille, climbing into a melodic jazz riff that was left hanging on a single clear note. The birds rose from the surrounding trees and the crows flew away in a cawing flock.

"Maynard Ferguson," Ginsberg said. "The keeper of the gate."

A bearded face popped out of the tower window.

"Who goeth and what foreth?"

"We be the Merry Band in search of the Inner Freedomites," Kesey said. "No need to *lithp.*"

The gate rose and Cassady eased through. A long, winding lane lay ahead. We moseyed ahead beneath leafy trees alongside a green lawn.

"Steam blowing up, and you don't play with yourself when that's happening," Cassady said. "She put my car in second gear. Wide open at eighty-five and she said, 'I thought that motor was awful loud.' Fifty miles later right through the block—*BLANG!*—goes the rod! Oh, I see we are here."

"There is going to be a smoke grenade set off during our entrance," Kesey said. "What color is it?"

"Green," I said. "Compliments of the Marine Corps."

"Green is a healing color," said Cassady. "I feel much better already."

"The great house, the great house," Hassler said, as we approached a three-story, white wooden building with a metal roof and covered porch, a tower at each end. One tower was painted red with an upside-down white triangle in the middle. A large white-and-yellow, cross-eyed face with a handlebar mustache and drooping earlobes was painted on the third floor of the mansion: "The Turned-on Man."

"Okay, we're coming in," Kesey said.

"Landing gear down. Smoke bomb released."

I pitched it out the window. A green cloud covered the porch and blew into the open windows of the house.

"Oh man," Hassler said. "It's like the Huns knocking on the gates of Rome."

Dick Alpert, high forehead, glasses, a multi-colored, short-sleeved shirt, walked out of the smoke, coughing, and waved to clear his face.

Cassady had eyes only for Peggy Hitchcock on the porch, green smoke swirling around her blue bikini, her butt sticking over the porch railing.

"We have been through the campaign at Wikieup and the fever at New Orleans," I announced, voice booming out of the speakers, as the porch denizens, including a small boy, walked toward the bus.

"To introduce all around," I continued, "at the wheel we have Speed Limit, now Sir Limit, knighted after coming down the Blue Ridge Parkway with the brakes gone while never missing a gear."

"Thank you," Cassady said. "Yes, I did that."

"Hardly Visible, you can barely see him hidden in his bright colors. Sound Man, scratching between his toes and searching for the foot powder. Highly Charged, sawing on his fiddle, and Equipment Hassler, contemplating the lovely Millbrook ladies. I have to pass this information on to you in order to explain what's exactly going on."

"We're high and they're coming down," Kesey said.

It was early in the morning and we had already reached our stride. They thought we were there for the four-hundred-meter, but we were there for the four-thousand, we the young upstarts from the West Coast, they the established legions of the East.

Tooting and fluting whistles and banging on tambourines, the Pranksters walked through the smoke and climbed the steps onto the porch.

"You look pretty beat and strung out," Dick Alpert said. "Unwind, and later on you can cool down in our waterfall and wash off."

I stayed on the bus to tidy up, then crossed the lawn to the house.

"Oh look, a wisenheimer," Cassady said, pointing at me.

A little brown dog was walking along my side. I wondered if Cassady was making fun of me again.

"It's not a wisenheimer," I said, "it's Veener Schneetzel, *mein herr.*"

The Pranksters broke out sleeping bags and blankets and crashed on the lawn in the warm sun, everyone sprawled out like Albanians, too sleepy and too tired to acknowledge the nibbling of insects. I stayed on the porch and talked with Alpert.

"Last night about twenty of us did acid," he said. "A very intense and profound trip, sitting by the fire, huddled together, a lot of intimacy in a profound deep trip that went all night. By seven or eight this morning everyone was in a mellow, delicate, vulnerable spot and drifting off to bed when your bus drove up, full of energy, so disparate from what was going on; you were speedy, we were mellowed out."

"What kind of experiments are you doing here?" I asked.

"Things like setting up an imaginary experimental typewriter. With a keyboard that has different states of emotion and planes of consciousness, instead of letters. We also do slideshows for people who were alcoholics or having marriage breakdowns, seeing what kind of therapeutic value acid has."

The experiments weren't exactly scientific, he admitted. They were developing maps and guidebooks of the mind. Exploring the brain, not just dosing people to see what would happen. They would come back like neuro-nauts and share the experience, telling about what they saw.

Noticing some of the Pranksters stirring and rising from their naps, Alpert said this was probably a good time for everyone to get in the water and wash off the fetid dust.

I joined them and we hiked across a field. Little Veener Schneetzel had adopted us and ran alongside, short legs churning. We came to a stream with a dam that formed a waterfall showering into a pond. We stripped to our underwear and gamboled in the frolicky waters like a whooping cowboy band of Wild-West saloon carousers invading a pastoral Indian village, sat under the falls, water cascading down our bodies, until Zonker yelled, "What's this?"

He plucked off a black leech that had glommed onto his shoulder.

The suckers were everywhere. We screeched and scrambled out of the water, picked them off and threw them squirming on the ground. Veener Schneetzel growled and pawed at the leeches, shook his head, *whew, bad stuff,* backed off.

On the way back to the house we spotted a horse grazing in the field. A big old feller, Percheron or Clydesdale. Hagen and Hassler and Zonker and I stopped to pet him. He kept chomping.

"Let's ride him," I said.

"It's a workhorse," Hassler said.

"He won't mind."

"How we going to steer the sucker?" Zonker asked.

"Easy," I answered. "We'll use my belt."

I pulled it off and fastened it around the horse's neck.

"One person can ride, or two even if you want; he's big enough. I'll lead him with the belt. Who's first?"

"I'll go," said Zonker.

He grabbed the mane to pull himself up just as the horse stepped backward and put his hoof on Zonker's bare foot, pinning it to the ground.

"Shit fire," Zonker yelled. "The fucker's got me! Get him off!"

I pulled on the belt. Hassler pushed from the rear. Veener Schneetzel yipped at his heels. The horse munched on. Hagen picked some green grass and held it front of the horse's nose. The horse lifted his foot and moved forward, tongue out. Zonker looked down, not a mark on him, only a deep imprint of his foot in the marshy grass.

"Still up for a ride?" I offered.

No takers. I recovered my belt, we left the old feller eating the grass, and arrived at the house in time for chow. A buffet had been set up on the porch, and the others were already digging in: brown rice, cooked squash with steamed Brussel sprouts, cabbage, broccoli and mung beans, and more broccoli; also papaya, mango, strawberries and blueberries over a bed of lettuce, spinach and kale.

Sandy wandered in, wan and haggard.

"What happened to you?" Hassler asked. "Someone work you over?"

"You might say that. They took me down to the crypt, what they call their private meditation room, and shot me up with DMT."

"Gawd, what was that like?" Dale Kesey said.

"A seventh dimensional carnival ride with tinges of yellow around the edges."

"Did they say anything about objecting to the way we came in and the way we acted?" Hassler asked him.

"They were not objecting but we came in with a lot of theatrics. They are operating here with what they call "the loss of ego," and the bus, in those kinds of terms, has a lot of ego. What they're good at is a very opposite thing to what we're doing. They're sitting back a good deal, sitting back because they have created a sort of utopia, a utopia that's contained in their own scene. These people at Millbrook are all New York people and a good number of them are what can be called sick people, although Alpert claims that *sick* and *healthy* and these mental things are merely individual models that people have built, just another game, just another role, and he gives some very convincing arguments."

"Jesus Lord," Dale said. "That the way this IFIF works, get high and then lay the psychobabble on you?"

"The term IFIF is used merely as a convenient reference. IFIF is gone, they're way beyond any kind of federation or internal freedom idea. It's not consciousness expansion so much as unconsciousness contraction. In other words, it's not turning you on more, it's turning off what turns you off."

"Well, Pranksters," Kesey said, "if we want to see Pennsylvania this evening, we better mount up."

Cassady was already in the bus, fussing with his overnight bag, stowing his spare clothes, pulling on his driving glove, adjusting the mirrors.

Dick Alpert cornered me and said, "We need some money to pay for dinner. Kesey said to talk to you."

"Okay. How much do you want?"

"We generally leave it up to what the guests consider it's worth."

"Fair enough."

I dug some dollar bills out of the plastic sack.

"Seventy-eight bucks, how does that sound?"

Alpert grimaced, then smiled and took the wad. He stuck it in his pocket without re-counting.

"Happy trails," he said.

"Thanks. Catch you on the rebound."

Alpert said something to Kesey. Kesey nodded and motioned to me and the two of us walked behind the house. Timothy Leary stood waiting for us.

He said the reason he didn't see us sooner was that he had just fallen in love with a woman, so needless to say that was distracting him. He was not only lovesick but had also come down with the flu, so he went to bed. He didn't know if history was being made, a meeting of the acid tribes; he was too pre-occupied. But now he wanted us to know before we left that we were on the same page.

"It is our mission to liberate the world," he said. "Why? To bring down the American empire. It's completely materialistic, and of course exercising complete power all around the planet."

We couldn't argue with that.

"We have very positive feelings about you guys," he said, "but we knew you were different. We use words like *session* and *lysergic acid* and you use the language of the psychedelic culture from the streets, dance halls and the buses. Some of the people here feel like you are making fun of us for being so formal. We can learn from your tribal nature. A true sense of humor runs through everything you do—a rollicking, good-natured, hit-the-road quality—and that's just what we need. We can learn from that."

We shook hands and left. I looked back. Tim stood watching us, Veener Schneetzel at his side.

O ver the years, we became good friends with Leary and saw each other often. By then, the Millbrook scene was over and Leary was traveling around the country on his own, giving talks and meeting with other psychedelic spokesmen. When-ever he came to Eugene, Kesey and I would pick him up at the airport and squire him around in Kesey's convertible, even one time to a University of Oregon football game. Tim loved the opportunity to get off his high horse and be one of the guys, hanging with our families and friends.

If you heard the bell or the song "Hit the Road Jack,"
that meant the bus was leaving. I never got left behind.
My spot was on the top of the bus. They played oldies
like "Love Potion Number Nine." Being on the bus was
the way summer was supposed to be, and every morning
was like the first day of summer vacation. They gave me
my summer back and I will love them forever for that.
  — Anonymous

30

Bored Out of Her Mind

No more Cassady. While we were staying at the Madhattan apartment, unbeknownst to us, Neal had arranged for his pal, Bradley Hodgsman, to drive Neal's car to Madhattan and be on the alert for Neal's call to pick him up. The two of them drove straight to California so Neal could get back to his recapping job at the tire place in San Jose. Plus, that house was waiting to be painted.

Without Neal at the wheel, we took turns driving, George Walker bearing the brunt. One night, Dale Kesey took over while everyone else slept. The bus moved along smoothly, then suddenly went over a bump and everything lurched to the side. Another smooth run and another bump and lurch, waking everyone up. The bus hit another bump, lurched, and all six bunks in the back collapsed.

Dale heard the screaming from behind, looked around, big smile on his face, *what's the problem?*

The bus coasted to a stop. The sun rimming the eastern horizon lit up a supermarket parking lot. Dale had followed the road to the entrance and drove in. He drove around and around the lot, hitting and driving over the curbs.

"Why? Why, Dale?" everyone wanted to know.

Dale shrugged. "I thought I was on the road and we were headed toward home. What were all those bumps in the road?"

"Look around you," Hassler said. "Does this look like any kind of road?"

Dale laughed. "I better get some sleep," he said, and slumped in the driver's seat.

We pulled the broken bunks apart and pitched the wood out next to some dumpsters. Spread the mattresses on the floor. Eased Dale out of the driver's seat, onto a mattress, covered him with a blanket. George took the wheel.

The engine was acting up. A cylinder which had been getting weak finally died. The five working cylinders kept us going until, approaching Minneapolis, the bus wheezed and sputtered to a stop. A tow truck pulled us into the International Harvester garage. George told the head mechanic the problem and asked him if they had any replacement engines.

"Come with me," he said, and led George into the shop.

A pile of six-cylinder engines were stacked against the wall.

"All the big trucks are switching from gas-powered engines to diesel."

"We'll take one," George said. "Pick out the best and I'll roust up the money."

George called Chuck Kesey, who had flown home from Madhattan. Chuck wired the money, 800 dollars. The mechanics went to work on the bus. We left them to it and walked around town, visited the parks, threw stale bread to the ducks and geese in the ponds, bought sandwich material in a store, ate a cold supper on the grass, then continued walking through the night.

A man stood leaning against the wall outside a bar. He asked one of us for a light. I handed him a book of matches. He lit up and looked us over.

"What are you characters doing wandering around here in the dead of night?"

We introduced ourselves and gave him the short version.

When he said his name was Ernest Gann, I asked him if he was the writer. He nodded.

"I read your book, *The High and the Mighty*," I said. "Really liked it, maybe that's why I became a pilot."

We spent an hour or more talking to him before parting, wandered some more, and returned to the International Harvester garage at dawn.

The engine replacement was finished. George fired up the old gal and she purred like a newborn pussycat. A burly, grease-splattered mechanic handed George a flag wrapped around a pole. George unwound the flag and whipped it back and forth: INTERNATIONAL HARVESTER in big letters.

George taped the flagpole to a post on the back of the bus and, leaving the garage and driving in the street, the flag flapped in the breeze.

From North Dakota, we crossed the border and drove across the Canadian Prairies. Coming to the Rockies, we stopped in Calgary where the Calgary Stampede was in full swing. We parked, roamed the midway, came to a big tent full of dancing people, the music loud and pulsating. We joined the dancers, a song and beat we'd never heard before:

"*When I touch you*
I feel happy inside.
Now, let me hold your hand,
I want to hold your hand."

When the song ended, we walked back to the bus where a large crowd had gathered. Mike Hagen was off to the side talking to a girl: medium height, round-faced, dark black hair to her shoulders. She said she was fifteen years old, was just walking around and her mood was down.

"High school has become a drag," she said. "I wasn't looking forward to the end of summer vacation. My folks let me come to the Stampede and when I saw the bus and the people around it, I walked over to take a look."

Kesey stepped out of the bus and said, "Let's mount up and head out. What have we got here?"

"Linda Klein," the girl said. "Can I go with you?"

Kesey looked her over. No sign of a spaced-out drug-head, but a sharp-looking, intelligent person, competent on her own.

"Alright."

In two days, Kesey's wife Faye was arriving on a train, so to kill time, we drove to a lake and camped out. We cooked over a wood fire, swam in the lake, hiked around the perimeter, and took naps until it was time to leave.

Kesey, not remembering our new passenger's name, called her Anonymous, and soon everyone followed. She accepted it happily, glad to be with us on the bus while at the same time not part of our team. Anonymous was not just a bus name but an apt description of her role.

We parked in front of the train station, tootled and flootled the arriving Faye onto the bus, then tooled out onto the street and through town, departing Calgary for home.

The cops stopped us before we reached the city limits. Two officers came aboard, saying they were looking for a fifteen-year-old runaway, a high school girl. Her mother had sent them a picture and they showed it to us. Anonymous, who had been hanging back, shoved through and said, "Let me see that."

It was a picture from a yearbook. The girl's face was tilted, away from the camera. Her hair was parted on the side and shaped around the sides of her face. Her lips were open in a slight smile.

"Oh, God," Anonymous said. "Who is that lame-looking kid? I can't see her ever getting on this bus."

She handed back the picture. The policemen gave the inside of the bus a cursory look-over and sent us on our way. When we crossed the border into the States, she hid in the back, bundled up in blankets behind Faye Kesey who was napping on the back seat. The customs inspector never saw her.

She stayed with us clear to Kesey's house in La Honda, and on to LA where we were going to a rock concert. While in LA, not telling anyone, she went off by herself to visit a boy named Mel whom she met when he was with his stepfather in Calgary.

"You know, your mother called," Mel's mom told Anonymous, "wanting to know if we'd seen you."

There was a knock on the door. It was Kesey.

"We found a letter in the bus with this address on it," he said. "Are you ready to go home?"

"No," Anonymous said. "I'm going to stay awhile."

"Alright, then."

Kesey left, the cops arrived. They took Anonymous to LA County, had her change into jail clothes and wait in a cell, then drove her to the airport and escorted her to the departure gate. She went into the ladies' room, threw her jail clothes in the trash and, putting on her regular outfit, flew home to Calgary where she went back to school.

She exchanged letters with Kesey and Faye, graduated from high school and after a few years returned to the States, ending up in Eugene, Oregon, and joining up with the bus on its tours through America and the British Islands before finally moving to Roseville, California.

Evil has its teeth in us and is chewing on our minds.
We the few can beat the evil in society because we
can count the number of seeds in an apple, but not
the number of apples in a seed.
  — *Ken Kesey*

31

What Were They Expecting?

K esey and I were walking through downtown Eugene when we came upon a kid selling homemade brownies. A sign said "25 CENTS." We stopped and looked at his wares. He stared up with big eyes.

"What's in those brownies?" I asked.

He looked puzzled. "Chocolate."

I raised my eyebrows up and down. "Are you sure there's no P-O-T in them?"

The kid looked up at his dad. His dad shrugged. The kid turned back to me.

"What's that?" he asked.

Kesey spoke up before I could reply.

"Power of Transformation," he said.

The kid nodded. We bought some brownies and moved on.

"Fast thinking," I said. "Good work."

"I had to do something to save your ass, you numbskull."

The dad yelled from behind us, "What ever happened to that movie, Kesey?"

Kesey turned around and said, "We were arrested."

T he setting sun glowed through the redwoods at Kesey's place in La Honda. Inside the house, a pile of movie reels sat on a table next to a 16 mm projector loaded with a four-hundred-foot reel. A Sony four-track tape recorder was on the other side of the table.

Pranksters sprawled on chairs and the couch and cushions. Everyone was primed with a bottle of Romilar cough syrup to stay mellow, and two Dexedrine crosstops to stay awake. We were going to watch, starting Friday night and going through the entire weekend, the entire forty hours of bus tapes and film.

Joints were passed around, everyone sipped drinks. Outside, the redwoods swayed in the night wind, whispering their secrets. The creek murmured in response.

"Roll 'em," Kesey announced.

He turned on the movie projector. I pushed the play button of the reel-to-reel.

The back of Neal Cassady's head filled the screen. Cassady waved his gloved hand, the one he used to change gears. A joint poked between his fingers.

"I tell you, Chief, if we don't get some food in these Pranksters' bellies soon, we'll have a mutiny on our hands and *athousandratburgerswon'tsatisfy* them sa-a-*a-y* it *isn't* *so* *we're* *not* *going* *too* *fast* *we're* *going* *too* *slow*..."

I hit the stop buttons. What the fuck? Everything was going along nicely when suddenly the sound went faster and faster, then slower and slower while the film chugged along at a steady rate.

Didn't take long to figure it out. The camera ran at a steady twenty-four frames a second, powered by a battery belt. The Sony tape recorder ran at seven-and-a-half-inches per second on 110-volt household current supplied by a generator on the back of the bus.

Due to a carburetor malfunction, the generator would sometimes run too fast and sometimes too slow. That screwed up playback.

We restarted everything and fought through the screwup for

the whole weekend. Monday, we crashed. On Tuesday, Kesey and I went to work.

Using scenes in which the sound was steady, we edited the film, cut the tape to match, and glued the pieces together. Every Saturday night we showed the week's results.

Word got out around the Bay Area. It wasn't long until the Saturday night showings drew crowds that spilled into the yard, an all-night party. It was out of hand, as was the mess we cleaned up the next day.

At the same time, unbeknownst to us, things weren't going well for William Wong, a narcotics detective in San Francisco. He hadn't had a headline bust in months and was feeling the heat. Unless he came up with something soon, he was facing a transfer to Missing Persons.

A fifteen-year-old girl at Woodside High School, close to Kesey's house, was caught with marijuana. That grabbed Willy Wong's attention. He zeroed in on Kesey, the cars going in and out, the number of people living there. He IDed Neal Cassady.

Cassady had already been busted twice for possession of weed. That clinched it for Agent Wong: Kesey's place was the hub of a major pot operation—and Neal Cassady made the deliveries.

Wong set up surveillance on top of the hill across the road. We were aware something was going on. We found cigarette butts and boot prints on the hill, more footprints in the path alongside the house. We took safety measures. Kept all the pot in one jar. Rolled up just enough joints to get us through the day, then hid the jar outside. I tried to get one of my old Marine friends to fix me up with a trip flare, but he said civilians weren't allowed.

"Not even us Marines?"

"You're a long way from the Marine Corps, Babbs!"

Kesey sent Faye and the kids to stay with her sister.

One evening Agent Wong was walking along Grant Street in

San Francisco and he overheard a guy say, "Let's go down to Kesey's and get wasted!"

Wasted? *Drugs!* That was all he needed. He put in for a search warrant. At the same time, George Walker found a bag of pot under the floor of the back shack we were tearing down. No one could remember putting it there; only thing we could think of— it was a plant.

We added it to our stash.

On a Friday evening in April, Kesey and I were working in the editing room. The Pranksters relaxed in the living room, reading and sewing and talking. The ten joints we rolled up earlier were stashed in the front pocket of my shirt.

Suddenly, Mike Hagen charged through the front door and yelled, "The cops are here, and they've got a warrant."

Kesey bolted from the editing room. *What the hell?* I shut down the equipment and headed for the noise in the bathroom.

Kesey was hunched over the toilet, one hand holding down the handle to keep the water flowing, other hand tipping a quart mason jar into the water. The one day we didn't take the jar outside and hide it.

A man was holding Kesey by his thick wrestler's neck, whaling on his back.

Sheriff's deputies poured in. George Walker stood agape, paintbrush dripping red glops on the floor. The entire bathroom was an ongoing art project, collages of photos, magazine pictures, headlines and original paintings covered the walls. James Brown sang about Papa's brand-new bag from a radio.

I grabbed the man beating on Kesey and yanked him, tumbling ass-over-teacups into the lap of Page Browning taking a bath.

Eyeglasses skewed, clothes sopping, the man spluttered up, waving a soggy paper. Deputies surged forward. The window at the end of the tub blew in, the muzzle of a pistol stuck into the room.

"Narcotics Agent Wong," declared the man standing in the bathtub. He brandished a paper in my face. "And I have the search warrant right here."

"Let me see that," I said in my sternest Marine Captain voice.

I tore the paper from his hand and looked at the ink smeared across the page.

"This is no good. Incomprehensible. Can't read a fucking word. You people get out of here."

An arm reached around and held a piece of paper in front of my face.

"I've got a warrant, too," the deputy said. "And this one is good."

"Papa's got a brand-new bag, eh?"

We trooped into the living room where the rest of the Pranksters were being held.

I couldn't figure it out. All this for a little pot? Seventeen armed deputies and a police dog? The ten joints were a heavy weight in my shirt pocket. I snuck one in my mouth and started chewing, then wandered around the room, palming joints to individual Pranksters, making chewing motions with my mouth. A woman I'd never seen before sat in a chair at the end of the room.

"Who are you?" I asked.

"One of the deputies."

She didn't look like a cop. Dressed in jeans and a button-down shirt, she'd been watching me all the time I was wandering around the room, but never said anything. I could have kissed her.

Taking us one at a time into the bathroom to be searched, they finished by morning and hauled us down to the San Mateo jail where we were fingerprinted and incarcerated, men in one cell, Gretch, Ginger Jackson, and Mountain Girl in another.

Ginger was a friend of Hagen's. We had a game called the Five-Day Stay, where people who showed up to hang around would have to sign up for five days, help out, then leave. Ginger was on her third day. When the bust went down, she was sitting on a log by the creek, enjoying the quiet and solitude until a deep voice behind her said, "Don't move."

"Okay," she said, and stayed there until they took us to jail.

Mountain Girl, nineteen, willowy with long, black hair, a bright smile and sharp mind, had come from North Carolina to work at Stanford University. One day she was sitting in St. Michael's Coffee House in Palo Alto drinking a cup of tea when Neal Cassady walked in. He told her about the Prankster scene and offered to take her up to Kesey's. When they got there, she was immediately taken with the scene and the bus and became a regular.

In the male section of the jail, the men already there sat with their backs to the wall. We formed our own group in a corner. Cassady was into his jail mode, quiet and subdued. One of the inmates, obviously drunk, wandered the room muttering to himself. A big bruiser, sleeves rolled up to show off his biceps, glowered at the drunk.

"Knock that mumbling shit off," he yelled.

The drunk glanced up and continued muttering.

"I told you to knock that shit off."

He stuck his fist in front of the drunk's face.

"You don't want to taste this, you better keep that fool mouth shut."

I walked over.

"Say, fellers, we're all in here together. What say we get along, maybe catch some shut-eye?"

The bruiser turned on me, red-veined eyes bulging.

"Who the fuck are you, getting in my business? Beat it, or maybe you'll get a taste of this, too." He held up his fist.

"Hmm," I said. "Where's the tattoos? You know, a letter on each knuckle, spells L-O-V-E."

"That does it, knucklehead, I'm going to..."

Jerry Anderson, a short, blond-headed guy with a lot of energy who had picked that day to visit Kesey's place, rushed up to the brute and got in his face. Jerry's head came up to the bruiser's shoulder. A banty challenging the cock of the walk.

"You want trouble?" Jerry said. "Then you're going to get it. More than you can handle. See those guys over there? You mess with one of us you mess with all of us. Ain't that right, men?"

Kesey stepped forward, then George, Hagen, Dale, Page Browning, Hassler and Lee Quarnstrom. Cassady stayed back, sticking to his credo: *The only excuse for violence is when making love.*

The brute snarled, walked away. He grabbed the bars.

"Jailer," he yelled. "Get me away from these crazies or there's gonna be a riot."

A deputy came around the corner.

"What's going on?"

I said, "You might want to house him in a different cell; he's about to beat up on that drunk."

He unlocked the door and led the bruiser away.

We were all pretty mellow. Those joints we ate might have had something to do with it. I turned to Jerry.

"What ever possessed you to get in that guy's face?"

"Couldn't let that ignorant lout treat you like that, Captain. Gotta stick up for each other. Only way to deal with bullies."

The next morning, they trucked us to the courthouse where we pled not guilty and were released on bail, thanks to our lawyer, Brian Rohan, an old friend of Hagen's from their days together at the University of Oregon.

Rohan tried to get the search warrant quashed, arguing there wasn't enough hard evidence to support it. Everything was hearsay. The "getting wasted" comment Agent Wong overheard didn't necessarily refer to pot. The expression was more commonly used for drinking alcohol. Rohan's argument didn't fly; the police had found marijuana.

Rohan cut a deal with the DA: Kesey and Page would take the hit, the rest of us cut loose, the deal made to protect Cassady from another felony rap, his third, which in those days meant a ten-to-twenty-year sentence. Kesey was found guilty of having a place where marijuana was confiscated. I didn't know where they found it; I thought it was all flushed down the toilet.

The DEA had been after Page for a long time, knowing he was running pot from the Mexican border. On his last run, Page had a feeling something was wrong. He pulled into the Arizona desert and buried his load. A half hour later, he was stopped by three cop cars. They tore his car apart, but had to let him go. Catching him at Kesey's was what they needed to hook him in.

One of the things they confiscated at Kesey's was the manuscript of a novel I had written about a Marine helicopter squadron in Vietnam. They must have thought it would reveal our drug shenanigans. The day the plea bargain went down in court, Rohan strode up to the evidence table, grabbed my manuscript, its pages held together with a rubber band, walked down the aisle and dropped it in my lap.

"This whole charade is bullshit," he said to me in a low voice, unusual for him, loud volume being one of his courtroom characteristics.

Another item on the evidence table was a syringe—proof to the cops that we were injecting hard drugs. When it was revealed we used the syringe to squirt lightweight oil into the moving parts of the tape recorder, that was quickly dropped.

When I appeared in front of the judge to enter my plea I told him, "Your Honor, I can explain why I threw Mister Wong into the bathtub."

The judge looked down at me.

"Young man, I will not tolerate any frivolity in this courtroom."

I was happy to comply and sat down.

Kesey whispered, "And just what were you going to tell

him?"

"I'd think of something."

"Never at a loss," Kesey said.

With Kesey and Page out on bail, we went back to work putting the movie together. The effort petered out. We were in a holding pattern day-to-day, cooking, cleaning, painting, tearing down the backhouse; but we were too used to playing the fool for errant kings to be content with ordinary tasks. Other capers were afoot.

The Acid Test was a thinly veiled excuse
to show samples of the movie
the Pranksters had filmed on their bus trip.
Certain unknowns placed a garbage can
full of Kool-Aid in the middle of the floor.
The Merry Band of Pranksters
set up at one end of the hall.
At the other end the Grateful Dead
played rock and bluegrass
and psychedelic wanderings.
Sometimes both bands played together.
And wasn't it Ray
who asked, "What'd I say?"
and the Dead who answered,
"No mercy in this land."
  — Ken Babbs

32

It Was Come to Jesus Time

It wasn't really an Acid Test. It was a Halloween party at The Spread, where I lived in Soquel, California, east of Santa Cruz. Our instruments and amps and microphones filled the living room. I played the electric bass, Kesey the electric guitar, George Walker on drums, Gretchen Fetchen on electric piano, Mike Hagen on guitar.

We did a sound check and then went outside to commune with the moon. We were in costume: Mountain Girl was Little Bo Peep; Lee Quarnstrom, ace reporter Clark Kent; George Walker, Flash Gordon, moving so fast you couldn't see him; Mike Hagen, an Eastern Oregon wheat rancher; Gretch, Wonder Woman. I was the Spirit; Kesey the Wizard of Oz.

We stood in a circle, held hands and hummed. A cloud covered the moon and everything went dark. We began to elevate—the cloud passed—we hovered an airy foot off of the ground—the moon spotlighted us—and out of the house rose the voices of an off-key chorus and the notes of a mangled celestial orchestra:

"*Judge decreed it, clerk he wrote it down,*

Give you this jail sentence, you'll be Nashville bound."

We floated inside. Garcia, Weir, Lesh, Pigpen, and Kreutzmann were playing our instruments and belting out the song:

"*Some got six month, some got one solid,*

But me and my buddies all got lifetime here."

We sidled in, singing and rapping. They eased out and we took over, the only song we knew:

"*Have you ever heard the story of Peggy the Pistol?*

She didn't shoot a gun but she shot a lot of crystal."

After that we took turns with the band until early morning, when the music wound down. We sprawled on the floor, held microphones, rapped long nonsensical poetic free jazz wordplay that morphed into deep religioso, talking about meeting on the other side—whether we believed in it or not.

Cassady, the Catholic, said, "Doggone dogma, Dog Man."

Kesey, the Baptist, said, "Want to fervently believe."

Robert Stone, the iconoclast, said, "Are you shitting me?"

Babbs, the delayer, said, "Won't know till we get there."

George Walker, not committing himself, said, "How about it, Allen, what's the Buddhist take?"

Allen didn't hesitate. "There was a chicken on the side of the road who saw another chicken on the other side. 'How do I get to the other side?' he yelled. The other chicken yelled back, 'You are on the other side.'" He smiled benignly.

Dawn crested the eastern ridge, everyone packed up and went home, leaving a mess and a three-day job, sweeping, mopping, scouring, bringing in the furniture, restoring the home.

T he second party—still not called an Acid Test—was in San
    Jose, at a nondescript house in an ordinary neighborhood.
The owner was a tall, slightly stooped acidhead with a bushy
Afro.

   A white van pulled to the curb. Five musicians began unloading their equipment. The Pranksters were already inside,
gear piled in a corner: movie projector, two tape recorders, microphones and speakers and, for this occasion, an overhead projector belonging to Roy Sebern, who had originally named the
bus *Further.*

R oy had us over to his house the week before the San Jose
    party to demonstrate his latest artistic endeavor. An over-
head projector, picked up at a school equipment sale, sat on a
table. We lounged on cushions, sipped drinks and smoked joints
while Roy mixed paints and gels in small dishes. Roy turned off
the light and turned on the projector. The wall filled with a
square, white image. He placed a piece of cellophane on the projector and the wall turned bright yellow. He dribbled oils and
gels on the cellophane, creating a swirling canvas.

   Changing cellophanes, using different oils and gels, he made
flamboyant, exotic, ever-changing wall paintings. We had never
seen anything like it.

   Late in the night, after Roy wiped the glass clean and white
light filled the wall, a black beetle walked across the projector.
The beetle was gigantic, antennae waving like pliant spears,
beady eyes glowing. At the edge of the frame another beetle,
even larger, scuttled across the glass with its jaws wide open
and clamped down on the first beetle. A tremendous thrashing
ensued. The smaller beetle bent in two, reached back and
grabbed the bigger one in the midsection. Shells cracked, pieces
flew.

   Eyes wide, we shouted, "You can do it, little guy!"

"That's it, gouge him in the eye!"

"No, no fair, no biting off his leg."

"Oh, shit, that's his guts leaking out..."

The smaller beetle fell limp. The bigger beetle ate it up.

Knowing there'd never be another show like that, we said goodnight to Roy and headed home. The light show, a staple of every rock-'n'-roll show to come, was born.

T here was a ruckus going on in the street in San Jose. The musicians were muscling a Hammond B-3 organ out of the van. It proved a challenge.

"Don't drop it," Pigpen yelled. "It's not paid for."

"Get back here and help lift," Phil Lesh retorted. "This fucker weighs two tons."

"In your head, maybe," Bill Kreutzmann said. "What are you doing, Bobby, it's gotta go this way."

"Maybe in China," said Bob Weir. "Just gotta get past that corner, two inches to the left."

"My fingers," Jerry Garcia warned. "Don't squash my fingers."

They grappled the organ onto the porch and into the living room, where they slid it into place.

T he sound system tested, the movie projector loaded with a four-hundred-foot reel of the bus movie, Roy's overhead projector beaming on a blank wall, everything was ready. The first arrivals stood in clumps waiting. The band hit it:

"*Wall I'm a super sloth, honey.*

Nosing around your hole.

I can make you breathe freely

Sucking out the bugs

Making your whole nose whole..."

Once the music was cranked up, the room came to life. No differentiation between performers and audience, no elevated

stage. Dancers peered into our tape recorders with reels spinning, stared at film moving through sprockets, looked over our
motley collection of musical instruments. No costumes, no
painted faces. All that was yet to come.

Sometimes the Warlocks played, sometimes we played, other
times we played together. Then there were short spells when no
one played, the flow unplanned, non-directional. When the
light of dawn blazed through the window, we called it quits,
packed up and cleared out, another Keystone comedy routine
moving the Hammond B-3 organ out of the house and into the
van. A toot of the horn and they were off. We followed in the
bus, winding down from our all-night high, worn out and ready
for bed.

W e were into a whole new ballgame. Our dreams of being
big-screen moviemakers had been arrested. We began
putting our efforts into a weekly Saturday night show.

Paul Foster drew up a generic black and white poster with
the words "CAN YOU PASS THE ACID TEST?" on top. Below
was printed "HAPPENERS ARE LIKELY TO INCLUDE THE FUGS, ALLEN
GINSBERG, THE MERRY PRANKSTERS, NEAL CASSADY, THE GRATEFUL
DEAD, ROY'S AUDIOPTICS, MOVIES."

At the bottom was a blank white square where we wrote the
location, for this, the first official Acid Test: Muir Beach.

We added a new twist to the show. Not only the name, but a
table at the door with a sign: "ADMISSION ONE DOLLAR." The dollar bought you an ID card. On the opposite side of the card was
a drawing of a stern Uncle Sam pointing his finger: "CAN YOU
PASS THE ACID TEST?"

What did it mean to pass the Acid Test? The real acid test is
a chemical experiment to see if an object is gold or not. You put
acid on the object and, if it is gold, the object takes it okay; if
not, the acid eats the surface away. In our case, the question
"Can you pass the acid test?" meant *can you get high and still*

function? There were no specific goals. It was discovering what was out there when you moved away from the norm.

Two large plastic garbage cans of Kool-Aid sat on the floor in the middle of the room, one labeled, "FOR KIDS," the other, "FOR ADULTS ONLY." Who put the acid in the Kool-Aid? We never knew or cared; our bit was to put on the show. The only rule: stay until dawn, no roaming the bricks, swaying and singing and attracting undue attention.

The Grateful Dead played the music that was in the air, the vibrations stirred up by the participants. As Kesey described it, "The Dead were supple enough to read the notes written on the wall. It's like a magic trick. When it happens, there's a crack in your mind. You know it's a trick but you can't figure it out and that crack lets in the light. It opens up all the possibilities and that's what puts you in touch with the invisible."

Stanley Owsley hit the Kool-Aid hard. He was calm until the Dead jammed on a long riff that brought him to his feet, dancing like a puppet on strings pulled by a crazy jerkoff. He pushed a wooden chair across the floor. The feet of the chair screeched. He lifted the chair slightly, changing the pitch of the screech, playing the chair to the beat of the Dead.

Neal Cassady blew through the double doors of the kitchen, pulling a dishwasher by its hose. He weaved through moving bodies until he walked alongside Owsley, adding percussive *glops* and *splurts* to the chair screeches as he blew into the hose and agitated the water in the bottom.

The Dead rose to perilous heights, the chair screeches grew frantic. Cassady added his gravely voice, "Fried and fricasseed, *glug ugg*, harried and scarried, *gurgle blurp blop*, left turn made me learn, *blastus-smashus*, no doom in the room," as dancers leaped out of the way.

Jerry laid into the guitar with a frenzy. Phil hand-slapped the bass, Pigpen wailed on the harp, answering Jerry note-for-note. Bill the drummer banged a multiple beat on the snares and Bobby strummed wild chords, determined to keep up.

It was hallelujah, come to Jesus time. When the last note shrilled, a long-haired, scraggly-bearded guy grabbed me by the shirt and screamed into my face—"I seen the light, I seen the light and *it is good!*"—then spun away into the crowd.

"That was intense," Kesey said.

"Like a fire in a circus. But that guy put it out by spitting all over my face."

When the light of dawn lit the surface of the ocean, Kesey and Jerry and Phil and I stood on the porch and smoked a joint. I slapped Phil on the back.

"Quite a night. Just like the big time, huh, Phil?"

"This is the big time. We could cut a chart-busting record."

"We taped the whole thing," Kesey said. "Press and release a disc tomorrow."

"Yeah," Jerry quipped, "and a year from tomorrow we'll be recording a 'Things Go Better With Coke' commercial."

Cracked us up. I swallowed the roach and we split for home. Walked away from another one, as Cassady always said.

O ver the years, people would ask Kesey, "Whatever happened to that movie?"

His reply was always the same, "We were arrested."

Moviemakers would tell him, "We can make that movie."

"Go ahead," Kesey answered.

They loaded up the film and tapes and left. A few months later, Kesey would go out to get the paper and find all the boxes piled on the porch.

"Many have tried to climb that mountain and all have failed," he said.

Hogs are coming.
In a world where everything is placed neatly on a ledge,
On a Harley Davidson the Angels ride on the edge.
In a world where you know what's gonna be happening tonight,
The Angels get off their bikes, you don't know if they're gonna play or
    Fight.
Ain't nobody likes a Hells Angel.
One of the things that makes them Hells Angels,
You gotta be villains in everybody's book.
You gotta be disliked by the cops and by the guy who dislikes the cops.
You gotta be disliked by the citizenry and the guy who opposes the
    citizenry.
If you're gonna be a Hells Angel, you gotta start off by being bad.
How you gonna be bad in everybody's book?
That's tricky business.
And he looked up at me from the hole he was in and smiled,
Looked up at me from the hole he was in and said you gotta go wild.
    — Ken Kesey and Ken Babbs

33

We Don't Pick Them, We Recognize Them

O n a warm summer day in August, after a tiring legal session with his lawyer, Kesey was walking down Grant
Street in North Beach San Francisco, taking in the sights and
sounds, when an amplified voice drew his attention to a hall
called The Place. A sign outside advertised, "Poetry Night."

Kesey stood at the open door and listened:

"*Two young ladies*
go to a drug store

to buy some gin
What kind?
asked the counter clerk
We have oxygen
nitrogen and phosgen.
Francis looks at
Maybelline and
Maybellline blurts,
there are three kinds of turds
mustard, custard
and you, you old bastard."

Kesey went inside and stood at the back. Onstage, a lanky, long-haired man in a leather jacket and oil-stained jeans stood with his hands in his front pockets. He didn't move or show any emotion, spoke in a clear steady voice.

"Minions by the millions
huddled at the locked
gates to the Ganges
no more room
in the water
the Ganges is nothing
but a movement
of mud from
the Bramaputra
to the Bay of Bengal
where it sludges
to the open sea."

He looked straight ahead, paused between lines, paid no attention to the small audience seated on folding chairs.

"Hasbro has applied
for a zip line permit
similar to a zip line
of the Taj Mahal
to the top of the mast

of a beached freighter
with styrofoam britches
to protect the rider
from attracting lost
and partially charred
body parts and
bits of smouldering pyres
seeking a connection
to the material world
so quickly left behind."

He turned away and Kesey saw the Hells Angels rocker sewn on the back of his jacket. The audience applauded lightly, the man left the stage and stood alongside the wall. Kesey walked over and said, "I liked your poem."

He eyeballed Kesey.

"Thanks. Let's go outside and have a smoke."

Kesey introduced himself and the man said his handle was Freewheelin Frank. They talked for a while, Kesey inviting Frank down to La Honda: hang out, share some weed and unwind, enjoy life in the redwoods.

A backfiring Cadillac convertible bounced over the bridge into the yard. Freewheelin Frank drove. Alongside him sat a big, bearded man, in the back three more. Hells Angels had come to scope out Kesey and his place. After an afternoon of beer and smokes and sizing each other up, the Angels decided to return with the whole chapter, have a righteous party.

We heard them coming from a long way off, guttural roar rising and falling, a line of motorcycles snaking around curves, the noise overwhelmingly loud on the bridge, where they geared down and turned around the drive to park their bikes in a row. Engines off, kickstands dropped, boots hit the ground and crunched the gravel as the Angels and their womenfolk walked to the porch.

"Been a quiet afternoon," Kesey said. "What say you grab some beers and take a load off."

We joined them at the firepit where a tub of beer in ice waited. Wooden stumps served as chairs. We sat and got acquainted and, as the day wore on, a raucous scene developed with fifty or sixty Hells Angels milling around the yard.

They had their rules: If you were smoking joints and ended up with two because you were too slow passing, then you had to smoke both of them all the way down; if you threw an empty beer can over your shoulder and it hit another beer can, then it was time to leave. None of the cans ever hit another.

The cops who had followed the Hells Angels from the freeway to La Honda sat out on the road. They stopped and shook down everybody who tried to leave.

The Angels brought Hunter S. Thompson to the party. We didn't know who he was. He was so messed up he couldn't talk. He was barefoot and skinny, dressed in a trench coat and a pair of underwear. We didn't know why he was there or what he was doing or why they were mistreating him so badly. They dragged him around, literally yanking his chain, for Hunter was chained to a Hells Angel, a dog was chained to Hunter, and a cat was chained to the dog. A chain of fools.

Ron Boise's sculpture *The Hanging Man*, welded from cut-up car hoods and fenders, hung from a tree limb. Allen Ginsberg sat beneath the tree and looked across the yard at the Pranksters and the Angels drinking and yakking. He listened to the music echoing through the Redwoods and jotted in his notebook:

"Hot breeze in the overhead trees
Bodies sprawled on the ground
Fire burned down to blackened coals
Beer bottles kicked all around
Cops asleep in cars on the street
You'd think this party had all wound down."

W e got acquainted with Tiny, Terry the Tramp, Buzzard, and Gut, whose brother was in the band Blue Cheer. Outcasts and outlaws who did whatever they wanted.

Kesey asked, "How do you pick your members?"

Pete from Frisco said, "We don't pick them, we recognize them."

In our lives as Pranksters we had learned how to move and dance in crowds without creating hostility, to find the cool spot in others, and it paid off at the party. It helped enormously that the Angels were having a psychedelic experience, not getting mean on speed and booze.

Mountain Girl swapped clothes with some Hells Angels and ended up wearing someone's vest. When it started to look like it might cause trouble, she gave it back. Puff, President of the Frisco Chapter, offered to let her drive his Harley. She agreed and climbed on.

I asked her, "You ever drive one of these things before?"

"Not this big, but plenty of others."

"Leave her be," Puff said. "She'll be alright."

She drove down to San Gregorio Beach with Puff riding on the back.

We played our instruments and the Angels broke out harmonicas and sang:

"Remember when we stuck old Nelly in the eye
and she went down to the hospital
and they stuck something up her ass
and next thing you knew she was
wired from stem to stern."

Freewheelin Frank said to me, "Hey man, see that bike?"

"Yeah, I see it."

"Go for a ride on it. Go on. Take it."

"No thanks."

I couldn't play that axe. Drop one of their instruments and it breaks, you're liable to break with it.

Someone in the house changed the record blaring out of the speakers. "Subterranean Homesick Blues" played over and over again until Mountain Girl, sick of hearing it, threw the record in the creek.

They stayed up all night, took everything in sight: reds, whites, Seconal, bennies and a new little tranquilizer, light blue as a robin's egg. Drank themselves into oblivion, collapsed on their motorcycle seats and slept. The next morning it was all anyone could do to light a joint and chug a beer. Partying was exhausting work.

Tiny had two pair of pants. One was ten years old. His good pair was five. He wore both of them at once, said it reminded him he was alive. Tiny was about six-eight, an enormous, hairy beast. All you had to do was say the word *communist* and his eyes went *CLICK*.

One of the Angels said, "Ah, man, we're something like communists, like what we got going is sort of a communal living thing, that's what communism was really meant to do."

Tiny's eyes went *CLICK*.

"Don't say that," he said.

Kesey said, "Wait a minute, Tiny."

"Don't say that," Tiny said. "Take it back."

"Wait a minute, Tiny," Kesey said.

Kesey strummed his guitar and sang:

"*In America, I can take the red,*
I can take the white,
but the blues leave me wondering,
if America's still all right.
The reds make you sleepy and mean,
you know what I mean.
The whites make you jump,
keep you up on the hump.
But those little blues,
those tiny blues tease,

they only make you geeze."

Cooled Tiny out.

Inside the house, Gut stared at a hamburger nailed to the kitchen wall. John Babbs put it there after the bus trip to Madhattan. The last ratburger. Petri*fried*. Gut pried the burger loose, turned it in his hand, sniffed, and took a bite. Chewed with a thoughtful look, then spit the bite into the sink and jammed the hamburger back on the nail.

"How was it?" Pete from Frisco asked.

Gut shrugged. "Stale."

Outside, just when things seemed to be most chaotic, when the noise reached its loudest, everybody banging and wailing for all its worth, Cousin Roy leaned over to me and said, "I likes to listen."

"Them's few that do," I said.

"I'ma one of the few. But I like to get in everybody's ear. Three inches from your mouth is where you want it. Everybody's ear. Three inches from your lips."

The party wound down. The Angels gathered their sleeping bags and jackets, kicked beer cans out of the way, mounted up. The last unmuffled hog rolled over the bridge and the parade wound around the curves down the hill back to the city.

"When the Angels were gone," Kesey told me, "Faye said, after cooking and fixing for them, 'I'd never been called *ma'am* before.'"

*Line me up with theaters where I can perform
my children's stuff. It makes a lot more sense;
also, it's a lot more colorful. When you're up
there with robes and masks and monsters and
dance and drums, the story gets up off the page
and moves around.*
  — Ken Kesey

34

Go Home and Enjoy
Yourselves

We weren't through with the Angels. We hooked up with them again when Kesey invited them to join with the bus at the anti-war Vietnam peace rally in Berkeley. The Hells Angels' avowed goal was to use fists and clubs to stop the peace marchers at the boundary between Berkeley and Oakland before marchers could stage a protest at the Oakland Induction Center. It was shaping up to be a big dust-up, giving the cops a chance to beat on the Angels and the peaceniks both.

The day before the rally, Kesey and I drove to the Luau Club in Oakland to talk to the Angels. On the way we listened on the radio to a commentator talking about the situation: "The Hells Angels, an illegal society, too vast to be controlled by law enforcement agencies, take illicit drugs, swallow pep pills or inject methedrine into their arms. But most will get high by smoking marijuana or gulping the strongest drug of all: LSD."

The Angels were at the Club, drinking and smoking pot. Kesey broached the subject: perhaps they could see their way not to be busting heads the next day; why add to the fray, save their fight for another day, when it wouldn't be the cops holding sway, everyone ending up in jail with busted bones or worse.

They got a kick out of that, and right on cue, Allen Ginsberg walked in. He'd been trying to track Kesey down and when he found out we were at the Luau Club, he came to see what was going on. His beard, round, soft body, balding head and tremolo voice had the Angels laughing and pretty soon the talk about to fight or not to fight got lost in shoving, grappling, arm wrestling and hollering insults at one another until late that night, when we wandered over to their clubhouse. Allen took off his clothes, sat cross-legged on the floor, tinkle-tinkled on his finger cymbals and hummed deep *OM* sounds as the Angels lounged on the beat-up sofas and ragged armchairs.

Kesey and I slipped out and made our way home, we had to get ready for the peace rally.

Somehow Allen made it to his place on his own.

We painted the bus bloody, Martian red, covered it with war-like symbols, reminiscent of a Viking warship. We donned surplus fatigues and armed ourselves with cheap toy weapons, fortified ourselves with juices and chemicals and, with Cassady at the wheel, headed for the anti-war rally at Sproul Plaza on the UC Berkeley campus.

A radio voice blasted through the bus's speakers: "Perhaps the most bizarre incident threatening the day is the rumor that the Hells Angels motorcycle gang will attack the Vietnam Day marchers if they attempt to enter Oakland."

In the field in front of Sproul Hall, thousands of protestors had assembled, from college professors to peaceniks, hillbillies and pacifists. A pacifist was screaming his tail off: "You must keep going, you must march, you will go down the street to Oakland, you will not stop, you have a vision, you are right, you are completely in the right, for you are pacifists and you will fight for that right."

Cassady drove the bus into the middle of the throng and

parked. The crowd was restive, harangued by voices screaming over loudspeakers. We walked through a circle of people jostling and arguing. Some threatened the protesters; the protesters pushed and shouted back. Cassady stopped and pulled out a pack of gum.

"Dentyne anyone, stick of Dentyne, *mmmm*, juicy, sweet, slams that light-giving delight straight into the old brain."

He extended the gum, handing it out to both sides, completely discombobulating everyone; hot air of strife and hate whooshed into the sky and gone. We walked on, leaving them wondering what happened.

Kesey was introduced to a great roar. He looked the throng over and shook his head.

"What are we doing here? Beautiful sunny day, having a Mussolini-like rally? Forget it, go home and enjoy yourselves. Look at the whole war thing and say, 'Fuck it.'"

At the fringe of the crowd people started drifting away. Kesey turned his back and started playing "Home on the Range" on his harmonica.

"Talk to them, Babbs," he said out of the corner of his mouth.

"See those guys with the shined shoes and colored pins on their lapels?" I asked. "They are agent provocateurs. Don't let them suck you in."

Below me, men in suits pulled pins out of their lapels and threw them on the ground. I took a chattering-teeth toy out of my pocket and held it up to the microphone. The irritating chatter grated across the crowd. I tied the toy to the microphone with a piece of string. Kesey and I left the stage and headed for the bus, teeth chattering behind us.

Someone yanked the toy off the microphone.

The Hells Angels didn't show. President Johnson said that if the motorcycle riders came, they'd all join in, not just the Angels but the Rattlers and the Gypsy Jokers the whole motley pack of them, and it would have come loose at the ends.

While the protesters were gathering to march into Oakland, we drove the bus to the Luau Club, parked, and went inside. The Angels lounged around, down on reds and getting drunk. Terry the Tramp slouched in a chair.

"What's the haps?" Kesey asked.

"Chilling," Terry said.

"So, you're not making a stand at the Berkeley-Oakland border?"

"Naw, we said to hell with it, lost our edge last night after watching that naked little Jew sit there cling-clinging his tiny cymbals and chanting. Wore us down to sleepy nubs."

We hit the bar for drinks and settled in. Figured we owed them that much and it turned into the goddamnedest party in the back of the blackest hole you've ever seen.

The biker club band, Dribbling Pee and the Peckerwoods, cranked up their instruments and mangled a song at ear-splitting volume.

"If you're gonna live in a dim room,
you're gonna have to learn how to howl.
If you're gonna live out in the midnight hour,
you're gonna have to learn how to see like an owl.
If you're gonna live out in the woods,
You gotta learn how to howl.
If you burrow beneath the ground
In a deep dark hole
Gonna have to learn how to get around.
Let it all hang down."

Sonny Barger, chapter president, wrote a letter to President Johnson offering the Angels to serve as guerillas in the Vietnam war, only he spelled it *gorillas.* They considered themselves true American patriots.

A guy in a suit pays his dollar, comes in, gets
the customary cup of Kool-Aid and walks around
carrying his umbrella, which by midnight he's
opened and he looks down and sees his shadow
and begins to strut. "The King walks." He turns
around. "Now the king will dance." The Dead,
supple enough to read the notes written in the
room, played to the king dancing.
   — Ken Kesey

35

Nothing But Mindless Chaos

W e ratcheted it up. Our lawyer, Brian Rohan, went to the
Fillmore Auditorium, a stately old building on the corner of Geary and Fillmore in San Francisco, and introduced himself to Charles Sullivan, who leased the building to rhythm and blues shows: James Brown, Bobby "Blue" Bland, and Ike & Tina Turner.

"Is the hall available for rent?" Rohan asked.

Charles looked him over. "Well, that depends, Mister Rohan. When would you want it?"

This was on a Wednesday. Brian took a chance. "Saturday night."

Charles nodded.

"You're in luck. Doesn't usually happen this quick but Saturday just happens to be open. What do you have?"

"It's a local, up-and-coming band called the Grateful Dead. They've been playing to bigger and bigger crowds around the Bay Area and they're ready for a larger, better-known place to perform."

"Never heard of them, but that's what this place is all about:

the music. It will cost you seventy-five dollars, up front."

"We can handle that."

Brian counted out the cash and passed it over.

Charles recounted it, stood up and stuffed the cash in his pocket.

"Good to deal with you, Mister Rohan. You can load in any time after five. You'll be handling the publicity and posters?"

"That's right," Rohan said.

They shook hands. That was the extent of the contract.

The band set up on the stage at the front of the hall. There was a balcony at the rear where we put our mixer, tape recorders and microphones. We placed speakers at both ends of the balcony. Our movie projectors pointed at a white sheet hung next to the stage. Roy and his overhead projector were set up down on the floor, so he could do his light show on the walls.

My voice boomed out of our speakers.

"As prearranged with the owner of the auditorium, the Acid Test will remain embarked on its perilous voyage the remainder of the night. I see someone on the stage waving his arms. The engines are cranking up. The evening's adventures are about to begin."

Pigpen hit a note on the organ.

"Let's all tune up," I said. "Everybody get in tune."

"I had to turn off our bass player," Bob Weir said into a microphone, "because he was walking around the stage making horrendous..."

Phil thumped a bone-vibrating bass note.

"The Acid Test is everywhere in this spaceship," I decreed. "Everywhere you are, you are acid testing and acid tasting inside the confines of this inner-spatial dome."

Pigpen came in on the harp. Bill the drummer added a low beat.

"Ain't no fucking power no place," Pigpen said.

"There has been a slight loss of power, according to the reports we are getting," I answered.

"I found it and it's plugged into that little box there," Bob Weir said, "but it still doesn't work."

"Okay," I said. "Turn the house lights on. We're going to have to mill around and reexamine the plugs."

"These three microphones don't seem to be working," Weir said.

"They fucked up, babe," Pigpen said.

"This is one of the invariable Acid Test problems," I said.

"Ah, gaze upon it, folks," Bob Weir said. "The electronic wasteland."

"How about a taste of microphones?" Pigpen asked. "Come on, now."

"Keep a'playing boys," I said. "Keep on a'playing. She'll come through one of these days."

"There ain't no power on the stage," Pigpen said. "No electricity on the stage. Fix it."

"This is the captain speaking. We have reached our first emergency and we haven't even gotten by the boundaries..."

"Why don't you rectify it pretty damn quick?" Pigpen demanded.

"There are wires all around here plugged into electricity," I said, "just reach down and..."

"Hey man, stop your babbling and fix these microphones," Pigpen said. "We need some power. Power."

"*Pow-er. Pow-er,*" the crowd chanted.

"*Hey, you got the power?*" Pigpen sang, a bluesy lilt.

"Come on, now."

The speakers came to life with a hum. Jerry hit it with fast licks up and down the strings.

"It seems as though it may work yet," Bob Weir said, and the band broke into song:

"*I'm a super sloth, honey, nosing around your hole...*"

"I believe we have accomplished it," Kesey said, through his microphone. "At least up here."

"I hope so, Mister Coward," Cassady answered. "That's Noel Coward, my dear, the same fellow I fear."

"I think I'll make a roam to the stash," Kesey said. "I've got a lot of tether. And it's decent weather."

"The best part of the trip," Cassady replied.

"But it would be nicer with a crystal atmosphere. I'm thinking about coming down to crystallize it."

"Kesey, the chief engineer, has left his station at the TV console to go down to the engine room and prepare the rocket fuel needed to steer this new configuration," I reported. "Cassady will remain at his post in the projection booth in order to keep driving the ship through whatever meteor shower we may encounter."

"*Well, I'm a piggy for your honey*
I need'a somethin' sweet from your lovin'."

The band was interrupted by a commotion on the floor.

"This is unbelievable," I announced. "Someone has brought a live pig into the spaceship and he's loose on the floor. We've managed to pick him up on our roving microphone."

Grunts and snuffles of the pig boomed through the hall.

"Somebody do something about that sucker," I said. "Gotta get him out of here. Call in reinforcements."

The Acid Test revelers formed a phalanx and, chanting like a platoon of Marines, charged the pig. Someone blew a whistle. The pig, panicked, wheeled and ran. A quick-thinking woman opened the fire door and the pig shot out into the street.

"*We are the best, we are the best,*" the pig herders chanted. Marching to the front of the stage they stomped their feet and sang along with the band:

"*Hogs are squealing*
Piggies want out.
Fenced in so long

They got the dry snout."

A large loudspeaker hung upside down from the ceiling. Music pounded from it. Dancers gyrated beneath a flashing strobe light. Someone banged on a metal, tubular sculpture. A sound generator thrummed a low, pulsing growl. Streamers and balloons swirled and waved from the ceiling. A video camera ran continuously. People standing and dancing in front of it could watch themselves on a large-screen TV. A man in a white fullbody suit stood in front of the camera; words painted on his suit flashed across the screen: "AND THE MAGIC NEVER STOPPED."

The band took a break. The stage filled with men and women carrying flutes, whistles, bongos, tambourines, congas, rattles and wooden scratchers. They chanted and sang: tribal rhythms guttural words. Sopranic wails filled the hall, dancers writhed and whirled.

The lights went out and a loud voice boomed from the loudspeakers:

"YOU PEOPLE OUT THERE, LISTEN TO ME. THIS IS LOTHAR SPEAKING."

A cheer erupted.

"THIS IS A TRAP. YOU ARE ALL BUSTED."

"You must be down in the swamp," Kesey said into his microphone.

"I HEAR A VOICE. MUST BE THE LOUDSPEAKERS. THE PHANTOM SETS OUT TO INVESTIGATE. SHOOT WHATEVER MOVES—NO, MOVE WHATEVER SHOOTS."

"I'm going to put a hex on you," Pigpen sang.

"WELCOME TO THE INNER SANCTUM. GOING FURTHER THE PHANTOM FINDS A VAST AMMUNITION CHEST. AH, THIS WILL BE MY BARGAINING CARD."

"You can't seem to get out of that swamp," said Kesey.

"WE ARE TRYING TO FIGHT PARANOIA. THERE IS NO NEED FOR PARANOIA TO EXIST IN THIS AUDITORIUM. THANK YOU, MY FRIENDS. CONTINUE. HAHAHA HA HA."

Another voice came over the speakers, younger, higher-pitched, stuttery, having a hard time getting the words out.

"T-those people were p-playing games with m-me, m-me and you s-said to me, 'N-no, they're not, they're d-doing the b-best they can.' S-so, you g-gave me s-something I was asking f-for."

"There he is, the sneaky little rascal," Kesey said, "lurking beneath the concrete. Come on out, justice awaits in the long table of dawn."

"Is that typical of your usual program?" I asked him.

"Let me tell you before I go. This virtuous louse that has come into our countryside like an ox has a wooden memory."

"I like that treat but it's like a knob," Cassady said. "Let's check in that other brain, okay? Don't agree with anyone from now on. I'm saying no to everybody this week. I haven't thought of that three times in a row. It develops a certain independence. I suppose I'll just have to say no to everything, especially... Ah, shush. It was *please*, that's what it was, and I didn't want to use it. *Please*, it's just too much."

The Dead came back to life, interrupting Cassady:

"Look in the coffin and what do I see
My dead family staring at me.
Why didn't I take them away from the plague?
And why was I spared with only the ague?
No place you can hide from the man with the scythe
He's going to insist on his godforsaken tithe."

The instruments went dead. The house lights came on and a short man in a striped shirt with a bow tie stepped to the microphone: Charles Sullivan, the Fillmore Auditorium boss.

"Everybody out," Charles Sullivan repeated. "The dance is over. Clear the hall."

"This is incredible," I said through the balcony speakers. "The chief security agent has suddenly taken over and informed us..."

"Everybody out," he interrupted. "The dance is over. Clear the hall."

"He's made his extraordinary announcement," I said, "and has pulled the plug on the band, completely nullifying the engine. We've lost all power."

The other microphones worked too.

"Total chaos," Bob Weir said.

"Wrack and ruin," Jerry said.

"Everybody enjoyed themselves," Charles Sullivan said. "Let me hear you say *yeah.*"

Our lawyer, Brian Rohan, took the microphone: "We're planning on having other gigs in other cities and if we have a hassle here there's not going to be another hall that will have us, so we'd appreciate it if we go a little bit more, and then turn on the lights. Everybody use their heads."

"Everybody stay calm," said Garcia. "Don't press forward and hurt any thirteen-year-old girls."

"All right, listen, you guys," Mountain Girl said into the microphone on the floor. "I'm not leaving. They can't drag me off this spaceship."

"Rumors about insurrection," Jerry said. "There's nothing to worry about. We're having a party."

"Utter chaos," Weir said. "On the road again. Get the people on the road."

An inflatable, multi-colored beach ball, caught and flung back in the air, sailed across the crowd. A large paper airplane made out of a concert program flew through the auditorium.

"Oh-oh, the cops," a voice from the floor microphone said.

Four policemen stood inside the doors taking it all in.

"When you come to one of these things, you want to have a lot of clean fun, you know," Jerry said from the stage. "Enjoy yourselves and not hurt anybody. That's what everybody came here to do. To have a good time."

"Arrest everybody, but don't hurt any of the equipment," Weir said. "It's our livelihood you know."

In screeching voices and horribly off key, the bandmembers

began singing the National Anthem:

"*Oh say can you see*

By the dawn's early light..."

"We're just signing off," Weir said. "Signing off with 'The Star-Spangled Banger.' I'm just a hired band member."

"Good old mindless chaos," Jerry said. "Happily ever after."

"Hey man, you don't have to be like that on the microphone," Charles Sullivan said. "Tell everybody to go."

A guy in the crowd yelled, "Fuck you."

"Now, now, now," Charles Sullivan said.

"Nobody seems to tell us how we're supposed to turn off this PA," Weir said.

"Enjoy one of America's most fabulous..." Charles Sullivan mumbled.

"We can stay here till hell freezes over," Jerry said. "But we've got to turn everything off."

"Okay, that's it, everybody go home now," Charles Sullivan said. "Everything is over. I don't have any choice in this."

"That won't work," Jerry said. "That won't work here."

"Everybody go home now, please."

"The cops are trying to turn everything off," I said. "And they have asked everybody to be turned off. That's impossible. We're not machines, we're human beings."

"You can't turn us off," Jerry said. "Hell, no."

"Our switches have all been short-circuited." I said.

"Let's let it run out," Jerry said. "Let the energy just eventually run out."

"Yes, at the end, nothing but mindless chaos," Weir said. "Even as it started. Even that same old dude."

The cops started herding everybody out the doors. I sat down on a chair at the back of the hall. A cop came up to me and said, "Come on, you have to get out of here."

"I'm part of the show," I told him, "waiting till everybody leaves so I can help clear out our gear."

He grabbed me by the coat collar to yank me to my feet. I leaned forward and let my coat slide off. He fell back and landed on the floor.

"Oh gosh, I'm sorry, are you okay?" I asked, offered my hand and helped him to his feet.

"How about you and me go outside and talk this over?" he said.

We went out and stood on the corner.

"What the hell is going on in there?" he asked.

"This is a show Ken Kesey and I put on, with music and lights and people in costume. We stay all night so that they can come down before they go home."

"Okay, so where do you live?"

"Santa Cruz."

"How often do you come up here?"

"Not very often. Just to do these shows."

"Okay," he said, and wandered off.

I went back inside. The place had emptied out, so we gathered our gear and drove away. A very successful night, considering.

We're not here for self. We're here for service.
We're here to multiply. Subdue ye the earth and
all that. We're here to make like three-dimensional
chess. We're here to accentuate. In other words,
everything is speeding up in this decade, what
you might say a form of Armageddon in many ways.
— *Neal Cassady*

36

Sanity Is Found in Harmony

O rganized by Ramon Sender, the electronic music composer and co-founder of the San Francisco Tape Center,
Stewart Brand, former Army parachutist working to obtain a
photograph of the entire earth, and Zach Stewart, who worked
with Brand to create the America Needs Indians show, the Trips
Festival was a three-day event in late January 1966 at the Long-
shoreman's Hall in San Francisco. It featured disparate psychedelic groups of dancers, musicians, artists and performers.

The poster read, "THIS IS THE FIRST GATHERING OF ITS KIND
ANYWHERE. THE TRIP—OR ELECTRONIC PERFORMANCE—IS A NEW
MEDIUM OF COMMUNICATION & ENTERTAINMENT. IN THIS FESTIVAL,
AUDIENCE & PARTICIPANTS WILL SEE HOW THE TRIP HAS BEEN
DEVELOPED FOR THEATER, MUSIC & DANCE, EDUCATION,
LIGHT & SOUND, ROCK 'N' ROLL, SCULPTURE, NOVELISTS &
POETS."

Saturday night's lineup: "KEN KESEY, MEMBERS OF THE S.F.
TAPE MUSIC CENTER, THE DANCE WORKSHOP, THE LOADING ZONE
ROCK 'N' ROLL, THE DON BUCHLA SOUND-LIGHT CONSOLE, THE MER-
RY PRANKSTERS AND THEIR PSYCHEDELIC SYMPHONY, NEAL CASSADY,
THE GRATEFUL DEAD ROCK 'N' ROLL, ROY'S AUDIOPTICS, MOVIES,
RON BOISE AND HIS ELECTRIC THUNDER SCULPTURE, THE BUS, MANY

NOTED OUTLAWS, AND THE UNEXPECTABLE."

Two days before the event, Kesey, Mountain Girl and I met Stewart Brand on the sidewalk in front of the hall. Stewart had a big smile on his face, deep wrinkles from cheeks to eyes, a floppy canvas hat atop his head. We walked up the steps into the building: cavernous, rounded ceiling, crisscrossed rafters forming an open dome with no beams. Balconies ran alongside each wall.

After looking at the hall, we went to Stewart's apartment. The sun had set and the air was cool. Kesey and Mountain Girl decided to go up on the roof with a blanket.

Stewart and I heard a commotion through the open window, something on the roof. I went up to look and found Kesey hand-cuffed by a cop.

"Tell them, Babbs," Kesey said.

"It wasn't his pot," Mountain Girl said. "It was mine."

"What pot?" I said.

"He threw it over the side, into the alley," the cop said.

"I'll go tell Stewart," I said, and went back down the stairs. Instead of going into the apartment, I went down to street level, out the front door, around the side of the building and into the alley. I looked around but couldn't see anything.

A cop emerged from the shadows.

"Forget it," he said, holding a pot-filled baggy. "What do you have to do with this?"

"Nothing," I said. "Just looking for a place to take a leak."

I turned and left, the cop yelling behind me, "Get back here."

"I found out Kesey and Mountain Girl were tossing pebbles off the roof," Stewart told me, when I was back in his apartment, "and one of the neighbors called the cops."

The next day newspaper headlines proclaimed: KEN KESEY ARRESTED AGAIN FOR MARIJUANA.

Our lawyer, Brian Rohan, posted bail with the proviso that Kesey couldn't associate with any of the Pranksters. Kesey laid low until Saturday night, when he showed up at the Trips Festival disguised in aluminum-painted mechanic coveralls, modified to look like a space suit. A welder's helmet painted the same aluminum color covered his head. A plastic, opaque shield that slid up and down hid his face.

Kesey and George Walker and I went out into an alley to confer. Kesey had his face plate up so we could see him.

At the end of the alley people were climbing over a fence and heading for a side door into the hall. A grim-faced man carrying a clipboard came into the alley.

"Wait a minute," he yelled. "What's going on? You can't come over that fence, you have to go in front and pay!"

They shoved past him into the hall. The clipboard man noticed us standing there.

"What are you doing? Why didn't you stop them?" he said, distraught and demanding, a man who expected his orders to be followed.

Kesey slammed his face plate down.

"*No comprende, vamooso.*"

He went through the door and vanished into the hall.

"Who is that guy, anyway?" Clipboard Man said. "Why was he letting those people in?"

I shrugged.

"Some spaceman, just landed, looking for directions."

George shook his head.

"Couldn't understand a word, he don't speeka dah Anglish."

We walked past him into the hall. Clipboard Man turned and saw more people climbing the wall. He held out his arms.

"Stop! You can't come in here. Go back! You have to pay."

They pushed him aside and hurried through the door.

The hall was filling with costumed revelers. A poster proclaimed: "THE GENERAL TONE OF THINGS HAS MOVED ON FROM THE SELF-CONSCIOUS HAPPENING TO A MORE JUBILANT OCCASION WHERE THE AUDIENCE PARTICIPATES BECAUSE IT'S MORE FUN

TO DO SO THAN NOT. MAYBE THIS IS THE ROCK REVOLUTION. AUDIENCE DANCING IS AN ASSUMED PART OF ALL THE SHOWS AND THE AUDIENCE IS INVITED TO WEAR ECSTATIC DRESS AND BRING THEIR OWN GADGETS (A.C. OUTLETS WILL BE PROVIDED)."

Onstage, the Grateful Dead hassled with their gear. Up on the balcony, Don Buchla, the sound engineer who invented one of the first synthesizers, spread out ten speakers on both sides of the hall. Running his fingers over a touch keyboard, he was able to send musical notes zooming around the room.

I merged our sound gear with his so we could record what was happening on the stage, the balcony, and the dance floor. A lady made up to look like a daisy rode around the floor on a bicycle. She twirled an umbrella as she pedaled and, when asked who she was, replied, "Space Daisy."

A strobe light flashed on and off inside a big upside-down speaker. A trampoline artist bounced up and down in the light, somersaults and leaps frozen for an instant, then dark, then frozen in another attitude.

Local filmmakers Bruce Conner and Bruce Baillie set up projectors in the corners and showed movies on the walls. Anna Halprin led her dance troupe through acrobatic moves inside a cargo net strung overhead on poles.

Kesey, anonymous in his space-suit garb with the visor down, sat on the balcony and wrote cryptic messages on an opaque projector beamed onto a screen at the back of the stage: "*Know those you love are safe.*"—"*Sanity is found in harmony.*"— "*The spirit is what matters.*"—"*Live to dance another day.*"— "*Getting old is a riot.*"—"*Find your sweet spot.*"—"*A card laid is a card played.*"

On the stage, the Grateful Dead navigated through chaos: a horde of people banging on hand drums, playing flutes, chanting, peering into the backs of the amplifiers.

The band gave up. They couldn't clear everyone off the stage, couldn't get their instruments plugged in and working, couldn't do a microphone check. Someone even stepped on Jerry's guitar and broke it. They joined the random activities on the floor. The canned music and spontaneous word jazz from atop the balcony took over the soundtrack for the rest of the night.

After the event was over, I looked around the hall. Where was Kesey? There was no sign of the mysterious spaceman.

Ramon Sender came up to me and said, "You know, Ken, I think Bill Graham and I were the only ones here who weren't high tonight."

"Who is Bill Graham?" I asked.

"That guy standing over there."

I laughed.

"What's so funny?"

"I wondered who that man with the clipboard was."

As above, so below. One as vast as the other. Those who
have gone before have left their experiences to draw upon.
Touchstones to be crossed until the further shore is
reached and once more, we move into the unknown,
purging all thoughts of mistakes previously made,
pouring energies into artistic triumphs, so elated with
success we fantasized that we should go into a recording
studio and get even better recordings, not stuck with the
setup in the bus.
— Ken Babbs

37

We Have Nothing Else to Do

A couple of days after the Trips Festival, Kesey, still out on bail, was having a bagel in the Place Cafe and Bar in North Beach when a man came up and offered to buy him a drink. They sat down with coffee and then the man made his pitch.

"I've got a state-of-the-art recording studio on Sixth Street, a couple of blocks off the Bay Bridge," he said, "and I'd like you and the Pranksters to come in and cut a biscuit."

"This is the real deal?" Kesey asked. "No strings attached?"

"Just like an Acid Test. You do whatever you want and it can go until you're done, all night if that's what it takes."

"That's our usual MO," Kesey said.

He pondered a bit, looking Jim Seagrave over: medium-tall man wearing a medium-expensive suit, with a medium-slight smile on his face.

"I have a good description of my operation," Jim Seagrave said, pulling a business letter out of his coat pocket. "I lay it on pretty thick, but the information is real. Here, I'll read it to you: *I take pleasure in announcing the formation of the West Coast's finest and most complete audio and recording facilities. We are in the process of holding auditions for our own Sound City record banner in an all out attempt to furnish an opportunity to the burgeoning talent on the West Coast."*

He looked up from the letter.

"Needless to say, you and the Pranksters would be a major score for Sound City."

"I don't know," Kesey said. "We're slated to go to Los Angeles in a week. How could we fit a recording date in?"

"I was thinking this coming Saturday night. We do the recording in one long take, I edit it in the studio and have the records pressed here in the city. With your name and the Pranksters and the success you have had locally, I think it would be a good sale."

"I'll talk to the team and let you know," Kesey said.

"That's fabulous," Jim Seagrave said. "I'll keep Saturday night open."

They shook hands and Kesey walked away, whistling Coltrane's version of "My Favorite Things."

"Hot shit," George Walker said when Kesey told us about the record deal.

"So, the big time is chasing us now instead of the other way around," Mike Hagen said.

"It's the complete circle," I said, "as portrayed by the snake eating its tail, at thirty-three-and-a-third rpm."

We dragged our equipment in from the street, the setting sun a red glow behind us, a cool breeze blowing in from the bay. Jim shook all hands, showed off his studio, told us to set up however we wanted. We mumbled our thanks, our eyes glowing, our energy pulsing, already taking off on a long trip destined to last through the night.

Open suitcases held tangled cables. JBL fifteen-inch speakers inside three-foot-high wooden boxes painted in bright fluorescent patterns stood in the corners. Tape recorders, mixers and amplifiers were piled on a long table.

Jim the Host never expected us to take so long putting together our figure-eight feedback loop: voices going through two microphones into a mixer, from there into two reel-to-reel tape recorders spaced a foot apart, with the sound recorded on the first tape deck then played back with a long delay on the second deck, going from there into two speakers with microphones in front of the speakers and back into the tape recorders, creating a long delay, repeating and adding onto the loop, very carefully, else the feedback would fry everyone's ears...

"What about the Grateful Dead?" Jim the Host asked.

Kesey glanced up from the microphone mixer. "They said they'd come by after their gig at the Matrix, so it'll be in the wee hours."

Jim the Host checked his watch. Approaching the witching hour and the only recordings so far were a few questions and answers between him and Kesey into the one microphone working.

Owsley showed up. He looked everything over and pulled Jim the Host aside.

"You mean you're letting Babbs mess with your gear? You know he's a maniac. You'll be lucky anything's still working when he's done."

Jim the Host's eyes got big. *Better get this herd of crazies corralled before the whole night goes to hell.* People wandered in from the street, stood around and slouched on couches.

"Ken," Jim the Host said, "this is Frank Fey, a local radio personality. He's got a working microphone."

"If I could ask you a few questions," Frank said, "fill me in on the details of what you're going to be doing."

"Well, you've already answered a lot of your questions by the tone of your voice, which says it's obviously ridiculous to ask such questions."

Frank Fey rolled his eyes.

"As navigator of this venture," Kesey said, "I try as much as possible to set out in a direction that in the first place is practically impossible to achieve and, along the way, mess up the minds of the crew with as many chemicals we can lay our hands on, so it's almost certain that we can't get there."

"Would you say it was deliberately self-defeating then?"

"About as deliberately self-defeating as anything that has ever been recorded in history. Most of the people here realize there's nothing to be gained. That every time you try to lay your hands on something and get hold of it, you've sold yourself down the river. The first Prankster rule is *nothing lasts*, and if you start there and really believe that nothing lasts, you try to achieve nothing at all times."

"If you're trying to achieve nothing, then why do you put so much effort into achieving nothing?"

"We have nothing else to do."

Everyone listening cracked up. Zen idiocy taken up to the mountaintop, raised into the clouds. I walked forward playing my harmonica.

"Who is that man?" Frank Fey asked.

"That's Ken Babbs," Jim the Host said.

"What are you doing, Ken?" Fey asked me.

"Just fun," I said. "A hard day's fun. Sometimes I put in an eighteen-hour day of fun."

I hadn't yet shed the wisenheimer mode Cassady laid on me months earlier. Kesey was always straight with everyone, but I goofed on people. Not mean, just ornery.

"Eighteen hours a day?" Frank Fey asked, deciding to go along with this nonsense.

"Yep, when I really get going, it builds up and pretty soon I'm having fun all the time."

"What about death for you?"

As if he'd like to kill the harmonica.

"What about it?"

"That's the termination of your fun, right?"

Maybe it was me he'd like to kill.

"Who knows? I'm not dead yet."

"Would you like to die?"

His true feelings were rising to the surface.

"What a question. Is that a threat? What do you want, my money? My harmonica? That's all I've got. My bandana? My knife? No, you'd use that to kill me. You can't have my knife."

The speakers in the room erupted into echoing delays of a chorus of harmonicas soaring through loops and circles that rose and fell like a platoon of madmen loose in the instrument storeroom.

"Take two," Kesey said, his voice rich and clear. "Take two, ladies and gentlemen, exposed, as it were, at this end of the Sound City situation, and we're trying to take two. Of what, may I ask?"

"You've got my interest now," Frank Fey said. "I'm learning some basics tonight. I'm as smart as you in one way, you know that."

"We're all as smart as one another," Kesey answered.

"No, no, I mean cleverly. I can talk as fast and as quickly and can write as well. It's the other thing that you have, the other philosophy, the basic thing that you have, the beautiful thing that you have."

Kesey didn't answer.

The gear was working good, the acid edge mellowed out. Settling into a comfortable groove, we went into one of our extemporaneous Prankster raps.

"There's always somebody there at the alley," Kesey said, "waiting for you to go slipping past and say, 'Hey buddy, you want to buy a hot trip to heaven?'"

"He's passed outside the sphere of verbal communication," I said. "Does this mean it is not heaven?"

"Not heaven? You mean after I finally got everything that I've been working all this time for, after I finally made all these marks on the wall, after I got all this stuff stashed away, now they've put it down that this ain't heaven?"

"I've got some bad news. I been offering this one-way ticket and it's fake."

"I've heard some crazy critters in my time but if you think I'm paying three dollars and ninety-five cents for an album like this, I say America doesn't need that kind of impudent young snot."

Jerry Garcia and Phil Lesh walked in. It was the wee hours of the morning, onlookers half asleep.

"Bells and fairies and Pan the Piper danced," I said. "A kid on the bank of the stream added his water to the water."

"Get him off of there, get him off of there," Kesey said. "Do you want the kids hearing this?"

"No. I'd like to lay this thing down," I said. "Give it up."

"I'd like to lay this thing down, too," Kesey said. "Let the Dead sing something. How's about it, Jerry? You up for something?"

"My voice is completely shot, Ken. I can't even hold a pitched note. *Ahh.* See. *Uhh. Nnnnnhhhh.*"

On that unpitched note, the session ended. Fourteen hours of tape edited down by Jim the Host into forty-two minutes. He wrote a blurb espousing the album:

"*The purpose of the recording was to produce an album of the unusual sounds and mental manipulations of the sometimes considered genius of Mr. Kesey and his cohorts during the actual happenings of a 'sugar' party. The results are different to say the least. The album was released three days ago and in the Bay Area has caused a minor mental earthquake.*"

Not securing a distributor, Jim the Host made the album available by ordering it from his recording studio address. He died shortly after and his wife took over the business. When she died, the album descended in obscurity, except for a printing in the UK. It was resurrected by Isaac Slusarenko, owner of Jackpot Records in Portland, Oregon. The original didn't have liner notes on the back. For the re-issue I wrote liner notes. The album, once relegated to obscurity, was brought back to life, like Frankenstein on the operating table, and *The Acid Test* reached number fifty in the national top fifty of sales on Record Store Day 2017, the year it came out.

*Breath comes quickly, eyes close in squinty
anticipation, head lowers until chin point is
almost vertical, feet spread as heels raise
slightly, hands seek nearest object with
fingers quiveringly, tantalizingly, caressingly
poised, belly tightens, from each buttock
twin masses of balled nerves join at base
of expectant spine.*
   — *Neal Cassady on writing*

38

A Sample of
the Riotous Escapades

I was getting ready for bed at my house when Kesey came in, looking drawn and down.

"What's up?" I asked.

"It's come to a head and about to boil over."

Still out on bail from both the pot bust at his house earlier in the year, and the later arrest on the roof of Stewart Brand's apartment, he was due to face the judge in two days for sentencing. He decided he wouldn't go.

"They're going to fry me, and I can't take the heat. I'm skipping the whole charade."

"What's your plan?"

"You don't need to know. Take the bus and the crew to LA and do the Acid Tests there."

He pulled a handful of hundreds out of his pocket and peeled off five.

"See you wherever our travels take us," he said, and left.

A lot to absorb but, as it was, keeping with the unexpected

being the norm. I went to bed. I'd worry about the next step
when I got up.

T he headline on the front page of the morning paper blared:
KESEY COMMITS SUICIDE. The accompanying article reported
that a note inside a pair of shoes was found on the beach: "*I, Ken
Kesey being of (ahem) sound mind and body do thereby leave the
whole scene to the Faye Corporation... Cash... The works... Last
words: A vote for Barry is a vote for fun... Ocean, ocean, I'll beat
you in the end. I'll break you this time. I'll go through with my
heels at your hungry ribs.*"

"Well, that's a laugh," George Walker said. "A fake suicide if
I've ever heard of one. Now he disappears. So much for him being the Big Cheese. What next, Captain Babbsaroonie?"

"Load up the bus; we're headed to Los Angeles."

The Grateful Dead followed in their van and, lucky for us,
we had compatriots in LA: Hugh Romney and the Hog Farmers.
They lived on top of a hill east of the city where they took care
of hogs owned by their landlady. They did shows and performances around town and, knowing we were coming, set up an
Acid Test at Pauley Pavilion, the basketball arena on the UCLA
campus.

"That's too big and too fancy for us," I told Hugh. "How did
you ever latch on to that?"

"Friends of friends," he said, giving me a wink. "We have to
be on the campus at noon and do a preview of the show in the
Student Union cafeteria."

We arrived after lunch was over. Only a few students were
there, sitting around tables in the back of the room.

Neal Cassady sashayed onstage. He pursed his lips, tilted his
head and leaned into the microphone.

"Whenever I hear the sound of the wind out there, I think of
a doll, the eyes opening and closed. Blackberry-bittersweet Larry from Okefenokee, in a foster clue, followed through the worst

of the poetry of Shelley. They decided then and there to name the fountain after old Lady Lou, or was it Beer Barrel Nelly? What a belly I know; it was a result of faroking you. I don't know, Mister Elgar, if your pomp and circumstance could ever come quite close—dear me, roll up your pants. They seem to be waiting for, yes, the sunrise from Montebello—no, no, another fellow."

He began singing to the tune of "The William Tell Overture."
"Hurry up, hurry up,
we must prevent that crime.
Hurry up, hurry up,
We'll get there in the nick of time,
We're going to make it all in rhyme
unless there's a problem in the kerosene-oh,
unless there's water in the gasoline-oh."

Then, continuing talking: "If you need air, there's no air in the spare but plenty out there. There's always a problem somewhere, anxiety that comes across the wheel but we'll come to it soon, the foe you know is not a foe, no, unless there is another fate. I am going to find the Custer's group, I'm going to find the group and then I will be with her soon, very soon."

Neal crouched, pulled the microphone down with him, then let it loose. The microphone rose up, tilted forward, rocked back and forth and found its balance. Neal spun on his heel and exited the stage.

Tiny Tim, skinny, dressed in a black suit, waltzed onstage, strumming a ukulele and singing in a falsetto voice:
"Looking out the window and what do I see
Gazillions of flowers looking back at me
Makes me think of my honey and all things sweet
In the garden of love, that's where we'll meet."

He finished the song, blew a kiss to the students and departed the stage.

The Grateful Dead ran on and surrounded a grand piano. Bill

Kreutzmann raised the lid and randomly plucked the strings. Jerry Garcia and Phil Lesh stood at the keyboard and played "Chopsticks." Bob Weir climbed on the piano and banged on the strings with his shoe. Pigpen, in full cowboy regalia, pulled a toy pistol out of its holster and pretended to shoot the piano. The ear-grating cacophony ended as quickly as it started and the musicians, laughing and slapping one another on the back, exited.

Hugh Romney, wearing a tie-dyed jumpsuit, strode to the microphone. "This is only a sample of the riotous escapades you can expect to encounter and participate in tonight at Pauley Pavilion at eight p.m. sharp. Wear your wildest outfits and boogie till you drop."

We stood outside, getting ready to leave, when a young man in a suit and tie came up to me and said, "Mister Flamson would like to talk to you."

"Who's he?" I asked.

"The man in charge of Pauley Pavilion."

I followed him into the building, up the stairs and down the hall to a swanky office where three older men in suits sat in chairs, two in front of a desk and one behind. The one behind the desk stood and said, "Mister Babbs, I'm sorry to say, we're cancelling your show at Pauley Pavilion tonight."

"What?" I said. "You can't do that. We have a contract."

"You'll see in the contract that if we deem the show to be unsuitable we can cancel it."

"Unsuitable? We've done this performance all over San Francisco to packed houses and now, by popular demand, have brought it to Los Angeles. Where do you come up with 'unsuitable?'"

"We watched your so-called performance preview in the caféteria and that was evidence enough."

"Evidence of what?"

"First, some maniac came out blabbering incomprehensible

nonsense, then a girl dressed up as a man sang the most ungodly song in a distorted voice and, if that weren't enough, a bunch of insane throwbacks to the Neanderthal age practically destroyed a valuable grand piano. Doesn't that speak for itself?"

"Oh, don't be such fogbound stiffnecks," I said. "This is performance art. It's the latest craze. The arena will be packed and we'll all make money."

"Money isn't the issue and the answer is no. The show is cancelled."

He and the other two suits were stolid, impenetrable, so I gave them my best Marine Corps glare and walked out, leaving them to "*their sad worries, their dreary highs,*" as Cassady once said, reminding myself, as I walked down the hall, of Cassady's closing line, "*Never knock the way the other cat swings.*"

I broke the news to the Pranksters and Grateful Dead and Hog Farmers. Everyone was down in the dumps, our grand entry into the LA scene thwarted, but Hugh pulled out a local entrepreneur's business card and called him. He directed him to a small movie studio on Sunset Avenue. Hugh rented the place for the night.

We spent the rest of the day altering the posters, putting the new address on them in big letters, then sent the Hog Farmers scurrying out to put the posters up in store windows and staple them to telephone poles.

There was a big turnout and the band gave one of their best performances. Hassler had earlier cut each of the movie reels into three sections and we projected three different images from the same sequence of events onto the walls through three movie projectors. Cassady, with his shirt off, danced all night, and in dawn's creeping light we shut it down and backed the bus in through a big side door and loaded up. The last scene shot on our movie camera was Jerry Garcia wielding a push broom, sweeping dirt out the door as it closed behind him.

*Pranksters are not just about acid. It's part of the
picture, but on a personal level. If you push the
use of the drugs, you lose people who are interested
in spiritual development, the search for enlightenment,
and the seeking of expanded consciousness. Following
that, the actions of helping one another out, being
kind to others and, most importantly, not adding to
the polarization and arguing going on all over the place.*
  — Ken Babbs

39

An Idle or Dissolute
Immoral Life

The Youth Opportunities Center in Compton, on the fringes
of Watts, was a cavernous concrete block structure. There
was sparse attendance at the Acid Test we were holding there
and the vibe of the building itself made its gloom hard to overcome, but gaiety managed to prevail.

Late at night a dark-haired woman, heavy into the Kool-Aid,
moaned and thrashed around and screamed, "Who cares?" over
and over again.

I took a microphone on a long cord and held it front of her.
Her cry filled the building, bounced off the walls and echoed off
the ceiling, so loud the band was drowned out.

"Who cares?" over and over again, everyone in the room
joining in and chanting until the Who Cares girl wound down
and eased into the arms of the Hog Farmers surrounding her,
patting her and cooing her, settling her down, bringing her back
into present time and present place.

Some guy, not having had enough, grabbed the floor microphone. "Nobody cares."

Another added his voice, "Freak freely."

Pigpen took over, from the stage.

"Everything's gonna be alright now. I wanta know, do you feel good?"

"Yeah," voices on the floor responded.

"I wanta know, can you find your mind?"

"Oh, yeah."

"If you can't you better get out of this place."

"Yes, yes."

"Who cares?" Bob Weir asked.

"Do you understand about it now," Pigpen said. "Well, if you don't understand, you better listen to what I've got to say. 'Cause if you don't, then there's something wrong with you. I'm gonna tell everybody in the house right now that there's many, many things you gotta do one more time. You got to think about your neighbors. You got to think about your friends."

Bill the drummer emphasized it with a drumbeat.

"You got to think about your brother. You got to think about your sister."

Another drum beat of punctuation, then one after every line.

"You got to think about everybody that means something to you."—*BAP!*—"I'm talking about it now."—*BOOM!*—"Do you think that you know something?"—*WHAM!*—"If you think you don't know something, goddammit, what's wrong with you?"—*WHUMP!*

He quit. Laughter in the background, then Pigpen came on again.

"Before I got interrupted by that drumming, I was trying to talk a little bit. I was trying to say something to all you people here. And my main point of business is, you got to love everybody. Walking down the street one day, somebody may come along and point a pistol at your head and say, 'Give me all your money.' Now if you have any sense, you know you're going to give him your money. You have reason to hate that man but you know there must be something wrong with him. I'm talking about somebody who lost a little bit of love. Somebody who lost a little bit of friendship. I want to know if you're hearing what I'm saying?"

The hall filled with a loud chorus of "*Yeah, yeah, yeah.*"

Paul Foster, black-bearded, imposing Hog Farmer, dressed in a garish jumpsuit, his face painted blue on one side and white on the other, was using a long walking stick as his dance partner, wheeling it around the room and thumping it on the floor.

We first met Paul in La Honda one night when we were high and had covered our eyes, experiencing what it was like to be blind. I crawled around on the floor and came upon two boots and felt them, then ran my hands up to encounter two thick legs.

"An elephant," I cried, "there's an elephant in the room."

We found out he was a stutterer when two of the people he came with were arguing about something and one of them said, "We're all brothers and sisters, right?"

Paul Foster said, "I'm n-n-n-nobody's s-s-s-sister."

Kesey said this about Paul: "Paul Foster is not crazy. He won't give us that relief. He looks crazy, acts crazy, and certainly talks crazy, but actual? He can't really claim such. For one thing, the son of a gun has a kind of backhand grip on wisdom. Or wisdom has a grip on him—it's hard to say which. Disconcerting... And his work—his writing and his art—gives one the same problem. At first it strikes one as straight-ahead crazy. Then at the second look, one notices a disturbing trickle of sanity. And this leads again to the sighing admission of wisdom stirring beneath the crazy look. It is always a rather uncomfortable recognition. Paul Foster is not crazy. But I have to admit he can put on a pretty good crazy act. Once you get past that you gotta give him the benefit of wisdom, damn him! He deserves it."

T he big double doors of the Opportunity Center burst open. Six LA policeman came in and stood watching. They knew what was going on and wanted to see it for themselves. Bill the drummer started a riff and the band broke into "The Midnight Hour," Pigpen singing:

"I'm gonna bang on the big bass drum
And my gal on the strings will thrum.
We'll make whoopie and dredge up delight
From the midnight hour till dawn's new light."

The microphones on the stage went off and the song dribbled to an end.

"They shut us off again," Jerry Garcia said. "That's what always happens."

"The story of our life," Bob Weir said. "You play somewhere and somebody turns you off."

The cops moved forward, through the revelers. The band laid down their instruments and hightailed it out the back door. Barney Laird, who had driven down from San Francisco with two new amplifiers, grabbed the amplifiers and ran out the door, pausing to wrap a chain around the handle. Two cops chasing him couldn't get out. They headed for the front door but by then Barney had hustled around the building and jammed a broom between the handles.

Out back, the band had scattered. Jerry Garcia beat it down the street and came upon some huge, weird, metallic spires that stuck high in the sky. The Watts Towers, built over many years from scrap materials by an artist, Simon Rodia. Jerry went in for a closer look, tripped and banged his head on a metal outcropping. He held his arm to his head, stopped the bleeding with his shirt sleeve, and headed back to the hall.

By then the cops had broken the wooden broom handle and opened the front doors. They stood outside in a group. LSD was still legal and they couldn't bust anyone, could only watch and scrutinize the crazies, who by then were leaving as the first light

Thanks, Babbs. 1995

aw, shucks!　　*Paul Foster*

I need to be a Wobbly.

1966: The Breakers

To Ken Babbs in thanks for six great weeks in L. A.

see you later.

Scene: Watts district of L. A.

Time: After the Watts Acid Test and the Watts Riots, both infamous. What a
feeling in the air! The pie was so thick you could cut it with a knife.

* * * * * * * *

We thought it fair game to destroy wisdom.

We had the authority of Kesey and Cassady,
brazen authority of huns sweeping down from the North.

A LIGATOR

We upset L A and maybe the cops
but there was no law
against LSD
to impishly dismantle our audience.

SIR, WOULD IT NOT BE REDUNDANT OF ME TO PRETEND TO BE A

We made chaos of order with beauty thrown in
and hints in low whispers from behind the Gray Curtain.

fool?

We were bumbling and awkward and broke all the forms
but in Watts we redefined hip.

We were the Acid, they were the Test,
but by 5AM on some far town hall clock
we were all of a similar lump.

If you would set this piece to music, we might chase & sanborn,

We ran like young gods, chasing what we could never quite see.

We eventually influenced everyone under thirty and

We thought it fair game to destroy wisdom.

the Prankster Hymn.

A letter Paul Foster sent me after the Watts Acid Test.

of dawn was cresting the eastern rim and the Test was over.

Then Paul Foster strutted outside, waving his walking stick. Needing someone to bust, the cops grabbed him, handcuffed him, led him to a car and drove away, lights flashing.

The other cops soon left. I wished they had stayed longer, for, as we were putting the gear away, I noticed someone stole my electric bass.

"Nothing lasts," Hassler said, and I let it go.

I caught a ride with one of the Hog Farmers to the jail and bailed out Paul. The driver dropped me off at the LA house where the Pranksters were staying, a two-story wooden place owned by an acidhead. We camped in the front part of the house. The Grateful Dead hung out in back.

Early every morning, the owner went downtown to Skid Row, picked up two men passed out on the sidewalk, and brought them back to the house where he gave them LSD and had them look at mandalas on the wall, hoping the experience would counteract their alcoholism. We never found out if he was successful. Every day there were two more men in the little room set aside for that purpose.

We decided to take the bus down Sunset Boulevard to advertise the next LA Acid Test. Before we headed out, I took Cassady aside and told him, "Neal, let George drive the bus on this run."

Cassady was indignant. He turned, stomped his foot, lit a cigarette.

"I, who after having driven all the way from California, was knighted on the Blue Ridge Highway, and who cooled out the cop on the New Jersey Turnpike, who regaled the people of Madhattan with a driving monologue while navigating the streets of the city? Now you tell me I can't drive today?"

"I want you to drive, Neal. I always want you to drive, but this goes beyond want, this is a need."

"*Hurrmph*, a need indeed. Speed is a need, this is a dastardly deed, goes without explanation."

"The explanation is simple. You don't have a valid driving license. We're going to be stopped for sure and they'll haul you off to jail and you won't be able to drive for the rest of our trip."

"Trip. I thought it was intrepid trip, but now I see it is insipid trip."

He threw the cigarette butt on the sidewalk, stepped on it, kicked it into the gutter, spun on his heel, strode across the street and walked away.

We were stopped before we drove three blocks. George passed muster with his driver's license and we continued on. Ahead of us a street was blocked off; people crammed on the sidewalks. A parade, featuring floats and horses and a marching band. We walked over and watched. A flatbed truck came by with a rock band playing on the back.

"Hey," I said, "That's my bass."

I ran out into the street and yelled at the bass player, "That's my bass, buddy."

He recognized me right away. He stopped playing, *what now?*

He looked so stricken and panicked, I laughed. I waved my hand at him.

"Ah, hell, don't worry about it," I said. "Keep the goddamned thing!" I walked back to the sidewalk.

"That was big of you," Mike Hagen said.

I shrugged. "Easy come, easy go."

I had traded a shotgun for the electric bass at a pawn shop. It would be easy to find another.

B ack at the house I was in the kitchen, my head in the fridge, poking around for something to eat, when Zonker yelled at me from the living room, "Hey, Babbs, come look at this."

Everyone was watching TV. A commercial was playing: Robin and the Seven Hoods doing "Things Go Better With

Coke."

"What about it?" I asked. "Am I missing something here?"

"Not the commercial, doofus," Hagen said. "It's *Dragnet* and the show is about the evils of LSD."

"*This is the city,*" the actor Jack Webb said over shots of Los Angeles. "*A fine place for people to enjoy life. One thing's for sure, whatever they're looking for cannot be found in a number five capsule. When they try, that's where I come in. I carry a badge.*"

Camera shot of Sergeant Joe Friday and his sidekick, Officer Gannon, walking into police headquarters, Friday doing the voiceover:

"*A powerful new drug, creating weird and dangerous hallucinations, had found its way onto the streets of the city. We had to try and stop it.*"

A call came into the police station about a young guy acting crazy, trying to chew the bark off of a tree. Sergeant Friday and Officer Gannon headed over. The guy's face was painted blue on one side and white on the other.

Everyone in the living room laughed.

"Just like Paul Foster," Hassler said. "Where'd they ever come up with that? Couldn't have possibly been the Watts Acid Test."

"*What's your name?*" Friday asked the guy.

"*Don't you know my name?*" he answered. "*My name is Blue Boy.*"

More laughter.

"*I'll make book he's been dropping that acid we've been hearing about,*" Officer Gannon said.

"*Let's get those sugar cubes over to the crime lab,*" Sergeant Friday said.

"*It's colorless, tasteless, can be used as a liquid or powder, even found on the backs of postage stamps,*" the chemist at the crime lab said.

"Where do you get those stamps?" Hassler asked. "Down at the post office?"

"*Is it addictive?*" Friday asked the chemist.

"*No, but every case we've had,*" the chemist said, "*the person has a psychological dependence on the drug.*"

Friday smiled knowingly. A man they had released from jail and picked up later showed all the same symptoms six months after first being arrested.

"*Users believe they have turned into monsters, and want to kill themselves, yet don't have the urge to commit suicide,*" the chemist said. "*They suffer extreme nausea, have severe vomiting, aches and pains, panic, depression.*"

"*Sounds like it's going to be a big problem,*" Officer Gannon said.

"*And as of now there's no law prohibiting the use and sale of LSD,*" Friday said.

"Lucky for us," I said.

"*One pound of the stuff could turn every person in Los Angeles County into a hopeless psychotic,*" Friday said. "*Seven million people.*"

They took Blue Boy to juvie, charged him with being in danger of "*leading an idle or dissolute immoral life.*"

"Oh, the danger, always the danger," Mike Hagen said. "God preserve us."

"*He was being held for his own protection,*" Friday said.

"*It's really getting popular,*" Gannon answered. "*Have you seen that bus up on the strip? Big sign on it, says* Can You Pass The Acid Test?"

"Oh boy," Hassler said. "You can't buy that kind of publicity."

"*For a buck you can find out. Pay your dollar and you get into an acid party,*" Sergeant Friday said.

"*Pretty soon they'll have it listed in the yellow pages,*" Officer Gannon said. "*Takes a couple of days to stir up a batch of acid. A lot longer to stir up a law against it.*"

Not all that long. That evening we got the news. The next day, LSD would become illegal in the state of California. That put a new wrinkle in things. We were getting ready to do a photo shoot. A photographer, Larry Schiller, had contacted the Hog Farm and told them *Life Magazine* was doing a special on LSD and they had hired Schiller to take pictures for the cover and for the article inside. Schiller had rented a sound studio and decked it out like an Acid Test. We were supposed to drive there, park the bus in front and, along with the Hog Farmers, go in and simulate an Acid Test for the camera.

I t was big time, pictures in *Life* and on the cover, so everyone did their best to play their roles. Schiller was constantly shouting instructions.

"More people under the strobe light. Dance wilder, crazier. Turn up the music."

I shook my head. It was a choreographed imitation, not a spontaneous exultation of the freedom of the spirit.

As the clock approached midnight, I went around the room and tapped Pranksters on the shoulder and told them to come out into the bus.

When we were assembled, I told them, "We're pulling up stakes. Acid is illegal in another half hour. I want to be out of LA. We've got all our gear on the bus and we can leave right now. You can stay if you want. The Hog Farmers will be glad to take you in, or you can beat it back to the Bay Area."

No one bailed out.

"Where we going?" Hassler asked.

"Mexico."

I still had the five hundred dollars Kesey gave me. Enough, I figured, to bankroll the trip.

Down to five pesos from five thousand dollars,
Down to a jungle from a five-acre home,
Down to a dope fiend from a prize-winning scholar,
Down to the dregs from the lip-smacking foam.
What used to be known as a promising talent,
What folks once called a real likeable lad,
Now hounded and hunted by the police of two countries.
Tarnished Galahad, did yore sword get rusted?
Tarnished Galahad—there's no better name.
Keep a'running and hidin' till the next time yore busted
And locked away to suffer your guilt and your shame.
    — Ken Kesey

40

It Was in Us to Be Superheroes

The ocean surf boomed outside the door of a motel in Mazatlán. We had driven the bus there from LA after talking to Faye Kesey on the phone. Ken had earlier called home and given instructions for us to meet him in Mazatlán. Everyone knew by now Kesey's suicide was a fake and that he was on the run. An article in the Santa Cruz newspaper said he was in Mexico.

The bus was parked outside on the street. We were gathered in the combination living room and kitchen of the motel. Hassler had something going on inside his rectum. A doctor had given him medicine he had to apply internally. He couldn't do it very well himself so he tried to get me to do it.

"I am not a doctor," I said. "I am a non-doctor and I will use my methods. Nurse, get the hair straightener."

"No, no," Hassler cried, "not the hair straightener."

George said, "Oh shit, I'll do it."

Hassler bent over and dropped his pants. George slavered on the ointment, stuck his finger in and went to work.

"You guys know how to work the crude," Mountain Girl said.

"Where is the camera?" I asked. "Get the camera, we need to record this for posterity so the future can see what we're like in real life."

Kesey walked in the door.

"Has it come to this?" he said. "Tell him you love him."

Kesey plopped down on the couch. I popped a cold Dos Equis and gave it to him. He took a big gulp and let out a sigh.

"Be damned if I was going to go in the calaboose," Kesey said. "I wrote that suicide note, stuck it in my sneakers and got my cousin Dale, who looks enough like me to pass a quick look-over, to drive to the beach in my old crummy and leave them in the sand. My only worry was Dale not taking into account the tide. But everything worked out okay and by then I was in Ron Boise's truck along with Zonker on our way to Mexico. We crossed over in the most desolate spot on the border that Boise knew: Sonoyta, south of Gila Bend, Arizona."

Zonk picked that moment to walk in, followed by a dark-haired girl.

"Just showing Maria the bus," Zonk said. "This is the gang," he told her, and introduced us to Carolyn Hannah, an old friend of his from San Jose State.

"We stopped at a seedy bar a hundred miles south of the border," Zonk said. "Boise figured no one would know Kesey in there, but to be sure he went inside first to scope the joint. She walked in right behind him. When Kesey and I went inside, I recognized her and told Kesey, 'You're going to be spotted now. That's a girl I knew in college.' Two drinks later he and the girl were good friends and Kesey had given her her bus name, Black Maria, because of her black hair, dark eyes and black clothes. She stayed with us when we went to Puerto Vallarta and came along to Mazatlán."

I stood up and grabbed more beers from the cooler.

"So, what's next?" Hassler asked Kesey.

"Find a place that's enough out of the way, we can hang out for a while. How long are your visas good?"

"Six months," I said.

"I don't want to be seen with the bus. Boise is parked a couple of blocks away. Zonk and I will meander down south with Boise. Maria wants to ride on the bus. Where's that place you heard about, George?"

"I ran into an old friend, Bill Bodle, at the bar here. He was with his uncle Pierre, who was the unofficial cultural ambassador to Mexico. When I told him we were looking for an out-of-the-way place, preferably on the ocean, where we could live for six months, he thought for a minute and said, 'You want to steer away from the tourista towns. I know—Manzanillo. It's a small fishing town with only one road to it that runs from Guadalajara over the mountains to Colima and down to the coast. That would be your best place.'"

It sounded good. Kesey finished his beer and stood up.

"Let's go, Zonk, before some gringos are attracted by the bus and come to check us out."

It was a long, slow, two-day haul in the bus through summer heat, a stop at the Guadalajara city market for iced coffees and warm pastries, then over the mountains to Colima and down a winding road to Manzanillo, a quiet fishing port with a promenade along the seafront. We took a paved road north for a few miles, then pulled off onto the sand next to a water spigot sticking out of the ground. I turned on the spigot and water gushed out, clean and clear.

George backed in next to the spigot, went a little farther, then pulled forward to straighten out. *Further*'s rear wheels spun and dug into the soft sand. He tried reversing, then went forward, then back, then gunned it, something popped and the wheels stopped turning.

He kneeled down and looked the situation over.

"What do you think?" I asked him.

"My bet is we broke an axle," he said.

"Looks like this is our campground."

No shade but the ocean was right at our doorstep, and while everyone else went for a swim, George, Hassler and I rounded up some planks that had washed up and hauled them to the bus to make a solid platform for the jack to sit on.

With the bus jacked up and the rear dualies off the ground, George wrestled the lug nuts off with the four-way wrench, then rolled the heavy dually wheels and tires aside.

"Where's Cassady when we need him?" Hassler said.

"Wandering the streets of LA," I answered.

George unscrewed the bolts that held the axle. He slid the axle out. The gear teeth at the end had come apart.

We stared at the broken axle. Now what?

"Someone's going to have to take it to a wrecking yard, see if they've got a used one," George said.

"How's that going to happen?" Hassler asked.

"I suppose there's a bus from Manzanillo," George said. "Probably have to go all the way to Guadalajara."

We looked each other over. No one was eager to volunteer.

"I'll do it," Black Maria said. She had changed out of her bathing suit and was standing behind us, taking it all in.

Mountain Girl, standing next to Black Maria, looked her up and down.

"Why you?" she asked.

"I'm the only one who can speak Spanish."

George wiped the axle clean with a rag. I dipped into the plastic sack and counted out a hundred dollars. Black Maria packed a small shoulder bag and set out, walking toward town, the four-foot-long steel axle over her shoulder, black hair hanging down her back.

"*Vaya con Dios,*" Mountain Girl shouted.

"What a woman," Hassler said.

"Considering she can't really speak Spanish worth a shit," George said.

We cooked beans and rice, spread them on tortillas. Swam in the ocean. Sat outside and watched the sun go down. A couple of days later, Maria came walking down the road, axle over her shoulder.

"How did it go?" George asked, relieving her of her burden.

She rubbed her shoulder.

"All right. Tedious bus rides, but Guadalajara was nice and the wrecking yard was a real trip. They couldn't figure me out for a while but caught on real quick when I showed them the broken axle. Twenty dollars, American, then the long haul back. What's to eat?"

We cooked up enchiladas and tacos and salad and shrimp, washed it down with beer and tequila as the sun sank into the ocean's edge and the moon rose over the jungle behind us.

Next day, George installed the new axle and, with everyone pushing, we eased the bus forward onto solid ground. The next day, Boise dropped off Kesey and Zonk when he saw the bus parked on the beach.

We spent the evening eating and drinking outside the bus, then went down to the edge of the ocean, hoping we would see the green flash as the sun dipped below the horizon. No luck, everyone moseyed back to the bus. Kesey and I stayed down by the water.

He told me he had been throwing the *I Ching* one night when a sudden storm blew in from the Pacific.

"'What's next?' was the question I asked the *Ching*, 'I can't spend the rest of my life eating frijoles and dodging federales. What should I do?' And before I could even consult the answering hexagram, there was lightning everywhere. I pointed to the sky, lightning flashed and all of a sudden I had a second skin of lightning, like a suit of electricity, and I knew it was in us to be superheroes, that we could become superheroes or nothing."

He looked at me meaningfully.

"Who can argue with the *Ching*," I said.

Kesey didn't say anything. I remained noncommittal, reluctant to pledge allegiance to such a grandiose notion, no matter how tempting. Me, a superhero? Save the world? A tall order, but better than a poke in the eye with a sharp stick.

"Go for the gold," I said.

"Yes, the brass ring."

We contemplated the cosmos for a while, then went back to the bus and crashed.

Kesey practiced what he talked about:
non-confrontational creative measures
employing the knowledge that there are
never just two opposing answers or sides,
but a multitude of other opportunities open
between the two, and the way to deflect
the antagonisms and the blockheadedness
of the sociopaths is to interject another spasm
of play in the game.
  — Ken Babbs

41

A Sad Situation, Sorry to Say

We found two places for rent, on the beach just off the road: one a cement house we called the Concrete-Block House, replete with kitchen, dining room, big wooden table, two bedrooms and a bathroom, hot and cold running water in both the kitchen and bathroom; the other place was next door, a Purina warehouse, red-brick building with a long, empty room and a small apartment with all the amenities. Kesey had enough money to pay for three months, and we settled in, the bus parked between the two buildings.

Mike Hagen showed up, driving a '50 Ford four-door sedan with the trunk taken off and the rear seats removed. A plywood platform stuck out the back, Mike's version of a homemade Mexican pickup truck.

"Look at that," he said, getting out of the car.

He pointed upward at a buzzard carrying a head of a hog, a hawk hot on the buzzard's tail. The birds flew over the house and across the road before disappearing in the jungle-covered hills.

"Hope that's a good omen," George said.

"Is there any other kind?" said Hassler.

"Not when the planets are aligned like today," Maria said, being of the astrological persuasion.

We swam in the ocean every day. There was a drop-off and the waves rose high and smashed down with a strong undertow. Get caught in one of those, the only thing to do was dive down and swim underwater away from the beach and resurface in the lull between waves, then catch another wave and ride it to shore.

Big sea turtles came in close, so calm and slow we swam up behind them, grabbed their shells and caught a ride. Manta rays, with languorous flaps of their wings, glided under the surface, frightening at first until we found out they paid us no attention, black eyes looking for other kinds of food.

We set up our musical and sound and recording gear in the empty room of the Purina warehouse and at night made tapes. Overdubbed the first track on the four-track and then again on the two-track; long stereo recordings of made-up stories backed by the Prankster band: Kesey on lead guitar, Hagen on rhythm, me on electric bass, Gretch on electric piano, George on drums. We felt so good about the results, Kesey decided we needed better equipment. He gave George a wad of cash and George flew back to San Francisco where he hooked up with Cassady, who knew about a '55 Chrysler sedan they could get for practically nothing if George could get it running. Turned out to be a faulty coil, easily fixed. They drove around looking for guitar amps and sound effect machines. They took so long, Kesey told me, "Go up there and make sure they're getting the right stuff. Buy a truck to haul it back here."

When I got to San Francisco, I called Jerry Garcia and told him what I needed.

He said, "Let's take a look at what they've already got."

When he checked everything over, he said, "You need better instruments."

First I had to get the rig to haul it with. I found a '52 Dodge window panel truck with front and back seats, windows along the sides, big storage space in the back, double doors in the rear. I bought it.

Jerry and I drove to Oakland to a pawn shop specializing in music equipment. Jerry tried out some guitars and picked a blond National with a wah-wah bar.

"Kesey will love this," he said.

He chose for me a solid body bass with a deep thump. The *piece de resistance* was an amplifier rigged with tremolo, echo, and reverb. We removed the back seat of the truck so everything would fit in. I dropped Jerry off and left to find George and Cassady.

"I'm flying back," I told them. "How do you want to do the drive?"

"The Chrysler for me," Cassady said.

"And me," George added.

"Who's going to drive the truck with the gear?" I asked.

The who we found was Page Browning, loose and carefree, loving nothing better than a trip to Mexico, a trip he made many times under less-than-legal circumstances.

Chloe Scott, our old friend from Menlo Park days at Stanford, wanted to come along. She rode in the Chrysler with George and Cassady. Page, driving the truck, dropped me at the airport and the two rigs headed south on 101.

Cassady kept his speed down, not to lose the slower truck, but finally took the bit in his teeth and sped up. Soon Page and the truck were no longer in sight. They came to the border between Arizona and Sonoyta.

"Oh-oh," George said. "It wasn't like this when we drove the bus through."

Instead of two sleepy border guards, there was a squad of

Mexican soldiers with machine guns firing them on full-automatic at rabbits hightailing it across the desert.

They halted fire and came over to check out the gringos. Formal at first, they had everyone step outside the car and show their IDs and answer the usual questions: where were they going and what were they going to do when they got there. They got the usual replies: touristas, come to enjoy the pleasures of your beautiful country.

Chloe took charge. A beautiful woman of English stock, mannered and with a slight accent, she bowled them over with her charm. The sergeant stamped their visas and, showing off his white, perfect teeth in a beautiful smile, sent them on their way.

M eanwhile, back at our digs in the Concrete-Block House we were awakened every morning at dawn by a man standing on the doorstep and calling out, "Hel-l-o-o."

We all called back, "Hello."

Later in the morning, someone would go outside and step in a puddle of water. I was up early one day and heard the "Hel-l-o-o," and went outside to see who it was. A short Mexican chap stood with a block of ice on his shoulder. He said it again and I realized, even with my sparse Spanish, he was not saying, "Hello," he was saying, "*Hielo.*"

The iceman had cometh. As he had cometh every morning. And now he would like to be paid. I went in the house to get the money. On bus trips, I had always been the one to carry the cash and keep track of expenses. Julius, our road manager, took over when we were doing the LA Acid Tests. He gave up the job when we came to Mexico. I didn't want to be pestered by it, and declared, "I'm putting the money in a coffee can. Take out what you need for the necessities and put the receipts in this cigar box."

I pulled a wad of pesos out of the coffee can and took them outside. "How much?" I asked, holding out the money.

He plucked out twenty pesos.

"*Muchas gracias*," he said and walked back to his cart.

On Sundays we went into Manzanillo and walked the promenade along with the locals dressed in their finery. The west side of the promenade faced the bay, on the east side buildings lined the street. The ends of the promenade were open and a paved walk went around a center park with benches and palm trees and a fountain in the middle. Kesey bought me a sombrero with a huge brim and I wore it as we walked. I felt something hit it, then something else. I took the hat off and looked. Pesos were sliding around in the brim. I looked over at the side of the promenade where teenagers were sitting on a ledge laughing. I got it, my sombrero provided a perfect target for their coins. I slung the outlandish hat on my back by the cord around my neck and kept it there. When we returned to the Concrete-Block House I hung it on the wall and never wore it again.

Cassady took the four-pound hammer from the tool compartment in the back of the bus—the hammer was used to pound the tires off of the rims when we had a flat—and, shirtless and barefooted, standing on the sand facing the ocean, spent hours flipping it in the air and catching it, doing double and triple flips, catching it with one hand, then the other, pirouetting in a circle to catch it behind his back, missing the catch, falling on a knee and scooping it up, flipping it back in the air, not missing a beat, his daily regimen, his exercise, keeping his body lean and muscular, reflexes sharp, mind at one with the action. He never went in the water and it never occurred to us, maybe Cassady didn't know how to swim.

One day Neal fashioned a new game out of two sticks he found in the jungle. One long and the other small. He held the long stick in his hand and with his other hand knocked the short stick into the air, keeping the short one aloft as long as he could. Two hits were ordinary and three were good, before he blew it and the short stick fell to the ground.

After weeks of constant practice, lurching and staggering, thrusting and sweating, plowing football-field-length trenches in the sand, flailing like a swashbuckling Errol Flynn fighting off hordes with cutlasses, Neal achieved a record number of seven hits.

He was triumphant. "It's a classic example of a great accomplishment performed by a member of the fifth root race emerging from the penalty box after being punished for trying to second-guess God," he said. He firmly believed he was a forerunner of the Aquarian Age, and Aquarius was his sign.

But he was a working servant who never wanted to be the king or the leader. After his record seven hits, he was happy with ordinary fives and sixes. He showed off for hours and drew a small crowd of interested Mexicans. One was an old man in black pants and open-neck shirt who made Cassady nervous with hawklike eyes, assessing Neal's game like a scorer keeping track.

All right, Neal would show him. He did a four, then a five, another four, then a triumphant six. The stranger picked up his own stick and approached boldly. He bowed, held his stick in front of him and smilingly spoke the universally understood words, "En garde."

Neal turned his best profile to him and crossed swords. "Lead on, MacDuff," he challenged. The old man whacked with a lusty vengeance and, before Neal could move, he had been belted half a dozen times and poked another three more. He immediately covered up but it was too late.

The stranger knew his business. He raised welts of pain and whelps of aches and yelps of hurts before Neal could drop his stick and hold his hands up in defeat.

The old man raised his sword and bowed. He whipped a liter of tequila out of his hip pocket and offered it to Neal. It was a statement, not a question, and Neal took a big swig. He then brought the old man to the house and introduced him, saying, "Whatever you do, don't pick up a stick in front of this guy."

Neal was humbled but not bitter. He gave up the sticks and returned to his hammer. That and his verbal virtuosities became his stock-in-trade whenever newer, younger, curious seekers gathered, looking to be instructed.

A '53 Chevy pulled up in front of the house. Three guys got out: Mike Hagen's younger brother, Johnny, Larry Shurtliff, and a guy named Drew—we never did know his last name.

Johnny and Larry, like Mike, were from Pendleton, Oregon: cow and wheat country. One time, Larry and a pal stole a bottle of whiskey out of a rancher's pickup because the rancher had run them off of his place for stealing watermelons. They got caught with the whiskey and were sent to the MacLaren Youth Correctional Facility in the Willamette Valley, seven-hundred miles from Pendleton. When they were released, they drove the '53 Chevy to Santa Cruz, California, where they met Drew and decided to drive to Mexico and see Mike.

A couple of days after they arrived, Kesey said he'd like to go up to Puerto Vallarto and catch the action in Mismaloya, where they shot the movie *Night of the Iguana.*

Hagen and Kesey and Johnny and Larry and Drew piled into the '53 Chevy and headed north on the unpaved road, winding up the coast. They couldn't find the cutoff to Mismaloya and parked alongside the road to talk things over. A blue Volkswagen Beetle pulled up and two young Americans got out, Arnie and Ray. They said they could take Kesey and the gang to the movie set in the Volksie. Kesey took one look at the car and the number of people and said, "We need someone to ramrod this operation."

"Ramon Rodriquez-Rodriquez, the famous Mexican guide, at your service," Larry said, and jammed seven people into the Beetle. Kesey gave him the name Ramrod for his feat, and he was called Ramrod from then on.

They drove the bug as far as they could on the dirt road until it dwindled into a path. A Mexican fellow came along leading a burro with a load of wood on its back. Arnie could speak enough Spanish to find out there was no road to Mismaloya. You had to take a boat from Puerto Vallarta. That settled it. They'd gone far enough. They drove the Volkswagon back to the Chevy, the VW went on to Puerto Vallarta, and Kesey and the gang headed back to Manzanillo in the Chevy.

Halfway home, they ran into a roadblock. Three unshaven, raggedy-uniformed Mexican policemen made them all stand alongside the road while the cops checked the car.

"Hmm, what's this?" the cop in charge asked, holding up a big hunting knife.

"You like that, huh?" Ramrod said. Ramrod made a take-it gesture with his hand, no mention of money or anything so crass between friends. The policeman gave him a big smile.

"*Jefe*," one of the other cops called, pointing inside the car.

The Boss Man went over and looked.

"*¡Mota!*" he cried.

"We're fucked," Hagen said.

Back in Manzanillo, George had punched holes in the bottom of a number ten can of peanut butter and filled the can with marijuana so he could shake the can and have the weed fall out the bottom while keeping the seeds and stems in the can. The cop held the can and studied it. He shook it and pot came out the bottom and swirled to the ground.

Kesey came over and reached into the back seat. He lifted out a roll of toilet paper and made motions to go into the bushes. They were too interested in dealing with the golden opportunities their discovery had provided to pay any attention to him and he walked away.

No one had enough money to buy their way out, a sad situation, sorry to say. They must go with the policemen to the nearest town. The Boss Man looked for Kesey but he wasn't in sight. He sent one of the cops into the bushes to find him. The policeman came out shaking his head. *Vamoosed.* Didn't matter, the gringo would be out soon and on foot would be easily caught, this day or one soon. They drove away.

Things were glum around the house on the beach. Mike and Johnny and Ramrod and Drew in jail and Kesey wandering around in the jungle.

He showed up three days later, clothes in tatters, scratches all over his arms and chest and legs. Filthy and sore. Shoes flapping on his feet. He headed straight for the ocean, dived in and came up howling, all those scratches and all that salt water.

He hit the outdoor shower and ripped off what was left of his clothes and shoes. Faye, who by then had flown down with the kids, brought him a pair of pants and a shirt. I brought him a cold Dos Equis. He collapsed on a chair.

"I headed away from the road where the cops had stopped the car," he explained, "and beat my way through the brush to get as far away as I could. I hadn't gone more than an hour when I hit some railroad tracks and walked south on the ties between the rails until I heard the rails humming. I went down the embankment and waited until a slow-moving freight train came along. I screwed my courage to the do-or-die bone and loped along with the train until I was able to grab the ladder and climb on the roof of a boxcar. I sat there until almost dark when the train slowed down and turned east toward the mountains. I climbed down the ladder and jumped off and fell and tore my pants and skinned my knees. I walked until it got too dark to see, then bedded down under a big tree and tried to sleep but there were a gazillion bugs and loud shrieks and calls of animals all around me. I huddled in a ball until dawn when I started walking again. Seemed to take forever but I finally got here."

He stood up.

"Now for bed."

What is this foolishness we call fooling around
instead of god-fearing, legitimate, money-making,
moral-lifting endeavors of a productive kind?
Like wiping the condensation from the windshield
of memory, he swiped the rag across his forehead
and had a revelation... I smell a rat! Wait...
That was me...
  — Ken Babbs

42

Meat for the Grinder

The Pot Bust Four—Hagen, Johnny, Ramrod and Drew—
were incarcerated in the Tepic Prison outside of Guadalajara. We contacted Paul Robertson, our lawyer friend in Palo
Alto, and he flew down, saying he could get them out. He had a
blond girlfriend with him and they stayed in a hotel in Guadalajara and lived the high life. Paul occasionally went around to
various officials, trying to find out how to spring the men, but
he didn't get anywhere and they languished in jail.

It wasn't too bad a scene, if you had money. I rode a Mexican
bus and visited them on Sunday when relatives of the inmates
lined up at the gate with baskets of food and clean clothes. Hagen and Johnny and Ramrod and Drew lived in lean-to palapas
built against the prison wall. The lean-tos faced a big courtyard
where prisoners and families and visitors sat at tables and on
blankets spread on the hard-packed dirt. I brought as much
money as I could come up with and a basket of tortillas and
hardboiled eggs and, hidden under a napkin, a six-pack of beer.
They didn't give a shit if you drank, Hagen told me, as long as
you kept it under cover and didn't get drunk and rowdy. If you
did, you'd end up in the tank inside the prison instead of out in

the sun.

It was Drew who came up with the angle to get them out, for, by then, we had given up on Paul Robertson. Drew had a pal in Santa Cruz, a guy we already knew, Mickey McGee, big and roly-poly jolly, so full of crazy antics and goofy talk he seemed like he was all of the Three Stooges wrapped into one person. We ended up calling him Stooges.

Stooges and Drew knew a tall, straight-spined guy they called Tall George. Drew said if anyone could get them out of there, he could.

They could make phone calls out of the prison. Drew called Santa Cruz and talked Tall George and Stooges's brother into coming down to spring them.

A few weeks later, a '38 Ford Woody station wagon, restored to the nines, came driving up to our house on the beach. Tall George was the most serious-looking, imposing legal beagle we'd ever seen. Stiff black suit, white starched shirt, with a high collar like something from the 1800s. Broad-brimmed flat hat. He was the son of a former ambassador to Germany and had a red diplomatic passport, the kind issued to ambassadors and their families. That would be his ticket into the official portals.

Stooges's brother was a carbon copy of Stooges, only not wound so tight. After one beer and a short palaver with us, they drove away in the Woody wagon, eager to get this thing done.

It took only a few days of Tall George in his imposing black suit and erect carriage and red passport to gain admittance to the judge sitting on the case, and he was only too happy to take care of this small inconvenience for a son of his good friend, the former ambassador.

With the papers signed and stamped, Mike and Johnny and Ramrod and Drew, with their small parcels of belongings, walked out of the prison and drove away in the Woody while swigging celebratory get-out-of-jail beers.

Once back at our digs on the beach, Tall George, Stooges,

Stooges's brother, and Drew wasted no time pointing the Woody north, back to the States. Ramrod and Johnny Hagen followed them a couple of days later. Before he got in the '53 Chevy, Kesey took Ramrod aside and told him, "You go to the Grateful Dead and tell them Kesey sent you."

W hen Ramrod arrived in San Francisco, he went to 710 Ashbury where the Grateful Dead lived. Mickey Hart, one of the band's drummers, heard a knock on the front door. Mickey looked out the window and said, "Who's there?"

"Name's Ramrod. Kesey sent me. Said you needed a good man."

"Come on in," Mickey said.

Ramrod went to work as a lugger, then head lugger, and eventually was in charge of the equipment.

Johnny Hagen also got a job lugging equipment for the Dead, leading to a whole line of Pendleton men who worked for the band.

J ulius Karpen was an old pal of ours in San Francisco and, for a while, Janis Joplin's manager. Short of frame, skinny arms and legs, wire-rimmed glasses hanging on the end of his nose, sparse hair that went in all directions. One time I was at his house in San Francisco. He was screaming on the phone, "Fuck you and the tramp steamer your mother came over in, you'll never get another chance to sign her up."

"What was that all about?" I asked.

"Some bastard Jew promoter in LA won't pay Janis three grand to come down there and sing. The cheap prick would only pay her a grand and a half."

"Aren't you Jewish?" I asked him.

"What's *that* got to do with it?"

Had me there. We shot the shit for a while and I left. Shortly thereafter Janis fired him. Julius could be adorable one minute and a stone maniac the next, she said.

When we were doing the LA Acid Tests, Julius told me we were at the point where we needed a professional manager. He'd be willing to take on the job, but it meant he would have to handle the money. We managed to keep going on the little bit we made at the gate of the shows plus everyone throwing in on the food and gas, but when I said we were going to Mexico, Julius told me we only had twenty some dollars left in the kitty.

I dug out the five hundred Kesey gave me to save for a rainy day and, figuring it wasn't pouring down in buckets yet but definitely *was* wet as hell, handed the money to Julius.

He went batshit. Screamed holy hell at me.

"You've had this money all this time and you never told me? What the fuck kind of deal is that, holding back on your manager? Where's the trust? Where's the professionalism? This is an insult to me and all the rest of us."

Mountain Girl interceded before I could say anything that would make things worse.

"Come on, Julius," she said. "Lighten up. Do you want the money or not?"

Bottom line, he took it, but he gave me the evil eye to let me know he wasn't going to put up with that crap again and he'd be keeping close track of how the money was spent.

By the time we were settled in Manzanillo, Julius had pretty much retired from the managerial position and, like the rest of us, was enjoying the weather, the ocean, the trips to town and the absence of the angst that went with putting on the shows and stretching every penny to make things work. He didn't say a word when I put the coffee can in the middle of the kitchen table and said that's where the money would reside.

Hassler, Zonk and Hagen decided to take a trip up into the hills in the '50 Ford sedan homemade pickup, the plywood platform sticking out the back. Julius said he'd like to come along, so the four of them—Hagen driving, Julius in the front seat, Hassler and Zonker facing backwards on the plywood—cruised up the winding dirt road until it started to get dark. They decided to head back home, beer and chips and salsa gone, the mood mellow and sleepy, Hassler now in front with Hagen and Julius, Zonker sprawled out asleep on the plywood. Mike braked hard going down the hill, but couldn't keep up with the force of gravity. They were going too fast when they went around a corner and plowed into a trailer loaded with sugarcane.

The front end of the Ford was crushed. Steam rose from the radiator. Mike had a big gash on his knee. Julius's leg was bent back, broken. Hassler had a bad cut on his cheek. Zonk, in back, was shaken up but otherwise okay.

The first we heard about it was when we got word they were in the Manzanillo hospital. Someone had come along, saw the wreck, and went for an ambulance to haul them to town. They stitched up Hassler's face. Zonk came home but, before he left, he stole Hagen's shoes, Mexican huaraches with the tire-tread soles. He figured Mike wouldn't be needing them with his gashed knee. Julius was in the hospital for two days and then released, his leg in a cast, his pocket full of sleeping pills. They kept Hagen for three weeks, fighting an infection, putting up with him constantly imploring the nurses, "*Mas codeinetas, por favor.*"

At the Concrete-Block House, Julius staggered out of bed every morning and stumbled into the kitchen, his hair wild, glasses slipping, crutches barely keeping up with his legs as he collapsed on a chair. Someone brought him coffee. He dug into a plastic bag and took out a red and an orange capsule, saying, "I get up in the morning, I take a Seconal."

He put the red capsule on his tongue and washed it down with a swig of coffee.

"Then I take a Nembutal," and washed it down with another

swig of coffee.

"Then I go back to bed."

He pulled himself to his feet and lurched out of the kitchen on his crutches.

It was going on too long with no change in sight; he still had a shitload of pills. We decided we'd better do something. I snuck into Julius's room when he was sleeping, found his plastic bag, and took it into the kitchen where George was using a spoon and cup to mash crosstop bennies into powder. I opened the Seconal and Nembutal capsules and dumped their contents in the sink. We spent the rest of the night loading the emptied capsules with speed. I put the plastic bag on Julius's nightstand before he woke up.

The next morning, he staggered into the kitchen, did his coffee-and-sleeping-pill routine and went back to bed. The next day he repeated the routine but instead of saying, "Then I go back to bed," he said, "Then I go outside and take a walk."

A week later he was his old, crotchety self, still on crutches, but nimble enough he decided it was time to get back to San Francisco and find some meaningful work.

He stood at the open passenger door of the Dodge window van and looked us over. Shook his head and gave us a wave.

"Goodbye, Julius, goodbye, old pal," we said.

Cassady sat at the wheel, waiting. He cranked the starter and the truck began to roll, heading for the Guadalajara airport.

"God, it's good to see the old Julius again," Hassler said, "free of all that managerial shit and money worries."

"Plus, he's wide awake and sharp," George said.

"And smiling," Kesey added.

We trooped back into the house.

Hassler walked to the front window and stood looking out.

"What's going on over there?" he said.

The house across the street had been vacant all the time we had been in Mexico. Now there was some kind of activity. We saw furtive shapes that seemed to be looking out the window at us. We conjured up the worst: Police doing a surveillance. Were they looking for Kesey, having gotten word he was hiding a scant couple of miles from downtown Manzanillo?

"Let's flush them out," I said.

Our old pal, Bob Stone, now a published author, had wrangled a writing job from *Esquire* to come to Mexico and do a story about Kesey on the lam. He stood behind me, looking and listening.

"Are you kidding?" he said. "You're dealing with some mean heat down here, and I don't mean the weather."

"It will be all right," I said. "Kesey can lay low. None of the rest of us are under the gun."

Hagen broke out the 16 mm Arriflex camera we'd used on the bus trip to Madhattan two years earlier. He mounted the four-hundred-foot magazine on top so it looked more professional. He screwed the camera onto the wooden tripod and took it out front and set it up, camera pointed at the supposedly vacant house. There was no film in the camera. But who knew?

A few minutes later the front door of the house opened and two men walked out, the first, a slick-haired, mustachioed, portly gent with an authoritarian mien, the second man a slimmer version than the first, seedier around the edges, both dressed casually in short-sleeve shirts and lightweight trousers.

"I am Federal Agent Numero Uno," the first man said. "We received word there were suspicious characters in a wildly colored bus renting two houses on the beach and I, unhappily, was taken off another assignment and ordered to investigate the circumstances."

"I can understand the confusion, seeing us as an unsavory element," I said. "But we're here on a six-month vacation from our work as filmmakers and musicians in *Estados Unidos*."

He smiled benignly. "That is, *Estados Unidos del Norte*, to be correct, for I assume you are from the red, white and blue."

"Absolutely *correctamente*," I said, my high school Spanish almost forgotten, reduced to mostly adding an *o* to the English word: *foodo*, or *gasalino*. *Cerveza* I knew by heart. "Why don't we get out of this heat and retire to *Las Haciendas de Bufón*, and cool off over a cold drink?"

He bowed. "Lead on, MacDuff."

I raised my eyebrows at Bob Stone. What did we have here, a Shakespeare buff? Bob shrugged. We walked the short distance to the bar. Hagen stayed behind to break down the camera and put it away.

They have us by the balls and
can't keep from squeezing us
out of Cuba and Venezuela.
Next thing you know
it will be Mexico.
They've got a screw loose.
Sometimes it is looser
than others and this
is one of those times.
    — Ken Babbs

43

Eastern Mustard
and Western Grit

The English name of *Las Haciendas de Bufón* was *The House of the Jester*. Inside, the walls were covered with paintings and pictures of jesters in European courts and Mexican night clubs.

"The reason we seem like suspicious characters to the locals is the sign on the top of our bus," I told Numero Uno. "It reads *Further* but, according to what the shrimp seller on the waterfront told us, everyone thought it meant *Führer*, and that we were Nazi-Party members hiding out in Mexico."

Numero Uno laughed. "Our information was even more bizarre. We received reports that Russian submarines were hanging around the coast, surfacing at night to study our defenses. As if Manzanillo would be a target for invasion. You were suspected of being agents put on the mainland to radio information to the sub. We noted the amount of electronic equipment you installed in the Purina warehouse."

"Our musical and recording instruments," I said. "You'll have to come listen to one of our nighttime sessions."

"No need. I can see now these suspicions were unfounded," Numero Uno said, sipping a margarita. "I had to leave the finest assignment of my career in Mismaloya, where a Hollywood company was filming *Night of the Iguana*, to come here. On the movie set, I was supposed to make sure everything went smoothly between the locals and the American moviemakers. But what I was really doing was keeping an eye on the stars of the film, to step in if fireworks exploded."

Bob Stone leaned in. Savory meat for the grinder. *Esquire* would eat it up.

"The leading actor and actress were Richard Burton and Ava Gardner, Burton a well-known lady's man and Ava a beauty of great renown."

"She, who had so many male idolizers," I said, "created the saying that swept across our nation: '*I wouldn't mind being a wallflower if Ava was my gardener.*'"

"*Pfffft.* Movie fans talking in jest. They never saw her in the flesh. She drew you like a sultry magnet. Dark, flashing eyes and come-hither look, a body to make you drool. Is it any wonder Richard Burton, the paramour of Elizabeth Taylor, separated from her by hundreds of miles, stoked a fire between himself and Ava Gardner and she warmed to the flames?"

Numero Uno stood up straighter, a stern look.

"Elizabeth Taylor heard about the fire brewing between Burton and Gardner and she wasn't about to let anyone else get their claws into her man. So, who should appear on the set? Elizabeth Taylor herself. From then on, she was with Richard every chance she could get; stayed with him at the hotel in Puerto Vallarta, sat next to him in the boat on the ride to Mismaloya, dark glasses covering her eyes, a white scarf wrapped around her head. But the one place she couldn't be next to him was in front of the camera."

Numero Uno slapped his hand on the bar.

"She seethed, having to stand with the rest of us behind the camera, watching Richard and Ava do their love scenes."

Kesey—wearing a sweat-stained Stetson, faded jeans held up by a wide leather belt with a bucking-bronc buckle, cowboy shirt with the sleeves ripped off at his armpits, red, white and blue painted sneakers on his feet—picked that moment to come into the bar.

Bob Stone blanched.

Numero Uno looked Kesey over. *Who was this gringo?* They hadn't seen him while doing their surveillance.

Kesey gave him a big smile and stuck out his hand.

"Sol Crackdancer," he drawled, "of the Durango Crackdancers. Heard my compadres here were indulging in our mutual countries' favorite pastime, so I decided I'd better join in a'fore they get falling-down-drunk without me."

Numero Uno smiled and shook Kesey's hand.

"Don't let me interrupt your palaver," said Kesey. "I'll mosey on down the bar and order me up a tall cold one."

Seeing no threat or signs of guilt from this oafish cowhand, Numero Uno went back to his story: how he had become the conciliator, a government official who wanted nothing more than friendship and peace among everyone on the movie set. Between him and John Huston, they kept everything running until the movie was completed.

"And now, as you can see, I am back to the mundane jobs, like being sent to Manzanillo to investigate the presence of possible spies."

We could see the sadness in his eyes, how he wished he was not here at the bar, but on the beach in Mismaloya, standing between two gorgeous American women.

"Therefore, my friends, I thank you for the drink, I hope you enjoy your stay—what do you call it, *woodshedding*—in our beautiful country. And now I must take my leave, for duty calls."

We shook his hand, lauded him with accolades, breathed a sigh of relief, and clanked our glasses together when the door closed on his dapper frame.

"I don't know how you guys do it," Bob Stone said. "Too brazen to be true."

"What are you gonna do?" I asked. "That movie was shot two years ago and the poor fuck is still mooning over it."

Back at the Concrete-Block House, Hassler told me he heard from Larry Schiller, of *Life Magazine* cover-shoot fame, that Schiller was putting together an LSD record and wanted something from us.

"I bet he does want something from us," I said. "He wants something from everyone. But I haven't heard him giving anyone anything."

"Ha," Hassler chortled. "He says he'll pay us seventy dollars."

"Well, that's a different kettledrum of starfish," I said, and went over to the Purina warehouse, renamed The Rat Shack, where we got high and made audio tapes all the cool and quiet night long.

I dubbed off a ten-minute piece onto a reel-to-reel tape, put it in a box, and took it back to Hassler.

"One of our finest numbers," I said. "'Mumbley Peg'—featuring Cassady mumbling, what else—and us singing and playing behind him:

"*Mumble-y peg, mumble-y peg,*
One wooden eye and one wooden leg,
Mumble-y peg."

Hassler and Zonker would fly back to the States, deliver the tape to Schiller, and wire the money to us.

"We are professionals, after all," Kesey said.

We heard about a great beach south of Manzanillo; packed up food, drove through town, turned onto a dirt road that ran alongside the ocean. George passed out capsules of LSD and we swallowed them with swigs of beer. The beach was in a small cove. On the south side, dunes ran toward town. The north end of the beach butted against a row of rocks, twenty to thirty-feet high, descending into the ocean.

"That looks like Nat King Kong's place," Kesey said.

We spread blankets on the sand, weighed them down with coolers full of beer and food. Kesey's daughter, Shannon, and his son, Jed, splashed and swam in the water. We ate and drank and watched the sun go down.

"There it is," Kesey cried. "Do you see it?"

Just as the orange rim of the sun disappeared below the horizon, a green light ran along the line where the ocean and sky met—a momentary flash—and then it was dark.

Kesey and I climbed up on top of the bus and sat with our feet dangling over the side, arms folded on the rail. He put his hand on mine, I clasped his, and we allowed electric impulses to pass through our hands and arms and into our bodies.

"Eastern mustard and western grit," he said.

"Midwestern corn and Great Plains wheat," I said.

He gnawed on that, then was interrupted by a yell: "Where's Shannon? Shannon is missing."

Kesey jumped up, scrambled down the ladder and loped across the sand in search of his six-year-old daughter. I followed him into the dunes. Everyone searched along the edge of the water, calling for Shannon, fears at a height—she was playing in the waves—got swept away. Then Hagen called out, "Here she is." Not near the water at all, but digging in the back of a sand dune; burying treasure, she said, irritated by all the fuss.

We loaded the bus and drove back to town, Cassady gentle on the controls. Wound through narrow streets, saw shadowy forms behind the curtains of second-story windows. Street lights cast a golden glow, white shirts and trousers danced on clotheslines. The streets were so narrow it seemed like we

would scrape the walls. Then we left town, drove to the Concrete-Block House, parked and unloaded the bus. With the kids
in bed, we retired to the Rat Shack for a quiet, thoughtful session on the instruments.

S oon it was time to return to the States. Our six-month visas
were about to expire. We put the recording gear and musical instruments in the back of the Dodge window truck. Left a
space along one window to stretch out. Bob Stone and Gretch
and I would take the truck, everyone else would go in the bus,
which was too slow to keep up with us. I drove ahead, toward
the crossing in Arizona.

Loaded on bennies and caffeine and weed, we blasted clean
through the Mexican night, my hands tight on the wheel, eyes
bugged out, watching for huge Mexican trucks barreling in both
directions. Bob Stone sat tense on the edge of the passenger seat
while Gretch slept in back.

Suddenly, a herd of cattle filled the road ahead. No time to
brake to a stop. I shot through the herd, zigging and zagging,
and came out clean. Bob Stone keened a high-pitch scream.
Hearts hammering, we poked along at a crawl until the vision
of sharp-horned steers faded from our retinas.

The road was pitch black, no white lines to mark the edges,
the line down the middle faded. A hulking machine appeared in
the road. Two vertical sides going up from wheels, a cab on top
and no taillights. Nothing I could do but shoot through the gap
between the sides of the machine. We emerged unscathed.
Neither Bob nor I were able to say anything. Finally he muttered, "I don't know if I believe that happened or not. What was
that thing? You did see it, didn't you?"

"Not until our front bumper was kissing its tail end. Took me
a while to figure it out. One of those tall wood haulers you see
in lumberyards. They straddle a pile of boards and squeeze their
sides together to hold the boards, that's how they move the lum-

ber around."

"In the middle of the night?" Bob said. "I can't wait until we get out of this country."

The wind picked up, tumbleweeds blew across the road. I blasted through. Bob Stone whimpered at each hit, until a sudden gust caught the front of the truck and tore the hood loose. It slammed against the windshield. The road blotted out.

Bob's whimper became a scream: "Slow down, slow down, stay on our side of the road."

"I'm trying," I said, holding the wheel steady, foot off the accelerator, tapping the brake. I stuck my head out the window. We were in the middle of the road, drifting to the left. I swung back into our lane and stopped on the side of the road.

"Now what?" Bob Stone said.

I walked around the van and tugged on the hood to pull it down off the windshield.

"Give me a hand," I said. "The fucker's stuck."

We yanked it back and forth until it slammed down over the engine. There was a dent in the middle from front to back and both sides of the hood. The front end stuck up six inches from the back. I dug some rope out of the back of the truck, tied the hood down, and we set out again, both of us quiet, intent on the road.

We crossed into the States at dawn, border guards barely checking us out.

"I'm done in," I said. "How's about taking the wheel?"

"I don't have a driver's license," Bob said. "I don't want to take the chance."

"Oh, come on, we're in the most desolate place in Arizona. What's the chance of a cop stopping us?"

"I don't care. I can't afford a ticket."

"Here, I'll give you my driver's license and I'll sleep in the back so if we do get stopped the cop will only see you and Gretch."

Bob grumbled but finally agreed. We hadn't gone fifty miles before a red light came up behind us. Bob cursed and pulled over. He beat his head on the steering wheel.

"I knew it. I knew it."

"Cool down," I said. "Act natural and tell him the truth. We're heading home from a vacation in Mexico."

Bob handed the license to the state trooper. He looked at it and looked at Bob and said, "This isn't your driver's license, is it?"

"It's mine, officer," I piped up from in back. "I told him to use it, so if you're going to write a ticket, give it to me."

"The driver gets the ticket. And from here on someone else has to drive."

Gretch and I took turns at the wheel and we had an uneventful silent drive to the Bay Area, where Bob got out and walked away without a word.

"I think he's mad at me," I said.

W hen the bus with everyone else on it approached the border, Kesey said, "Let me out here. They might have a flyer about the bus, and for sure one about me. Once you're across, go down the road a ways and wait."

Cassady drove on. Kesey spied a Mexican on a burro, the Mexican holding a guitar, a big sombrero on his head, serape over his shoulders. Kesey told Cassady to stop, then he walked up to the man and palavered for a while with gestures, then handed over a fifty-dollar bill.

The border guard was half asleep in his chair when a burro came ambling along. The man riding it had a sombrero down over his eyes, a serape around his shoulder. He strummed his guitar and sang:

"*Ay yie yie yie,*
mi madre es muy bonita,
mi esposa mi da un cerveza,

mi casa es un elegante,
y mi perro es uno delgado,
solo tengo un peso,
todo lo que quiero es una siesta."

Meaning, roughly:

My mother is very beautiful,
my wife gives me a beer,
my house is elegant,
my dog is skinny,
I only have a peso,
all I want is a nap.

The guard waved him through. The man rode a ways, dismounted, and went into the bushes.

"It's Kesey," Black Maria said when he emerged.

Dressed in his regular clothes, he walked toward the bus. Behind him the Mexican stepped out from the bushes and mounted the burro. A sombrero shaded his eyes, a serape covered his shoulder. He strummed a guitar and sang softly as he ambled back into Mexico:

"Todo lo que quiero es una siesta."

There's room. We don't all have to be the same.
We don't have to have Baptists coast-to-coast,
we can throw in some Buddhists and some
Krishnas and people who are thinking totally
strange things about Irish leprechauns; there's
room spiritually for everybody in this universe.
— Ken Kesey

44

Nothing Less Than Saving the World

"T hey couldn't find their underwear if it were hanging on the clothesline," Kesey said, staring into the camera.

The TV reporter smiled, and said, "That's sure to get the FBI's attention."

Kesey waved goodbye and walked down Grant Street into Chinatown.

Later in the day, the same TV reporter interviewed the agent tasked with catching Kesey: "What's your take on Kesey taunting you?"

FBI Agent Cramwell said, "Mister Kesey can spout off all he likes. It's the last hurrah of a desperate man who knows his days are numbered."

Kesey wasn't worried. He'd been back from Mexico for a week and wasn't trying to hide or lay low. Too big a city, too many people, too many friends willing to provide him a bed and place to stay. His lawyer, Brian Rohan, wasn't as *laissez-faire* about Kesey's chances of remaining free. He made arrangements to meet Kesey and give him some realistic choices of how and where to lay low, out of the public's eye.

Driving Hassler's car, Rohan picked Kesey up on Market Street. Kesey walked around to the driver's side and said, "Let me drive."

He headed across the Bay Bridge into Oakland.

"No one even knows my name over here," Kesey said, turning to Rohan with a smile.

"Look out!" Rohan yelled.

Kesey looked but it was too late. He slammed on the brakes and slid into the back of a car that had stopped at a crosswalk. Kesey's head snapped forward and his face hit the steering wheel.

"You alright?" Rohan cried.

Kesey looked at Rohan.

"Oh, shit," Rohan said.

Kesey's lip was swelling, blood welling from his mouth. Kesey held out his hand and spit a hunk of tooth into it. He lifted his upper lip. The inside was lacerated. His left front tooth was broken, only a jagged tip remaining.

"Come on," Rohan told him. "You've got to get out of here."

Kesey opened the door and walked around the car to the sidewalk. He held his bandanna to his mouth.

"Here," Rohan said.

He handed Kesey a handful of money.

"I'll tell them I was driving," Rohan said. "Get back into the city and call me when you're settled somewhere."

Hassler had a dentist friend who lived in the hills outside Santa Cruz. The dentist told Kesey he could make a new tooth that fitted over the stump of the old one.

The dentist asked Kesey if he wanted anything special, gold or platinum or a color that matched his other teeth. Kesey sketched the tooth he wanted on a piece of paper. The dentist looked at it, and broke into a big smile.

"I can do that," he said. "Take a couple of days but I can do it."

Kesey hung out at Hassler's until the tooth was ready. When he emerged from the dentist's office he gave Hassler a big smile, showing his pearlies. The new tooth was shaped like a shield, the bottom half alternating green and white vertical lines, the top, silver with a gold, five-pointed star in the middle.

"Whaddaya think?" Kesey asked.

"Only you," Hassler said. "Only you."

Kesey continued to taunt the FBI. One afternoon he was in Hassler's car—front end dented but still roadworthy—tooling down the Bay Shore Freeway. A dark blue sedan pulled alongside. The passenger looked out the side window and saw Kesey, who looked over and grimaced, caught in the steely glare of FBI Agent Cramwell.

Kesey skidded to a stop on the shoulder, jumped out, raced around the car, crossed a ditch, climbed over a chain-link fence, then hightailed across a grass field. He looked over his shoulder. The two FBI agents were scaling the fence. Kesey slowed down.

"Shit, piss, corruption, snot, seventeen assholes tied in a knot," Kesey said to himself. "This is the way it will always be, running from the feds. Is that how I want to spend the rest of my life? To hell with it."

He stopped and turned around.

The agents came puffing up, suit coats open and chests heaving. Agent Cramwell had ripped his pant leg from crotch to shoe climbing over the fence. The loose fabric flapped like a rag on a clothesline.

Kesey held out his hands.

"Cuff me, men, I'm yours."

Agent Sykes reached for his handcuffs.

"No need for that," Cramwell said.

They walked to the fence, followed it to a gate and hiked along the freeway to the agency car.

"We get to the office," Cramwell said, "call your friend to

come get the car before it's towed."

Kesey stood contritely in front of the judge, who read him the riot act, closing with, "Jail time for you, young man."

The gavel slammed down.

"Your honor," Brian Rohan said, "we would like bail for my client."

The judge leaned over and stared at Rohan.

"Bail? He was out on bail and hightailed to Mexico. You have the nerve to ask for more bail?"

"If my client can explain," Rohan said.

Kesey stood up and told the judge he had indeed changed, that he realized LSD had made him think he could do whatever he wanted, but now he knew that was a mistake and he had come back to exhort the acidheads to give up the drug and go in a new, positive direction. He was going to bring everyone together at an Acid Test Graduation to be held at Winterland. The Grateful Dead would play.

He promised this was for real, his lawyer would be with him all the time and ensure, when the event was over, Mister Rohan would bring him back to court.

The judge pondered.

"I will go along with this, as cockamamie as it sounds. God knows someone has to speak out against the drug and I suppose its greatest spokesman would be the best person to do it."

The TV cameras outside the courtroom zoomed in on Kesey. He was through mocking the FBI and instead hawked the upcoming show.

When Bill Graham saw the news clip, his hackles went up. Did Kesey have a hidden agenda? Big events were Bill's turf. Was Kesey planning to muscle in? Bill Graham promptly booked Winterland and the Grateful Dead for Halloween, depriving Kesey of both.

Undeterred, Kesey found an abandoned building off of Market Street with an empty warehouse on the first floor and he rented it. The band Anonymous Artists of America said they would play.

We painted a sign on canvas and hung it on the side of the bus—ACID TEST GRADUATION—and drove around town, Pranksters on top tootling and fluting. That was the extent of our advertising.

Mountain Girl bought some white, Can't Bust 'Em coveralls and sewed round pieces of dark blue fabric on the back with large, five-pointed white stars in the middle of the blue pieces and thirteen small, white stars around the edges. The front had a blue patch with a white star in the middle sewn over the left chest.

While we were inside the building getting things ready, Cassady, wearing a pair of the star-festooned coveralls, stood alongside the bus and did his throw-and-catch routine with the four-pound hammer, attracting a crowd that stood and watched.

The night of the graduation, during a short briefing in the bus, Kesey ran down what we'd be doing. George passed around a jar of orange juice. We all took a sip and went inside.

A small but exuberant crowd. A stage at one side of the room. The ACID TEST GRADUATION banner hung behind the stage, a red-and-white parachute above the center of the room. Below, a large space for dancing. To the right of the stage, a comfort area with bean bags and couches.

The Anonymous Artists of America played a set. Everyone danced, then Neal Cassady went onstage and called out names over the microphone. As each person came up, he handed him or her a personalized Acid Test diploma, shook hands and said a few encouraging words: "Nobody bugs you, that's what you do; men pick up a little blond or a brunette on the other side of the floor, women loosen up, make ready to boogie; that's right, do a little jive, make like a beehive."

The lights went out. There were shouts and nervous laughter

and catcalls. A slow roll on the drum, faster and louder, ended with a big bass drum boom, and the lights came on.

Kesey stood at the edge of the lighted space, black maw of the empty warehouse behind him. He wore a top hat and a black suit. A purple cape hung from his shoulders.

"Welcome to the world of magic," he said, "where the mysterious rules and the fog are peeled back. You can see new possibilities revealed."

He pulled a pack of cards from his pocket. Ripped off the cellophane to show the pack had never been opened, and called for a volunteer. A man dressed like a lumberjack—striped shirt, suspenders, thick trousers, boots—stepped forward.

Kesey handed him the pack of cards.

"Open it and shuffle the cards, look at one and memorize it, put it back in the deck and the deck back in its box."

Slowly and carefully the lumberjack did as he was told, making sure Kesey didn't see the card. He handed the box to Kesey, who in one motion threw it in the air. The box came open, the cards flew in all directions, and fell on the floor. Kesey reached behind his head and pulled a card out of the headband of his hat.

"Is this your card?" he said.

He held up the four of hearts.

"Damn," the lumberjack said. "How'd you do that?"

"It's a mystery. That's what you'll remember."

He called for two more volunteers and a couple of burly guys stepped forward. He had them tie a thick rope in double and triple knots around his ankles and pull them tight. They threw the end of the rope over a rafter and pulled Kesey upside down two feet off the floor. They tied the rope to a beam and left Kesey hanging.

Hassler and I held a curtain in front of Kesey. The Anonymous Artists of America broke into "Brokedown Palace." Grunts and sounds of a struggle on the other side of the curtain, then a thump. Hassler whisked the curtain away. The rope hung limply from the ceiling, the knots untied. Kesey, wearing white wrestling tights, lay slumped on the floor. His chest heaved as he gasped for air. He struggled to his feet, lurched over to the Pranksters and plopped on the floor. Cassady passed him a bandana. Kesey mopped his face and rose to his feet.

"We opened a crack in the wall and let in the light," Kesey said, once he caught his breath. "Now it's up to you to widen that crack. Wake people up. And once awake, keep them awake. Use your skills as performer, wizard, magician, raconteur, teacher. Humor works all the time. When the teenage student's mother was asked why she volunteered to help in the high school cafeteria, she replied, 'Youth must be served.'

"Did someone mention LSD as a catalyst for change?" Kesey continued. "When meatball hit, it hit everything. The trees, the rocks, the people, the houses, the institutions, and now everything is psychedelicized. There's no need to reopen that door. You don't use acid to leave the world. You use it to get into the world. Be one with the people. Embrace the ordinary. Happiness for all. Rich or poor. Affluent or destitute.

"Follow your bliss. You have to participate in the material world. You're not going to be here all that long. Don't sweat the screwups. Try to get it right the next time. Just like fixing the carburetor on a pickup truck. Those screws are tiny. Enjoy the tussle. Don't forget the benefit of a good nap. We are few but we are powerful. The love we create will never die. Thus endeth the lesson. Now, party down."

Kesey leaned back with his head in Faye's lap. He closed his eyes and let the night wind down around him.

After the Acid Test Graduation everything went sideways.

A ghost's whisper simpering in the forest,
branches creaking, leaves tickling,
owls hooting. A random thought
if said aloud may soon attract a
raucous crowd. The spotlight can turn
into crosshairs. Our art is to fall and
stumble, bumblefuck out of the spotlight.
That's when the magic happens.
  — Ken Babbs

45

His Blue Metal Cup

The Summer of Love, Ken Kesey was in jail. Not in the slammer, but instead doing six months at the San Mateo County Sheriff's Honor Camp which, coincidentally, adjoined the property in La Honda where he had been busted.

With Kesey gone and San Francisco invaded by pilgrims with flowers in their hair, followed behind by sharks preying on easy fare, the Pranksters decided to beat feet. We headed in a new direction. Under the asphalt. Out of the spotlight. We moved to Oregon where Kesey's dad had bought a sixty-eight-acre farm near the Willamette River, fifteen miles east of Eugene.

There was a big hay barn with cattle stalls. The beat-up travel trailer where a caretaker had lived now stood empty.

Hassler found a little place in the barn to live, and George fixed up a room. Faye and the kids slept in an outbuilding. Mike Hagen lived in the back of a boxy 1938 Railway Express truck. Gretch's brother helped me build a cabin by the pond. We also built a cookhouse with a kitchen and dining hall where we prepared and ate our meals.

There were chickens. There was Bam the Ram. Don't bend

over or you got butted from behind and your noggin would be in the dirt. Stewart the Dog, a black-and-white crossbreed of shepherd and something mysterious, wandered in and adopted us. He begged you to throw stones or sticks. A spaced-out pilgrim gave him some speed one day and he sat by the pond, pounced on a rock, spit it into the edge of the pond and pounced on it again, over and over, until he was so wore out he keeled over, his nose on the edge of the water. There was a mule and a white horse, a steer, a hutch full of rabbits, and a big garden.

The Dodge window van truck I drove from Mexico still had the dented hood with a rope tying it down. One day, George Walker and I bent the hood back with a crowbar and wrenched it closed again. I painted a big blue star over the dent, and below the star, outlined in red and black, like something from a Marvel comic book, the word BAM. I covered the whole thing with clear acrylic. The hood gleamed like a big fist coming at you. From then on it was the *Bam Truck*.

Sonny Barger, Oakland Chapter President of the Hells Angels, showed up one day, roared in on his hawg. By then we had roughed out an office in the second story of the barn. The window looked out on the drive and the cow pasture. I brought Sonny up to the office and we reminisced about the party in La Honda. Bemoaned the fact that Kesey was in jail rather than at the farm. I heard a vehicle start up. I looked out the window. Someone was driving off in the *Bam Truck*, a guy who'd wandered in the night before, a hitchhiker, wanting a place to crash.

"Shit," I said, pulling back from the window.

"What's up?" Sonny asked.

"Some fucker is stealing the *Bam Truck*."

Sonny stood up and looked out the window.

"You want me to chase him down?"

I laughed.

"That would short his circuits for sure, leave him twitching on the ground. Thanks, but he won't get far. The truck is out of gas. That's why it was parked heading out."

The truck turned out of the driveway onto the road. A hundred yards later it jerked to a stop. The guy got out, kicked the side of the truck, and trudged off down the road.

I opened the window.

"The *Bam Truck*'s in the road out of gas," I yelled at George Walker. "Can you go get it?"

He waved his arm. I shut the window and Sonny and I sat down on our chairs.

"You ever smoke PCP?" he asked me.

I shook my head. I'd heard of it. Angel dust. Elephant tranquilizer. Powerful shit.

"Want to try some?"

"Sure."

He loaded a pipe, took a drag and handed it to me. I did the same, held it as long as I could, let it out with a rush. My head swelled big as a watermelon. My limbs went dead. My body rose from the floor and I hovered by the ceiling, looking down at Sonny watching me with a bemused look. The floor spun in circles, the walls leaned in, almost bursting, the desk elongated and everything on it flopped crazily. I crashed back down into my seat.

"That was like a fire in a circus," I said.

"Pretty hot, huh?" Sonny answered.

"Intense," I said.

We shot the shit for a while until everything was back to normal. Sonny and I shook hands. He went out, fired up his hawg and, with a deafening roar, scratched gravel out of the drive and burned rubber onto the road. The rumbling roar faded as he disappeared around the curve, heading for the highway and home.

L ater that summer, with Cassady at the wheel, we loaded up the bus and drove to California to visit Kesey at the honor camp. When we pulled in, the parking lot was full of cars. We found an empty spot on the edge and piled out, carrying baskets of food, and boxes full of crayons, pencils, colored sharpies, pens and inks. We lined up at the gate where the guard was checking each person on a list, then he'd let them in. When it was my turn, he looked at the list and shook his head.

"I don't see your name. You'll have to wait outside."

I plodded back to the bus. Couldn't figure out what happened. Sat on the couch behind the driver's seat and mulled it over. Some kind of a fuckup somewhere, but what're you going to do? Remembering Cassady's line, I said out loud, "All you can do is blast. *Blastus-smashus, begorgeous* and *begashus.*"

Cassady vaulted into the bus and gave me a look.

"Went wrong on some curve," he said, plopping down in the driver's seat. "Set us up for this."

His name wasn't on the list either. He lit a cigarette and we sat and waited until dusk.

Visiting hours over, everyone trooped onto the bus, a tinge of sadness in their faces, tempered by the happiness of seeing Kesey. They said he was in real good spirits, considering. He lamented that no one came to visit Page Browning, but he'd pass him our love and share the eating goodies. Kesey was particularly pleased with the boxes of art supplies, for he was keeping a jail journal and could spice it up with drawings and color.

"He said he was sorry you couldn't come in," Faye told me. "He thought he put your name on the list but something must have happened. He also told me that one day when he was in the woods on a work crew, they were up on the hill that butts against La Honda and he was chopping out blackberries and kept going up the hill to the spring that comes out of a pile of rocks. His blue metal cup with the white star painted on the side was still hanging from the branch of a tree, so he filled it and drank the water down, and crouched to savor the moment, then hurried back to the work crew. No one said anything and the guard didn't notice. Ken said he was relieved because if he had been caught, he would have been sent back to jail in San Mateo to serve out his time."

Heading home we drove through San Francisco. Haight Street was crammed with pilgrims, come to revel in the liberation from bodily hang-ups, to enjoy the ecstasy of newly created relationships, and the bonding of being part of a new movement, expressed by sharing and love.

We continued to the ocean, turned right on the coast road and over the Golden Gate Bridge, our only appearance at the legendary Summer of Love.

The summer droned on, hot and dry. Chuck Kesey and I hooked up irrigation pipes from the pump in the field, and kept the cow pasture green.

There was another pump alongside the pond. I ran a hose to the bottom of the pond and sucked water to a float in the middle. A nozzle shot a geyser thirty feet in the air in a wide spray that fell back into the pond, aerating it and keeping it cool.

The days were getting shorter. The leaves turned red and fell from the trees. The tomatoes and corn and beans and lettuce were harvested. Apples were crushed for juice. The bright orange color of the pumpkins stood out among the decaying brown vegetation. The steer was butchered and the meat stored in the freezer at Chuck and Sue Kesey's creamery in town. Rain turned the brown fields green and, in California, Kesey was about to be released from jail.

George and I drove down to Chloe Scott's house in Menlo Park, California, around the corner from Perry Lane where Kesey and Faye had lived while he was going to the Stanford graduate writing class and finishing *One Flew Over the Cuckoo's Nest*.

Chloe taught dance in a big open studio that she added to the back of her house. She offered her place for Kesey's Get Out Of Jail party. A Monopoly game was the motif: big cards with drawings from the game hung on the walls, a Monopoly board painted on the floor, the poster paint deteriorating as people staggered across the squares and fell to their knees, victims of too big of a toke on the blue nitrous tank in the corner of the room.

Bottles of booze and jars of pot covered the table. Glasses clanked, the smoke was thick. People sprawled on the couch and sat on the floor. The kitchen was crowded with loaded loonies looking for ice or scarfing the food laid out on the table.

I borrowed George's car and drove to San Mateo. Parked in front of the jail and went inside. The waiting room was full. The door to the cells opened and the inmates emerged. Their faces broke into big smiles when they saw their friends and loved ones.

Kesey was next to last in line, behind him an elderly Black man, bent over and dragging a leg.

I embraced Kesey, then looked around. "Where's Page?"

"Some kind of paperwork problem. He gets out tomorrow."

Kesey motioned to the older man behind him.

"This is Charles. He doesn't have anyone to pick him up so we'll give him a ride home."

We headed for the door. A man wearing an immaculate white suit with matching vest, trousers and shoes, leaned against the wall. Damned if it wasn't Tom Wolfe. Hadn't seen him since the Acid Test Graduation a year before. I only had time to smile and give him a wave before the door slammed behind us and we headed for the car.

A raucous crowd greeted Kesey at Chloe's house. A gin and tonic, a joint, and a balloon full of nitrous oxide were thrust at him. He ignored the balloon and joint, downed the gin and tonic in one gulp, handed the empty glass off and plopped on the couch. He looked at the flushed faces and beaming smiles and took in the greetings: "So glad you're here, Ken," "Out of the joint at last, have another joint, Ken," and, "Oh, Ken, I am so glad to see you again"—the last by a luscious young lady, skirt rising on her thighs as she sat down on the couch next to him. He tried to place her face.

"Remember? The ride in your bus to your house in La Honda and then down to the beach where we had that intimate talk."

She pressed against him. He stood up and she fell sideways on the couch. He cut through the crowd into the dance studio, out the sliding glass door, into the backyard: a green lawn bordered by flowering shrubs, a large redwood tree sitting in the center. He leaned against the tree and stared at the sky.

I walked out and stood next to him.

"Get me out of here, Babbs."

"Where do you want to go?"

"Home, back to Faye and the kids."

"What about your probation? You can't leave the state without permission."

"Fuck that. They'll never know."

Reminded me of what he always said: *You ask a bureaucrat for permission, you'll never get it. Just go ahead and do it.*

"Okay, let's go."

George gave me his car keys and I drove Kesey to the bus station.

"Here," I said, handing him eighty-seven dollars, all I had.

He smiled for the first time. We shook and he headed for the bus station.

"See you in Oregon," I said.

He waved and disappeared through the door.

It's all very well, taking twelve hits a day, but where's
the health? It's the same problem as with India. Self.
All those fakirs holding their arses for a thousand years,
or standing on their nose for self! It's a hang-up.
We're not here for self. We're here for service.
We're here to multiply. Subdue ye the earth and all
that. We're here to make like three-dimensional chess.
  — Neal Cassady

46

My Kingdom for a Light

B ill Graham was going to put on the biggest outdoor rock-
'n'-roll show ever held and he found the perfect place. He
called Kesey to come check out the location. Kesey said he'd
bring the bus and pick up the Grateful Dead on the way.

The site was in New Mexico, on a two-lane road out in the
boonies. Cassady parked the bus on the side of the road. A black
luxury car pulled up behind. The driver's door opened and Bill
Graham stepped out.

"Get that green envy look out of your eyes," he told Cassady.
"It's only a rental."

"Lincoln Continental," Cassady said. "Ooh la la, those backward doors—but that was the earlier model."

Bill Graham turned to Kesey and began praising the wonders
of the place.

"As you can see, the field next door is plenty big enough for
parking and a camping area. From here, we look down at the
arena."

The hill descended to a natural amphitheater that flattened
out at the bottom.

"That's where we'll build the stage," Bill Graham said.

"Well, nothing to do but check it out," Cassady said, "and what better way than to take the car."

Before Bill could object, Cassady jumped into the driver's seat of the Lincoln.

"*Bo-ard*, all aboard," Cassady cried, and we piled in. Kesey in front, Bill Graham, Jerry Garcia and me in the back.

Neal drove back and forth across the hillside going down. The car slipped on the grass, the front end rising and banging on the ground as he straightened the wheel and sped down the hill, Bill Graham screaming, "Slow down, Neal, this isn't an all-terrain vehicle."

"At this point all you can do is blast, Bill," Cassady said, spinning a donut on the grass before slamming to a stop. He dropped the gear into park with a tremendous clunk, turned off the ignition and jumped out. He pulled a cigarette out of a pack of Camels, lit it by striking a stick match with his thumbnail.

"Cassady, you maniac," Bill Graham started to say.

"Never mind that," Kesey interrupted, "what do you make of this?"

He pointed to a large black object lying on the ground.

"Right where the lead guitar ought to be, don't you think, Jerry?"

Garcia shook his head.

"Not with that thing there. Whew, what a smell."

We walked over, holding our hands over our mouths, and looked down at a dead cow, bloated with gas, vital juices leaking into the ground.

"We'll have to get rid of that," I said to Bill Graham.

Not waiting for his answer, I walked over to the car and popped the trunk. Just as I hoped, a can of gasoline, for roadside emergencies.

I carried the can to the cow, unscrewed the lid and poured the gas over the dead animal.

"A light," I said, "my kingdom for a light."

"No," Bill Graham said, but he was too late.

Cassady struck another match and tossed it on the carcass. The fumes exploded with a tremendous *WHOOMMMMP*, and a thick column of smoke rose in the air.

It billowed high, then spread out in a black cloud. Moisture formed and fell on us—not water, but snowflakes—thick, fat, wet drops that stuck to the ground as we brushed off our shoulders and arms, to no avail, the snow too thick and fast. The carcass burned fiercely, snow melted and sizzled, and the smoke disappeared into the cloud above. Snow covered our shoes, up to our pant cuffs. If we were to get out of there, we had to do it fast.

We piled into the car, wet shoes forming puddles on the carpet. Our heads shook snow onto the upholstery, the interior stinking of wet clothes. Cassady eased forward slowly, then, gaining traction, switchbacked up the hill.

"You can do it Neal," we encouraged him together. "That's it, easy does it."

"Breaking this car in nicely," Neal said.

"Keep moving... No... Don't stop, don't stop..."

The engine coughed, then quit, halfway up.

"What the hell, Neal?" Bill Graham yelled. "Don't pull your car-driving tricks now. We have to get out of here."

"Out is right," Cassady said, "we're out of gas. But never fear, help is near, right at the rear."

He popped the trunk.

"Oh dear."

He started walking up the hill. The rest of us followed, all but Bill Graham.

"What are you doing?" he yelled. "There's a can of gas in the trunk."

Came the dawn, he stopped talking and started walking.

We beat him to the bus. Cassady had already started it and was easing forward when Bill Graham appeared alongside, banging on the door.

"Wait a minute," he yelled, "what about the car?"

Neal cracked the door and hollered, "It's fine, Bill, just wait till spring when it thaws and you can get it out then."

He hit the gas and pulled away.

After we had gone down the road for a ways, Kesey said, "Slow down, Neal."

"Certainly," Cassady replied, "just like I did when she grabbed the Vicks VapoRub instead of the Vaseline."

Kesey said, "Okay, stop here."

Neal pulled off the road.

"Right over there," Kesey said, pointing across a field, "is where my dad and Chuck and I were driving along in the motorhome and saw a movie being shot out in the meadow. We decided to check it out. Stopped and watched from a distance. A man in a Cavalry uniform trotted over to us on a white horse. It was John Wayne. He looked down at us and said, 'What have you pilgrims got going here?'

"Daddy said, 'I'm traveling with my boys on a vacation and we saw the movie set and thought we'd look it over,' and then, to my embarrassment, added, 'This here's my oldest boy and he plays a pretty good harmonica.'

"John Wayne looked down at me and said, 'Let's hear a lick, son,' so I pulled out my harmonica and played."

Kesey put his hand to his mouth and, making the sound of a harmonica, started humming.

I recognized the tune and sang along:

"*Around her neck she wore a yellow ribbon.*

She wore it for her lover who was far, far away."

Everybody on the bus joined in,

"*Far away, far away, far, far away.*"

"John Wayne gave me a big smile and said, 'That's right smart playing, pilgrim. My hat's off to you.' He raised his hat, wheeled the horse around, and galloped back to the set."

Neal started the bus.

"How meaningful," he said.

Easing onto the pavement, he accelerated to a steady fifty-five, and we rolled down the road into a fiery sunset. Bands of purple, red and orange hugged the ground. Above, lighter hues of brown and hazel clung to the bellies of billowing clouds. The colors dimmed as the sun dropped below the horizon, greys and blacks covering the land.

In the back of the bus a song rose up, Pigpen singing while cuddling a winsome lass:

"There was no warning, it just happened
You kissed me goodbye and that was it
No, no, no, I couldn't accept my fate."

Red and orange colors rose and splashed against the side window.

"Holy shit, the bus is on fire," Jerry Garcia yelled.

Cassady pulled off the road and we piled out. Flames were shooting out of the rear wheel hub.

Kesey quenched them with a fire extinguisher. Neal looked closely and said, "Rear-end oil leaking out of the seal, friction of the turning wheels set it on fire."

"What now?" Kesey asked.

"We slow down, limp on in, otherwise it's a long night waiting for a tow truck and a large cash outlay to pay for it."

"Didn't know Neal could slow down," Jerry Garcia said out of the side of his mouth.

"Just shows to go you," Phil said, "there are stranger things than we know under the sun."

"I heard that," Cassady said. "We're dealing with the lack of the sun, or is it the sum of the parts that determine the fates of those whose eyeball-kicks get burned by dastardly doubt? No, according to Edgar Cayce, it's the kundalini rising from the base of the spine to open the chakras that propel the energy to the skull.

"Who was Edgar Cayce, you ask?" Neal continued, once we

were aboard, rolling along at a sedate thirty-five. "Only the greatest spiritual medium and seer we've ever known in America, although he wasn't a medium; he was a *large*, as evidenced by the size of his seer sucker suit, ha ha. He was able to go into a trance and see the future and the past, and related it to whatever a person was seeking, be it health, wealth, or solutions for life turmoils, you name it. I admit I am a follower, not as a religion, you understand, but as lessons in life closely aligned to his predictions, like saying California would fall clean into the ocean—this in the late Forties after the Second World War. The reason California had to go was that the vibe, the spirit, particularly in the Los Angeles Basin, was sinking to lows never before seen, due to embracing the evils of gluttony and greed, and falsification, while abandoning the truths of kindness and charity; but dig this, he also cautioned that California could be saved from a watery grave if the spiritual level were to rise to acceptable levels through some kind of all-encompassing positive movement."

"It's happening, Neal," I shouted. "Right now. We're all part of it."

He jerked around. "What? Is this coming from your experience on the basketball court, having dabbled in the sport long enough to give you some kind of greater understanding?"

"No, it's from the music. Think about it. What was Pigpen singing? 'Turn On Your Love Light?' That's what's happening all over California. Like the Quicksilver Messenger Service: 'Who Do You Love?'"

"How about the Jefferson Airplane?" Bob Weir said. "'I Need Somebody to Love.'"

Everyone began shouting out songs: The Lovin' Spoonful, "Do You Believe in Magic?" Big Brother and Janis Joplin, "Piece of My Heart." The Beach Boys, "Good Vibrations." Country Joe and The Fish, "Waltzing in the Moonlight." Blue Cheer, "Just a Little Bit."

The titles and songs became more obscure: The Electric Prunes, "I Happen to Love You." The Incredible String Band, "First Girl I Loved." Moby Grape, "Come in the Morning." The Chambers Brothers, "Time Has Come Today."

The list went on until everyone ran out of bands and songs. Kesey said, "I'm convinced, all the evidence is in, and the fact is clear: California is still here. It was music that saved the day."

"Hallelujah and praise be," I cried. "I now have the answer to all the sourpusses who say nothing good's ever going to come outta the Sixties: 'Well, we kept California from falling into the ocean.'"

You can't go any faster than you can go,
but still, you want to get more. Your life
gets in your way, as it were. What is there
but one force? That is, of the soul. May I
say a word about comedowns? Comedowns
are what one works with all the time.
It's a form, what the hell? So, why
concentrate on it. The end of this bit.
Thank you. Thank you...
   — Neal Cassady

47

Potholes to Be Avoided, Mental Spinoffs Corralled

K esey and I drove down to California to visit Lee Quarn-strom, who was working for the Watsonville *Register-Pajaronian* newspaper. Passing through San Francisco, we drove past the Fillmore Auditorium, the setting of the San Fran Acid Test.

I told Kesey about the time after the Acid Test when I went to the Fillmore Auditorium with Cassady looking for a place to show our bus movie. It was a Saturday and Graham was putting on a concert. People were lined up on the sidewalk waiting to get into the venue.

"The perfect place," Cassady said.

I pulled to the curb and Neal jumped out. Bill Graham, clipboard in hand, was haranguing the fans to stay against the wall, not block the sidewalk.

Cassady interrupted Bill and asked him if we could use the building to show our movie this coming Monday night. Graham was his usual frantic self and he tried to put Cassady off: "Not now, can't you see I'm too busy to talk. Come back on Monday."

"Monday?" Cassady shook his head.

"Yes, Monday. What's the matter with Monday?"

"I know you'll be here on Monday and I'll be here on Monday," Neal reasoned, "but what about the building?"

It didn't register on Graham. He flapped his arms, yelled at Neal that he couldn't talk now, ran over and pushed a kid against the building. I grabbed Neal.

"Forget it."

We drove on.

Cassady said, "Can't forget it, nor forget the time I was walking down the sidewalk in front of Bill Graham's house. He was on the steps talking to some people, saw me coming, ran down and knelt in front of a car parked at the curb. When I got next to the car I said, 'Oh look, there's Bill Graham down on his knees checking the tires to see if a dime got stuck in the tread,' and you can count on him not forgetting about that, either."

Kesey laughed. "That's Neal, going wrong this curve, set up for that."

L ee Quarnstrom's house in Zayante—a redwood canyon in the mountains near Santa Cruz—was a nondescript frame building, sad unwatered bushes in front, a cracked concrete walk to the porch, sagging couch along one side, front door with triangular windows.

Inside, a hallway with coats and sweaters and hats hanging from hooks, a large living room dominated by a regulation-size pool table lit by an overhead light.

A parrot on a perch in the corner of the room squawked: "*Biscuits for peace! Biscuits for peace!*"

"That's Captain Crank," Lee Quarnstrom said, welcoming us in. "He never shuts up, but his vocabulary is limited to one one-liner."

Lee was tall and slender with a droopy mustache. He had a babble of monkeys that lived in a greenhouse next to the living room, and their constant chatter and shrieks were a background discombobulation to the shrieks of the parrot. Lee's wife, Space Daisy, standing in the corner of the room, waved to Kesey and me.

The front door burst open and Cassady walked in talking and gesticulating. He gave us a surprised look, not expecting to see Kesey and me at Lee's house.

I rolled the cue ball across the long green and asked Neal, "Care for a game?"

"You know my nature, Ken, never one to turn down a sporting challenge. Gives me a chance to test your mettle, Ken, see what kind of metal you're made of. A steely feller, or lead in your pants. What shall we play?"

"How about rotation?"

"My thought exactly. Numerical sequence, lined up in conjunction with the planets, with the added degree of difficulty of dropping the balls in successive pockets, clockwise. Who's to break?"

"Flip you for it." I dug a quarter out of my pocket. "Call it, Neal."

"By its name, then, would any predicted action be known by any other than that which describes it perfectly? In this case it would be heads, since tails would imply furtively slinking away from the game."

I flipped the quarter and let it fall on the table.

Neal leaned in to look.

"I knew it, I felt it all the way from my head to my toes, all the way to the very bottom. Rack 'em up."

Lee and Kesey disappeared into the kitchen to drum up some chow, leaving us to the game with Space Daisy to spectate.

Cassady aimed in on the cue ball, pulled the stick as far back as he could and shot it forward. Solids and stripes flew in all directions. The twelve ball hung on the lip of a side pocket and tipped in.

Neal slapped his stick on the side of the table.

"Since we're playing rotation, it was the one ball that was supposed to fall, not the twelve, and that would have started me in the correct numerical sequence, but a ball laid is a ball played—so go at it, Ken."

He turned to Space Daisy and began chatting her up. The balls were nicely scattered on the table and I dropped the one and the two before I missed.

"Back in a mo'," Cassady said to Space Daisy, then quickly sank the three and four balls before missing. I sank the five. He missed on the six. I ran the table through to the nine ball and was lining up to shoot the ten when Neal said, "You didn't put that nine ball in the corner pocket like you called it, Ken."

I could have said, "If you'd been paying more attention to the game and less attention to Space Daisy, you'd have seen me make the shot." Instead, I tapped the pocket and said, "I laid it in there just like I said I would."

"You put the nine ball in the wrong pocket," he said. "I know it. You know how I know?"

He turned to Space Daisy.

"Babbs lies."

My body went cold as if somebody had opened the door. Talk about a pregnant silence. This was like a ten-month-term baby about to burst the walls of the womb. I hunched over the table, poised for the next shot, eyeing Cassady along the pool cue. The monkeys were quiet, the parrot watched through one bright eye. Cassady waggled his finger at me.

"One time when we were on the bus trip," he told Space Daisy, "I was standing in line behind Mister Babbs at a ratburger joint and when it was his turn to pay, he told the cashier he had bought ten burgers when I knew for a fact he had ordered and received, not ten, but"—he pounded the tip of his cue stick on the floor for emphasis—"*twenty*. I was behind him in line and heard every word."

I relaxed. Cassady hadn't seen me shoot at all. He based his assumption on an outdated but unfortunately true dishonesty on my part. I shook my head.

"You're not so purely snow-driven yourself," I said. "How about the time the cop stopped you and asked if you were on anything and when you were your usual, evasive self, he told you to empty your pocket and you pulled your pocket inside-out, concealing the bennies in your hand and showing the pocket empty while, with your other hand, you grabbed your nose and blew snot out and flung the snot onto the cop's spit-shined shoe while apologizing up a storm—then leaned down on your knee and stuck the bennies in the cuff of your pants, while whipping out your hanky and swiping it across the cop's shoe as he retreated as fast as he could before you made everything worse?"

"I never did tell him I was on anything, so you can't say I told a lie," Cassady said smugly. "Now what's your excuse?"

"*Biscuits for peace!*" Captain Crank squawked. "*Biscuits for peace!*"

"Yes," I said. "I was a liar, one of my many character flaws, but after spending time with you, Neal, and picking up on your standards, like you saying, 'Don't spit in the swamp,' I saw the error of my ways and made the necessary changes in my behavior, and thus I do not lie anymore."

"Aaah, pulled that one out of your ass. Keep shooting."

I leaned over the table, rifled the ten ball in and missed the eleven. He shot, missed, and walked over to stand next to Space Daisy.

"Can't concentrate on trivial matters now, m'dear. Not when courageous bounds have been breached and hearts leap toward a greater game."

He glanced at the clock on the wall.

"I have to be in San Jose in exactly fifty-two minutes, so I can't dally. I'll shoot quickly and we'll soon be done."

He was no longer interested in the outcome and let me run the table. Before the fifteen ball dropped, his cue was racked, his coat was on and he was out the door without looking back.

Lee came in, carrying a platter of grilled cheese sandwiches, followed by Kesey with a tureen of soup. They set them on a table butted up against the wall.

"*Biscuits for peace! Biscuits for peace!*" squawked Captain Crank.

"Don't get your feathers in a twist," Lee scolded the bird. "I'll bring you something too."

Gravel hit the outside wall like buckshot.

"Dammit," Lee said. "I told Cassady a thousand times not to spin out when he leaves here. Lot of good it does."

He looked at me.

"You didn't let him throw you when he called you a liar did you?"

"He didn't call me a liar. He said, 'Babbs lies.' You were watching the game. Did I make that shot or not?"

"I don't know. I was watching Cassady kissing Space Daisy."

It shouldn't have mattered but I was rankled, not by what Cassady said, but because of what he believed about me. It was important to me that Cassady didn't think I cheated.

After Kesey and I had been back in Oregon for a few days, Cassady showed with a woman and a couple of guys he was going to drive to San Miguel de Allende, Mexico, along with his new girlfriend, JD, who knew about a house where they could stay. They'd be leaving Oregon soon and Neal wanted them to meet Kesey before they set out.

A couple of days later, after the sun set and the lingering rays were staving off the night, Cassady showed up again, driving an old beater. I was standing alongside the barn, watching. He came up to me and said, "I have to change a flat down at the gas station and it needs a tube and they have one but they want a dollar for it, which I don't have, and they won't take my ten-inch Crescent wrench in trade. Do you know of any wheels around here that still have a tire and tube?"

"Let's look around," I said.

We searched behind the shop but couldn't find anything.

"Looks like you're out of luck," I said.

"No such thing, occurrences happen as preordained, for I follow the teachings of Edgar Cayce, who told the world that by using the force of positive thinking, seemingly disastrous events can be altered to produce better outcomes."

"In that case," I said, "let me follow you down to the gas station and see what we can come up with."

The wheel rim of his car was lying on the ground, the tire next to it, tire irons and tools alongside.

"You see the way everything is laid out," Cassady said. "No hard angles, mostly curves, a few straight lines, it should indicate a completion in the works."

"I agree."

I reached in my pocket and pulled out all the change I had. Ninety cents, a dime short.

Cassady opened the car door and felt around the seats. He slid his hand in the tight space where the seat was bolted to the floorboard, grimaced, and pushed harder. His eyes lit up.

"Got it." Pulled out a dime. "My boy, the heavens are in alignment again."

He went in the gas station and came out with a tube. Three new patches were stuck to the rubber.

"And I know they will hold," Cassady said. "For I put them on myself."

He inserted the tube in the tire, used the tire iron to force the tire on the rim, rolled the wheel over to the air hose and inflated it. He knocked on the tire with the Crescent wrench.

"Thirty-two-pounds pressure, perfect."

He jacked up the car, took off the spare, replaced it with the one he'd fixed, put the spare in the trunk, gathered the tools, threw them in the trunk and slammed the lid shut.

He rose, wiped his hands with his hanky, and gave me a big smile.

"Captain Babbs, you have once again, relying on your well-honed basketball skills of improvisation, plus your military doggedness, alleviated the shortfall in the material realm. My thanks to you."

We shook hands, he jumped in the car, and started it up. He leaned out the window.

"You know, Ken, I think you made that pool shot after all."

"Thanks, Neal, that means a lot to me."

He gave me a wink, hit the gas and roared off, red taillights vanishing in the night.

A month later Ramrod called and told Kesey that Cassady had died in Mexico.

Cassady and JD had been at a party in San Miguel de Allende, and it was getting late. He'd been drinking, which he rarely did, took a couple of downers and was bullshitting with four other guys. One of them proposed they go out on the railroad track and count the number of ties between here and the next town. Neal was all for it but the others were jacking him around and didn't follow through. Neal was disgusted—agree to do something and then not do it?—and struck out on his own—bareheaded, short-sleeved shirt, thin windbreaker, chino trousers, worn-out leather shoes—into a cold, misty night, water dripping off the trees and bushes.

They found him at dawn, lying on the tracks, a half-mile from the party. They tried to rouse him but could only get a slight quiver from his body.

"His lips are moving," one of the guys said.

They bent in close.

"Sixty-four-thousand-nine-hundred-and-twenty-eight," Cassady murmured.

"What was that all about?" the guy said.

"He did it," another answered. "Counted the railroad ties to the next town and back to here."

"Shee-it, what a thing. A number. Hardly what you'd call famous last words."

"Don't put your mouth on it. None of us had his nerve."

Neal died four days short of his forty-second birthday.

K esey and I mentally kicked ourselves in the ass when we heard. Not about his last words, but that we weren't with him when the challenge went down, how we'd have gone on the tracks with him, wouldn't have left him on his own.

Kesey shook his head, set his mouth in a grim line, went in the house and upstairs to his office and didn't come down until the next day. He and Cassady had a special relationship. Both with brilliant minds. Kesey was the chief who laid out the plans and assigned the roles to be played. Cassady was the working-man star, who used his voice and stories to lift us into higher realms of thought. Together, they kept the varied personalities of the Pranksters pointed in the right direction; potholes to be avoided, mental spinoffs corralled, kept the whole furshlugginer package lurching forward.

Kesey received a phone call from San Francisco a few days later. Somebody he didn't know. The guy had heard about Cassady and wanted to cheer Kesey up.

"Just got the word," he said. "Cassady's spirit is back in the states. Came across the border on the sole of a migrant farm-worker's sneaker."

K esey went to work on his *Jail Journal* in the caretaker's
trailer, cutting up the pages he drew while in the Sheriff's
Honor Camp, gluing them down on large, thick, white cardboard, then adding additional words and drawings.

The Pranksters drifted off to their own places. The commune
thing was over; the farm was now Kesey's home.

At the Black and White Ball in
San Francisco, the roadies had to load
the equipment into the elevator to take
it up to the third floor and I said just drive
the truck into the elevator. The truck broke
the elevator. They had to carry the equipment
up the stairs. Then Owsley took so long
setting up the sound and PA equipment,
the band never played until after midnight
and when people complained, I told them, "The
Grateful Dead is like the tides: they come
and go at their own speed."
  — *Ken Babbs*

48

Gross Materials
Turned into Gold

The new year in 1969 found me working as the warehouse-man for the Grateful Dead in Novato, thirty miles north of San Francisco.

The previous summer I'd bought a Fort Ord Army bus that had been converted into a motor home, replete with all the necessities—best of all, a ceiling high enough I could stand up with a couple of inches to spare, unlike *Further*, a former school bus in which I had to bend halfway over to walk around.

Gretch and I became an item on the bus trip to Madhattan in 1964 and afterwards began living together. Now, she and I and our two little kids lived in the bus in the courtyard of the warehouse, which was fenced-in on all sides: to the rear a child care center; beyond that and on all the other sides, Hamilton Air

Force Base, where fighter jets roared off the runway, hit their afterburners and exploded into the sky.

An office sat in the front of the courtyard. Inside the office, a desk and chair and couch. The landlord, an older, friendly-faced gent in casual dress—leather shoes, comfortable pants, open-collared shirt—came in every week or so to collect rent and check up on the place.

There was a bathroom next to the office and I installed a tub to go along with the sink and toilet. First, I laid down a wooden floor over the concrete. When the landlord saw that he shook his head: "That'll never work."

"Why not?"

"Urine," he said.

I covered the wood with urethane to waterproof it.

The landlord was full of homespun homilies he'd collected over his lifetime as a businessman. His most important lesson—repeated often—"Ken, remember as you climb the ladder of success, there will be many hands holding the ladder for you."

He took a puff on his cigar and pointed it at me.

"There will come a time when you've reached the top of the ladder and, when you start your way down, you'd better be damned sure you didn't step on any of the hands holding that ladder."

A ugustus Owsley Stanley III, the grandson of the Kentucky governor and congressman of the same name, was the sound engineer for the Dead and was at the warehouse every day working on the practice space. He drilled holes in the concrete, laid down a wooden floor on top, and covered the floor with carpet. Theater drapes hung on ropes across the middle of the room, creating a mock stage. The amps and Hammond B-3 organ and drum kits had their places, with monitor speakers in front and stacks of speakers on the sides.

Owsley named the warehouse "Alembic," an ancient, alchemical word meaning a vessel or crucible where gross materials were transformed into gold.

He held court on the second floor in rooms that ran along one side of the building. There was a walkway in front of the rooms and railings where you could stand and watch the band down below.

"We don't practice," Jerry Garcia told a reporter once, but they worked and reworked the songs at the warehouse, changing and reshaping them before and after their public performances.

I was giving the kids a bath in the office bathroom one day when Owsley came in. He stopped short and said, "Oh no, don't ever give them baths."

What now? He was always coming up with some dogmatic cocksurety or other until everyone was sick of hearing it—like, we all had to eat only red meat, because that's what the cavemen ate, and their bodies were pure healthy temples, even though they lived to the ripe old age of twenty-five or so.

"Why not baths?" I asked.

"Sitting in that dirty water after you soap off, that's why. I hated baths and refuse to take them to this day and you shouldn't subject your children to them."

"To each his own," I said and began rinsing the kids off.

"Talking to you is like trying to teach something to a rock," he said and stormed out.

At least I hadn't called him Owsley. He was adamant that his name was now Bear and everyone had to call him by that or get a good tongue-lashing.

I pulled the plug, the water swirled down the drain. I noticed it wasn't all that dirty.

Jerry Garcia was outside waiting for me. Gretch was taking the kids in Jerry's car to Mountain Girl's while Jerry and I drove in my bus to San Francisco for a Grateful Dead photo shoot.

"Aw, rats," Jerry said, climbing aboard. He sat on the box next to the driver's seat. "These photo sessions are a drag. But what you gonna do?"

I eased into the traffic and headed down the 101 for the Golden Gate Bridge.

The Dead's new record, *Aoxomoxoa*, was about to come out and Warner Brothers needed publicity shots. The band had learned by now that this was part of the deal. You did what you wanted to in the studio, but when the fun was done, you had to play their game. I slipped a Van Morrison tape into the deck and concentrated on the road, humming along, when the engine coughed and sputtered and, despite my pumping the gas and pulling the choke handle in and out, the motor quit running. I coasted to the side of the road, got out, and opened the hood to suss the problem.

Jerry stood alongside, peering into the oil-splattered guts. I took the air filter off of the carburetor. A clip holding the choke had come loose. I could get my hand on the clip but couldn't hold the rod and slip the clip in the slot, too.

"Jerry," I said, "reach in here and hold this rod with your finger, will you?"

He didn't say anything or make a move. I turned and looked. He stood holding up his hand, fingers extended, revealing a space where one finger had been cut in half. He shook his head.

"Can't do it man. Can't take a chance on hurting any more fingers."

"Okay, so be it."

I went in the bus and got a screwdriver. By holding it in my teeth, I was able to move the rod in place and stick the clip back on.

I cranked her up, the engine caught with a roar. I eased onto the road and we continued on our way.

The photo session was in the loft of an old warehouse off Harrison Street, the seediest part of San Francisco. Rent was cheap, and a cooperative theatrical company had taken over the warehouse as a practice and storage space. Ten o'clock in the morning, the building was deserted. Climbing the stairs, Jerry said he knew the loft would be deserted, too. When were the guys in the band ever on time?

We wandered around the room. Huge, blown-up posters of the Dead, Jefferson Airplane, Quicksilver, Big Brother, Harlequin, The Sons of Champlin and The Charlatans covered the ten-foot-high walls. Old, saggy, dilapidated couches sat beneath the posters. A huge, eight-foot-in-diameter wooden wire spool served as a table. Jerry looked out the window. He had to wipe the smudge to see into the trash-littered alley, another bleak warehouse directly across.

"This dump could give a timid-hearted fella the creeps," he said.

The door burst open and the rest of the band came in: Bob Weir, Bill Kreutzmann, Mickey Hart, Phil Lesh, Tom Constanten, Ramrod the head roadie. Pigpen brought up the rear, decked out in cowboy garb: boots and jeans, Roy Acuff shirt and grand-champeen belt buckle, Levi's vest, a dozen-gallon hat up top and, strapped to his waist, a cartridge belt and holster weighted down by a .22-caliber Colt Frontier replica six-gun.

"Hi-yah, pards! Le's get this yere shindig a-shootin'," Bob Weir said.

"Yar, its'a r'al shootin' match, ain't it?" Bill the drummer replied.

"You bet your boots," Phil Lesh said. "Those were our marchin' orders—mount up for a shootin' session."

"But whar's that dad-blame shooter?" Mickey Hart asked.

"Right here," Pigpen said, twirling his pistol.

"Put that thing away," Garcia said, "before somebody gets hurt."

"Relax, it ain't loaded."

Garcia shook his head and sat down at the big round table. The rest of us pulled up chairs. Ramrod whipped out his Buck knife and popped it open. We'd all received Buck knives for Christmas. Everybody reached in their pockets for their knives. Ramrod flung his at the table and it stuck in the wood. The rest of us followed, some knives sticking, others clanging on their sides. We laughed and then everybody had the same thought. Seven hands reached for the knives, making sure they got the right one.

The front door of the loft banged open and a scruffy group of men walked in. They eyed us sitting at the table, then collapsed in the couches on the other side of the room. They began talking quietly. Snatches of conversation drifted over: "Bloody hell... C'mon, mate... A farthing says it isn't..."

They were quieted by the door opening. Rock Scully, the Dead's manager, came in, all smiles. He greeted the scruffy newcomers warmly before heading over to the round table, where he was verbally accosted by the troops.

"Whar you been, boy?"

"We gon' be tied up here *all* day?"

"Don' fancy having to wait for no photog!"

"Jest who am those fancy primroses what interruptin' *our* session?"

"Easy, easy, easy." Rock raised his hands in supplication. "The photographer will be right along. Hush your voices, now. Don't you hicks know who *they* are? That's Led Zeppelin."

"Oh my... Why, I declare... Bless mah soul... Aren't we the honored ones... Kiss my stinky finger... What the fuck they doin' here?"

"Not so loud! They'll hear. They're on an American tour and Warner's figured it'd be simpler and cheaper to shoot two sessions at once."

"Not on our time, they ain't... No, we ain't waitin' 'round for *no foreigners...* Where they come up with a crazy name like that anyway?"

"It's a joke, don't you get it?" Garcia says. "Goes over like a lead balloon, er, zeppelin."

"Ho, ho, ho," the others chanted, getting up and conga-lining around the loft, sticking their legs out in time with the *ho, ho, hos.* Garcia lit a cigarette and stared at the dirty window, ignoring them. Pigpen grabbed an overstuffed chair and pulled it around so it faced the center of the room. He piled a bunch of pillows in the chair and ceremoniously paced off twenty steps. He drew his pistol and held it in the air. He turned and aimed.

The report sent feathers flying from the pillows. Garcia jumped.

"Hey, I thought you said that thing wasn't loaded?"

"Who ever heard of carrying an unloaded gun?" Pigpen said. "That's how people get killed."

He fired off another round. Feathers flew and the pillow flopped off the chair.

"Got him, daid center."

"Let me try that," Weir said.

"Come on," Garcia said. "Knock it off."

Stealing looks at the Brits sitting on the couches, gazing calmly at the muzzle flashes, the smoke curling to the ceiling, the guys kept banging away until the door flew open again. The photographer had arrived. Rock Scully immediately got everything organized, making sure the Grateful Dead went first.

When the Dead were done, they left without saying anything to the other band, who were being herded by the photographer into their photo shoot. Jerry and I wandered off to the back corner of the loft which had been walled off to form a separate room.

"Let's see what's in there," Jerry said.

Garcia pushed open a door. A shrill scream erupted. "What the hell?"

A bare bulb swung from the ceiling on a spindly cord, splashing the room with garish light and twisting shadows. Below the light, an old, black, ink-stained printing press dripped spectrums. A bald-headed man wearing thick, rimless glasses, eyes wide as the lenses, cowered behind the press.

"Hey, Chromedome, what the hell you doing up here?" Garcia laughed. "I thought you guys were hiding out over in the Haight."

Before he could answer, the door banged against Garcia, and another man, as skinny and tall as the other was fat, emerged from behind it. His hair lay down his back, stringy and matted. His hands were black with ink. He lifted a shaking finger.

"J-J-Jesus, man, don't ever sneak up like that without a warning. You like to s-s-scared us to d-d-death."

"Sorry, Snake Eye, I had no idea. So this is where you're doing your dirty work now, huh?"

"One s-s-step ahead of the law," Snake Eye said, wiping his brow with a dirty rag. It left a thick smudge. "But," he said proudly, "there she lie, issue number three. Another m-m-masterpiece," he cackled hoarsely.

Garcia picked up a copy.

"You speed freaks," he said. "I know the routine. Four days without sleep, cranking out the hottest item to hit the bookstores since Henry Miller."

They were printing *Zap Comix*. Feelthy, rotten cartoons and comic stories drawn by R. Crumb and the rest of his underground cronies—so blatantly big-dick porny and lopped-heads gruesome, the San Francisco fathers had immediately banned them and ordered the cops to raid every bookstore, making the comics an even hotter number in the subculture.

"No way the cops ever going to stop this," Jerry said. "It's too good. Whang the truth bell and it gonna reverb."

No telling how many times they'd had to move their press, but not to worry, it was just good ol' Jer finding them out.

"Cool it," Garcia said. "Lock the door and we'll never tell anyone we were here. Your secret is safe with us."

"G-G-Gawd, Jer, you're the greatest."

Chromedome scraped forward on his knees and grabbed Garcia's hand. Garcia snatched it away.

"Back off! Back off! Jesus! I'm not your fucking savior."

Jerry pushed past me and fled the room, flailing his hand with his bandana.

He laughed. "They're probably hiding under the printing press again. Might be days before they get up the nerve to come out. Leave it to the band to up the action. They always gotta be putting it on, and I bet those Brits thought it was simply your normal American working day here in the wild, wild West."

He patted his pocket.

"I'll be the first on my block to have the new *Zap*," he said. "This was worth the whole goofy shooting match. Great fun, eh Ken?"

He slapped me on the back. I faked a recoil like I was falling down.

"Hotsa mama," I said, and sang, "*In the meantime, in between time, ain't we got fun?*"

We split from the loft and headed back to the warehouse.

*There's four things you have to do before you can
continue on the path of Enlightenment. First you've
got to give up ambition, yet work like a man that's
ambitious. You've got to kill out desire. You've got
to kill out the need for comfort. And lastly, you have
to remove the wound from your voice. Because the
master will not listen to the wound in your voice.*
— *Ken Kesey*

49

Heathen Camel Dung

The Grateful Dead hired a new manager, a minister of all
things, and he was, by God, gonna elevate these boys to
the su-preme heights.

Dross to gold.

The band was in the warehouse, running through a sassy
R'n'B song. Pigpen sang, Jerry responded on guitar, Phil walked
the beat, Billy brushed the cymbals, Mickey tapped the snare,
Bobby stroked the chords. It was coming together nicely, when
in walks—nay, *strides* their new manager. He deposited his
briefcase at the feet of the band, ending the song with a resounding thud.

He asked me what I was doing there.

"Jes' listening to the dingdong bell of the church of lost consciousness, boss, waiting for Monday morning to come down
and give me a newborn glimpse of reality."

"Oh," he said and turned away, dismissing me.

"It's happening, men," he said. "The very thing needed in
order for you to jump to the higher rung and grasp once and for
all the success you so rightfully crave."

"Can the shit and give us the news," Jerry said. "I can tell it's not going to be good, or you wouldn't be baring your surplice so obvious."

"The new tour schedule is in and, for the most part, it's an easy swing, but there's one leg that's going to be tough. You have to play New York City on a Friday afternoon and Austin, Texas, the next night."

"That's impossible," roadie Rex Jackson hollered.

"No way we can load out and load in that quick," Ramrod said.

"We'd need a miracle," Bobby said.

"It'll never happen," Billy said.

"You a flat-out numbskull," Pigpen said. He drew his .22-caliber six-shooter from its holster, held it up, and spun the cylinder.

The manager blanched.

"Boys, the lord will give you strength."

"Strength we have. What about sleep?" Phil asked.

"You'll have to make do. This was the only way I could set these shows up. Don't forget you hired me just for this purpose."

"Yeah, but not to kill us," Jerry said, and they sang together:
"Holy moly, where is the door?
Why am I crawling on the floor..."

"Sorry, boys," he interrupted, "the contracts are signed. Either make these dates or you'll never play another hall on this planet. I'll help you every way I can."

"You gonna lug that equipment?" Jackson said.

"You gonna play your ass off on these gigs?" Phil said.

"No, my job is to stay home, scheduling you even deeper into the ecstasy of success, and with the blessing of the lord to support you..."

"Take that lord shit and shove it," Billy said, hitting the bass drum for emphasis.

"I wanna hear you sing some gospel," Pigpen said, "about

how you gonna make us rich and all."

"You know I can't sing, I can't dance, I can't play an instrument, but I am one lord-lovey businessman."

"Alright, alright," Jerry said. "You're gonna help us any way you can, right?"

"Of course I will."

"Then get us some speed."

"Speed?" he sputtered, wringing his hands. "*Speed?*"

"Yeah, and not just any no-good kitchen shit, either."

"But I know nothing of such matters."

"Time to learn," Jerry said. "I want some obetrol. Yeah, it's gotta be obetrol, simple as that."

"I'm a man of the cloth, I can't stoop to such..."

"Do what you have to do," roadie Rex Jackson interrupted. "I'm with Jerry."

"Me too," Ramrod said. "Get enough for us all."

"I'll take one small hit," Bobby said, "but you have to score or your name isn't Reverend."

"It's camel dung," Billy said.

"Heathen camel dung at that," Phil said. "You'll be so low that snail shit on the bottom of the ocean is gonna look like shooting stars to you."

"*In the sky*," Pigpen sang.

"Boys, boys, stop it. You're not being fair. I've been working 'round the clock to put thy house in order and it's a mess, a real mess, and what do I get in return? Opprobrium at every juncture. Why are you treating me this way?"

"Because it's your birthday," Mickey Hart said, and the band laid into a rollicking version of the old song as Bill Kreutzmann brought forth a cake, brimming with burning candles. Up in the loft, the angelic voices of the golden-tressed backup singers joined in,

"*Happy birthday to you, happy birthday to you!*"

W e polished off the cake and the ministerial manager left, still disgruntled. The roadies began breaking down the equipment and moving it outside into a chartered bus that was taking the Dead to Fresno for a concert. I was going along but didn't want to be just a spectator, so I had put together an audio-visual rig stacked on a handcart: at the bottom an amplifier, above it a microphone with its cord plugged into a mixer. I duct-taped a long metal pole to one arm of the handcart and stuck a clamp-on electric light on top. A long extension cord hung on a hook on the back of the cart.

We arrived in Fresno an hour ahead of the gig and the roadies started hauling the gear into the hall. It was a small auditorium with a large wooden dance floor and a stage set back into one wall.

People were already filtering in and I got to work assembling my multimedia cart. Once everything was in place, I unrolled the long extension cord and plugged it into a wall outlet. Turned everything on, tested the microphone, set the sound at a good level, and then broke out the Polaroid camera I'd brought along with three eight-packs of film. I set the camera on flash. With that and the light on top of the pole, I'd have plenty of lumens for good pics.

The audience, dressed in tie-dye and brightly colored outfits, wandered the room. I decided to get to work. With the light on top of the pole guiding my way, I pushed my handcart through the crowd.

"Say," I said into the microphone, amplified voice causing people to turn and look, "there's a fine-looking gent in his paisley suit and Bullwinkle-size bow tie. Howsabout I take your picture and give it to you for your scrapbook?"

He grinned and nodded. I aimed in with the Polaroid, the flash went off, and the picture popped out of the side of the camera.

"Here you go, bro," I said, handing the photo. "Don't touch

the surface, and the image will start to appear. Make sure it's dry, then you can put it in your pocket or paste it to your forehead or whatever else your creative mind can conjure."

I trundled past him and went on, stopping to snap pictures and talk. I circled around in front of the stage. A familiar form was crouched on the front edge, his head poking into the back of one of the speakers.

"Look there's Owsley," I said, voice blaring out, "jiggling and giggling wires and poking and probing cosmic connectors trying to find a wholesome meeting of mind-melding hearts."

He turned, eyeglasses glinting as he glared into the flash of the Polaroid capturing his pissed-off visage.

I pocketed the picture and continued the rounds of the dance floor. The sound system came on and the Dead began to play. Everyone surged to the stage and I made for the fringes, studying the pic I took of Owsley, waiting for it to develop, when my light went out and my sound system died. I parked the cart and, using my flashlight, looked around for the problem. No power going into the equipment. Had to be the extension cord, probably unplugged, tangled in someone's foot.

I followed the cord to the wall. It was still plugged in. I pulled out the plug and looked at it, used the screwdriver blade on my pocketknife to pull back the insulator protecting the wires. Everything seemed okay, but I went in deeper and unscrewed the wires and found one of them cut, inside, where a cursory look couldn't see. I looked up on the stage. I didn't see Owsley, probably busy backstage, but I knew it was him. He didn't like anyone pointing him out, putting the spotlight on him. He tried to stay incognito. I fixed the plug and went back to my ditzing around, but I was bummed. What the hell was I doing at these Grateful Dead concerts making a fool out of myself when I could just as easily be doing it on my own without anyone cutting me off?

O n the way to the bus after the concert, Owsley came up and grudgingly gave me credit for finding the break in the power cord. I let it slide. He didn't think I had it in me, thought I had no prowess putting together electronic sound systems and keeping them working, even though I'd been doing it with Kesey for years before he ever came on the scene. Plus, being an old Marine, used to building whole camps from scratch, I knew what it took to make things work.

I felt pretty morose on the way back to the warehouse. I just wasn't cut out for the world of rock 'n' roll. I decided to retire from my job as warehouseman and head back to Oregon, see what I could drum up there.

There is no plan that includes all people,
there is only you in front of me and what
I can do to help you out. Kesey talked
to every homeless and down-and-out bum
just like he was talking to the president.
This is what America is all about,
you never want to give up that freedom.
   — Ken Babbs

50

Sea of Tranquility

T he kid walked in just as everything was up and running.
He stood and waited, fifteen years old, bright red hair,
ripped jeans, sneakers with laces untied, tie-dyed T-shirt, worried look on his face.

"Look what the marmoset dragged in," Kesey said. "Where'd
you come from?"

He looked around nervously.

"Uh, my mom dropped me off, said Kesey would take me in
for the summer."

"Oh, your mom? And who would that be?"

"Lou Ann Olsen. She said you'd remember her, that you told
her to come by the farm and bring your boy."

Kesey gave him a puzzled look.

"Not that I doubt you, but why didn't Lou Ann come in with
you?"

"She and her new boyfriend are going to a lake somewhere
in Washington and she said they didn't have time to stop and
visit."

Kesey stuck out his hand.

"I'm Kesey and these are my pals: Babbs, in the white shirt

and pants; George Walker, wearing his trademark multicolored pants and shirt; Hassler, the only normal-looking one of the bunch, in jeans and brown T-shirt; Mike Hagen, with the long-sleeved cowboy shirt."

We were standing and sitting, facing a long table that held a big TV, two reel-to-reel tape recorders, a microphone mixer, a sound effects machine, an amplifier, and a large speaker at each end of the table. Both tape recorders were running, one playing music, the other recording sound from the TV, the input from my microphone and another microphone on a stand to my left, plus one in front of each speaker so we could crisscross the sound in stereo, creating a figure-eight feedback loop.

"What's your name?" Kesey asked the kid.

"Jake."

"Well, Jake, grab a spot. Control Center is up and running. There's a table with glop in the back of the room; help yourself if you're hungry."

Kesey turned to me.

"Ready to rock and roll?"

I gave him the a-okay and turned up the sound.

"*Buzz Aldrin is erecting the photo window screen now,*" TV announcer Walter Cronkite said.

"*When I step back a little bit from the landing module,*" Aldrin said, "*I can see exactly what the pictures on the camera show. The module's outer surfaces of foil. It looks like it's close to the surface of the moon when in fact it really isn't.*"

"*You're standing in a soft spot where we see footprints nearly an inch deep,*" Houston said.

"*Those footprints will be there for an awfully long time,*" Walter Cronkite said.

"No shit," Hassler said. "I hope we check on that in a few hundred or thousand years."

"They'll be covered over with a gazillion other footprints by then," George said.

"Houston, Houston, this is Barn Control," I said, "there is some conflict over when the footprints will be obliterated. Ah, crap, why don't they answer?"

"Your space link is breaking down," Kesey said. "Here, have a toke on this. It will cool your frying synapses from the effect of the acid."

Jake shook his head. *Acid? This could get crazy.*

"*I believe they're setting up the flag now,*" Houston said. "*I bet they're the only persons alive who don't have TV coverage of the feat.*"

"*How does it look on TV,*" Michael Collins said from inside *Eagle*, the landing module.

"*They've got the stars and stripes up now, Mike, and you can see it from the window inside the module,*" said Walter Cronkite.

"You going to stand at attention and salute?" George Walker asked me.

"Right on," I said. "Upside down with the peace sign to the forehead."

"The Stars and Stripes Forever" blared from the speakers in the barn. Jake the Red put his fingers in his ears; this was louder than the Grateful Dead in Winterland.

"*There was talk about putting little flags of all the countries on the pole, but Congress said no,*" Walter Cronkite said. "*It's an American flight and we want the American flag and that's all. They do have the flags of a hundred and twenty other countries in the Eagle. They are returning them to earth and giving them to the other countries.*"

"Yes," Hassler said. "Generosity, one of our country's greatest attributes."

"As witnessed by us watching for free on TV," George said.

"Except for the ads," Kesey said, "which we can mute and play our own music."

"Right on," I said.

Buzz Aldrin was out on the surface walking around.

"*You do have to be careful of where your center of mass is,*" Houston said. "*You have to take two or three paces to make sure you have your feet underneath you.*"

"Oh, is that where they are, Houston?" Hassler said. "I was thinking I had to stand on my head to get a good look at them."

"*Like a football player, you can step out to the side and cut a little bit,*" Houston said.

"*He is like a football player in that outfit,*" Walter Cronkite said.

"Not to mention *touchdown* a while back," Kesey said. "More of the all-American analogy of this mission."

"*Do you believe what you're seeing, David?*" Walter Cronkite asked.

"*Even though I know I'm seeing it, I don't believe it,*" David Brinkley said. "*It's off the charts.*"

"I hope it doesn't give rise to a conspiracy theory that this is all happening in a movie studio in Hollywood," Hassler said.

"It's happening right here in Kesey's barn," I said. "We're conspiring to make it into a musical play."

"*I don't suppose it's necessary to say so,*" Walter Cronkite said, "*but this is not just for fun. They are supposed to be bouncing around like this, walk this way, that way, turn left, turn right.*"

"Hup two—hup two—keep in step, men—chest out—stomach in—you're in front of the reviewing stand now," Hassler barked, dredging up his military background.

"*Neil and Buzz,*" Houston said. "*The president of the United States is in his office now and would like to say a few words to you.*"

"*That would be an honor,*" Neil Armstrong said.

"*Go ahead, Mister President. This is Houston, out.*"

"*Neil and Buzz, I'm talking to you by telephone from the Oval Room at the White House, and this certainly has to be the most historic telephone call ever made. I can't tell you how proud we all are of what you've accomplished. For every American, this has to be the proudest day of our life. And for people all over the world, I am sure they join too with us, emphasizing what an immense feat this is. Because what you have done, the heavens have become a part of man's world. And as you talk to us from the Sea of Tranquility, it inspires us to redouble our efforts to bring peace and tranquility to earth. For one priceless moment in the whole history of man, all the people of this earth are truly one. One in their pride in which you have done. And one in our prayers that you will return safely to earth."*

"Hey Jude" rose out of the speakers in the barn, joining with the voices from the TV.

"*Thank you, Mister President,*" Neil Armstrong said.

"*It's an honor for us to be able to participate here today,*" Buzz Aldrin said.

"*Thank you very much,*" President Nixon said, "*and I look forward—all of us look forward—to seeing you on the* Hornet *on Thursday.*"

"Yes, yes," Hassler cried, "we are all looking forward, onward and upward, the moon today, the stars tomorrow..."

"With just a tad more of that LSD," George interrupted.

Say it isn't so, thought Jake the Red, *how much further will they go?*

"As above, so below, Mister President," I said.

Jake peered closer at the TV. *What was that astronaut doing now out there on the moon?* Bending down and reaching out with something in his hand.

"*Neil Armstrong has the scoop for the bulk sample collecting,*" Walter Cronkite said.

Moon dirt. Jake shook his head, not knowing little baggies of the stuff would be worth big money back on earth, were the baggies ever to get out of the hands of the scientists.

"*These are destined to become the most closely studied objects, I suppose, in history,*" Walter Cronkite said.

"The Shroud of Turin now falling into second place," Kesey

said.

"*I believe the hundred and forty scientists scattered all over the world are extremely eager to get even a tiny portion of it for their study.*"

"*I don't know what color to describe it,*" Neil Armstrong said, "*other than an ash cocoa color. It appears to be covering most of the upper part of my boot, tiny particles...*"

"*This is Houston. Neil, you are cutting out at the end of your transmissions. Can you speak a little more closely into your microphone? Over.*"

"*Roger. I had it inside my mouth.*"

"Eating the microphone?" George said. "Do you get a medal for that?"

"*Sounded a little wet,*" Houston said.

"Ah, sweet badinage," I said. "How totally American. Team palaver in even the most trying of situations."

"*Neil's been on the surface an hour now,*" Walter Cronkite said. "*Even on the television it's interesting to see how black the astronaut looks when he is in the shadow, because there is no air to diffuse the light, so in the shadow, even though there is sunlight all around, it's pitch black.*"

"Whoa," Hassler said, "perspicacious analysis by our astute commentator."

He looked at me.

"See, I know big words too."

"We are all college grads here, Hassler," I said. "Big words are the norm, even if you did get your degree from Way Below Normal U."

"I went to the School of Hard Knocks, myself," Mike Hagen said, "and they never used any big words there."

"Is that why your head is so lumpy?" George said.

"*Heart rates of both crewmen are averaging between ninety and one hundred,*" Walter Cronkite said. "*Flight surgeon's report: they're right on the predicted number of the BTU expended in the energy of work, and he thinks they are in great shape."*

"*I look around,*" Neil Armstrong said, "*the contrast in general is completely by virtue of the shadows very light colored gray with a halo around my own shadow and around the shadow around my helmet as I look across the surface, the contrast of the strongest tendency of surrounding colors still fairly light, the larger amount of shadowed area looking toward us, considerably darker in texture where we've walked, footprints in the terrain of this surface vale, a darker contrast rather than color.*"

Jake the Red shook his head. Incomprehensible. *Were those guys on the moon tripping too, or weren't they getting enough oxygen?*

"I knew it," Hassler said, "Neil Armstrong's a poet, extreme free form."

"Just what you'd expect free of earth's gravity," George said.

"That's it," I said. "One-sixth of our gravity, so mundane earth descriptions are lighter weight, floating into unbefore-reached regions of the mind."

"Dull, plodding, mush-mouthed, hackneyed layers burp, bubbles erupt, and pop-colored icicles melt hogwash into pure liquid words," Kesey said.

Jake the redhead shook his head. *I knew it, they're all crazy here.*

"*Neil is filling the bulk sample bag attached to a scale,*" Walter Cronkite said. "*As seen in the picture. Buzz is behind the LEM, at the minus-Z strut.*"

"And Kesey is groping around behind the recording and playback array, fucking with the sound effects mixture," Hassler said.

"*That's the landing directly opposite the ladder,*" Walter Cronkite said.

"The toilet door is right next to the steps going up into the loft of the barn," Mike Hagen said.

"*I'm now in the area of the minus-Y strut,*" Buzz Aldrin said.

"Kesey is about to stab the sound array table with a screw-driver," Hassler said.

"*Buzz is making his way around the LEM, photographing it from various angles,*" Walter Cronkite said, "*looking at its conditions from all sides.*"

"*Yas,* thank you," I pontificated. "Thank you, Houston and moon people and TV commentators and worldwide watchers in awe and heightened awarenesses from penthouses to railroad shacks to the bus barn on the Kesey farm raising the awareness to even greater heights of enjoyment and creativity recorded on the reel-to-reel for generations to come, carried into the future by our unexpected guest, Jake the Red."

Jake shook his head. He was having none of it.

Sparks flew and smoke rose from the delay and reverb effects box.

"*WAA, WAA, WAA,*" I cried. "Fire! All hands to emergency stations."

George ran for the fire extinguisher.

"Dirty, weasel-snot, beetle-brain, mudder-jumping, piece of burnt-toast shit," Kesey said, swatting at the smoke. He jumped back as a bolt of blue flame shot out of the effects box.

"Should I call 911?" Hassler shouted.

"Too soon, too soon," I answered. "Give it a shot, George."

George squeezed the handle and a burst of foam blanketed the mixer. There was a hissing and a sad moan and the flame went out.

"*WAA, WAA, WAA,*" I yelled. "Secure emergency stations. I repeat, secure emergency stations."

"*The surgeon says everything looks fine,*" Walter Cronkite says.

"Yeah, but what does he say about the effects box?" Mike Hagen said.

"Toasted," Kesey said.

"*Neil Armstrong has been on the life support system for two hours now,"* Walter Cronkite said.

"Ah, poor guy," Hassler said. "Let's hope they don't pull the plug on him."

"Not as long as he's breathing," I said. "Where there's breath, there's life..."

"And where there's life, there's hope," Kesey interrupted. "And we better hope this show ends pretty quick because we're about to run out of tape."

"*The panorama is complete,*" Houston said.

"*I'm not having too much success, juggling these PSE experiments,*" Buzz Aldrin said.

"*Just dump them in the slot on the LEM,*" Houston said.

"And hightail it out of Dodge," Kesey said.

"*They are installed, the bubble is level and the alignment appears to be good,*" Buzz Aldrin said.

"Oh, oh, that's it," Hassler said.

The tape came to the end and flipped around and around on the reel-to-reel recorder. A shrill ringing caught everyone's attention.

"What's that? Emergency, emergency!" Hassler cried.

"It's the phone, for Christ's sake," said Jake the Red.

He walked over and lifted the receiver; listened, and held it out: "It's for you, Babbs."

"Hello. Yeah, it's me. Hi, Stan. Uh huh. Sounds good. Sure. No sweat. Okay, see you there."

I hung up.

"That was Stan Goldstein, calling from the Hog Farm," I said. "Pack your bags. We're going to Woodstock."

Hitchhikers, bus riders, longhairs on foot,
Dust rises from the road, cars stalled on the edge,
A large meadow beckons, the word is out.
Music all day, party all night,
A three-day celebration, dawning of the light.
　— *Joni Mitchell*

51

Journal to Woodstock Nation

The cock crowed and the chicken cackled, "An egg, an egg." John John the white horse nickered in the pasture. Bam the Ram waited for someone to bend over for a butt to the butt. Stewart the dog roamed with a rock in his mouth, imploring someone to throw it. The cows buried their muzzles in the grass. The smell of hot coffee and pancakes on the griddle wafted from the open window of the cookhouse. Inside, the group self-named the Farmsters wolfed down flapjacks and guzzled coffee. The sun edged higher, promising another hot clear day.

In the grassy area behind the cookhouse, three decrepit buses lined up facing the driveway. Little kids, some in diapers, ran in and out. Hassler, hair tousled from wrestling with a pillow all night, and Dale Kesey, eyes hidden by a ball cap, stood in front of the buses. Dale chewed on a blade of grass. Hassler whipped dental floss in and out between his teeth.

"This is just like Ken," Dale said. "Takes off in *Further* just when we're needing to get the bus ready for the trip."

"He said he'd be right back," Hassler said.

"I'm about ready to call a prayer meeting," Dale said, "get some help bringing him back."

"Roust out your fiddle and play him in. You know he's just fiddling around over there. This show is ready to hit the road."

The show had been solidified the night before at a meeting when everyone who was going along signed on in the logbook. Stan Goldstein, a main man in the Hog Farm, had wired me $1,650, which I changed into one-dollar bills and afterwards made the first purchases: a logbook and a briefcase to hold the log and the loot.

Kesey decided he wouldn't go to Woodstock and, at first, wasn't going to let his bus, *Further*, make the trip either. But when he found out David Butkovich would take charge and drive and maintain the old gal, Kesey gave the go ahead. Then, while everyone else was making the final preparations to leave for Woodstock, Kesey took the bus on a trip to the coast.

"He comes, he comes," David Butkovich said.

The bus lumbered in and pulled to a stop. The door opened and Maria got out, frazzled and irritated. She shook her head, no questions, and went into the barn.

Everyone gathered, eyes wide, gasps, stunned silence as a man who seemed to have taken a bad beating emerged from the bus. Hair full of briars, face covered with dried blood and criss-crossed with scratches. Shirt and pants in torn rags, arms and legs a mess. Shoeless. He licked his lips. I stepped forward with a cup of coffee in one hand and a pint of rye whiskey in the other.

"Looks like you could use a pick me up," I said, topping the coffee with a generous hit of rye.

Kesey swigged it down and wiped his mouth, leaving a bloody smear across his lips.

"Balm of the beast, I mean breast," Kesey said. "What's that sound?"

I looked around. *Sound? What sound?*

"Hot water filling the tub," Kesey said.

He handed me the cup and shuffled toward the barn.

"Wait a minute. What happened?" Dale Kesey yelled.

Kesey waved his hand and kept walking.

"We picked up Billy T," Kesey said, after he was cleaned up, still black-and-blue, covered with scabbed-over scratches, nose red and puffy. "For those of you who don't know him, he's the Black guy standing in the back there, a drumming speeder. For a cheap natural tweak, he filled double-aught capsules with cayenne pepper and dropped them with a cup of coffee in the morning. Thought he invented it. I told him we were doing that on Perry Lane in 1958. Billy T got on the bus in Florence and guided us out of town down a trail to the edge of the dunes where we parked and walked to the ocean. When the sun went down, we hiked back to the bus and found four bikers sprawled on the ground. We started a fire and ate weenies and beanies and drank beer with them until one of the bikers began putting the make on Maria and wouldn't back off, and you know Maria, she tried to cool him by talking soft and friendly but it just made him more aggressive, so I had to put my mouth on it and that aggravated the situation to the point where we began wrassling. I put my moves on him, pinned him to the ground, then one of the other bikers whaled on me from behind and next thing all five of us were into it, rolling around in the blackberries until Billy T leaned over us with a bottle of booze in one hand and a bottle of pills in the other and said, 'Lay off, mother-fuckers. I've got Tequila and quaaludes.'

"He popped the lid with his thumb, threw down a pill, opened the Tequila with his teeth and took a slug. The bikers untangled, let me up and we sat around the fire drinking and toking and dropping pills until the wee hours when we dropped off until this morning, when, with the bikers sprawled unconscious in the sand, we slunk away and headed for home."

Kesey headed to the barn for a nap. Everybody split up and turned to. Plan was we'd leave the next day, July 29th. Hassler and George Walker told me they'd decided not to go. Then Hagen took me aside and said Kesey told him that tonight he was going to snatch *Further* and, with an all-male crew, meet Hagen at Sutro's Tunnel in Nevada. Leaving me to stew on that, Hagen split for San Francisco with the 16 mm camera to buy film and supplies.

Four buses were in the final stages of preparation for blastoff: My bus, *Fort Home*, with Gretch and the little feller, Simon, a toddler, and his older sister, Casa, age three; Dale and Diane—she called herself Tillie—in the *Brown Hound*, also known as the *Double D* bus, with their three kids, Nathan, Kerry and Captain Eon; Keith Haxby's bus, the *Hitchhiker*, full of men and women who showed up at the farm and signed on for the trip; and Kesey's bus, *Further*, crew still not assigned, although David Butkovich was in charge, with Roy Sebern as his assistant.

I was writing in the logbook when Ramrod showed up, just in from San Francisco. He said he'd be going with us and catch up with the Grateful Dead in Woodstock, where he'd return to work as their equipment manager. Now he wanted to spend some time with his wife, Patty Cake, and their son, Strider, who were passengers on *Further*.

Ramrod handed me a couple of slips of paper, cut out of a newspaper and magazine.

"These are from Garcia," he said.

"Perfect," I said, "Just like from the book, *Message from Garcia*."

"Believe that's *Message to Garcia*," Ramrod said.

"Still works."

I glued the newspaper clippings into the logbook, first: *The young cavalrymen left Fort Leavenworth as raw recruits; they returned as seasoned veterans of Indian strategy and tactics.*

Then the other from a congressman's speech: *As I see it, Ladies and Gentlemen, finding answers to our present day problems is just as much our responsibility as it is the government's and if we are going to win this battle, we must provide the leadership that these times require. It is up to us and our counterparts, all across the land, to make the real voice of America heard. I say it is time for all of us to stand up and be counted.*

"We are doing that," I said, and wrote Ramrod's name in the logbook.

The *Bam Truck* roared in, back end full of foodstuffs we unloaded on the concrete pad next to the cookhouse: 100-pound sacks of brown rice, oat groats, brown sugar, dry milk and whole wheat flour. Sacks and jars and cans of salt, pepper, tea bags, cottonseed oil, peanut butter, raisins, kitchen matches, toilet paper, buckwheat pancake mix and tomato sauce.

Dale, working on *Double D*, cursed like a Christian each time he dropped a wrench: "This goldurn, mother-forsaking gasket needs a sealant if there's any chance in heaven of stopping that oil leak."

Having finished tuning up the engine on *Hitchhiker*, Keith Haxby muscled a refrigerator through the door.

Paul Sawyer, the Unitarian minister we met in California when we held an Acid Test at his church, drove in with his girlfriend, little Carole. They had driven hard to get to the farm before the caravan took off. A welcome addition, for they would drive the shuttle car, a necessity in a venture like this, as buses were inevitably going to break down and need someone to go for needed parts.

By nightfall, food and bedding and clothing were stored aboard the buses. We sat around a bonfire, played music, sang, groused about things left undone, then accepted the fact we had done as much as we could in the short time we had to get ready. With Dale bestowing blessings all over the place, we called it quits for the night; no big issues to settle. We'd deal with unexpected things as they happened.

I n the middle of the night when all was quiet, Kesey and Page Browning headed for the buses, intending to steal *Further* and drive it to Woodstock. The inside of the bus was lit up, full of women: Jeannie Whitman (aka Gas Girl), Maria, Erica and Patty Cake. They were folding clothes and making up beds, talking and laughing quietly, not wanting to wake up Patty Cake's baby, Strider, asleep in a crib.

"Jesus Christ," Page said, "I've never seen such a..."

"Shush," Kesey said softly. "Don't let them hear us, we'll be swamped with femininity."

"What's going on, men?" David Butkovich asked, appearing out of the gloom.

"Shhhh," Kesey said. "You want to tip the applecart?"

"What applecart?"

"The bus. Can't you see what's happening?"

"Well, yeah, sort of."

"Let's get back behind the cookhouse," Page said, "out of their line of fire."

"So, what's going on?" Butko said.

Kesey ran his hand over the top of his head. "We were going to grab the bus, beat it out of here, man it with men and go our own way to Woodstock. That's out of the question now, the way the bus is packed with women and kids."

Butko chuckled. "Impossible to roust them out, I can grok it. Now what?"

"Page and I slink back into our hidey-holes and pretend this never happened."

"Not a very satisfying outcome," Page said.

"It's up to you now, Butko," Kesey said.

"Me? What's up to me?"

"To take charge of that flock of hens and get them and the bus safely to Woodstock and back."

"Just call me the rooster," Butko said.

"Cock-a-doodle-doo," Page said.

"Good luck," Kesey said and put out his hand.

Butko shook his and then Page's.

"Use the farm as Info Central," Kesey said. "Let us know if

anything's needed and how things are going."

Butko nodded. Kesey and Page walked away into the darkness.

After they left, Billy T stole in out of the night, crawled up on the platform on the back of the bus and lay down on his bedroll.

B lastoff was at noon on July 29th, the day hot and clear. We made it to Bend by suppertime for sandwiches, then drove on into flat sagebrush country, where we parked alongside the road and spent the night.

That first day we covered 160 miles and spent $367. At that rate it would take us twenty days to get to Woodstock and cost $7,340. By then the festival would be over.

"Seems," David Butkovich said, "we might tighten this operation up."

Hot, hard driving the next day, from Burns, Oregon, to Idaho to swim in the Snake River, eat supper in a park in Boise, and drive to Mountain Home, where I led the caravan into a cul-de-sac where we parked. In the morning we had to back out, inspiring Butko to award me a "HAVE BUS WILL DEBACLE" card.

Word came from Info Central at the farm: Hagen was still in San Francisco gathering camera equipment. He will make a speed run to meet us en route or in New York State.

Before we hit the road again, I called everyone together and told them, "Just so we don't lose touch with one another, keep an eye on the bus behind you and if it's in trouble and needs to stop, the driver will flash his lights and the bus in front will pull over and we'll all stop and find out what's going on."

That plan lasted until the late afternoon when we noticed *Hitchhiker* had disappeared. A side road pointed to a campground on the Snake River. *Further* and the *Brown Hound* went there to wait. I parked *Fort Home* on the side of the highway to stand watch while Paul Sawyer and Maria and Carole drove back in the shuttle car to look for Keith and his bus.

Paul returned a while later to say *Hitchhiker* had broken down and was being towed back to Rigby, Idaho. We spent the night alongside the river. The next morning, when we were cleaning up from breakfast, Keith and his bus rolled in. They had replaced a broken crankshaft by working all night.

"A nice homey garage and small-town friendly folks," Keith said. "They let everyone sleep in the bus and we had coffee and donuts before we left."

One of his passengers, Donnis, had enough to pay the bill and I reimbursed her $189 for the towing and repair.

We hadn't gone another fifty miles when Dale's bus, the *Brown Hound*, broke down. The other buses drove on a side road down to a river and parked in the shade while up on the side of the highway men leaned over the *Brown Hound*'s engine and started tearing things apart, getting more and more frustrated as the sun beat down and the sweat in our eyes kept us from seeing what we were doing.

Rancor was boiling to the surface.

"Nothing to do at this point, lads, but ride the monkey," I said. "Have a hit of this."

I lit up a fat doobie, took a hit, and passed it to Ramrod. He passed it on, then popped a Grateful Dead tape in the boombox:

"*Nothin' shakin' on Shakedown Street,*
used to be the heart of town.
Don't tell me this town ain't got no heart,
you just gotta poke around."

A grooving calm overlay the fray, the repair job relaxed into one slow step at a time, the turning of the wrenches, the tightening of the screws, the testing of the circuits, the discovery of the problem: bad coil, no juice to the spark plugs. Easy fix: replaced the coil with a spare.

O n the road again to Yellowstone National Park. Paid the four-dollar entrance fee and drove through to Old Faithful.

"There's Billy T's car," Butko said. "Looks like his old lady's inside."

Billy T emerged from *Further* where he had spent most of his time, rarely emerging. He walked over to the car and got in.

"Well, that explains why the only thing Billy T got excited about was whether we were going to Old Faithful or not," Butko said.

With Billy T and his lady following, we drove to Firehole Lake, where we soaked in a hot pool and sacked out afterwards on the grass nearby.

At midnight the park rangers arrived and rousted us. No overnight parking except in designated campgrounds, which they said were full, so move on.

Dale lost his headlights but no excuse, move on. So we drove away in the night with Dale sandwiched between two other buses. Exited Yellowstone and drove through Gardiner, Montana, and pulled off on a dirt road to sleep.

Early in the morning we were rousted by a deputy sheriff who told us we were parked on the approach end of an airport runway and had to move pronto—*no, you can't fix breakfast—go on down the road.*

"Looks like Billy T is gone," Butko said. "Snuck off during the night."

Neither the *Brown Hound* nor the *Hitchhiker* would start, dead batteries. Butko hooked a chain to one, I towed the other. When the engines caught, we hit the road.

Some guys have all the luck
the rest of us have to
get by on mere talent.
How's that for a sucker deal?
The best and I won't
settle for anything less.
That's when feathers will fly,
as will the fur,
although no one
knows just how far
or how fast
they'll apply the tar
when they run you
out of town on a rail.
  — Ken Babbs

52

In Reasonably Good Shape

Saturday, payday. When we stopped to cook breakfast, I broke out the logbook and the cash. Everyone lined up and received a dollar bill and wrote their initials alongside their names. Just like when we were paid in the Marine Corps, all in cash.

We stopped for gas in Livingston, Montana, and were informed by the sheriff that police radios were monitoring our progress, the cops having been advised by Yellowstone Rangers that we were on our way.

After looking us over, the sheriff said, "*Pshaw*, they're family people, not troublemakers."

His partner said, "Shore must have taken a long time to paint that bus." They sent us on our way.

Made it as far as Billings, Montana.

The axle on *Fort Home* broke, rear end spraying oil. We stopped, I took the axle out and drained the rear end. Cut a gasket out of cardboard, put the axle back in, refilled the rear end and, with it still leaking, drove to Billings where I found an F-5 Ford truck in an abandoned wrecking yard, ponies wandering among the rusty 1940 Plymouths. After long deliberation and consultation with the owner, I removed the two axles from the wrecked truck, replaced *Fort Home*'s cracked axle and took the other with me as a spare.

We left Billings, Montana, late for our first all-night speed run. We would stay in line and keep track of one another. If in trouble, flash your lights at the bus in front. The women decided to drive. Gretch piloted *Fort Home*, Gas Girl followed in *Further*. Maria and Carole drove the shuttle car, and behind them was Tillie at the wheel of the *Brown Hound*. Kay, in the *Hitchhiker*, brought up the rear. I was asleep in my bus when I was awakened. Something was wrong.

"What's going on?" I yelled.

When I got no answer, I yelled again: "Slow down, you're shaking the bus to pieces."

In the morning, when we stopped for gas in Forsyth, Montana, I found out the women had been racing the buses, trying to pass one another on the two-lane road.

The cafe next door to the gas station was open so we went in for ratburgers. They were better than ratburgers, good old cafe hamburgers, from all-beef country. The place was packed.

"There must be something going on here," I said. "A hullabaloo of sorts."

A cowboy on the other side of the cafe rose from his chair.

"What's up with all that hair?" he said.

"Saturday night," I said, "when we all gets drunk and lets our hair down."

The cowboy, lean and hard as a fence post, with a pocked

face and attitude to match, made a pass at Tillie as she passed.

"There's our cowboy," Tillie said, motioning at Dale. "He's a champion, all-around cowboy."

Holding her burger and milkshake, she went out the door. The cowboys glared at Dale who stood leaning against the counter. For a change, Dale kept his mouth shut.

The cowboy turned to me. "How about you? Are you an all-around champion cowboy? You don't look like any kind of cowboy to me."

"That's because we're farmers from Oregon."

He checked me out. Figured me for a fuzzy-faced nobody, no sport there. He turned back to Dale, but he had split with his burger. We followed him outside. I was looking for Ramrod to borrow some money. The cowboy and one of his swarthy buddies bypassed Dale standing there and went up to Ramrod, told him they were going to cut his hair.

"Get me a knife and I'll get a lock of that mop," the swarthy cowboy said, grabbing a handful of Ramrod's hair.

"Got any burger money?" I asked Ramrod, interrupting their play.

"Yeah," Ramrod said.

He reached in his pocket, pulled out some bills and handed them to me. The ordinariness put a wet blanket on the action.

"Where you from with all that hair?" the cowboy said, starting it up again.

"I was born in Dillon, Montana," Ramrod said.

"Why then, you're a disgrace."

"My granddad and grandma homesteaded right there."

"How'd you ever come to such a pass?"

The cowboy shook his head.

"Are you really a cowboy?" Maria asked.

He ignored her and walked away, his pal following behind, and the whole thing dribbled away to nothing. We loaded up the buses and drove into the day.

T he next morning, on a hot, dry day—sweat running down the cracks of our asses, everyone stripped to their underwear, air like a blast furnace blowing through open windows— we crossed the Missouri River, stopped, jumped in the water. Later, that evening, 1,426 miles from Oregon, money halfway gone, we parked in front of the courthouse in Minot, North Dakota, sat on the lawn, ate supper, then loaded up and headed into the fading sunlight for another all-night run.

In the wee hours, the *Brown Hound*'s generator quit. Ramrod, at the wheel, kept going with no lights, cradled between *Further* and the *Hitchhiker*, the *Brown Hound*'s battery providing enough voltage to the spark plugs to keep the engine running. Dawn found us in Grand Forks, Minnesota. My bus was leaking oil, its valves screaming. We stopped at a parts store and, when it opened, bought a new gasket for my bus and a generator for Dale's.

I towed the *Brown Hound* with *Fort Home*, 'round and 'round the parking lot to pull-start it, then out onto the road, but there was not enough juice in the battery to keep the *Brown Hound*'s engine running. So we changed batteries; I gave Dale mine that had a full charge, and put Dale's in my bus to charge it up.

"I told you we'd ruin that battery driving on it all night," Tillie said when I was making the exchange. "I knew it, nothing's going right. We should have stopped and slept, but no, it was press on, press on."

Dale didn't answer. He replaced the voltage regulator and, with his bus running on the juice from my battery, we returned to East Grand Forks—to Sandi's Body Shop and Auto Parts, where we took out the generator and put in a new generator that didn't work—and took out that generator and put in another generator—and finally had a take.

Where was Hagen with the camera? This was our ongoing road drama: men working on the bus, mothers watching and playing with kids, other women making sandwiches, cops overseeing the whole operation, Auto Parts Sandi and Larry supplying us with generators and voltage regulators. A street crew arrived and began tearing up the pavement, noise so loud we couldn't hear each other talking.

On the road again, long haul across Minnesota to arrive at International Falls at midnight and cross into Canada. Paid a six-dollar toll to cross the river, then had to wait two hours while an immigration officer took me into his shack and grilled me—*where you coming from, where you going, why are you entering Canada?* He came to the conclusion that ours was a shady operation, not up to historical standards of conduct, business, appearance and who knows what else. The upshot was, they wouldn't let us into Canada and they wouldn't refund us the six dollars we'd paid to cross the bridge, although as a sop they paid our way back into the States.

We pulled into US Customs knowing we would be putting ourselves in the hands of officialdom, forced to humbly receive all that was doled out: putdowns, searches, questions, harsh naked lights, machinery humming, concrete and steel, badges, uniforms, Nixon smiling from a framed photo on the wall.

The scene teetered on the edge of an all-night bummer. I broke out the blond guitar, Butko fired up the generator, and we plugged in the guitar amp. Paul Sawyer turned on his light gun and began taking 8 mm movies. The Farmsters joined in musical disarray, and the scene tilted into the realm of a good time; uniformed inspectors relaxed, the charade droned to an end and, after taking Butko inside to sign a receipt for items confiscated—one plastic jar of miscellaneous pills and capsules; one butt of tobacco-like substance; a plastic bag containing tobacco-like substance—we were free at last, shrieks of hallelujah as we drove away, a happy cry out the window of the *Brown Hound*: "Well played, Farmsters!"

A hard drive south through Minnesota and Wisconsin into Michigan to stop in Powers at an archaic, rundown park with slides, swings, tables, a rusted, four-burner wood cookstove, with warming ovens above and a cooking oven below. A starling flew out of the leaning metal smokestack when Butko pulled the oven door open. He shook his head.

"No cooking on this beast," he said, and turned to a large brick and concrete-block fireplace which had a flat metal shelf to cook on and a big chimney with a place on top to heat water in a teakettle.

"This'll do," Butko said.

He scrounged firewood, got a blaze roaring and mixed up pancake batter. We wolfed flapjacks in the ravaged splendor of the park, looking as if civilization had crumbled, leaving the brick and iron junk lying around intact, without any social upkeep to entangle time and toil. Tillie huffed over from the outhouse and said, "I sat down to take a shit and two rats ran out from a hole in the floorboard."

"Be not alarmed," Paul Foster said. "When nearing completion we should remember the magic that drove us to life in the beginning."

"Speaking of driving," I announced, "the great rock debacle of Woodstock awaits."

We gulped down snacks and beer in Flint, Michigan. The kids swarmed around the parking lot of the laundromat where we stopped to wash clothes. Two cops showed up, said someone called in that we were drinking in the laundromat.

We shook our heads, no. No beer in sight, they started to leave when they spotted Dale with a bottle of it. Just as they were pinching him, Paul Sawyer walked out of the laundromat with a sandwich in one hand and a beer in the other.

"You're both under arrest," one of the cops said.

"I don't know about Dale and Paul Sawyer," Ramrod said, watching the cops take them away, "but I'm going to nix drinking beer on the street in this burg."

"And the hippies came in from the woods, free as loons, so

put a couple of them in jail and let them know, this is White Man's Country," Paul Foster said.

The next morning, I paid the fines for Dale and Paul and we went back to the campground where we had spent the night. There was a shout from behind Keith's bus. A little boy, Jesse, had swallowed a mouthful of gold paint. His lips and chin were covered and he was sobbing, spitting out paint.

Paul Sawyer took Jesse to town to find a doctor. The rest of us drove ahead to Grand Blanc, where Paul would catch up with us.

We parked in an abandoned gas station and, per usual, every time we stopped, had to fix one of the buses: a leaking axle on *Fort Home*. Once again, I cut a gasket out of a piece of cardboard and sealed the leak.

Paul arrived to say Jesse had to spend another night at the hospital. Leaving the hospital, Paul's suitcase had fallen off the top of his car, scattering clothes across the highway. He was going back to see if he could recover anything.

We drove to Mosquito Junction Campground and settled in: fire, sky, trees, bugs, corn, watermelon, Jim Beam, guitar, flute, Vernors Ginger Ale, mosquito repellent, and mysterious Kool-Aid.

The next morning a guy walked over from the Shell gas station across the street and said, "You folks might want to think about moving on. I heard over the scanner that the FBI was looking for some buses."

We loaded up and, in the rush to leave, Keith backed into a brown Falcon. The driver, a gentleman in a suit and fedora, looked at the damage and said, "Not too bad, probably cost about fifteen dollars for repair."

Keith agreed the dent could easily be pounded out and said he would send the gentleman fifteen dollars as soon as he had it. The gentleman, a true gentleman, agreed, gave Keith his address, and left.

We drove to Davison, Michigan, and waited for Paul to catch up with Jesse. I gave Keith fifteen dollars. He walked to the post office and mailed the money to the gentleman.

Saturday morning, August 9th. Payday, one dollar each, $259 remaining. Twelfth day out, 3,012 miles since Kesey's.

Paul showed up with Jesse and drove straight through to Port Huron and another try at crossing into Canada, for we were going to give it our all to do part of the trip in Canada. Much to our surprise, we were waved through the border into London, Ontario, where the local police promptly pulled *Further* over. Ramrod had run a stop sign.

We were about to cause a traffic jam, double-parking with three buses and a car, when Ramrod yelled to keep going, he'd catch up with us on the road.

Jenny, who called herself "the English Ghost" was an eighteen-year-old from England traveling around the States with her pal, Wendy. While stopping at Kesey's, they'd decided to go with us to Woodstock. As we whipped down the road through Canada, Jenny, logbook on her lap, wrote down her impressions of what she was seeing and thinking:

Mood lightens crossing into Canada. No hassling about ID for the two English guests, or the dog demurely hidden. During stops for eats, there is a feeling of open curiosity rather than lurking hostility. Wendy suggests it is connected with an agrarian way of life—the Canadians are not overwhelmed by dirty faces, blue jeans, bare feet and certain toddlers.

Canada is lovely and green and down home, feels cool and fresh, however, soon we'll be in Woodstock and I hope I meet Dylan and get stoned with him. An old man on a horse-driven plough just blew everyone's mind. Two beautiful old horses stomping through the hay in a field, a dappled grey mare and a baby mare. I'm so happy. The bus is lovely today and my fever's not so feverish.

What she didn't mention was that when we left the Kesey

farm, she was down in the dumps and, as the trip went on, was getting more withdrawn and wasted, not taking care of herself. Everyone was worried about her but she turned down all offers of help. We did all we could, plying her with food and water she barely touched. Something was bothering her to the point where it was affecting her physically, but she refused to talk about it, so we kept a close eye on her, figuring once we got to Woodstock, we'd get her to a doctor.

We blasted through Canada. When we got close to Niagara Falls where we'd cross into New York State, there was still no sign of Ramrod and *Further*. Spotting a lit-up building with a VFW neon sign, I pulled over and walked to the building to make a phone call.

Kesey's farm was Info Central. If we got separated, we'd call Info Central and check to find out if someone from the missing bus had called in and said where they were. A tedious process, requiring handfuls of quarters at phone booths, but in its quirky way successful.

This time I wasn't going to call Info Central, but the Canadian police, asking them to keep an eye out for *Further* and, if they spotted the bus, to tell Ramrod we'd wait for him on the American side of the border at Niagara Falls.

When I walked into the VFW club, the men sitting at the bar and tables turned and stared at me. Older guys, World War Two and Korean vets. I nodded, went to the bar and asked if they had a pay phone.

A man, sitting on the stool next to where I was standing, said, "What you doing in here, mate? Don't you know we're all veterans and don't take a shine to you blokes running up here to avoid doing your military duty?"

"I came here because I saw the sign. My dad was a World War Two vet and belonged to the VFW when he got out. I thought this would be a friendly place."

Another man got up from a table and walked over. He was

as tall as me, broad and muscular, his roll of belly fat probably hard as a rock. He took my beard in his thumb and finger and gave it a little tug.

"And what about this? You one of them hippies?" he said.

I laughed.

"Too old for that," I said. "I'm in a caravan heading to a music festival and we're missing one of our rigs. I'm wanting to call a trooper and ask him to keep an eye out for the bus, tell him where we can meet up."

"Instead o' doing that, why don't you just give yourselves up and save the Mounties a heap of trouble rousting you?"

There were murmurs and low voices of agreement.

"I don't think so," I said. "Looky here."

I pulled out my wallet, extracted my discharge card and handed it to him. He turned loose of my beard and held the card up to the light, lips moving as he read. He looked at me, then turned to the room.

"Captain, United States Marine Corps," he said, and slapped me on the back.

"Helicopter pilot in Vietnam," I said, and pulled a wad of dollars out of my wallet. "I'm buying a round for the house, and a beer for me."

We shook hands, he went back to his table. The man on the stool next to me raised his glass in a salute. I went over to the pay phone in the corner, called the Mounties, gave them my message, came back and drank up. I thanked everyone for their *horse*pitality, and left.

That evening, when we crossed the International Bridge into New York State and pulled into the line at Customs, I looked in the mirror and saw *Further* come off the bridge into the States. I pulled over and waited for him, then we drove up to the customs inspectors, who looked us over.

"You know, they *could* be marijuana smokers," one of the officers said.

"Yeah, but if we start now, it'll take us all night," the other one said.

"Okay, let them on through."

S unday, August 10th, 3,339 miles and our thirteenth day on the road, rainy and cool, we stopped in a park for the night and were greeted upon awakening by a park ranger who requested that we immediately leave. We were held up at the exit for a registration fee and, as soon as we hit the road, were pulled over by two state cruisers and a sheriff's car, followed by more rangers who performed a full-fledged license and registration check, then sent us on our way. We stopped to gas up and immediately afterwards were pulled over again by an unmarked state cop who did the license and registration repeat.

A gulp stop in Ithaca, a gas stop in Damascus. Then, after a long haul into the night, we turned off the main road and at the turnoff were met by a guy on a motorcycle who had ridden out from Woodstock to meet us. He led us through White Lake, part of Bethel, the closest town to the festival. From there, we continued to the festival site—a six-hundred-acre farm owned by Max Yasgur—drove through the gate, across a pasture, parked in the grass, got out of the buses, and were greeted by Stan Goldstein and Hugh Romney and his wife, Bonnie Jean. Behind them, the Hog Farmers.

We made camp, ate and watched movies projected on a white sheet hung between two poles. Phase one—getting there—was completed. Equipment and Farmsters worn out, but in good order and spirits. 3,609 miles logged, $117 dollars remaining. Stan Goldstein wrote out a receipt on a wrinkled piece of paper:

R'cd 4 buses, 1 station wagon, 1 4dr sedan, 37 people, 1 dog, 1 cat, 1 rat in reasonably good shape. Signed, SG, 11:25 PM, 10 Aug 1969.

Q: What is something you will always remember?
A: Taking Jerry Garcia for a ride around the place in
a golf cart. Jimi Hendrix doing the "Star-Spangled
Banner" at dawn. Shaking hands with Ravi Shankar.
Digging the immensity of the festival; reminded
me of people in India gathering at the Ganges for
one of their religious ceremonies. Wondrous.
Q: Were drugs being experimented with?
A: You kidding me? Kids, wives, mothers, husbands,
single men and women. Sheesh, who has time for drugs?
  — Ken Babbs

53

Make It a Free Concert

The tents and buses and trucks of the Hog Farm encampment sprawled across the grass on top of a hill, then down a gentle slope into a large meadow with a pond at one side.

The Oregon buses were parked on a knoll looking down on the Hog Farmers. *Further* pointed its nose at our sound equipment in a clump. Butko and Ramrod and I sorted through the mixers, amplifiers, speakers and guitar amps. We would be running a funky free stage for music and making announcements, leaving the Hog Farmers and the rest of the Farmsters to deal with the Free Kitchen and the Freak-Out Tent.

The Freak-Out Tent had cushions and mats on the ground. When a person on a bad trip was brought in and laid down, the Hog Farmers hovered over the person and gently massaged and hummed the frantic soul back to peace.

We ran an extension cord from the generator on the back of *Further* to power the sound equipment and, in the waning hours of day, sent our version of music wafting across the meadow. I was on the blond guitar booming out the Fender guitar amp; Dale on his fiddle, also amplified. Some unknown plugged his guitar in and joined us while another stranger in a black floppy hat added his mish to the mash, pushing his mouth on a harmonica. Unrecognizable as any known tune, the music dipped and swayed, shrieked and screamed into a mellow groove that welcomed the arrival of a cool breeze softening the muggy heat of day.

The next morning we were awakened by a dusty pickup that parked next to the buses. Mike Hagen and a full complement of pals finally caught up to us with the camera gear. He was ready to start shooting. I led him on a tour through our area, then over to the main stage, a frenzy of activity in a frantic panic to get the huge structure finished before the concert started, still two days away. The workers kept everyone at a distance, out of the way, no interruptions now, no hanging around and gabfesting.

Hagen and I were standing at the bottom of a slope, looking up at the main stage when a bearded, shirtless guy ran at us, screaming, "You can't be here. Get out of here. Can't you numbskulls see we have work to do?"

"Keep shooting, Mike," I said. "This guy seems to have toppled over the edge."

Picking me out as the major troublemaker, he tackled me to the ground where we thrashed around, trying to get the advantage of each other; both sweaty, neither wearing shirts, both bearded.

"What's this?" Sonny Heard, one of Hagen's pals, yelled. "It's the Siamese Twins and we can't tell them apart."

"Then let's separate them," Ramrod said—a good thing for me, because I was pinned to the ground, grass and dirt digging into my back, big-lout belly squeezing the wind out of my lungs.

Ramrod and Sonny pried him loose. He stood up and yelled, "Now are you going to get out of here or do I have to let you have it with this?"

He picked up a two-by-four and swung it like a baseball bat.

I backed away. "So much for brotherhood, we're all in this together, and all that shit. You're as much a corporate thug as any stock market flunky. Come on, Mike, we'll go someplace else where the air is rarer."

I was steaming and took off out of there at a fast clip for the big pond, plunged in, pants and shoes and all. I was cooling off nicely when an authoritative voice boomed out of a bullhorn, *"Everybody out of the water. No swimming allowed. Noncompliance will result in a ticket and a fine and you will be eighty-sixed from the property."*

We ambled back to our camp. I turned the amp up to eleven, strapped on the blond guitar and rent the peaceful air with bloodcurdling, piercing cries; I ripped up and down the strings in a maddening blare of feedback and echo about to drive everyone crazy when some real music interjected its calming presence.

I stopped banging and whanging and looked around. Four guys I'd never seen before, one on acoustic guitar and singing, one on electric guitar, another on electric bass, and the fourth beating on a handheld drum added a blues line to the Prankster mayhem. We backed off and let them take over.

The acoustic guitar player stepped to the microphone and began singing:

"Looking up at the stars,
I could not sleep.
Legs are too restless,
Got promises to keep.
Gonna get up and take a walk,
Find me a woman and have a long talk.
She'll give me solace and I'll give her joy.
We'll dance and flirt and maybe a kiss.
I'll be her mister and she'll be my miss."

After a few numbers they quit and we got acquainted. They

were the Quarry, from Pittsfield, Massachusetts, playing together since high school. They were doing a gig at the Zodiac
in Manhattan when Michael Lang, the Woodstock organizer,
heard them and told their manager, Barry Hollister, to bring the
band to Woodstock. Guitarist and singer, Dave Carron; lead guitar, Mike Furey; bassist Dan Velika; drummer, Mick Valenti.
Longhairs. Down to their shoulders. They brought their own
equipment: guitar amps and a black-pearl Ludwig drum kit.
They set up camp alongside ours.

Our camp was on the path between the main stage and the
Hog Farmers, in the way of traffic to and fro, so we moved down
the hill to a flat spot. We'd run the free stage there, where performers could play music and do readings or give talks, from
late morning to not-so-late nights.

I wandered over to the main stage. Construction was still going full blast. A chain-link fence ran behind the stage along the
property line. There was a wide-open gate on the dirt road that
led into the festival. A trailer, serving as the security office was
parked next to the entrance. An older man, late forties, early
fifties, stood outside the trailer door. Short haircut, square face,
penetrating eyes, he watched the young people parading past
with a slight smile on his face.

I went over and we traded stories. He was Wes Pomeroy,
head of security, and curious about what I was doing there, obviously older than most of the crowd pouring through the gates.
I gave him a short rundown and it came out we were both
former Marines. We hit it off and he said he was waiting for the
security force to arrive: forty off-duty New York police officers.
Then he surprised me by asking if I would brief them on what
their function would be at the concert.

There I was, bearded, bare-chested with a red bandanna tied
around my neck, Levi's hanging low on my hips, sandals on my
feet, facing New York's finest, looking at me stone-faced, waiting to hear what this West Coaster—introduced by Wes Pome-

roy as one of the organizers—had to say.

"First off, this will be a simple casual job for you men. You'll be dealing with a crowd of people who are here for the music and to have a good time. I doubt there will be any hassles but if you see an altercation, step in and calm them down and hang around to make sure it's over."

I paused and one of the policemen said, "What about drugs?"

"There's going to be a lot of drugs, but for the most part it will be simply using, so let it go. If you see anyone selling and money changing hands, tell them it's not kosher and if they keep it up you'll confiscate the drugs and the money. Let's face it, these will be mostly potheads and acidheads and they're not here to make trouble. Mainly, enjoy yourselves and help out anyone who seems to be in difficulty. Wes Pomeroy here is the boss and if there's anything you need or have questions about, he's always available. Right, Wes?"

"Absolutely. Thanks, Ken. Okay, men. Go at it."

The line of people coming through the open gate was thickening. An organized troop, dressed alike in khaki uniforms, approached the gate. They marched in single file, led by a stout lady with thick brogans kicking up dust; a whistle dangled on her ample bust.

I looked at Wes Pomeroy. He shook his head and said, "Go see what they want, Ken."

I met them at the gate. The head lady blew her whistle and the troop came to a halt.

"What gives?" I asked her.

She looked me up and down and frowned. Who was this interloper with the nerve to question her?

"We are the ticket takers," she said. "All those people who have already entered will have to leave and re-enter and show their tickets."

I held up a finger.

"Hold on for a mo', ma'am, while I consult with my superior."

"At ease," the head lady bellowed. Everyone in the line relaxed.

When I told Wes what she wanted, he let out a long breath.

"How we going to manage that?"

"There's probably already a hundred thousand people inside," I said. "We'll never be able to get them all out and come back again. Who knows how many even have tickets?"

He rubbed his chin.

"Gotta be some way to work this out," he said. "Any ideas?"

"Like they say in the Marine Corps: '*Do it with a KISS.*' Keep It Simple, Stupid. We'll make it a free concert, do away with tickets altogether."

He chuckled. "That's so simple it might work. I'll check with Mike Lang over at the stage."

He went into the security trailer, talked on the phone, nodded and hung up.

"He agreed," Wes said. "Go break the news to the lady."

"Well," I said, giving her a big smile. "Turns out we won't be needing your team after all. The promoters have decided to make it a free concert, so nobody has to leave and come back in."

She glared, then spun around, yelled, "About face." When the line dutifully obeyed, she ordered, "Forward march," and they strode away.

"Well," I told Wes, "as Neal Cassady said, 'Walked away from another one.'"

Behind us, men and women rolled the chain-link fence away from the gate, leaving a fifty-foot opening so everyone could go in and out.

"Guess we're done here," I said.

Wes nodded, we shook hands, and I ambled through the woods and over the hills, singing, "*To grandmother's house we go, we go, to grandmother's house we go.*" I reached the free stage, went behind the buses and took a nap in the shade.

What's really neat about crowds at festivals
is the way that, even though it appears to be
tightly packed, when you get down in the thick
of it, there's room to move, everyone able to
move freely in a civilized manner without
banging into each other.
  — Ken Babbs

54

Screaming For More

A crew of Hog Farmers was building a stage in front of the semicircle of parked buses. They leveled a frame a foot off the ground and covered it with sheets of plywood. Another crew brought in a thick electrical cord from the main power grid running the main stage, giving us enough amps to run the Prankster and Quarry equipment, with extension cords into the buses for lights and kitchen appliances.

When everything was up and running, I announced over the microphone that the free stage was open to anyone who wanted to come up and play an instrument and sing, or just say their name and where they came from.

"Line up on the left," I said, "and walk to the middle, do your thing, and go off on the right."

A line formed immediately. Almost everyone merely said who they were, but some were musicians. I put a chair on the side and let my thoughts roam, not paying any attention until I heard a voice and guitar I recognized. Joan Baez was sitting on a chair in the middle of the stage, singing and playing. The crowd in front was enraptured, not making a peep.

"Look at the fire, look at the smoke,
Look at the man taking a toke.

I'll show you a wanderer who has no home.
He may be down on his luck but he's no bum.
And I'm not either, just chewing my gum."

In the middle of the song, a naked, red-bearded, red-haired, six-foot-eight-tall Viking raced across the stage, doing cart-wheels head-over-heels, passing a hand's breadth in front of Joan Baez, his balls and pecker flying. She shrieked, strummed wildly as the Viking landed on his feet, galloped through the crowd and disappeared over the hill. Behind him she sang:

"Show me the penis and show me the nads,
Show me the cartwheeler as he tumbles off the stage,
And I'll show you a young man with so many reasons why
He may be down on his luck but he's no bum
And I'm not either, just chewing my gum."

D avid Butkovich came hustling in from the main stage. "The Grateful Dead are here," he told me. "Ramrod is bringing over a bunch of their gear."

We shut down the free stage and worked new amplifiers, mixers and speakers into our system. In a few hours everything was up and running. We knocked off for supper and in the cool of the evening, the Quarry played. The space in front of the stage started filling up, and by dark the hill was crowded from top to bottom, people sprawled on the ground and standing in the back.

Before we knocked off for the night, the Farmsters joined the Quarry for a rollicking jam: Dale on his violin, Tillie on guitar and singing, me whanging on the blond guitar. Goofy, drawn-out, meaningless riffs winding through a cacophonic beat that tailed off into long, meandering chords, quieter and quieter, un-til we were done.

At midnight a horrendous storm hit with a relentless down-pour and thunder and lightning. In the morning, the camping places in and around the bus were wrecked. Everyone scurried around, gathering the shredded pieces of tarps and plastic and throwing them aside. During the storm, the power routed from the main stage burned out. Ramrod and John Hagen got busy and when they turned the equipment on, a guitar amp blew. Ramrod discovered that when they restored the electrical power, they brought in 220 volts instead of 110. Ramrod raced over to the main stage, found another power supply and installed it. The line voltage was straightened out and the free stage was up and running in the middle of a bright sunny day.

Towards evening, black clouds mushroomed on the horizon. I walked to the main stage to catch the Grateful Dead. The clouds opened, the rain poured down so hard you couldn't see from one side of the stage to the other. The force of the wind left one shredded piece of canvas dangling over the guitar amps and drums. The electricity shorted out, sparks dancing across the floor of the stage. The amps blew with a bang and smoke shot out their backs. The Dead huddled together, trying to keep dry. Jerry and Phil and Bobby clutched their instruments against their chests. Bill leaned over his drums, protecting them best he could. The sound techs and electricians worked frantically on the wires and connections. One working spotlight swung in the wind and threw a beam back and forth across the stage.

Out in the dark, the hill was a mass of shapes huddled under blankets and sleeping bags, bare skin glistening where the spectators had no covering.

I was standing in the back of the stage next to Pigpen when one microphone began to work. Pigpen said to me, "Go tell them a story, Babbs."

I gave him a look. Every time I was on the stage with the band and they were spending an endless time getting ready to start, Pigpen would tell me to tell a story, knowing that once I got on the microphone, the band would immediately begin singing and playing.

Not this time. It was going to take awhile before the stage was cleared of debris and the instruments were up and running.

"We come all the way from Ore-*ee*-gun," I said. "Forty people in four buses, departed from Ken Kesey's farm, leaving Ken Kesey behind, he didn't make it. So the other day Liz, one of the women who rode here in Kesey's bus, wired Kesey a hunnert-and-eighty bucks to buy a plane ticket to Woodstock, but we come to find out Kesey used the money to fly a kid named Jake, who'd been dropped off at Kesey's farm in Oregon by his mother, who never came back to get him—used the money to fly the kid home to San Francisco—so you can tell your chilluns that's the reason Ken Kesey never made it to Woodstock."

The other microphones onstage came to life. The guitar amps buzzed, but the techies were still scurrying around so the band couldn't start a song. Someone yelled something from the crowd.

"You want it louder?" Jerry said into his microphone.

The crowd yelled back answers and suggestions, words barely discernable on the stage.

"What I mean to tell you," Bob Weir said through his microphone, "is everything up here is falling to waste."

"I can see what the problem is," I said, mouth tight on the microphone. "You got to get right in here and talk loud. The problem is if you can't hear us down there, we can't hear you up here. But we're working on it. Trying to smooth it all out for the distance of the whaddaya call it."

"You call it what?" Bob Weir said.

"Wanta-call-it-more, of whatever-it-is."

"More microphone noise," Bob said.

"Yeah, right, more volume," I said. "It was like Jellystone Park was this place made for the people and by the people, like it was in Indian days, when tribes came to camp in a neutral ground where no warfare would take place. Established a holy place to take a bath and cleanse your body, a place you could be in the center of the world. In the great American tradition with all this apparatus that we have going here, it puts Old Faithful in a greater participation light for, like in a hot spring, you can sit here and bathe as long as you want."

"Bathe," Bob Weir said. "And if it don't work, we can pull one up in Peoria."

"It always comes a little bit at a time, you know, and it's a little edgy at first," I said. "Under cover of darkness, we slipped in and bathed in the Jellystone pools. Later on, we were run out because you're not allowed to park there overnight unless you're in a designated camping area, ha ha ha."

The crowd in front was getting rowdy, screaming and waving fists.

"Oh, too bad, the guys down below don't seem to like my microphone working," I said.

"More volume on number five," a sound man interrupted.

"Never attention, cats and moans and whales, but you can turn it up anyway," Bob Weir said.

"Bring up six," Jerry Garcia said again.

"In Detroit last year it was bring up two," I said. "So everybody was doing two and this guy came up on the stage and in a moment of great breakthrough said, 'Do three.' Just like last night when the Bible-thumpers came to the free stage and a bunch of them yelled, 'Revolution!' and another bunch answered, 'For Christ!' and I realized, by God, they were doing three, and some guy listening said, 'Three is fine but when you want to complete the thing, you want to do it like this'—he stuck three fingers in his mouth and slapped his forehead—'That way you got the three and the...'"

"How come you turned mine down?" Bob Weir interrupted.

"As the deathly silence settles over the pavilion," I said, "and we realize we overloaded everything and the final fuse was blown, the helicopters will still be flying out the wounded and the green-tab acid-takers will be saying to one another, 'I took the green stuff and I feel great, what's all the hassle?' That's when I can only be scared so long and I start saying, 'Hey man, I trust you, and if you're going to give me some stuff that's a bummer, I'm not going to quit taking it just because, you know, to blow the trust.'"

An old familiar character, familiar to us West Coast guys, stepped to the microphone.

"Hello, people, my name's Country Joe. I want to tell you something. You know a lot of us people from the Bay Area, we're real LSD freaks. We've taken a lot of LSD. We know what LSD is. But I'll tell you all one thing: there's something being passed out here today, may or may not be LSD, and there's a chance you won't have a great good trip. Now, if you've taken it already, don't worry because you're not poisoned and you won't die. Just listen to the music and wait till you get some stuff that you know is good. That's called common sense. Right on."

"Country common sense," I said. "From us folks out west. Beware the green-tab acid."

"Sit down," someone yelled from in front, and others took up the cry. "Sit down!"

They'd had enough of my bullshit, they wanted the Grateful Dead and, right on cue, the band hit the first notes of "Love Light." Then, in front of the musicians, appearing like some kind of pop-up toy, was a guy we'd never seen before: shiny face, thick, black, wavy hair to his shoulders, bushy-black eyebrows, deep-dark eyes, black mustache winding down his mouth to a Van Dyke beard around his chin, bright blue, wet sweatshirt zipped up to his neck, his eyes dilated.

He began talking into the microphone: "Whoa-a, yeah, I've seen the sunrise, the sun rise over the lakes, the great, the Great Lakes, and over the Pacific Ocean and over the Atlantic and there's something I'd like to say, that there's another coast, it's the *third* coast, the greatest freshwater reservoir in the world, and more miles of coastline, just measure it..."

Bob Weir came over to me. "Get him off of there."

I had two joints in my shirt pocket. I took one out and walked to the front of the stage. I lit the joint as I approached the bearded guy. He reared back, surprised by the sudden flare. I took a hit and handed him the joint. As he held it to his lips, I pulled him away from the microphone. As he took another hit, I passed him over to Ramrod who eased him off the stage into the arms of the crowd below.

Pigpen's voice came out clear and strong:

"There was no warning, it just happened.

You kissed me goodbye and that was it.

No, no, no, I couldn't accept my fate.

I beat my fist against my head.

Didn't want to live, better off dead.

A beggar pleading like a fiend,

Restore my senses, come back to me.

Don't give me any of that sick sympathy."

The band laid on the instrumentals, "Turn on Your Love Light" poured out of the speakers for forty minutes with back-and-forth singing between Bobby and Pigpen intermixed with long, loopy guitars, keyboard and bass, Billy's pounding drums. An over-the-top closing song that left the crowd screaming for more.

Everyone has to work the daytime job to do the
nighttime play, but the real work takes place
both at the daytime job and during the night-
time play: to be a force for love, peace and happiness.
— *Ken Babbs*

55

This Is Our Show, Not Yours

T he cows lowed and mooed in Max Yasgur's pasture, clear
of piles of trash, garbage, discarded clothing, sleeping bags
and tents. The security trailer and chain-link fence were gone
and the area where the stage and performers' tent stood was a
bare patch of ground.

At the Hog Farmers' Food Kitchen and Freak-Out Tent, everything was packed into buses and trucks, ready to haul ass.
Keith Haxby and Dale Kesey appropriated two-by-fours and
plywood from the remnants of the free stage to build shelves in
their buses.

Ramrod rejoined the Grateful Dead to take up his job as head
roadie. Jenny, the British girl, had gone downhill fast during the
festival. Not eating, she was down to skin and bones. Hair un-
kempt. Clothes dirty. Jenny, thinking she had a venereal disease,
was distraught over the thought of going back to England and
having her parents find out. A Hog Farmer who had a car offered to take her to a hospital in town. Maria said she'd go along.

Two of our buses had flat tires and *Further* wouldn't start.
We put spares on the buses and pulled *Further* with Yasgur's
tractor to get it started. *Further* sloshed through a ditch, up and
out. The tractor pulled the *Brown Hound* and *Hitchhiker* up the
hill. I tried three times to make it in my bus and failed, then hit

it hard and, with back-wheels mud flying like a geyser from a volcano, I made it to the top. Dusk settled in and we camped right there. Stan Goldstein showed up along with some of the festival workers. One of them was the bearded, shirtless guy I'd wrestled in front of the stage when it was under construction. He gave me a wry grin and I nodded. No more of that mano-to-mano baloney now, not after the uplifting spirit of the festival.

Stan asked me if the Pranksters would be willing to go to the Texas Pop Festival near Dallas and do a free stage. The Hog Farmers were going and would run a kitchen. We'd camp at a park a few miles from the festival, dealing with the overflow from the main stage.

Once again, we'd be paid $1,650.

Just then someone yelled at me, "You better get over here." I shook with Stan on the deal and walked over to see what was happening.

A guy from Warner Brothers had put out the word for everyone at Woodstock who had been shooting movie film to come meet with him. Young, curly locks and a lean build, he stood on a box and said he had an offer for everyone who shot film at the festival.

I split and rounded up Hagen. When we returned, a dozen men had gathered, all ages, from high schoolers to grizzled old groots.

"Reason I'm calling you here," the Warner Brothers guy said, "is if you give Warner's all the footage you shot, Warner's will process it for free, look at it and if anything gets used in the Woodstock movie, you'll be paid for it. Anything we don't use, you get back."

I looked at Hagen. He gave me the whaddaya-think gesture. I shrugged. Why not? Everyone was in. We broke up and Hagen and the other filmmakers went to get their film.

The next day I went with Stan Goldstein to the main stage area to get the money to go to the Texas Pop Festival. We met with Michael Lang, one of the Woodstock festival ringleaders. Stan asked for an advance for the work the Hog Farm did at Woodstock. Stan would pay me for the Texas gig out of that. After smoking hash and palavering, we got the okay from Michael.

With the cash to pay us for the Texas Pop Festival locked up in my briefcase, I gave the marching orders to the Pranksters: "Load 'em up, hit the road. Time's a-wasting."

Jenny was back from the doctor. Vaginitis and possible urinary tract infection. Treatment: antibiotics, keep her warm, lots of rest.

The Quarry band decided they'd stick with us for the Texas job. They loaded their gear in their van, would take turns driving while the rest of them rode in *Further*.

On Friday, August 22nd, we departed White Lake, New York, and headed west, scheduled to arrive at the Texas Pop Festival campground on August 28th. Twenty-nine people, three dogs, one rat and four buses. The Hog Farmers would meet us there.

On the road again, following the sun. Into Pennsylvania we drove, where *Further* ate a valve stem in a rear tire and chewed the tire to its bitter end, which meant replacing it with the bald spare. Butko threw a cigarette butt out the window and hit a state trooper's car on the windshield—the siren wailed, the lights flashed. Smokey Bear hitched his gun belt, walked alongside the bus, looked it over, top-to-bottom, stem-to-stern, and informed Butko he needed to get some mud flaps.

"Yes, sir," Butko responded. The trooper gave him a two-fingered salute and walked back to his cruiser.

In Ohio we crawled behind serious, black-clad families riding in horse-drawn buggies. Clear sailing through Kentucky and Tennessee, Mississippi and Louisiana, into Texas, to arrive at the little town of Lewisville. With the sun descending over the western plain, we drove into the park.

The Hog Farmers were camped in a wooded area at the end of a large field. A large, canopied tent covered the Free Kitchen. Behind the trees, the water of a lake lapped against the shore.

We parked our buses inside the tree line, under the shade.

"That's it for today," I announced. "Tomorrow we go to work."

T he next morning, we built a stage three feet off the ground and covered it with a canvas canopy. While the work was going on, Hugh Romney came over and said to me, "Let's go over to the main stage, see what they have going on there."

It only took a quick look at the grandiose layout being assembled for the festival concert at a car racetrack for us to realize this was far beyond anything we could deal with. The lineup of bands was impressive: Janis Joplin, Sam and Dave, Sly and the Family Stone, Santana, Canned Heat, the Grass Roots, B. B. King, Chicago Transit Authority, Tony Joe White, Spirit, Johnny Winter, Sweetwater, Ten Years After, Freddie King and Led Zeppelin.

It would be all we could do to handle our own scene. We drove back to the campground to find cops at the gate, turning everyone away. Cars were lined up on the road. I walked up to the cop.

"What's going on?" I asked.

He gave me his *who-are-you* look, then deigned to say, "This park isn't open right now. No one's going in, including you."

"I beg to differ. This gentleman"—I nodded to Hugh Romney dressed in flowing shirt and baggy shorts, bright red sneakers and jester's hat—"and I are in charge of running the campground for the duration of the Texas Pop Festival, to provide an alternate place for the people who can't make the big concert."

It was a mouthful but the cop was not impressed. I let him

have it.

"Listen, you fucking prick, let them in. This is our show, not yours."

"You, foul mouth, are under arrest. Turn around."

He slapped the cuffs on me and started walking me toward his cruiser. A plainclothes car pulled up and a large man dressed in khaki uniform, wearing cowboy boots, stepped out. He stuck a ten-gallon hat high upon his half-bald head. A white star gleamed on the front of the hat.

"What's going on, Charley?" the man asked.

"Howdy, Sheriff. All these people"—he gestured at the line of cars—"are wanting to go into the park but I told them it's not open and this bozo tried to tell me that he and that other clown are in charge of the park now. Then he sassed me and called me some nasty things and I'm taking him in."

"Well, hold on, Charley. Let him go a minute and come on over here."

They walked to the plain-marked car and talked. The deputy, obviously not happy, came back, took the cuffs off of me, stalked to his car, and drove away.

"I'm Sheriff Grady," the man in the Stetson said. "Looks like you and I, like it or not, will be ramrodding this venture together."

He'd leave it up to me, he said, to keep things orderly inside the park with no shenanigans of any kind. The festival people needed this place to handle the overflow from the concert. He'd be close by and if I dropped the ball, he'd be forced to step in.

We shook on it and he left. I waved the first car in and Hugh and I followed. When we reached the wooded area, I looked back at cars pulling into the field and parking in front of the stage, forming rows like at a drive-in movie theater. The Texans got out of their cars and trucks, leaned against their rigs, lit cigarettes and drank beer, and watched as we worked on the stage.

While Jenny was back on solid foods, taking antibiotics and regaining her health, her pal Wendy was in trouble. She had dropped mescaline the night before, wandered out on the road and was picked up by the cops, who took her to the police station, then to the hospital, and after that to the British Consulate where she was being held.

I wrote a note to the Consulate, saying if they let her stay with us and did not deport her, we would take care of her and she would get better, but if she were confined, her mental health would go downhill. They didn't answer.

By late afternoon the free stage was up and running. The Quarry talked the crowd into leaving the comfort of their cars to gather in front of the stage, drinking and toking and bouncing to the beat late into the night.

Dawn's red rim brought me up on the stage to welcome another day: "Up and at 'em, campers," I announced over the PA. "Coffee is brewing in the Free Kitchen, the sound gear is in A-one shape. Bring your gittars and mouth harps and Jew's harps up here and join in so the music never stops."

At the gate to the grounds, the cars kept coming. The cops wondered, *let them in, keep them out?* The Lewisville police chief, Ralph Adams, came to the stage for a confab and agreed to let cars come in and go out willy-nilly, but the nude swimming had to stop. Boats belonging to the townies who came to gawk were clogging the waters and the situation was getting dangerous.

Hugh Romney walked over to the edge of the lake and yelled at the swimmers, "Ahoy, nude-ohs. If you want to stay out there, you have to put on your pants. Can you dig it?"

He cooled the scene out.

Onstage, an Ernie Ford look-and-sing-alike—slick-haired guy in a bowtie, black mustache and cowboy hat—wowed the crowd with a song Ernie never knew:

"Could you see them in the lake?
They were there to wave to you,
bare-skinned maidens.
On the banks we were crowded,
hundreds thronged and nary a thong..."

Dope and booze freakouts moiled across the dusty ground, a swirling soup that roiled to the edge of the stage and back around the parked cars until dark, when as many as could fit clambered onto the stage where the freaks, drunks, frat rats, cowboys, bloods, hippies, rednecks and townies leg wrestled, arm wrestled, danced, sang and fought, while the light show pulsated and the music blared on.

David Butkovich took the midnight-to-six-a.m. shift, keeping a lid on things until a tear gas bomb was thrown and the free stage became a free-for-all stage that blew the fuses and killed all lights and sound.

Next day, Sunday, day of rest, but no rest for the weary. Everyone who had been up all night and those who grabbed a snooze were greeted by "The Star-Spangled Banner" booming through the speakers, followed by me giving the morning greeting: "Up and at 'em campers! Calling all volunteers for the trash detail: bottles and cans to your left, paper and garbage to your right, plastic sacks a-plenty."

An official-looking car drove in and parked in front of the stage; Sam Houston, the Lewisville mayor, got out, followed by Ralph Adams, the police chief.

The chief said, "We can't allow any more cars in. We're locking the gate. We got a call from California. The Hells Angels are on their way and they'll be here this afternoon to tear the place apart."

"Now, now," Hugh said, "there's no reason to be alarmed. I can assure you everything will be alright and Ken here will agree with me."

"Right," I said, and pulled my Marine Corps card out of my

wallet. "I've dealt with the Angels before and they respect this."

The police chief looked at the card and handed it to the mayor, who took his glasses out of his shirt pocket and bent in close to scan the card.

"Well, guess we can keep an eye on things from outside," Mayor Houston said. "But anything gets out of hand we're closing the place down. I'm arming myself with a pistol and preparing for the worst."

He gave me a stern look, nodded, and they got in the car and drove off.

"Hey Babbs," Maria said. "Jenny went to town to visit Wendy and the Brits kept her. Said they were going to send the two of them back to England."

"At this point, probably for the best," I said, and headed to the Free Kitchen for coffee and breakfast, thinking. We surely did all we could for the two Brits even though they were total strangers, but we've had many like them come around and we're used to dealing with it. Take them as they are, try to fit them in for the short time they are here, make them feel like part of the gang and give them a good send off when they leave. But that was close to impossible in this case, them being from another country and all, and youngsters at that.

*Where true equality lives, is Time. Every single
person in this world is given 24 hours a day. It's
their 24 hours to do with however they want. You
can sell your time to somebody and get some money,
which is okay. But it's still your time. I don't know
how many times I've had offers to do something
for money and I'd say, "Wait a minute, that's a waste
of my time." And they'd say, "Yeah, but I'm paying
you." And I'd say, "You can pay me all the money
you want, but I am going to waste My Time on
My Time."*
— *Ken Babbs*

56

Biggest Drive-In Free Stage

Another hot sultry day at the campground drive-in free stage, an ongoing outdoor concert party that had no agenda other than to pump out the music while keeping an eye on the disparate activities burbling and bubbling in and out of the cars. A cloud of dust rose in the middle of the field and rolled toward the stage. The Quarry picked up the beat and wailed a piercing anthem to the approaching dust storm.

A woman ran up to the stage and yelled, "It's Tennessee. He's taken way too much acid and he's freaking out and nobody can help him. He's someplace else, he's somebody else."

Behind her the dust cloud came closer. When the wind blew an opening, I saw Tennessee sitting on the ground, legs spread, arms sticking out, a person sitting on each leg, a person holding each arm as he struggled to get free. His face was contorted, mouth open, white teeth sparkling, dark hair a wild mop, eyes bugged out, chest bare and dirty. He shouted wild unintelligible sounds. I jumped down from the stage and bent over him.

"Tennessee, it's me, Ken. Tennessee, do you see me? Look at me."

He thrashed and pulled, trying to get loose.

"Let go," I told the people holding him down.

They looked startled but turned Tennessee loose. I got down on my knees and put my arms around his head and whispered in his ear, "You be what was meant to be and what is meant to be is that you be here with me."

I hugged him and, with my arms around him, rolled on the ground, around and around, him hanging on until I got to my knees and stood up, still holding him, helping him to his feet. We whirled one way and then another, the Quarry whanged and banged, the people around us clapped their hands and stomped their feet: Tennessee and I were joined as one, sweaty bodies slick and sliding to the ground, where we lay panting until someone poured a jug of water over us. We shook our heads, water drops flashed through the air, winged birds flew to the sun, we laughed and gasped and stood up straight and strong, clasped hands while the band played on.

For the rest of the day, Tennessee was the guardian of the stage, patrolling in front, keeping his dilated eyes on everything as the afternoon droned on and the anxiety over the arrival of the Hells Angels dissipated, for the motorcycle gang never showed up.

We had a late start the next day. Texans sprawled next to their cars were awakened by "The Star-Spangled Banner," followed by my booming voice over the loudspeakers: "Welcome again, campers, to the biggest drive-in free stage in America. Drop your cocks and grab your socks. It's cleanup time at the old corral."

Men and women stumbled to their feet and began cleaning up the place in anticipation of another day's mess.

The Quarry went over to the main stage at the speedway, played to a rousing reception, came back, and tore into a long set that drew a mixed crowd up onto the stage: Texans of all persuasions and colors packed so tightly together there was no room for movement. The Quarry were backed up against the amps, primal grunts and screams mixed with the music, everyone at a pitched edge—for the word was B.B. King and the Blues Band were coming to play on the free stage as soon as they finished on the main stage.

That night, Hugh Romney lay on his famous bad back, in the middle of the stage, crooning and babbling into a microphone. I hid behind the curtain cackling into another one.

An old frizzled-headed gent peering in from the backstage blackness yelled, "Say, who is that doing all that squawking anyway?"

I stepped into the light and said, "'Tis I, the Booger Wooger Man."

The old gent laughed, light glinting on his gold tooth. "You keep right on it, y'hear?"

Hugh Romney interjected from the floor. "If you're the Booger Wooger Man, can I be Wavy Gravy on the floor?"

"Of course you can."

Wavy Gravy raised himself up on an elbow.

"What's that I hear, someone offering to sell a joint for a dollar? Unheard of. All you folks with grass bring it on up here and let's roll it up and smoke it up for free. This is a free stage, isn't it?"

The joints were thick bombers. Eager smokers puffed and shared while the Old Booger Wooger Man and Wavy Gravy mouthed low fuzztones of encouragement, helping to stoke a party energy rush meant to fulfill the workweek promise of good times if you play your cards—*puff puff*—right, fellow 'Mericans?

Midnight and the big dawgs still hadn't shown. A somnolent

lull slowed everyone down. I dimmed the stage lights, the Quarry played a long, drawn-out note... We shut down the microphones and amplifiers, leaving nothing but quiet murmurings, when someone yelled, "They're here."

A big tour bus worked its way to the side of the stage. The door opened and B.B. King and the Blues Band trooped out, climbed onto the stage and plugged their instruments into the Quarry amps. David Butkovich turned on the power. B.B. King looked around with a big smile on his face when he heard a voice booming out of the speakers.

"Yes, ladies and gentlemen, campers and nudie swimmers," I announced from behind the curtain, "this is the Old Booger Wooger Man, introducing, as promised, a passel of all-time champion music-makers who have come to regale us till the cows wake up."

The band hit it:

"It's that same old thing day in day out,
I'm so alone I want to scream and shout.
Can it be true I'm not loved by anyone,
Doomed to spend my life a lonesome son?"

B.B. King had to watch his step to avoid a body sprawled underfoot.

"It's just me, Wavy Gravy on the floor," Hugh Romney said, "where the music I hear comes in the most clear."

B.B. King looked down at him and said, "If you want to be Wavy Gravy on the floor, then you be Wavy Gravy on the floor."

They started a new song. Dave Carron from the Quarry took my microphone and began singing from behind the curtains:

"I'm a crosscut saw
Drag me across your log
I cut your wood so easy
You can't help but say, 'Hot Dog.'
I got a double-bladed axe

That really cuts good
I'm a crosscut saw
Gonna bury me in your wood."

B.B. King looked to his left, then right, then turned all the way around, big wide smile on his face, as he listened to Dave's clear pure voice.

After it was over and the bus drove off into the light of day, Hugh Romney, still lying on the floor, grabbed my leg as I walked past.

"Listen," he said to me, "if B.B. King calls me Wavy Gravy, then that's who I am."

I clutched his arm. "What is deemed done is a fixed star in the firmament, and the Wavy Gravy star will shine with the brightest. Now get up and let's go to bed."

I pulled him to his feet and we shuffled off the stage.

A late wake-up the next day to pack up and clear out, we had to wait to get paid and, while waiting, drove out and parked on the side of the road.

The Quarry was going to continue to San Francisco with us and went off to rent a truck to haul their gear. The Hog Farm departed for their home in Llano, New Mexico, in a charter bus named *Indian Detours*. Keith Haxby and the *Hitchhiker* headed back to Oregon. Dale and Diane, in the *Brown Hound* decided they'd head out on their own, destination unknown.

The Quarry was delayed obtaining a truck and sent word they'd meet us on the road, so, in the darkening light of dusk, with the cash in the briefcase, we set out. A half-mile down the road we were stopped by the red lights of Sheriff Grady pulling us over for a comprehensive shakedown: Everyone stood outside while he searched my bus and *Further*. We were ready for a search and came through clean.

By then it was dark. Sheriff Grady checked our IDs one-by-one with his flashlight. David Butkovich gave the sheriff a ration of shit, got a ticket for a bad attitude. $45 dollars total, which I paid on the spot.

We reached Vernon, Texas, in the wee hours and spent the night at a roadside rest stop, a continuous line of trucks and trains roaring past.

We lingered there until the late afternoon. On September 10th, under a light rain and yellow-clouded sky, we fired 'em up, all but *Further*. Starter worked, but no fire. I found the problem. Someone had disconnected the wires to the battery. I put them back on and in the glow of sunset we headed out, only to stop again, *Further* coughing and cutting out and emitting a burnt smell. Wires were crossed and shorting out. We caught it before there was a fire and complete breakdown.

We drove through the night to Bernalillo where we crashed for sleep and eats at an old campground next to a river and irrigation ditch.

New Mexico and Highway 66: the old Okie route to California. After passing Glenn Canyon on the Colorado River, we stopped and set up a sweat lodge, hot bodies huddled inside a pop-up tent. Three ladies who came to fish were shocked by the sight of a nudie freako show bursting out of the tent, *hie-yee*ing into the water, blasting waves into the fish lines while singing, *"Good morning to you, fisherwomen, we're all in our places with smiles on our faces!"*—at which time the Ranger arrived, curious as to why we didn't sleep up on the hill where there were plastic rain roofs and concrete tables. "To keep people away from the riverbank, to help preserve the 'cology of the last bit of a natural riverbank you can still get to on the Colorado River," he said, "'count of that damn dam upstream."

Next time, we assured him, up on the hill, for sure.

A mile down the road, *Further* had a flat tire. Time again for Old Baldy, which was down to cords but always saved us. A supper stop at Pipe Ford on the Old Quarry Trail, site of the first telegraph line in Arizona, then we were back on the road, spurred on by Paul Foster, "Hey, we've been out of dope and have been out for how many days now? God, I've lost count."

A hot drive through Nevada. We pulled to a stop at a crossroads saloon where a sign said, NO FIREARMS. We played the slot machines and ate hamburgers.

We drove until tired and stopped at a graveled parking lot, then departed without eating supper. Sped down Montgomery Pass into California, where we stopped to sleep.

N ext day we rode into San Francisco and up the 101 to Novato, where we pulled into the lot at Alembic, the Grateful Dead warehouse and studio. Johnny Hagen, Mike's brother was the only one there, waiting in his pickup for the place to open.

He crawled through a window in the front office, opened the door to the lot and we parked and went inside, lugging our equipment and powering up our amplifiers. The Quarry started playing. Lenny Hart, the band's manager, came in, followed by the Grateful Dead. We played and sang together through the afternoon.

We hung around the warehouse for a few days, buses parked out front. When we were ready to leave, the Quarry stayed to look for work in San Francisco. We headed north up the 101 through grape country, stopped at a winery and bought three and a half gallons of red wine, then continued on to the Russian River, where we pulled off the highway, ate chicken, Brussel sprouts, bean sprouts, brown rice and drank all the wine.

A scruffy dog, some kind of short-haired terrier, snuffled into our circle, his nose twitching, tail wagging, not begging exactly, but displaying a lot of interest in the food.

"He a vegetarian?" Butko asked, holding out a chunk of Brussels sprouts.

The dog sniffed it, turned around and sat down.

"Okay, try this."

Butko held out a chicken-leg bone. The dog leaned forward, took the bone in his mouth, turned and lay down. Crunches, then silence. Next morning, he was aboard *Further*. Snuffy was his name.

We stopped for lunch at a state park in the redwoods. On this late summer's date the place was empty, no campers or picnickers. The dog was busy snuffling and pooping and got busted.

"Dogs must be on a leash," the park ranger said. He held out a slip of paper, which stated the rules in print.

"Sign here," he said.

I signed, glad to see there was no fine, and we mounted up, Snuffy leaping aboard.

That morning we crossed into Oregon and stopped for gas in Grants Pass. Some LA cat, down on his luck, his '56 Dodge broke down, said he had no money for smokes and wanted to know if we'd buy some cartwheels.

"Nope," I told him. "Don't use them things. Got any grass?"

"Two joints."

I went with him to his car where he broke out two rolled joints. We smoked the joints in the bus, I gave him two dollars, he went back to his car and we fired up and hit the road.

We pulled into Kesey's farm in the early evening, parked my bus and *Further* side-by-side behind the barn, smoked a joint with Kesey, helped him put his new pony in the barn, ate supper and drank tea. Snuffy got acquainted with the animals on the farm and, along with Stewart, Kesey's dog, peed on the fence posts until both dogs were peed dry.

Later, when everyone had crashed, I wrote in the log book that Intrepid Trips had returned to home port.

"The Farmsters pondered and wondered... What to do now

and wherever the wind blows ... Assignments may come and assignments may go but this is the time to settle for winter rates
when all else is done..."

"How and where do you want the bus left?" Butko asked
Kesey.

"Empty and where it is."

One time a guy asked Kesey for some thoughts on
something the guy was writing and Kesey said,
"I've got my own dragon chewing on my leg and
can't take on someone else's dragon."
— Ken Babbs

57

Hornswoggling

The hay was stacked in the barn. The sprinklers were in a pile in the field. The grapes were ripe and juicy, the apples red and wormy. The trees were turning; gold and orange hues gleamed among the green. Kesey and I headed to the swamp to cut firewood before the rains came and turned the ground to mush.

"Did you bring your gloves?" Kesey asked when we arrived at a downed ash tree.

"You kidding me? I never take a leak without putting my gloves on first."

"A dick like that, I'd wear a glove too. You got yours?"

"My dick? I never go anywhere without it."

"No, you lamebrain, your gloves."

"It just so happens I forgot my gloves," I said, not about to let him rag on me about forgetting my gloves.

"Here's a pair you can use."

He handed me a thick canvas pair, so stiff I couldn't bend my fingers. I silently cursed myself, for not admitting that the supple, tanned, deerskin gloves that fit my hands like a second skin were stuck, unseen, in my back pocket.

I decided to make the best of it and picked up the chainsaw. Watching me struggle with the chainsaw, trying to start it when

I couldn't get my fingers in those stiff gloves around the starting handle, Kesey said, "Once, four samurai were standing alongside a stream and arguing about who had the sharpest sword and how it made him the best warrior. The first samurai put his gleaming blade in the water and sent a piece of paper floating toward it. The sword sliced it in half. The next two samurai did the same thing with the same result. The fourth samurai, an old doof in tattered robes, thrust his rusty sword into the water and floated a single piece of paper its way. The paper approached the sword, swerved, and went floating past."

I eyed Kesey. He looked back blandly. Putting the chainsaw down, I ripped the stiff gloves off, threw them on the ground. Pulled my own gloves out of my pocket, put them on and, instead of picking up the chainsaw, went over and started pissing on a blackberry bush.

"Those three samurai weren't convinced," I told Kesey over my shoulder. "'Check this,' the first samurai said. He flashed his sword in the air and cut a fly in half. The other two samurai did the same. The old doof gave a half-hearted swing with his sword. 'Ha-ha,' first samurai laughed. 'Fly fly away.'

"'Yes, but fly will never reproduce again.'"

I shook my dick. The old saying bubbled in my mind's mire:
"You can shake it, you can break it,
You can pound it against the wall,
But you have to put it in your pants
To make the last drop fall."

I zipped up. There was a stirring in the swamp, a primordial shudder. A maple tree shrugged. Leaves fluttered and fell, leaving the tree as bare as a lady with her petticoats and skirts piled at her feet.

Through an open space between the trees a brown eagle stared at me, his talons gripping a cedar post. Then, silently, wings unfolding, he lifted and flew away. I looked at Kesey. His hand was raised.

"*Selah*, Grandfather."

We got to cutting. Trimmed the branches and bucked the tree into woodstove lengths. Shut down the saws and picked up the splitting tools.

Kesey used a wedge and sledge. I was a maul man. He set the wedge on the round and pecked at it with his sledge until the wood split down the middle. Then he split another chunk.

I set a round up, lifted the maul over my head and brought it down hard enough to split the round in half with one whack. If the wood was straight grained, that's all it took. Twisted, it took more than one whack.

Kesey reached back with his sledge, swung the nine-pound head close to me.

"Watch it," I said. "You're liable to squash my balls with that thing."

"I didn't think you wanted any more kids," he said.

Har, har. I let it pass and we started in again. After a while he said, "You know, you'd save a lot of energy using a wedge and sledge instead of that maul."

"Yeah, but it would take twice as long."

"Twice as long as what? You're not going any faster than I am."

"You kidding me? There's no way you can split wood faster with a wedge and sledge than I can with a maul."

"You want to bet?"

"Does a fox suck eggs? Name your wager and make it easy on yourself."

"I'll go twenty bucks for twenty minutes."

"You're on."

He nodded. I grabbed a round and started whacking for all I was worth. I could hear him hitting at a steady beat. This was going to be a cinch. After a while I had to take my jacket off. His forehead wasn't even damp. Pretty soon I was glancing at my watch. The twenty minutes were starting to drag, but no way was I about to let up. I pushed it to the end.

"That's it," I said. "Time's up."

He stepped back a pace and surveyed the pile. "Well," he said. "I guess you hornswoggled me this time."

You bet I had. It wasn't even close. He hadn't done piddling. The wood around me was piled up to my waist. His came up to his ankles.

"Well, come on," he said. "Let's throw the wood in the truck and take it up to the shed."

The flush of victory lasted about two minutes. It took me that long to realize I was the one who was hornswoggled. He didn't rub it in though. It might make me more wary the next time.

We drove to the house and threw the wood out of the truck onto the ground in front of the woodshed.

"We'll stack it later," Kesey said. "We've got just enough time to make a dump run before it closes."

I backed my truck to the garage and we hoisted the fifty-five-gallon cans of trash onto the bed. Then we drove to the dump in Creswell, paid the fee and backed up to the unloading bins. Together, we lifted the cans from the bottom and tipped them into the bin, which took total cooperation—the cans were heavy and could tip over if we weren't careful.

"This is how I got my front tooth broken," I told Kesey.

"At the dump?" he said. "I thought it was when that redhead slammed you face first into the wrestling mat when we were at Stanford."

"No, I didn't tell you then, but the first time my tooth was broken was when I was in high school working at my uncle's pig farm and we picked up garbage in fifty-five-gallon drums at restaurants and emptied the cans into the hog troughs. My uncle said, 'Ready?' and tipped the can before I said, 'Yes.' The edge of the can hit and broke my tooth. I was one pissed-off teenager."

"A lesson learned is a lesson practiced," Kesey said. "Let's do this last trash can right."

When I reached for the can I saw, sitting on top of the trash, three milk jugs, stoppered, full of an amber liquid.

"What's this," I said, hefting one. "Your beer stash."

"Might be. Give it a try."

I uncapped it. *Whew*. Pungent.

"Whassamatter," I said, "you don't piss off the porch anymore?"

"Faye says I'm killing all her flowers."

"Piss like that, I can believe it."

"Throw it away and let's get out of here. There's a whiff of Jim's Landing in the air."

"I'll be hornswoggled, I can smell it too."

I capped the milk jug and threw it in the dump.

At the bar we had our usual two gin and tonics and then I got up to leave. Kesey stayed seated.

"You go on ahead," he said. "I've got some things to take care of."

"How you getting home?"

"I've got it covered. Go along now."

I went home and the next morning at Kesey's, I noticed the wood we piled in front of the shed had been stacked inside.

"What's that all about?" I asked when he came out of the house.

"When we were at the dump, two deputies came roaring in and threw the wood all over the place. Faye yelled at them, 'What are you doing?' and they said someone called to say I hid pot in the woodpile. 'That's the dumbest thing I ever heard,' she told them. 'Now what are you going to do about all that wood scattered everywhere?' They hung their heads and said they'd pick it up. They even stacked it in the shed."

"Guess they got hornswoggled," I said.

We hopped into Kesey's convertible and drove up the hill to the highway, me gabbing all the way, Kesey not saying a word.

"I'm not hanging you up with all my jabbering?" I asked him.

"I'm not hung up, I'm hungover. I stayed at Jim's Landing until I was soused, then called Faye and had her take me to the community college. They wanted to interview me to be on the school board and I couldn't figure out a way to tactfully decline so I thought I'd go in drunk and see what happened."

"So?"

"So I don't have to worry about being on the school board."

We approached the Pleasant Hill school zone. Every time Kesey drove through the zone he complained about no one slowing down. He'd had enough, and he set up a meeting with Jim Howard, Superintendent of Schools, and a bigwig from Oregon Department of Transportation. We pulled off the highway onto the frontage road in front of the school and parked next to the administration building.

Jim Howard and the ODOT official were waiting for us. Kesey gave them his spiel about how dangerous the highway was and that they needed to do something about it. His words didn't seem to be having any effect, although Jim and the ODOT man listened politely. A steady line of traffic drove past, and then a loaded log truck whipped off of the highway onto the frontage road in front of us and went roaring past in a deafening roar, slinging gravel against our legs before turning left onto Enterprise Road.

Jim Howard and the ODOT guy looked like they had been hit with a haymaker. Kesey was grim-faced. Jim Howard turned to Kesey and said, "We'll see what we can do about this."

The ODOT official nodded in concurrence.

Two days later there were lights and signs on the highway:

SCHOOL ZONE

20 MPH

WHEN LIGHT IS FLASHING

When school was starting in the morning and letting out in the afternoon, cars and semis and log trucks on the busy east-west highway crawled along like dogs on a leash.

K esey held a volleyball game at his place every week. We started after supper and played until dark, then had drinks and snacks. One time, Kesey unobtrusively disappeared. A few minutes later a great white owl swooped out of the loft in the darkening light and floated over us with hardly a whisper, putting a scare in everyone.

Kesey not only liked to pull surprises, but he also passed along tricks and shortcuts he had learned. His dad taught him when you open a can of paint, you take a hammer and nail and punch holes around the inner edge of the can so the paint that collects in the gutter drips back into the can.

He also told me, "When you make spaghetti and you're stirring the sauce with a spoon, dip the spoon in the water that you're boiling the noodles in. The flavor goes into the noodles."

"Where'd you get that from?"

"Faye's been taking a cooking class at the community college."

"A cooking class? She's only cooked about 6,000 meals for about 10,000 people over the years!"

"Yeah, I know. But that's what they taught her at the class."

He also told me that when you cut a baguette for the spaghetti meal, you turn the baguette on its side to slice it.

One time when I was at his house for dinner, he gave me the baguette and the cutting board to slice the bread. I laid the baguette down and started to slice it.

Faye yelled, "Don't do it like that. Turn it on its side."

I looked at Kesey. He rolled his eyes to the ceiling, nothing to do with him.

I turned the baguette on its side and started cutting. Much easier. We settled down to the meal and then I headed home, another big day tomorrow.

Love the quick profit, the annual raise,
vacation with pay. Want more
of everything ready-made. Be afraid
to know your neighbors and to die.
And you will have a window in your head.
Not even your future will be a mystery
anymore. Your mind will be punched in a card
and shut away in a little drawer.
Love the world. Work for nothing.
Take all that you have and be poor.
Love someone who does not deserve it.
Denounce the government and embrace
the flag. Hope to live in that free
republic for which it stands.
So long as women do not go cheap
for power, please women more than men.
Ask yourself: Will this satisfy
a woman satisfied to bear a child?
Go with your love to the fields.
Lie easy in the shade. Rest your head
in her lap. Swear allegiance
to what is nighest your thoughts.
As soon as the generals and the politicos
can predict the motions of your mind,
lose it. Leave it as a sign
to mark the false trail, the way
you didn't go. Be like the fox
who makes more tracks than necessary,
some in the wrong direction.
Practice resurrection.
      — Wendell Berry,
      from "Manifesto: The Mad Farmer Liberation Front"

58

I'll Never Come This Way Again

"We're going to take you to the airport by canoe," Kesey said.

Wendell Berry laughed. Our old pal from the Stanford writing class, now a renowned essayist, poet, novelist and farmer, used horses instead of a tractor and didn't have a TV. People came to his house from all over to check out his composting toilet. A spokesman for sustainable farming, he had flown to Oregon to give a talk at the University of Oregon.

Long, lanky and laconic, ask him a question, he pondered a bit, then answered in a slow, measured voice. He spent the night at Kesey's, gave his talk to a packed house the next evening. The next day, a clear, bright Sunday with nary a cloud in the sky, he was scheduled to fly back to his home in Kentucky, and Kesey and I were going to take him to the airport.

We put the canoe in the Willamette River under the Jasper Bridge. Kesey jumped in the water and, standing in the shallows, wrapped his arms around a big salmon. The fish shrugged and sent Kesey splashing into the river. I grabbed the salmon by the tail; it whipped me back and forth like a dog shaking a weasel. I fell in and watched the dark-skinned fish swim away. Wendell Berry laughed uproariously at Kesey and me floundering in the drink.

While I held the canoe steady, Kesey and Wendell loaded our drinks and food and the paddles. Kesey sat in front with a paddle, Wendell in the middle, our passenger. Carrying my paddle, I pushed off and hopped into the back seat. We headed to the middle of the river and pointed the nose downstream. The Jasper Bridge disappeared behind us and we were quickly removed from all traces of civilization. Big trees hung over the riverbank. A blue heron rose and flew ahead before swerving off over the brush. We could have been the first ones to traverse the river; everything was the same as hundreds of years before. The only sound was the paddles knifing the water.

The river ran straight and true with occasional rocks sticking above the water. We came to a sharp left turn and I held the paddle hard on the side of the canoe to bring us around the curve. The water was racing and we picked up speed and swept in close to the bank before straightening out.

There was a rock-covered flat spot on the side of the river just ahead and we pulled over to take a break. I went off a ways to take a leak and heard Kesey telling Wendell, "That curve was where one time Babbs held his paddle on the wrong side of the canoe and, in the frenzy to straighten out, we tipped over and everyone went in the drink. We popped to the surface, grabbed hold of the canoe and splashed to this very spot where Babbs, stripped to his underwear, was taking a piss just like he is now."

"Yeah," I yelled over my shoulder, "and you announced to everyone, 'Look at Babbs, searching in his shorts for his dick all shriveled up from being in the cold water.'"

Wendell laughed. "Well, a shriveled dick is probably better than no dick at all."

"Unless it's Dick Tracy you call to find the remains," I said.

We pushed off into the river. Rocks jutted from both sides, creating a narrow channel. Water splashed over the front of the canoe. We sliced through, our paddles keeping us from hitting the rocks, and came out of the trough heading straight for a big oak that had toppled into the river, branches thick both above and below the surface. We steered to keep from being dragged under. After we were clear, Kesey said, "One time we were coming down the river with George Walker and we got caught in the branches of a tree and we all went in. Babbs and I got out from the entanglement, caught up with the canoe and, while hanging onto the sides and looking around, realized George was nowhere in sight. Just as we were about to dive under and look for him, he popped up downriver from us, a real relief."

"It's a wonder," Wendell Berry said. "Nothing like that on our slow-moving river back home."

"How about the time," I said, "when under one of those trees we saw a canoe turned over, all snarled up, and we pulled over to take a quick look, half-scared we'd find someone in there. We hooked a line to the canoe and pulled it out and luckily no bodies, no life jackets, no paddles, no nothing. We towed it home and Kesey's brother, Chuck, welded the tear in the canoe together and we've been using it ever since."

"This canoe?" Wendell asked.

"No, our spare," Kesey said, "for when we have more people making the run."

Wendell was quiet, enjoying the ride, watching the changing scenery. The osprey that had been circling overhead hit the water with a big splash. Wings beating frantically, it rose with a salmon clutched in its talons. It skimmed along the river, then flew up and landed in the top of a dead tree.

"I believe that's a yew behind that snag," Wendell said.

"It is indeed," Kesey said. "Grows for a hundred years or so and doesn't get very big. It's valued now for its bark, which contains Taxol, a cancer fighter."

"That could well be the reason the bark is poison to cattle who eat it," Wendell said. "In England they planted yew in churchyards so the cattle couldn't get at the church."

We came around a long curve and, in the straightaway, people floated in inner tubes and plastic rafts. Others were splashing in the shallows. The sandy bank was a turmoil of kids and teenagers running and skipping stones, standing and talking and drinking beer.

"Clearwater Boat Landing," Kesey said. "Sometimes we pull the canoe out here, but today we're going on, so we have to stick close to the shore because over there, in the middle of the river, is a whirlpool. You don't want to get caught in that. It doesn't pull you down into a deep spiral but keeps you going 'round and 'round in a circle and it's a devil of a time getting out."

Clear of the people, we disappeared into a tunnel of trees hanging over the water, once again seemingly far apart from civilization and its teeming masses.

"For a while," Kesey said, "I had an aluminum rowboat we took down the river. It seated four. We used that boat a lot. One time we had a tank of nitrous oxide with us. We smashed the boat into a rock early in the trip and it gashed a big hole in the bottom. We couldn't keep up with the bailing, and had to pull over, tip the water out, and duct tape the hole as best we could, then keep going until the leak got too big and the distance between stops smaller and smaller. At dark we decided to spend the night on the riverbank. We built a fire, cooked a fish David Butkovich caught. He didn't stay to eat it, instead went crashing through the blackberries to find a phone and call his wife and let her know we were okay and for her to call the other wives.

"The next morning, when it was light enough to see, there was the Jasper Bridge, our destination, right ahead. We got in the boat, bailed as hard as we could to stay afloat until we went ashore. That boat was never launched again. Uh-oh, decision time."

Up ahead the river separated around a small island.

"Which way, Babbs?" Kesey asked.

Oh shit, I couldn't remember for sure. I was leaning to the left so I said, "The left channel."

When we got alongside the island, the canoe grounded on a shallow rock bed. We got out, laid the paddles in the belly and pulled the canoe along, scraping the bottom, until the river joined together and we hit deep water. We clambered in and took up our paddles.

I said, "Reminds me of the woman riding her bike over the cobblestone street. She said, 'I'll never come this way again.'"

Kesey dug his paddle in the water and flipped a geyser into my face.

"Okay, I'll never tell that stupid joke again," I muttered, wiping my hand across my eyes.

We rounded the last bend for the straightaway to our destination. On our left, the railroad line to Roseburg; on the hill above the railroad, Interstate 5 roaring with traffic; on our right, the riverbank lined with mobile homes.

We passed under the Springfield Bridge, angled the canoe toward shore and pulled up onto dry land. We were in Day Island Park, green grass and bushes and paths and a short walk to city streets. We hiked two blocks to the Springfield Creamery, owned and operated by Kesey's brother, Chuck, and Chuck's wife, Sue. Their Health Food and Pool Store was next to the Creamery. Inside the store, Chuck had built a platform seven feet off the floor, with steps leading up, railings all around, and a regulation pool table in the middle. Out on the sidewalk, an eight-foot-long box sat against the building between the Creamery and the Health Food and Pool Store: The Free Box.

"This is where, when we're soaking wet from a canoe trip, we get dry clothes," Kesey said. The Free Box was overflowing with pants and shirts and jackets and hats, all donated. Put some in, take some out.

Wendell liked that. "Could use one of those boxes in most every town," he said.

Chuck came out of the Springfield Creamery and he and Kesey and I walked back to the river to get the canoe. We loaded the canoe on the top of Chuck's pickup. Faye took Wendell to the airport in the car, and Kesey and Chuck and I drove to the Jasper Bridge where we'd first set in. We transferred the canoe to the top of my truck, Chuck drove away, and Kesey and I hopped into my pickup.

"What say we go over to the Jasper Store and get a beer?" I said.

"Maybe even two," Kesey answered.

I parked in front of the store, next to another pickup. We looked in the back of the truck. A seven-foot-long sturgeon lay in the truck bed. It was still breathing.

"They can live quite awhile out of water," Kesey said.

"Looks like he's about at the end of the line," I said.

"We still have time. Grab the other end."

Kesey reached in and got his arm under the head. I picked up the tail. We lifted the fish over the side of the truck and stumbled across the street, down the hill to the river and pitched the fish in.

It lay motionless, gills slowly opening and closing, then with a flick of its tail, glided away.

"Let's get out of here," Kesey said.

We hustled to my truck. I spun the tires leaving the lot.

"Whew," I said, still breathing hard. "Lucked out there."

"Yeah," Kesey said, "too bad someone with a camera wasn't there to catch the look on that guy's face when he saw his sturgeon was gone."

"Gone, real gone," I said. "Just like that beer."

*"Hey Rube" is an old-timey phrase, coined in the
merciless culture of the traveling carnival gangs that
roamed from town to town in the early twentieth century.
Every stop on the circuit was just another chance to
fleece a crowd of free-spending rubes, suckers, hicks,
yokels, johns, fish, marks, bums, losers, day traders in
Portland, fools who buy diamonds from gypsies, and
anyone else over the age of one in this country who
still believes in his heart that all cops are honest and
would never lie in a courtroom.*
  — Hunter S. Thompson

59

I'll Never See That Movie

"Forty six-foot steel T-posts, six seven-foot treated poles,
three spools of barbed wire, staples, and wire holders," I
read from the list I'd written in my notebook.

"Oh, Lordy," Kesey said, "the planning comes easy, it's the
thought of the work that slows things down. I need more coffee."

He stood up from the table and walked to the stove. He was
pouring a cup when there was a knock at the door.

"What now?" he said.

Two dapper gents stood on the landing. Kesey ushered them
in and said to me, "Michael Douglas and Saul Zaentz."

I stood up. Hollywood luminaries. What was this all about?
Michael Douglas was his father's lookalike. Dark hair swept
back, smile on his face, white shirt with black vest. Saul Zaentz
was older, rotund with an oval face, balding head, silver short-
haired beard, wire-rimmed glasses. I shook hands and we sat
down around the table.

After the usual chitchat they got down to business. Zaentz and Douglas announced they were going to make the movie of *One Flew Over the Cuckoo's Nest.* Michael's father, Kirk Douglas, had bought the play and movie rights when the book was published in 1962. Kirk hired Dale Wasserman to write the play and the next year it opened on Broadway with Kirk playing McMurphy. Now they wanted Kesey to write the screenplay for the movie.

Kesey thought for a moment, then turned to me.

"It's lunchtime, Babbs. Howsabout making us some tuna fish sandwiches?"

I scrounged through the kitchen for the makings. Tuna, mayo, mustard, celery and relish. I opened the tuna and put the chunks in a bowl, cut up the celery and put it on top of the tuna, then spooned in some relish.

The conversation at the table was a low murmur in the background. I stirred everything together and reached for the mustard. As I was about to squirt it into the tuna salad, Kesey appeared at my side and said, "What are you doing? You don't put mustard in tuna salad."

I looked at him, mustard poised. Touch and glow, to squirt or not to squirt?

"It's the way my mother always made it," I said.

"This isn't your mother's house."

He snatched the mustard out of my hand. "Just make the damned sandwiches."

I didn't know what bee got up his butt, but wasn't about to make an issue out of it. I laid the sandwiches on a platter, added lettuce and sliced tomatoes around the edge, and carried it to the table.

"Here you go, gents. A snack to keep you on the go and some garnishes to please your palate."

Kesey put a bottle of red wine on the table along with some glasses. I backed away.

"Aren't you going to join us?" Michael Douglas asked.

"No, I have to run to town and get our fencing supplies. Big job in the works."

I picked up the list of supplies, waved goodbye and left.

The next day when we were out in the field, working on the fence, I asked Kesey, "What was that all about?"

"They were pushing me, wanting me to go along with their plan and I needed to do an end run. The mustard gave me some space. We finally reached an agreement. I'm going to write the screenplay."

He smashed a fence staple into the wooden pole, driving it in to the hilt.

Later, after some months passed, Kesey found out they didn't use his screenplay after all, but hired someone else to write it. Kesey was beaked but he knew the reason why. Like he did in the book, when he wrote the screenplay, he had Chief Bromden tell the story. They wanted McMurphy to be the main man, not the chief. They signed Jack Nicholson for the part, and were already filming at the Oregon State Hospital outside Salem.

Kesey stewed, then he sued. Breach of contract. The trial was held in Oregon. Right from the start, the head LA lawyer was on the attack.

"This is a frivolous suit with nothing in the mind of Mister Kesey but to get his hands on some money that isn't his. Where is the signed contract? What evidence is there that he was hired to write the screenplay?"

Kesey's answer was simple.

"We agreed on the deal and shook hands on it. Even I, with my limited knowledge of law, know that a handshake is as good as a written agreement. If you don't believe we shook on it, we can have Michael Douglas and Saul Zaentz testify."

The LA lawyer leaped to his feet.

"I object, Your Honor. He knows Michael and Saul are too busy working on the movie to leave the set."

He was bluffing. His team knew the handshake deal was true. The judge found in Kesey's favor and awarded him the agreed-upon money.

The trial over, the phalanx of big-time LA lawyers stood up and paraded past Kesey in their three-thousand-dollar suits. The head lawyer, the most sartorially resplendent, stopped in front of Kesey.

"You may have won this victory but I'll guarantee, you'll be the first in line to see the movie when it comes out."

Kesey looked at him and said, "I'll never see that movie."

I told him I never would either.

And neither one of us ever did.

T he Oregon premiere, held at the McDonald Theatre in Eugene, was a gala affair packed with Kesey's mom and his relatives and friends and as many Eugeneans that could fit in.

Kesey stayed home with Faye. I picked up Page Browning and we went over to Kesey's to keep him company. We had a few drinks, sat around talking and listening to music and, as the evening went on, I noticed Page was getting more and more antsy. Finally, he said, "Let's go outside, Babbs and get some air."

"What's up?" I said when we stood in the light of the full moon.

"I can't take this shit. All those people in town kissing ass on that movie and Kesey isn't getting any writing credit. Let's take a ride up to the corner, I want to make a phone call."

I parked next to a double phone booth in the gas station lot. Page jumped out and went in the booth. I could hear him yelling, something about a bomb, and that the movie was a slap in the face of people with mental illnesses and someone had to make a statement, get their attention.

He slammed the phone down and ran to the pickup.

"Take me home," he said. "I feel a bodacious drunk coming

on."

The next morning, I went over to Kesey's to see how he was doing. He met me at the door.

"Have you seen the paper?"

"No, why?"

He handed it to me. The headline read: BOMB THREAT EMPTIES MCDONALD THEATRE. The story went on to say everyone had to stand outside while the place was searched. Then, at the end, it added that a man who had been making a phone call at a booth in Pleasant Hill heard another man in the booth next to him screaming and yelling about a bomb in the theater. The screaming man left in a green pickup truck.

I gave the paper back to Kesey and jammed out of there. Drove home and parked the truck behind the shed. Inside the shed I found a can of red paint and a brush. I quickly painted the truck red. Stepped back to make sure no green was showing, then buried the paint can and brush in a blackberry patch.

A couple of days later I looked out the window and saw a black car pull into the drive. I peeked out from behind a curtain where they couldn't see me. From the spotlight next to the front window, I could tell it was an unmarked police car. The two men inside wore suits. Undercover cops. They sat for a while, looking around, then backed up and left. I took a deep breath and let it out. "Walked away from another one, Chief."

Religious forces are needed to overcome the egotism
that divides people. The common celebration of the
great sacrificial feasts and sacred rites, which gave
expression simultaneously to the interrelation and
social articulation of family and state was the means
employed to unite men and women. The sacred music
and the splendor of the ceremonies aroused a strong
tide of emotion that was shared by all hearts in unison,
and that awakened a consciousness of the common
origin of all creatures. In this way disunity was overcome
and rigidity dissolved.
　　— I Ching

60

Dogs Must Pay Full Admission

A Lincoln Town Car pulls up to the curb and parks. The radio plays a commercial jingle:

"*Go tell your neighbor,*
go tell your neighbor
that we're selling milk."

The driver punches the radio off.

"Ha, we'll see about that."

He looks up at the blue and white Springfield Creamery sign across the front of the building. Adjusts his homburg, checks that his tie is tight against his neck. Brushes a speck of dust off of the collar of his overcoat, brandishes a furled umbrella like a shillelagh. Strides purposefully toward the building.

"This is the place. I'll just slip in through the back here, and take care of these miscreants."

He smiles grimly.

"I hate to do this but an inspector's lot is not easy. I hope they're ready."

He marches into the milking room, takes off his hat, tips it in greeting. Chuck Kesey, dressed in white bottling duds and black rubber boots, nods and follows him through the room.

"So immaculately clean and all," the inspector says, smiling and gesturing with his umbrella. "I suspect you've cleaned up so it will be just the way I like it when I come in, ha ha ha...

"Ah, the office." He raps on the door with his umbrella then barges in.

"How do you do, young lady, it's good to see you." He nods and smiles at Nancy Van Brasch sitting at the desk.

Chuck Kesey and Page Browning have followed him in. Page lugs a crate full of one-gallon milk jars. The inspector turns to Chuck Kesey.

"I know you have been bottling milk reliably for the past number of years but now, due to the unfortunate incident the other night, that is out. I'm sure the Erickson Brothers will be happy to take over."

He pokes Chuck in the chest with the handle of his umbrella, thrusts a bundle of papers into Chuck's hand, salutes with his hat, gives everyone a big smile and strides out the front door.

T he unfortunate incident alluded to was no small-time dust-up, but a front-page scandal. A few weeks earlier, Bud Haxby, Chuck's partner, picked the apples off of the trees in his backyard and brought them to the Springfield Creamery where he and Chuck dumped them into a large vat in the back store-room and proceeded to brew up a batch of applejack. It was fermenting nicely but, unbeknownst to them, was driving one of the workers, a former alcoholic, nuts, tempting him with its easy access, and he succumbed to temptation; just a taste for a few days, then one night he went on a full-bore drunk. Stumbling home, he couldn't remember if he had turned off the spigot at the bottom of the tank.

When Chuck came to work the next morning, twenty-five cops, three reporters and two cameramen greeted him. The storeroom was flooded, the vat was empty and the smell of alcohol hung over everything. A large group of townsfolk stood outside.

The newspaper headlines screamed: "KEN KESEY'S BROTHER BREWING LIQUOR AT THE SCHOOL MILK BOTTLING BUSINESS."

Alluding to Ken Kesey's lurid past in order to draw in the readers. The initial furor had no sooner died down when the inspector arrived. After he so smugly marched out, Chuck waved the papers the inspector left and said, "What are we going to do? What are we going to do?"

They had lost the Springfield Public Schools milk account, and that was what had kept the Springfield Creamery afloat.

One of the employees, Jim Hyslip, said, "Let's have a concert, get the Grateful Dead to play and use the money to keep going."

What a notion. Only one way to see if it would fly, and that was to fly in Chuck's small airplane to Grateful Dead Headquarters in California.

C huck Kesey, Bud Haxby and Black Maria followed the path of the migrating birds, heading south, keeping Interstate 5 beneath the plane.

The band vacillated. Did they really want to do a benefit? They were playing their asses off trying to make money. Ramrod put a stop to the wrangling.

"You've got to do this," he said. "They're family."

That settled it. The 1972 Springfield Creamery Benefit Field Trip was a go, a free-spirited concert in a field which was the parking lot of the Oregon Country Fair in Veneta, west of Eugene. Everything would be put together with volunteer labor and, concurrent with the stage being constructed, a movie team was formed; the extravaganza would be shot in its entirety on 16 mm color film.

Word went out over the air: "Good morning folks, Poppinjay the Dee Jay, poppin dee jay all dee way, letting you know the Springfield Creamery benefit concert is on, and you heard it first right here and as for you innocent thousands who are hanging on the edge of your seats wanting to know... Yes, it's true, I'll be there live, poppin dee jay all dee day in every way from the first note to the last."

He flicked the mic switch off and brought the volume up on the record, Jerry Garcia singing:

"Play that song from my childhood years,
Play it so sweet it brings me to tears..."

The early morning sun beamed through the branches of a tree. Birds chirped and crickets fiddled. A rooster crowed. In the middle of the field, a child sat up in a sleeping bag and yawned. The sun beamed across the top of a tower constructed from logs impaled into the ground. A dog slept in the back of a pickup. A naked man took a leak next to the Hog Farm bus. People were up and moving around, the start of a new day, already warm, hotter to come.

Page Browning, shirtless, bandana tied around his head, was in charge of building the stage and brooked no shit. While others argued the merits of a plan, Page got right to work.

"*Woo-ee*, doin' good. By this afternoon I'll be even better. Energy's coming off me like sparks. Here's the marker stake I put in while the egghead philosophers were talking. Less talk, more action, I say. *Unh!*"—he pulled out the stake and picked up the posthole digger—"I'd rather have calluses on my hand than on my tongue."

Chuck Kesey, hand to his chin, looked at an empty spot in the field: "This used to be an Indian celebration ground. I found some painted rocks. Maybe I can do something to restore the spirit of the place, build a counterbalancing spire of freedom, reaching for the sky, a tower of some kind."

Porta-potties arrived on a trailer pulled by the suck-truck. No dogs, the concert poster said, but dogs abounded in abundance and a decision had to be made:

"Let them bring their dogs but they must pay full admission."

A low-slung Ford station wagon clunked across the field. Poppinjay's raspy voice railed inside, "All dee way, kiddies, just like dee man done say, whoops, careful on the ruts, and dee overhanging branches, dee jay ain't gonna be poppin in any way if we get stuck now."

"What's the deal on people that don't pay?" the ticket takers wanted to know.

"You're going to have to say something like, 'Have you got anything at all?'" Bob Laird, the man in charge, explained. "Don't really hassle them but give them a little shit. Go all the way down as far as you can, without spending more than thirty seconds on each person. If a guy wants to give his shirt, go ahead and take it."

Poppinjay walked through the crowd. "What's this? A shy man smoking a joint. Doesn't want it to be seen, he's nervous. Probably thinks I'm a narc. Oh shit, he spit it out. Too bad. I could have copped a hit. Damn, Poppinjay, you've failed again."

The crowd poured in carrying food and liquid. Concert tickets were pasted to their bodies and clothes. An undisturbed cobweb rested on a bush next to the path through the woods.

Ray Brock, the ex-husband of Alice of Alice's Restaurant fame, drove from the East Coast to Oregon to hang out with Kesey but when he got to the farm, Kesey wasn't there. After getting butted in the ass by Bam the Ram while rooting through his trunk, Ray wasn't going to hang around the farm. He drove to the concert site on the other side of Eugene.

He found Kesey in front of the stage being built and was drawn into a construction discussion with Kesey, Rock Scully and Sam Cutler, two Grateful Dead managers. When they found out Ray was an architect, they asked for his opinion. Ray hemmed and hawed and didn't answer.

"What's to say, really?" Kesey said. "There is an apparent job to do and it is getting done."

"But it's the way it's done that's important," Ray finally said. "There are age-old laws of construction that *have* to be followed."

"You've been through this at your old church," Rock Scully said. "Did the floor ever give you trouble? Are those two-by-sixes on the stage strong enough or should we go into three-inch stuff?"

"I say it's strong enough," Sam Cutler said. "Page Browning knows what he's doing."

"He tends to build over rather than under," Kesey said. "The point is not to get caught in a debilitating argument."

Ray Brock pulled Kesey aside.

"This is crazy," he said. "They think the whole thing is going to cave in. And they're asking *me* for advice now that it's pretty much already finished. Hell, Page built it. What are they coming to me for?"

"This is one of the problems encountered when great undertakings are attempted," Kesey said. "The divisive egotism that isolates and separates men is the burden being laid on you. Forget it. Remain true to yourself within, and be quiet and easily adaptable without."

"Hmmm," Ray muttered and headed for the parking area. He'd had enough of this shit and needed a drink. There was a bottle in his car.

"Say, is that a topless girl already?" Poppinjay asked, walking toward the stage. "Kids running loose and free, is it like this in Ohio at one of those church-lawn picnics behind the big brick Methodist? Do I detect the smoking of marywanna? When I get up to the stage, I must keep everyone up to date, provide a service, not an outlet for my extroverted ego, these folks cannot be ignored. Bearded, hatted, overalled, potsmokers, beerdrinkers, halter-topped, long-tressed, scantily dressed, talking, nodding, sipping. There, hanging on the fence, a mustachioed gent with carnal intercourse on the mind, prevented by the fence; always the fence, in front of the fence, behind the fence—whose idea was this fence anyway?"

Four burly Oregon men, Page Browning in front, pulled a log into place, resting one end next to a pre-dug hole. They hoisted the pole vertical and slid it in. Page peed into the hole.

A grand piano was rolled onto the stage, its protective blankets were pulled off. The piano tuner hit the strings with a small hammer and tightened the pegs.

The two-way radio Poppinjay held in his hand squawked. Brother Bartholomew, his broadcasting partner, hailed from the sound board tower in the middle of the field.

Kesey was Brother Bartholomew; I was Poppinjay.

"Bring in summer please," Brother Bartholomew said.

"Going to be a hot one today," Poppinjay answered.

"Listen, did you know, if it keeps up like this, it will break the Oregon record for the hottest day ever?"

"We have to conserve water. They're going to be wanting water desperately as it gets hotter. It's up to a hundred already."

"Yes, we've cracked through the energy crisis and we're moving rapidly into thirst. It looks like they're building a crucifix next to the stage. At sunset a horse is going to be crucified alive."

"They should have put the horse on it before they put it up," said Poppinjay.

"Gonna be hard now. Where's the crane?" Brother Bartholomew answered.

"We only have one ladder and the guy on it has only one arm. How can you crucify a one-armed man?"

A huge dispute arose. A one-armed man. Everyone was completely distraught. They couldn't crucify a one-armed man. The very act of crucifixion demands a cross.

Poppinjay said, "You now see looming over the stage a cross with a nub, and our pal, Joe Valentine, not crucified, is perched on top like a crow."

Poppinjay was interrupted by Sparky, one of the stage crew, offering some liquid.

"Here put one drop on your finger, it will help lubricate your throat."

"I dunno." Poppinjay said. "It's about the mouth, too tense. Must relax if I'm going to be talking to the people. Whatever I've got to say, just say it. Why be reserved?"

Poppinjay licked his finger and stepped to the microphone.

"Ladies and gentlemen, today's program is being brought to you by Morton salt tablets and our sponsor recommends everyone take one or two. Today they are absolutely free at the White Bird tent, where two guys just now dropped off a girl who was freaked out. Don't suppose she got into that bad acid do you? The blue tablet shaped like a pyramid with a white eye in the middle?"

"Why? What's up with that?" someone yelled.

"It kills you, so think how happy you'd be when you didn't eat one. John Lanning, you didn't take your insulin and you're going to faint in the crowd unless you run back to the Mu Farm where the guy wearing a gas mask has your medicine. Water is located in the water truck but don't wallow in it. It's right behind the kids' tent. Keep wet and keep salted up."

"Come in, come in on the stage," Brother Bartholomew radioed.

"Roger, this is the stage," Poppinjay answered. "Everything's coming in, coming in clear."

"Okay, got you now. Get them woke up, this is it. I've got a gallon of water hidden under the stage over in the back where they parked the trailer. Have someone send it up to the sound tower, will you?"

"Roger. I've got a very trusted messenger and he'll bring it to you."

"Okay, but be careful, just keep the container closed. I don't want anyone adding to it."

"No, we wouldn't want anyone to tamper with the water. Why, that's dirty pool. Just think what it could lead to.

"Hey, Page," Poppinjay yelled. "Come here a minute."

Page made the water run to the sound tower, came back and gave Poppinjay a thumbs up.

Brother Bartholomew called Poppinjay over the radio, "Hey, that water, is it, ah... Did you have any?"

"Did I have any? Yeah, I had some before it went out."

"Just checking. Over and out."

"Out and out and out."

*None of us are musicians or navigators. We're
completely bumbling amateurs. Anybody who
makes any kind of discovery, they do it by accident,
something to break ourselves out of the rut of our
doing the same kind of thinking for so many thousand
of years. We don't even realize that our thoughts are
going nowhere new. You can be enlightened, which
is like, AH, and to do that you have to wander into
new areas.*
    — Ken Kesey

61

Sing Me Back Home

B ob Weir walked onto the stage. Poppinjay greeted him by
hitting him up for a loan: "I already have thirty-five-hun-
dred, another thousand and I can start building on the house."

Weir was unfazed. "What about next week? Can I mail it to
you then? Hey! What are those guys doing with that nitrous
tank?"

What tank? When Poppinjay turned back, Weir was gone.
Jerry Garcia stood behind an amp. Poppinjay walked over.

"Hey Jer, we're really cooking today. Gosh, I don't know
what to say for a change, I'm so public but I can't help but be
too personal, just a little over the edge, you know what I mean?
There'll be time—shoot, we got all day—so don't mind me pop-
pin-dee-jay all over you. I'm trying to be the perfect host."

Garcia blew cigarette smoke in Poppinjay's face. Gave him a
smile and said, "Who needs a cranky landlord when there's a
perfect host around."

"Is there anything I can get you?" a young lady asked.

"Yeah, more beer," Jerry said.

She filled a cup from a keg. A table alongside was covered with bottles, cans, jugs.

"Last call for alcohol," someone shouted.

"They'll be balling on the ground in front of us," Phil Lesh said, looking at the bare-assed bodies, sweat glistening in the torrid sun.

"It's about this water problem," Brother Bartholomew came in over the radio. "Keep it under your hat but we've got a crisis here."

"You got a crisis there, great. Keep it back there," Poppinjay said.

"Here, we've got plenty of heat, but we're hurting for water. Women and children are going to have to be taken care of first. I was just back at the water truck, it was thirsty women and children and babies all around, and people underneath licking on the bottom of the water truck, and this one skinny dude comes up from inside the truck with a T-shirt full of water, squeezes it into a jug and says, 'That's all there is, sister.' It's dry out here, Poppinjay. What are we going to do? There's forty-thousand people in terror and if they make a run on the stage..."

"Keep calm. Hey..."

"Yes, calm. We've got to keep this crowd calm, Poppinjay. Don't let them get loose. If it gets like I think it's going to get, we better gather the kids and find some way out of here."

"Don't freak yet, I think we can make it. If we're coming into a crisis this is the time to be a lert."

"A *lert*—hell, you're a dolt. This is the time to get out of here, when there's forty thousand hippies running around looking for water."

"No, no, we've got a lot of confidence in these Oregon hippies. They are strong critters. Let's keep our eyes open and see if any of them start freaking. The first sign of freaks, then we'll worry. That fence in front of the stage is a bone of contention to me. A fenced-in area is fencing something in or something out, I'm not sure which."

"The logic and logistics of the scene can't help but win out. The fence is a necessity of the time."

There was a sudden movement toward the fence. Jostling and pushing, a bare-chested guy climbed on the fence, trying to get over. He poised on the top, then fell back, arm caught on the metal pole. Blood spurted—skin torn—a cry!

"White Bird!"

The crowd parted as two newly formed friends helped the injured guy toward the White Bird tent.

"If y'all refrained from tryin' to jump the fence," Bob Weir said over the microphone, "you wouldn't fuck yourselfs up."

"Say, when are we going to start this?" Phil asked.

"Before you begin," I said, "I would like to introduce the band."

"I don't know who he is," Bob Weir said, "but he ain't no Bill Graham."

"That's the nicest thing I've heard all day." I looked at the crowd, all these ecstatic folk in their promised land, squinting up at the stage, dope and booze lowering the barriers of social blundering, me yakking and swaying, filling time for the hot-hot high to come on. It was going to be a long day.

"Before you introduce the band," Phil said, interrupting my reverie, "we'd sure like to thank the Springfield Creamery for making it possible for us to play out here in front of all you folks and God and everybody. This is where we really get off the best."

I then introduced Bob Weir and handed him a black T-shirt.

Bob held it up and said, "When the sun goes down and it gets cool enough, I'll wear this thing."

"Yeah, when you sing the Texas song," I said, and gave Phil Lesh a bulging paper sack. Phil pulled out a walnut, tried to crack it with his teeth. Too tough, he dropped it back in the sack.

I handed drummer Bill a T-shirt with a painting of a mandala on the front. Bill pulled off his shirt and put on the new T.

"And over here," I said, "the lead Garcia player—no, the lead *guitar* player, a blast from the past."

A photograph in a wooden frame of a young boy dolled up in a robe, a scepter in his hand, very religioso-Mexicano. Jerry laughed and put the photo on top of his amp.

"And now, for Keith on the piano, something to help his reception."

I handed him a radio antenna. He held one end in his ear while running notes up and down the piano.

"For Keith's wife, Donna, authentic Indian rocks Chuck Kesey found in the meadow when he was digging a posthole."

Donna held one up for everyone to see and returned to her spot behind the band.

I had one more for the man who came out of Pendleton to lift equipment for the band for so long that he caught my bad back. I gave Ramrod my old back brace, shredded at the edges. Ramrod stuck his cigar in his mouth, wrapped the brace around him and, holding his back, disappeared behind the equipment.

"Sorry to say, Pigpen isn't here," Phil Lesh said. "He's sick and had to stay home."

The band broke into song:
"*Wandered away from the Carolina farm,*
Had a groovier place calling me.
Stuck out my thumb like Jack Kerouac
And rode with a back seat honey
Across the mountains and the plains.
Sent one postcard to the folks back home,
Telling them I found the nourishing rains."

"Poppinjay, you up there?" Brother Bartholomew radioed when the song ended. "Next time you're on the microphone, say something about the water."

"It's becoming very dry," said Poppinjay to the crowd, "with probably another three hours to go, but according to a report I just received there's going to be a fire truck moving through the crowd spraying water that's not drinking water. So save the drinking water and use this for the rubbery water, the body-soothing water."

"Look for a while at the china cat sunflower
Proud walking jingle in the midnight sun
Copperdome bodhi drip a silver kimono
Like a crazy quilt star gown through a dream night wind."

Underneath the stage, kids climbed all over the scaffolding, hanging by their knees, upside down, their faces streaked with paint. In front of the stage, three hands held a four-foot-long, big-bowled smoking pipe wrapped in leather while a bearded guy took a toke. A jitterbugging couple danced on a plywood platform in the middle of the field, the man in jeans and no shirt, she in white panties, sweat glistening on her body. Another lady paused dancing, swigged a drink of water out of a plastic milk bottle, then spun away.

"I know you rider, gonna miss me when I'm gone.
I know you rider, gonna miss me when I'm gone.
Gonna miss your baby, from rolling in your arms."

"I've got one thing to tell you before we go any further," Poppinjay announced to the crowd. "The mystery of the vanishing truck: or, what happened to the guy who was gonna spray the crowd. Never happened. Turned out the truck was the one that drains the shitters and we weren't about to have it be said that you were going to have shit sprayed on you at the concert."

"We're changing our name to the Sunstroke Serenaders," Bob Weir said, sweat dripping off his face.

"We can share the women
We can share the wine
We can share what we got of yours
'Cause we done shared all of mine..."

A little feller dressed in diapers, his face streaked with chocolate, remains of a brownie clutched in his fat little hand, a scowl on his face, sat on the ground in the middle of a spare tire. A shaggy-haired, freckle-faced dog, ears perked forward, stared at the brownie. The dog edged closer, nose inches from the goodie. The kid held the treat up, the dog took it daintily from his hand, and gobbled it down. The kid looked in wonder at his empty hand, then lowered it. The dog licked the remnants of the brownie off the kid's hand. The kid stuck his hand in his mouth and duplicated the dog, *lick-lick-lick.*

Paul Foster, bushy-headed, bearded, wearing blue coveralls festooned with patches, whirled and punched the ground with a stick, paused, then burst forward through the crowd. At the back side of the stage, a long-haired naked man climbed his way to the top one of the tree-poles. He sat there, ass on the wood, balls and dick hanging in front.

"Poppinjay," Brother Bartholomew muttered over the radio. "Do you feel weird?"

"I not only feel weird, I look weird."

"The sun should have set hours ago," Brother Bartholomew said in a strained voice. "It's coming apart, Poppinjay. Let's get the kids and get out."

"Calm down, calm down. We're not going to bail until a definite crash is imminent. Not yet, you got that?"

"*Dark star crashes, pouring its light into ashes*
Reason tatters, the forces tear loose from the axis
Searchlight casting for faults in the clouds of delusion
Shall we go, you and I while we can
Through the transitive nightfall of diamonds..."

The blazing sun descended, shining into the band's eyes. Jerry stared through dark glasses, crowd wavering in a gray mist. Guitar frets buckled. Strings stretched out of tune. Drum skins went soft. Piano strings loosened.

"*Shall we go, you and I while we can*
Through the transitive nightfall of diamonds?"

A bouncing beat and interstellar wanderings, the bass laying down a solid line while Jerry picked an intricate run that accelerated, bringing the rest of the band along, then a broken rhythm on the bass and an arpeggio on the rhythm guitar, slowing to a set of chords. Keith joined on the piano. Jerry fingered the fastest runs yet, then slowed to single clear notes. The crowd in the dark moved along, caught in the moment, long, slow chords announcing, after thirty-two minutes of "Dark Star," a new beginning, Bob Weir's voice rising from El Paso, of all places, crooning a gunfighter ballad. Overtones of sorrow and exhaustion followed. Strength tested and endured, guitar quietly plinking, Jerry Garcia's face strained, his voice worn:

"Play that song from my childhood years,
Play it so sweet it brings me to tears.
Drive away all my thoughts of the long, lost days
When I was wandering in a senseless maze.
Sing me a refrain that restores my calm.
Lay on me that lifegiving balm."

"Dark as it is, nobody got run over by a tractor," Brother Bartholomew said over the radio. "Something to be thankful for, I suppose. I didn't stub my toe."

"Hello, Earth," I answered. "We're back. How was the picnic? Call me on the phone, Mister Moon. Color me white with my valleys black. And then leave me alone."

Campfires glowed on the edges of Temple's Meadow. The water truck sat in the middle of the field, never refilled, couldn't get it started. Men and women wandered, snatches of conversation drifting in and out. Roadies loaded the equipment into the rental truck. The piano, covered with a tarp, sat by itself on the stage. The truck drove away, headlights shining down the road.

Look . . . Reality is greater than the sum of its parts,
also a damn sight holier. And the lives of such stuff
as dreams are made of may be rounded with a sleep
but they are not tied neatly with a red bow. Truth
doesn't run on time like a commuter train, though
time may run on truth. And the Scenes Gone By
and the Scenes to Come flow, blending together
in the sea-green deep, while Now spreads in circles
on the surface. So don't sweat it. For focus, simply
move a few inches back or forward. And once
more . . . look.
    — *Ken Kesey, from* Sometimes a Great Notion

62

Last in Peace, First at the Bar

We were tooling along, top down, in Kesey's white Cadillac convertible, our destination a logging site on the Oregon coast where a movie crew was filming *Sometimes a Great Notion.*

Kesey was filling me in on what he did after he graduated from college.

"I spent a year down in Hollywood, the classic small-town boy looking to break in as an actor, but covered my ass by pounding out scripts on a typewriter instead of pounding on studio doors looking for work."

He had the looks—perfect white pearlies, sparkling blue eyes, curly blond hair, erect frame on a muscular body. Little did he know the race to stardom was already won. Paul Newman was Hollywood's handsome blue-eyed leading man.

"I had a fallback plan," Kesey said. "I received a Woodrow Wilson Fellowship to go to grad school. Supposed to prepare me for a teaching career."

"I never knew that," I said. "I went to Stanford on a Woodrow Wilson Fellowship, too."

I slapped him on the leg.

"Think of it, Kesey and Babbs in the race for Teacher of the Year."

He glanced in the mirror.

"Damn, George, back off. What's he think, we're in a race to the coast?"

George Walker was behind us, pushing his multicolored, fluorescent-painted, top-down Lotus, lunging up close, then backing off.

Fern Ridge Lake, with an osprey nest atop a tree, was on our left, then on our right, the town of Noti.

"*Shall we settle for a tie, not I, not I,*" I sang out. "*Shall we wear a tie in a church or bar, not I, not I.*"

Then Lake's Trout Farm, where Kesey got the fish for his pond. Walton, where the county shut down the soft drink and ice cream stand for having no permit. The tunnel at the top of the hill, where Kesey leaned on the horn, *WAAAAAAAAAA*; George's answer from behind, *WOOOOOOOOOO*. We emerged from the tunnel into another world: roar of waterfalls, freshets, spouts, whirlpools and eddies assailing our ears with underwater words, *geeloop, glop, fissrish, susheeze,* the Wakonda Auga River rushing seaward, down the steep slopes of the Coast Range. Cedars, brackens, ferns and moss, and thick fir forests grew alongside stark clear-cuts. River words now sibilant whispers in a widening and taming run to the ocean. Log booms tied to pilings, small boat docks and ladders rising up to houses, then the town of Wakonda. A fishing fleet with booms and winches tied to the dock. Crab pots and fish boxes, ice machine. A narrow, refrigerated storehouse sat on the weather-beaten planks next to a stand advertising FRESH FISH AND CRABS. Across the street the post office. Bank, grocery, movie theater, laundromat, real estate office, cafe and, in the middle of it all, staring at us like a baleful evil eye, The Snag.

We drove around the bottom of the town, on our left the mudflat where Indian Jenny dug clams, and up a steep dirt road, stump farms on either side, around sharp S-curves, to emerge on a flat scar, the ocean and town far below. Old-growth logs lay next to a diesel yarder, metal pole stuck high in the air, thick cable with a haulback attached to pole's pinnacle. Below the yarder, a loaded log truck. Movie camera and sound gear rested in a pile. Woodsmen and film people were packing their gear after a morning's take. Totally out of context, a gold Corvette with its top down sat parked next to the logging equipment.

The director and star of the movie walked toward us with a welcoming smile, his blue eyes shining. He wore full logging gear: cork boots, thick black pants, red suspenders, hickory-stripe shirt with the sleeves rolled up, hard hat tipped back. We were face to face with a real-life Hank Stamper.

"We're just breaking up," he said, "and heading down to the The Snag. Is that your Lotus, George?"

George jumped at the bait: "Such-and-such an engine, so much-a-much power gear ratio, clutch manifold exchange rate, with more-on-the-floor, forward and back."

He led Paul Newman around the car, a slap on the hood, a swipe of a rag snatched from his back pocket. "Thirty-two coats of paint, lacquered and varnished, topped by sunscreen and it will top one-eighty in oh-so-many-point-seconds."

"Well," Paul Newman said, "my Corvette's merely a stock factory model but it's no slowpoke. What say we race down the hill to The Snag? Loser buys the beer."

George's eyebrows went up so high and fast his feet rose off the ground. He reached for the door handle. Paul Newman, ambling towards his car, turned and said, "George, howsabout filling Clarence there in on your gas situation. He's got some extra in a can."

George looked for Clarence, spotted him and called out, "I'm good, no need to..." A motion to the side caught his eye.

Paul Newman had sprinted to his car and jumped in. He scratched gravel off the landing. The race was on. I didn't have a checkered flag so I waved my bandana as George whipped past.

Kesey and I followed from a distance, watching the two cars spin around curves with no place to pass. George veered back and forth from one edge of the road to the other. Paul Newman blocked every move. They tore around the bottom of town and skidded to a stop in the front of The Snag.

The tavern was a square blue building with second-story rooms and balcony across the front, one window with THE SNAG painted on it, the other holding a neon beer sign. Inside, a lunch counter alongside one wall, the bar on the other side of the room, with tables in the middle; in the back of the room, a pool table, hooded stained-glass light overhead, cues in a rack on the wall and, beyond that, more tables with paper placemats that had ruffled edges and a black border framing a drawing of a tall fir standing on a knoll, the tree's top broken and snagged.

The walls hung with deer and elk antlers, a cap and ball musket, photographs of 1930s cars with fishermen standing alongside holding strings of fourteen-inch trout. In another photo, loggers stood at the base of a fir tree bigger around than three of them could reach. A light-blue painted sign hung over the top of the door: *REMEMBER... ONE DRINK IS TOO MANY. WCTU.*

George Walker and Paul Newman were standing at the bar cracking a beer when Kesey and I came through the door.

"Here's to victory," Paul Newman said, raising his bottle, "be it ever-so-degree of difficulty won."

"And to losing," George snorted, "though it was by a fluke lost."

"Thereby hangs the tail of a whale," I said, "which comes in last, so to speak, at the very end."

"Last in peace, first at the bar," George said. "What's your pleasure?"

"Henry Weinhard," Kesey said.

We clunked frosted bottles, took big gulps, washed down the logging-road dust.

An old geezer prowled the perimeter, brown-billed ball cap perched on his head. A brown leather belt held up brown corduroy pants, a brown flannel shirt tucked into those pants. His arm stuck out from his shoulder, then bent ninety degrees at the elbow, encasing body to hand in a thick cast.

His face caught the light, mouth a stern thin line, eyes boring straight ahead. Henry Fonda, playing the part of the Stamper scion.

"Old Henry, when he prepares for a shoot, doesn't socialize," Paul Newman said. "He's already into his role and won't leave it till we're done shooting. Everyone respects him for it. No one gets near him or talks to him."

Newman walked over to the pool table and picked up a cue stick. He started hitting balls into the pockets.

I joined him at the table and watched for a minute. Time slowed and a door came unhinged. Celestials and Mythologicals laid down bets.

"What do you say to a game?" I asked. "Loser buys the next round."

He turned his head and laid the big blues on me.

"You trying to hustle me, bub?"

"That's a laugh. I don't know how."

"The perfect hustler's answer. Let's see if you've got the scratch."

"Eight ball good for you?" I said.

"Good as gold. Flip for the break."

He dug a quarter out of his jeans and showed me both sides. "Heads I win, tails you lose. Call it."

"Let it hit the floor," I said. "I call edge."

"Just what you'd expect from a Merry Prankster."

He flipped the coin. It spun and twinkled in the air, tinkled on the floor, bounced, hung for an instant, then stood, stuck in a crack, edge up.

Paul Newman smacked his forehead.

"I shoulda guessed."

He loaded the rack, set the point on the marker and stepped back.

I smashed the cue ball as hard as I could. It scattered the balls in a crazed break, and zoomed into the end pocket. Scratch.

"That's more like it," Newman said. He lined up on the two ball—"Center pocket"—and dropped it.

"Solids for you," I said, "as befitting a man of your stature and standing. Stripes for me, hankering back to my Prankster days of red-white-and-blue striped T-shirts."

"Acknowledged," he said, sinking two more, then missing. He'd left me a straight shot across the long green.

"Fifteen in the corner pocket."

As I was lining it up, he turned to Kesey.

"What happened, Ken, after you finished *Notion*? Were you burned out on writing?"

"Not that so much. I had proved myself once and then proved myself twice and so I asked myself what do I have to prove now? The answer was, prove nothing."

"You still write, then?"

"I'm not a writer anymore. I'm a storyteller. I use the tools of music and magic, of fire and smoke and smarting eyes. Nature abhors a hollow frame and, if story doesn't fill that space, Pepsi will. And Chevrolet. And Ronald McDonald. This is war, and story is one of our weapons. The innocent heart is the prize we battle for."

"Hmmm," Newman murmured.

"Your shot," I told him.

He sank three in a row. I dropped two, he made another

three, then we traded shots until we were even at the end. He had to sink the eight ball to win but it was blocked by my lucky thirteen.

"Why's it lucky?" he glowered at me.

"Because it's the letter M in the alphabet."

"I don't get it."

"Marijuana."

"Shoulda guessed."

He whanged the cue ball off the back cushion; it hit the eight ball and it rolled to a stop in the middle of the table.

"Thirteen in the side pocket," I said and made the shot. "Eight ball in the left corner pocket."

Perfect hit, the eight ball dropped. I raised my stick in triumph just as the cue ball fell into the other corner pocket.

"Ha, scratched," Paul Newman said. "I knew that coin flip was a fluke."

I bought the next round. When we drank up, Paul Newman slammed his bottle on the bar top. Time to get to work. Kesey and George and I stood behind the camera, where we could watch.

They were shooting a scene around the pool table. Old timers, glum-faced and silent, sat watching in the back of the room. Up front, standing at the lunch counter, younger men glared and gnashed their teeth. They were loggers, out on strike, pissed off at the Stampers, an independent outfit, still working.

Henry Stamper whacked the cue ball with his good arm, the other one sticking out from his side. Floyd Evenright, the union boss, tall and wavy-haired, stood and shot daggers at Henry. Muttering something about the good old days, he grabbed a beer off the bar top and stomped across the floor to the lunch counter.

"Who's talking about the good old days?" Henry Stamper growled. "That damn pecker always talking about the good old days. Nothing good about it 'cept free Injun nooky."

Paul Newman, playing Hank Stamper, Old Henry's son, walked into The Snag.

"Henry," he said, nodding his head in greeting.

Willard Eggelston, the movie theater and laundromat owner, a mousey, mustached, glasses-wearing man, turned from his stool at the lunch counter. "Let me buy you a beer, Hank."

Everyone in the town was hurting, he told Hank. No one was going to his movie theater. Maybe he should show those tits-and-ass films. He's got a special going at the laundromat, three shirts for ninety-nine cents.

"We want your help, Hank," Willard said.

"I've tried, Willard, but my wife won't let anybody touch my shirts."

The union boss, Floyd Evenwright, interrupted: "Leastways you knew who your friends were. In those days you could trust your friends. They didn't knife you in the back."

Old Henry stepped toward him. Floyd rose to his feet.

"Floyd," Henry said, "if I was a couple months younger, I'd wrap that chair across your fat gut."

Hank stepped between them.

"Henry, be a sweet young feller and head on back home."

Henry smiled.

"Let me get my cane."

Henry turned to get his cane and banged Floyd a wallop on the head with his cast. Floyd lurched forward and cocked his fist.

"Hey-hey-hey," Hank said, grabbing Floyd's arm.

"I'm sorry, Floyd," Henry said disarmingly. "I didn't mean to do that."

He walked past and flashed Hank a grin, showing his teeth.

I let out a big guffaw and yelled, "Way to go, Henry, you shoulda KO'd him!"

"Cut," Paul Newman said.

Everyone stood still. The whir of the camera stilled. Paul

looked at me and shook his head.

"Babbs, this isn't a crowd participation shot. You're going to have to hold your mud."

"Ah shit," I started to say, but Kesey cut me off. "We have to go home anyways. This is a good time to pull out."

Paul waved goodbye and Kesey hustled me out the door. We trudged to the car in silence. When we were seated and belted in, I said, "He took me to the cleaners."

"What did you expect, dealing with a professional."

"What? He was a professional pool player?"

"Didn't you ever see the movie *The Hustler*?"

"Oh yeah, right. No matter. I gave it a good shot."

"Blunderbuss," Kesey said.

He fired up the convertible and, with George following behind, we hung a U-turn away from The Snag and headed east, following the river until we started the climb over the Coast Range, then down into the Willamette Valley and a straight shot for home.

There were so many
named the wizard
and all seemed to appear
then vanish behind a curtain.
Don't pet a burning dog.
Check your mail.
Cash on the way
is meant to sway
the odds on it being
a most meaningful day.
  — Ken Babbs

63

Trees Crying to Be Felled

Kesey and I read in the paper that in Holland they opened a man's third eye by drilling a hole in his forehead, the purpose being to let in vibratory emanations not seen by the two regular eyes.

Kesey and I mulled it over. Seemed like a simple enough procedure and the results, as outlined in the article, were mighty enticing.

"We can do that," I said.

"Certainly within our medical grasps," Kesey said.

Kesey went to get the drill. I swept a clean place on the table. We flipped a coin to see who would go first. Kesey won.

"This looks like the right size, big enough to let in the emanations but not so big as to lose too much brain goo," I said, putting the quarter-inch bit in the electric drill. I hit the trigger and the bit spun rapidly.

"Uh, perhaps a bit of the sterilization might be in order," Kesey said.

"Good point."

Water steamed in the tea kettle on the stove, whistling to become tea.

I poured some over the drill bit, then, sticking the drill ahead of me like a gun, advanced toward Kesey. He lay on the table, Buddha-like, impassive, resolved. I leaned in, aiming at a point in the middle of his forehead. The drill whirred, Kesey stared straight ahead, eyes wide and unblinking. I willed a steady hand and put the tip of the drill against his skin and started to push when the drill stopped, the lights went out and the tea kettle whistled in the dark.

Kesey blinked and stood up.

"The emanations have spoken. Let's see what happened to the electricity."

Going out, we met Page Browning coming in.

"*JAYSUS AND PISS-CALL!*" he roared. "I made it here in the nick."

Unashamed, unabashed and unapologetic, he fessed up. Yes, he threw the mains in the electrical box. Never let it be said he'd allow us to maim ourselves, no matter how high the motive.

Kesey shrugged. Wasn't meant to be. We'd have to stick to our tried-and-true mind-opening methods.

"What are you doing over here in the daytime anyway?" he asked Page. "I thought you were fixing the roof."

"Nadine was correcting every move I made and I couldn't take it anymore. I finally figured it out. It's a woman's job to give man shit."

"That's true," Kesey said, "but it's a man's job to eat it."

"Yeah," I chimed in, "and the illuminated man likes the taste."

Page shook his head. "I'm not there yet."

"Let's go to town and get a drink," Kesey said. "The sun is over the yardarm somewhere in the world."

We drove in my pickup, bought a bottle of gin at the liquor store. Purchased cups and mix at the 7-Eleven. On our way home, while driving past the community college, a cop pulled in behind us and turned on his lights. Crumpling the cups and stashing them under the seat, I led the cop into the school parking lot where Kesey jumped out and hustled down the hill to a baseball game. I put my hat over the bottle on the front seat. The cop, walking up, said, "I bet that fellow is leaving with the bottle."

Page started berating the cop: "Why you pulling us over? We weren't speeding or anything."

"Someone called in and said they saw you guys drinking in the truck."

"We never," Page yelled. "And you stop us on some stranger's word? It could have been someone who had it in for us and sicced you on us."

"Now, now," I said. "What's done is done and you can see we aren't drunk and don't have anything in the truck."

"You probably think you're putting something over on me," the cop said. "I'll be watching for you from now on. Now, get out of here."

He drove away. Page waved his arm, all clear. Kesey came back and we drove to his house.

P age and I had two things in common. We were both born in Columbus, Ohio, and we were both in the Marine Corps. He was with the unit that came ashore with the Marines in Lebanon. They stepped off the landing craft past bikini-clad women watching and laughing. After that foreign policy disaster, he was a brig guard aboard the same ship that carried him to Lebanon. When he got out of the Marine Corps, he had that same tough-guy attitude, although as time went on the rough edges smoothed out.

One morning he came rapping on my door. I was barely awake, hung over from the previous night's carousing with Kesey, and was slurping down my first cup of coffee when, bursting with enthusiasm, he exclaimed, "Come on, it's a beautiful fall day! There's crisp in the air, and there's trees crying to be felled."

I laid my forehead on the table. "Not today, I can't handle it. Too shot, too far gone 'round the bend."

"Ha ha," he laughed. "Never too far gone to get wood. Right now or the wood will be gone before winter is gone."

He cajoled and berated me into downing the coffee, putting on my work clothes and boots, and getting into my '53 half-ton pickup, saw and cutting gear in the back. Page leading the way, we started on the long, curved climb into the woods. Maple trees, mixed among the green Douglas firs, were bright yellow beacons, but I was too shot to appreciate the beauty.

Page spotted a couple of dead snags on a hill close to the road. Lugging our chainsaws, we clambered over a ditch and up to the trees. Page worked on a tree closer to the road while I started on one higher up. I made my kerf cut, aiming the tree so it would fall parallel to the road, then went on the other side and started cutting. The tree leaned, began to fall, then twisted and crashed down, not in the direction I planned, but directly on top of the cab of my truck.

I shut off the saw and went down the hill to ascertain the damage. The cab was crushed, the windshield blown out, door windows crushed. Together, Page and I wrenched the driver's door open. The roof rested on the steering wheel, bending the top of the wheel down.

"What now?" Page said.

"Cut the fucking tree up and throw the pieces in the truck. Be damned if I'm going to leave the wood here."

I went up the hill and retrieved my saw. Page bucked his tree into rounds and rolled them down the hill into the ditch next to his truck. He threw them in the back. I threw mine in my truck and crawled into the driver's seat. Bending low, there was a three-inch gap between the roof and the bottom of the windshield, just enough to look through.

Page came up alongside. "What's the plan?"

"You go first, slow."

I honked the horn. It still worked.

"If I'm in trouble, I'll honk. You slow down, I'll ease up to your bumper and use you as a brake."

We headed out, navigating around the curves, everything going okay until Page suddenly slammed on the brakes. His truck skewed sideways, I slammed on mine and stopped before hitting him. Page jumped out of his truck, rifle in hand, stopped, got off a quick shot, then half-crawled, half-ran up the hill and disappeared into the brush.

I started up the hill to follow him but he was already walking toward me, a deer hanging over his shoulders.

"Help me get him into the truck," Page said.

We threw the deer on top of his load of wood and moseyed down out of the woods, past farms and houses, going faster. Page wanted no one to see the deer. He drove to the shed in back of his house, pulled the deer off of the wood and carried it inside.

"Made it," he said, coming out of the shed. "Safe and sound, gutted and hanging from a rafter."

"That's all well and good," I said, "but what about my truck?"

"I was thinking about that all the way down. I've got something that will work."

He broke out his acetylene cutting torch and cut off the roof. We pitched it into the grass and went behind the house where his old, dead Ford station wagon sat on four flat tires. Page removed the tailgate window.

"Old school window, straight up and down, no curve," he said.

He rooted around in his metal scrap heap and found a steel rod he cut into two pieces. He welded the pieces to the front corners of my truck's cab and slid the back window from the station wagon into the grooves of the metal pieces. A new windshield.

"Perfect," he said. "You're a go-go again."

We didn't mess with the bent steering wheel. I drove home, unloaded the wood and stood looking at the truck. I now had a topless rig, not what you'd call a convertible, but a dumbvertible. I went in the house, downed a beer and crashed.

Page had taken a welding course at the community college and got a job at a rock-crusher manufacturing plant after obtaining his welding certificate. He was scheduled to start on the next Monday but, the Saturday before that, took his dirt bike for a ride in the field behind his house, and a stob sticking out of the ground punctured his leg. Monday, he couldn't go to work. It cost him his job.

His wife, Nadine, was already fed up with Page not having a regular job, and losing this one was the last straw. She took their three kids and headed for Canada, where she'd grown up, to stay with her mother until she got a nursing job and found a place of her own.

Page was so torn up he went to town and started drinking first thing in the morning. By afternoon he was soused and decided to head for home, but first he stopped at his friend Jake Mason's house. Instead of Page getting any sympathy, Jake tore into him, blaming him for Nadine leaving, poured it on so hard Page got pissed off, stomped out, stopped at the market and bought a bottle of port, sat on the bench on the store's porch and chugged the whole thing down.

He tossed the empty bottle in the trash can, staggered to his pickup truck, made it the short distance home, found his way into the house, and collapsed, lying on his back in the bed.

The next morning I got a phone call. I could hardly recognize his voice.

"Ken, come get me, I'm bad sick," he said, voice weak and

tremulous.

"Page," I said. "What happened?"

"Just come get me."

He was lying on the floor in the living room, the phone next to his ear. He opened his eyes.

"My stomach," he said. "It's killing me."

I hoisted him into the car and drove to the emergency room.

I waited, pawing through the most useless magazines in the world until a doctor came out and told me: "He's bleeding internally. He has a rare blood type and we can't supply it for him. Since he's a veteran, an ambulance is taking him to the VA hospital in Roseburg."

The next day I drove the seventy miles to Roseburg and visited Page in his hospital room. He was sitting up in bed and looking pretty good.

"Long as they keep pumping blood in me, I'm alright," he said. "Meanwhile they're trying to stop the bleeding, but no luck so far."

"What the hell? Why the bleeding?"

He grunted.

"Here's something to remember. Don't ever go to sleep lying on your back after you've drunk a lot. The alcohol pools in your stomach and eats holes through the lining."

We shot the shit for a while, then I pulled out my small cassette recorder and asked him if I could record our conversation. He not only agreed but said he'd like to put a message on tape for Nadine and the kids. He told them how much he loved and missed them and that he hoped to see them soon. He also said in case the unexpected should happen, he'd want Nadine to keep everything and share it with the kids. He said I could have his .30-30 Winchester, the one he shot the deer with.

I packed up the recorder, we shook hands. I left and didn't see him again until after they moved him to the Portland VA hospital. Roseburg couldn't keep supplying him with the blood type he needed, and in Portland they had a better chance to stop the bleeding.

Kesey and I drove to Portland. We arrived at the hospital in the early evening. Page was upright in bed and looking relatively chipper considering he had purple fluid injected into his veins that day. After the injections, they took pictures to see where the blood was leaking but they didn't get any results.

We talked for a while, then, realizing he was beat, said our goodbyes.

The next day we found out he had died during the night. All the shit they'd pumped into him had shut down his organs. Kesey was pissed off.

"If that had been a senator's son, he'd still be alive."

Page's family came down from Canada to take care of the details for his burial. Since he was a veteran they obtained a grave marker from the government, engraved:

JOHN PAGE BROWNING
PFC US MARINE CORPS

WORLD WAR II

SEP 24 1938 † NOV 18 1984

When Kesey saw that, he said, "That would make Page the youngest person to ever have been in the Marine Corps."

"Yes," I said, "and in World War Two, too."

"Not two," Kesey said. "He was three when the US entered the war."

"Droll," I said. "Very droll."

The funeral was on a clear cloudless day. Early that morning I went to the grave site in Pleasant Hill and hid a cassette player in the mound of dirt next to the grave. I ran a switch into the grass I could work with my foot, and hid two speakers next to the mound. The tape on the cassette was of Page talking to me at the VA hospital in Roseburg.

I was surprised by the number of people who came to the funeral. The small parking lot at the cemetery filled up quickly. The overflow of mounrers' cars parked on the shoulder of the road stretched for a half mile in each direction.

When the short service was over and everybody finished telling their stories about Page, it was time to cover the casket. I hit the play button with my foot and waited for Page's voice to rise out of the mound of dirt. Nothing happened.

I edged over to check the wire. It had been pulled loose. The opportunity was lost. I kicked the speakers farther back into the grass and gave up on the whole thing. When I turned around Kesey was standing next to me.

"You didn't think I'd let you pull that dumb stunt, did you?"

"No more than Page would let me drill a hole in your head."

The first clod of dirt struck the casket.

There is something men should know and understand
about themselves. A man should be allowed to be as
big as he thinks he has it in him to be. This is also a
goddamned good thing to base a story on. It's big;
the whole idea. It means giving the finger to any
notion about God or any other all-powerful beings,
and saying Man is it; Man has to be it; Man has to be
as big as he can possibly be or we ain't got nothing!
— *Ken Kesey*

64

A Chainsaw Becomes
a Typewriter

"What the hell happened to your tooth?" I asked Kesey. He looked at me grimly.

"I sneezed when I was down at the pond throwing grain to the ducks and geese and my tooth flew out. Before I could pick it up a goose swallowed it. I knew if I had any chance of finding it, I'd have to search through the goose shit."

He didn't find it and, bearing a temporary tooth the dentist glued into the gap, the two of us headed out in his black '66 Mercury ragtop in the dead of winter, on a speaking tour to points east.

Kesey and I had our routine down. He was the main attracttion and I was his Ed McMahon sidekick, except on this tour I was playing the role of a newspaper cameraman, carrying a 1950s four-by-five press camera and wearing a fedora with an Intrepid Trips business card stuck in the hatband.

The trip east was smooth sailing, top down, heater on full blast, cold wind blowing over the windshield, until we started climbing into the Colorado mountains and the road became snow-covered, frozen. Kesey grappled the wheel with gloved hands to keep the car from blowing off the road as we crawled up a 12,000-foot peak where the car slowed, almost to the top, wheels spinning, back end sliding.

"Keep her going," I yelled.

I jumped out and tried to push the car forward. The tires spun, the car inched ahead, I gave it all I had, and we made it to the mountaintop, where Kesey stopped with the nose pointing down.

I swept the snow off the seat and got in. Took a long pull on a pint of Old Overholt. The blasting heater thawed my bones. We slid down the eastern slope of the Continental Divide onto the Great Plains, Scorpio visible, Jupiter glowing, Sagittarius fading as the sky lightened. We passed an old cemetery on the side of the road. The right rear tire went flat.

An eighty-year-old cadaverous Christian who wouldn't talk money on a Sunday stopped and gave us a lug wrench, which proved too small. We found a Crescent wrench in our trunk and were able to loosen three lug nuts. The other two wouldn't budge.

A cowboy who said his name was John pulled over in his pickup and loosened the other lug nuts with a three-quarter-inch socket wrench.

We jacked up the car, switched the flat for the spare, and headed down the road, listening carefully—no hiss of a leak but a scraping noise, something dragging. We stopped to look. The muffler was hanging by a thin piece of metal. I yanked it loose and threw it in the trunk.

Driving slowly, we continued to the town of Hope, aptly named and gratefully fulfilled, for there we had the muffler welded and the tire replaced for fifteen dollars.

We sang that song about going to Kansas City as we drove away from Hope. Four hours later, we pulled into the first speaking stop—a university symposium on Robert Kennedy.

T he voice booming out in Pierson Hall at the University of Missouri–Kansas City was none other than Robin Morgan's, laying into the men: the sexist, domineering, glass-ceiling-defending assholes in the homes, the schools, the TV shows, the offices and the books.

"The history books tend to be written by white, straight males," she said. "Going one step further than the old Marxist dictum that workers must seize the means of production, we say women must seize the means of reproduction... She's made to feel if *he* can't have an orgasm in bed, it's *her* fault. If *she* can't have an orgasm in bed, it's *her* fault."

Spotting Kesey as he slipped into a vacant seat, she cried out, "And there's one of the worst of the lot, with his portrayal of men lording over women in his blatant male-domineering book, *Sometimes a Great Notion.*"

Kesey stood and said, "Viv is the strongest character in my book. She never wavers in her courage, despite the calamities raging around her; and when she finally has enough, she leaves. Who needs it?"

"Who needs all that criticism, anyway?" some guy in the audience yelled at Kesey.

"Yes, I wonder why it is such a necessity to pigeonhole everything. When people write about me, I begin to see paper reflections of me and I wonder, is that me? Two reactions: one, that it couldn't possibly be. Two, that it is me and that's too bad because you can get trapped inside the image that is being built up."

Not wanting to cut into Robin Morgan's time any further, Kesey walked out and, after snapping a few pictures, I followed.

The next day there was a lunch for all the symposium participants. Paul Krassner had flown in that morning and we took him with us to the lunch. Before we ate, Basil, the organizer, announced that Susan Sontag, the writer and political activist, was in Mexico and couldn't make it.

"Paul Krassner is here," Kesey said. "Put him on in Susan's place and pay him her money."

Nobody objected, and after lunch we walked back to the house where we were staying. Kesey opted for a nap. Paul said he was going to talk to his friend, Ed Sanders, who was in town doing a reading and playing music. A fan of Ed's from his work with the musical group the Fugs, I asked Paul if I could tag along.

We walked to a two-story house and went upstairs to a bedroom. After greetings, Paul said, "Babbs, Ed wants to talk to me about the book he is writing about Charles Manson, and he doesn't want you to listen in. The fewer who know what he's doing, the safer he will be from Manson's people. So you go in the bathroom and wait until we're done."

I sat on the toilet, twiddled my thumbs and finally was tired of the whole thing. What did I give a shit about Ed and his book? I pounded on the door. When Paul opened, I said, "See you back at the house," and beat it out of there.

That evening, Kesey and Krassner and I walked to the hall and waited at the stage door to get in. The door opened and a lady beckoned to Kesey. He went in and, before we could follow, closed the door on Paul and me. Krassner shrugged. I laughed. We walked around to the front entrance and sat down in back.

Kesey, wearing a short-sleeved, three-colored V-neck, with a bandana tied around his neck, sat onstage with the other panel members: suit-and-tie bedecked older gents, one of whom was on his feet talking into the microphone. Russell Kirk, the noted conservative thinker, author and speaker, expounded upon the need for moral imagination.

"Wait a minute," Kesey interrupted. "Where's Paul Krassner? He is supposed to be on the panel. Come on up here, Paul."

Krassner refused to budge until a student rose to his feet and said he had paid to hear Krassner. At that point Paul walked up onto the stage and joined the panel.

"As I was just saying at the lunch, Paul," Russell Kirk started to say, but Krassner interrupted him.

"The only thing I heard you say at lunch was 'Please pass the salt.'"

Russell Kirk shook his head and sat down.

Albert Murray, noted jazz critic and the author of *Stomping the Blues*, took the microphone.

"The blues as such are synonymous with low spirits. Not only is its express purpose to make people feel good, which is to say in high spirits, but in the process of doing so it is actually expected to generate a disposition that is both elegantly playful and heroic in its nonchalance."

Andres Guiterrez, a member of the pioneering El Teatro Campesino group, which toured the San Joaquin Valley playing for farm workers from the back of a flatbed truck, jumped to his feet and cried, "Foul! Foul! I speak for the oppressed Chicano minorities. Who do you know has given a life for oppressed minorities?"

"Caesar Chavez," Krassner said and, with this interjection, they opened the microphone on the floor for anyone to speak. The panel became a give-and-take forum of free expression and highly loaded stammering, but no loud arguments.

I shot a few pics with the Speed Graphic camera. By then everyone was used to me, ace reporter, roaming through the audience and on the stage, blinding people with flashbulbs.

As things were winding down, Kesey rose from his chair and walked to the front of the stage. He put his hand to his chin for a minute, then said, "I believe that the human being has been stagnant for maybe five thousand years as far as further development goes. We've worked very hard at playing with codes and signals and tampering a little bit here and there with communication. But I think now something else can happen.

"I think we are once more realizing that we are an animal, a sweating, moving, stinking, born-and-dying animal and that the myth that there is inside us some kind of little, beautiful person that drives this flesh machine around is not true. This chunk of meat here"—he thumped his chest—"is me. People aren't believing there is a prettier and more beautiful existence somewhere inside us. People are beginning to think that we've lost something we can't quite put our hands on.

"We are divided internally. We are never hitting on all of our cylinders at once because whatever we're doing, it's only half. If we are holding down a responsible eight-to-five, get-the-job-done thing, the artist side of ourselves is saying, 'Man, get out there and wail and fly.' But as soon as you're out there flying, there's the other side again, saying, 'Come back down here and toe the mark, you've got commitments to meet.'

"There's always this nagging, so wherever you are, at any position, you are being criticized by yourself. And that's true ninety-five percent of the time, even when you write. But that other five percent is what you write for. You don't know you're doing it until all of a sudden something shakes you and what a moment ago was a chainsaw becomes a typewriter."

He pulled a cassette player out of his pocket, held it to the microphone and pushed the play button. Stevie Wonder:

"Merry widows sing anthems to life's bliss,
Seal it with a hug, sign it with a kiss,
Meanness never makes you strong,
Forgiveness wipes away everything wrong."

Kesey pushed the stop button, stuck the player in his pocket, flashed the peace sign, jumped off the stage and, slapping hands with the people as he walked past, went out the door.

I t was a soothing end to the evening but there was no rest for Kesey and me, for we had to go to the offices of the campus newspaper to work all night with the journalists to put out a special edition about the symposium. We finished just in time for a seven-a.m. trip to the printer, then crashed until afternoon when Kesey woke me, saying we had to get to the Student Activities office before it closed to pick up the one thousand dollars, as per the deal. When we got there, we were informed we would have to wait five days for the check to be processed through headquarters in Columbia, Missouri. Kesey convinced Nancy, head of the office, to draw up a new contract, only to find out we'd have to wait until the next day to obtain the okay-ed contract and then take it deeper into Missouri.

Kesey and I left the office and went to the campus newspaper building to pick up a bundle of the newspapers we had worked on all night. Much to our surprise, we discovered the entire run had been confiscated by the university, all of the copies all over the campus picked up and destroyed because of, as one of the students at the newspaper office explained, that obscene poem we'd put in by Allen Ginsberg.

"Ah, what you expect, here in the heartland," Kesey said, "where they are still reactionary when it comes to reading about cocks and balls."

We went back to our digs for a lambchop dinner, washed it down with Old McKenna, and hit the sack.

We didn't manage to get up and out at six so we could make the two-hour drive to Columbia, Missouri, and arrive at eight when the office opened to get our check, but we were up and moving around in the house by eight.

Kesey peered into the top of the Old McKenna whiskey bottle. "Let us gird our loins." He poured the dregs into his coffee.

Our host, Basil, gave him a remonstrative look.

"Aren't you worried about being an alcoholic?" he asked.

Kesey took a long swallow and answered, "I'm not an alcoholic, I'm a lush."

"What's the difference?"

"I don't have to go to all those damn meetings."

Basil looked at me. "What about you, Babbs? Aren't you worried about having a drinking problem?"

"I thought having a drinking problem was when you woke up in a dry county."

"I give up," Basil said.

W e arrived in Columbia, Missouri, at 11:15, turned in the contract, and were told to wait in the coffee shop. The checks wouldn't be available until 1:30. We had a leisurely lunch until two checks were ready: one for a thousand dollars and another for two-hundred dollars. Kesey cashed the two-hundred at the bank, mailed the thousand home to Faye, and we blew out of town.

Crossed the Missouri and Mississippi Rivers into Chicago to stop for chow and, in the pre-dawn hours, rolled through Carl Sandburg country heading for Detroit, hoping the bad Eastern Truckers didn't eat us.

Snow and wrecks slowed us through Detroit and across the bridge into Canada, but Canadian Club with melted snow in paper cups calmed us enough that I took a snooze while Kesey drove. I was awakened by the sound of the left rear—the same tire that had been leaking ever since Kansas—finally going flat. We put on the bald spare and kept going, talking about starting up a small press magazine. We had the equipment: an IBM composer which justified the print to make straight lines down both edges of the page; a polaroid camera on a stand that copied black and white photos and put small dots on the picture so the image would be clear when printed. I was already doing paste-up jobs for a printer in town, and Kathy Wagner, who had moved to Kesey's from San Francisco, did the typing. Plenty of shops in Eugene could print the magazine.

A dust devil in front of us raised a funnel of snow and ice. When we drove through it, our thoughts were scattered like trash and debris blown into tiny pieces.

We crossed the border from Canada into New York state, then on to Massachusetts. A two-lane blacktop, covered with snow, bridged the Connecticut River on Route 9 to Amherst, where we rented a motel and bought another snow tire before going to Bob and Janice Stone's house for dinner.

After recounting how the newspapers in Kansas City had been confiscated, Kesey said, "It's time we did our own rag, only not a newspaper but a small literary magazine."

"Why not," Bob Stone said. "It's all the rage these days."

"Yes," I chimed in. "Take back publishing from the publishers."

"Do all the publishing you want," Bob said. "The movie starts in fifteen minutes."

The Godfather. We found center-row seats halfway down and settled in. The movie hadn't gone fifteen minutes before Bob Stone stood up and yelled, "Why are you people sitting here placid and uncomplaining and idolizing these gangsters? They are bastards without a shred of decency, only out for their own fiefdoms and ill-gotten gains and will do anything—murder, fires, major destructions..."

The lights came on and ushers appeared, tromping through seated patrons to take Bob by the arms and pull him into the aisle, Bob yelling all the while: "Walk out, people! Have nothing to do with this abomination! Be brave, protest the actions of the wrongdoers..."

Kesey, following behind him, said, "Uh, Bob, it's a movie. Those are actors..."

Bob glared. "Don't you see, it's the portrayal that's wrong! Why do they watch this?"

"Don't ever come back," the manager said as the ushers pushed Bob onto the sidewalk.

"As if," Bob said, then turned calmly to Kesey and me. "Let's stop at the pub for a brew."

We made it a short stop, just long enough to rehash the tumult at the movie theater before walking back to house and hitting the hay, another big day on tap.

Good words have power, like Shazam! *One single word can change a crippled newsboy into a superhero.*
Words can get you in trouble. Words can also talk you out of trouble. Words can keep you alive.
— Ken Babbs

65

There Is No Danger of the Dinochicken Escaping

The next night we motored to Amherst College for Kesey's speaking gig. It was scheduled to be at the chapel, but the building was already full with more people standing outside, so we moved to the Cage, a dirt-floored athletic building with a wooden basketball court laid over the dirt.

Kesey stepped on the stage, looked out at the faces, paused for a minute, then waded in:

"I went through a lengthy period of my life which I am going to go into now because it makes for a nice metaphor. Suddenly there were a bunch of us high and we realized that we had a chance to see the real books, the Karmic Books. Not the ones they keep in the principal's office or down at City Hall in the Library of Congress. These are the books that show where you stand in eternity, that show how you are doing: if you are a gentle soul; if you are a harsh soul; if you are afraid; if you are courageous—it is all right there. And we thought, 'Hey, that's far out. Let's leave these other books alone and go to the real books.'

"It was as though a big hand grabbed me by the back of the neck and said, '*YOU WANT TO SEE THE REAL BOOKS, HUH?*'

and forced me, nose to the page, to look for about thirty hours at the inequities of mankind, and at every ungentle act and lie and unkind thing that I had ever done. Finally, after seeing all the things that were wrong with myself and outside myself, going through all the wars and violence and finally out to everybody starving everywhere, I realized that is the real book. And it's what Hell is, for hour after hour to see where you really are and what the situation of the world really is. It scared the pants off of me.

"The only true currency is that of the spirit," he continued. "It doesn't make any difference how much electricity is in those overhead lines or how much gas is in the car. If you don't have the spirit, you don't do jack shit. And when we begin to think that the spirit comes from something outside of us, we're conditioned to try to buy it in some way. On the other hand, you can be broke and accomplish a great amount.

"Oh, about four hundred years ago, the Baal Shem Tov, the founder of modern Jewish Hasidism, came to the king and said, 'King, the wheat is poisoned with ergot and everybody that eats it is going to go crazy.'

"The king says, 'That's terrible,' and the Baal says, 'I thought you would say that, so I have stashed enough good wheat for you and me to make it through the year and we won't go crazy.'

"The king says, 'Now wait a minute. If I'm the king of these people and you're the rabbi, ought we not eat the same food and feel the same things so we have a better idea how to get through it?'

"The Baal says, 'I thought you would say that, too. So I figured we'd put an X on each other's foreheads so that when we see each other we will know that we *chose* to go crazy, whereas everybody else is just crazy.'

"And we did. On that first long-ago bus trip, we chose to go crazy and know each other."

He ended his talk to standing applause. He hung around and

schmoozed with the crowd for a while and then we headed back to the motel.

After a late rising we picked up his thousand-dollar check and sent it home. Then it was on to Yale for the next talk, set up and hosted by Rich "Rocket" Coursen, dark hair parted on one side, crewneck sweater with a woven string necklace hanging loosely. He surprised us by saying he was from Eugene, Oregon.

Room 100 of the Art Gallery at Yale was packed with a crowd milling around outside. Officer Ball of the Yale Police arrived and looked things over. There was a tank of nitrous oxide on one side of the stage, pot on the other. Officer Ball stood in the middle and announced, "The aisles must be cleared," which led to a shouting discussion over who was to go, who was to stay, shall we take a vote, shall we go to a bigger hall?

When Officer Ball left in search of a bigger hall, he received a standing ovation.

A girl filling balloons with nitrous oxide for the audience took a big hit and fell over. Kesey caught her and laid her down as the tank fell on both of them. Kesey waved his arm, *No problemo, amigos, merely a flash.*

Officer Ball returned to say there was no other place available, but by then enough of the crowd, bored with the whole thing, had wandered off. The problem was resolved.

"Talk to them Babbs," Kesey said, stalling for time.

"Quite an honor to be here," I said. "My first time at an Ivy League school, although they called Miami of Ohio the Ivy League school of the Midwest, probably because of the Georgian red-brick buildings."

I stepped to the chalkboard at the side of the stage, turned it to face the audience, and took a piece of chalk from the tray.

"Since this seems to be a science room of some sort, I figure it's the perfect place to expound upon the giggle properties of nitrous oxide."

I drew a circle in the middle of the chalkboard.

"This is the nitrous. You can see it's inert, laid back, no inertia at all, and next to it"—I drew another circle—"is the oxide. It's got energy. Not one oxygen molecule, but two, and they are squirming sons of bitches. Put them together"—I drew a big circle enclosing the two, turned the chalk sideways and made big, broad lines across all of the circles, then drew a mushroom cloud with bubbles rising to the top—"and you have created the giggle-property of the gas, which, when inhaled, causes you to laugh uncontrollably and fall flat on your face."

"Enough with the science," Kesey said. "Let's return to reality as we know it. Joseph Campbell says, 'Follow your bliss.' That makes a lot of sense except for the fact that there's billions of dollars being poured into TV right now to tell you what your bliss is. Tells you to watch this, drink this, gurgle this or wear this, so it's fuzzy for a lot of people. What is our bliss? It takes a certain kind of gyroscope, a compass to keep us on the right track, and that is one of the things that LSD will do for you: it will clear up your compass. It will correct your compass real damn quick. Suddenly when you're high and you're loose, you realize, what am I going to do now? This is me.

"Some spiritual traditions hold that before you can really expect to find enlightenment, you have to raise a child to maturity. Then get out once again on your own path. Maybe the kid we have to raise to maturity is ourselves."

The audience rose and clapped, yelled and cheered, crying for more. Kesey raised his hands and shushed them down.

"You don't want to get too deep into this stuff. There's other things going on. Paleontologists are attempting to recreate a dinosaur—or something a lot like a dinosaur—by starting with a chicken embryo and working backwards to engineer a Dino-chicken, in order to bring it out on a leash during lectures."

He turned to me.

"Babbs, get the creature out of his cage."

I stepped back and shook my head and began singing:

"Holy moly, where is the door?
Why am I crawling on the floor?
Jeepers creepers, molly weepers,
All I want is my jammies and slippers."

"You're no Paul Anka," Kesey said. "Forget the vocals and get the Dinochicken."

I went backstage, stomped on the floor and yelled so every-body in front could hear: "Come on, you! Get out of the corner, there's work to do. Dammit, why you always got to act like this?"

I returned to the front of the stage. Shook my head. "No use, boss. The Dinochicken is sulking, pissed off because he's always kept locked up in a cage and then dragged out like some freak to scare people. Don't we know he's an artist?"

"Leave it then," Kesey said. "Don't worry," he told the audi-ence. "There is no danger of the Dinochicken escaping and going haywire on Avenida Revolución in the middle of a feder-ales and drug gang shootout. Thank you all for coming."

After the talk, we had been invited to a professor's house, where as soon as we arrived Kesey headed for the kitchen. He was poking around in the refrigerator when the professor's wife, tall and elegant in a white blouse and black skirt, asked him, "What are you looking for?"

"*Huevos whateveros,*" Kesey said.

"What in the *worldeveros* are those? I'm Agnes, by the way."

Kesey set some containers on the counter. "You want the long or the short version?"

"From an author, the long version of course."

"Okay." He put more containers on the counter. "*Whateveros* are very popular the second or third day after the main dish that inspires them has faded from memory. Easiest, of course, are the leftovers from a bulky Mexican meal."

He reached under the counter and pulled out a skillet.

"I like to chop the leftovers all in a big skillet, like this, along with some fresh tomatoes, peppers, and even tortilla chunks if there are any."

He turned the stove on high under the skillet, took a butcher knife off the rack, and began chopping up a tortilla. He splashed olive oil on the skillet and threw tortilla chunks in.

"Cook until the tortillas are swollen and soaked, then carefully crack a half dozen eggs."

He cracked the eggs into a bowl and turned on the oven. The professor walked in, followed by a group of students. They crowded around the kitchen. Kesey poured the eggs into the skillet and stirred them in with the tortilla chunks and pieces of vegetables.

"Top with chile sauce and chunks of cheese. Then stick the skillet into the oven. Let it cook until bubbles can be seen, then turn off the bottom heat and turn on the broiler until the eggs and cheese are light brown.

"Serve for lunch or supper—even breakfast—or a late-night snack. The same thing can be done with leftover Chinese, using noodles instead of tortillas, or leftover corned beef, or Thai food, or anything that was good once and still has the body to be good again. I've never tried it with Spam. Best served with a cup of good Mexican coffee."

"I don't have the Mexican but I can offer a good bean from Costa Rica," the professor said.

"By the time it's ready, so will be the *huevos whateveros*," Kesey said. "Let's wait in the living room and have a drink."

He was the last one to leave the kitchen. Agnes, in front of him, turned and said, "I see you are very close to your inner child."

"Thank you, ma'am," Kesey drawled. "I tend to keep the little feller close by just to give me a nip with his teeth when I ramble on too faluting long. What's this?"

He pulled a quarter from her ear.

The next day we drove to Manhattan, our first visit since the bus trip of 1964. We cruised the avenues, took a turn through Central Park, then up Broadway. A smoke ring puffed from the Camel billboard in Times Square.

We had heard, from a phone call to Faye, that Larry McMurtry was in New York and she made a date for us to meet him for lunch. It was great to see Larry, in his western togs with cowboy boots sticking out from under his blue jeans. Kesey filled him in on our plan to put out a small literary magazine.

"Why in the world would you want to do that?" Larry asked.

I jumped in: "To take publishing back from the publishers."

Larry looked at me.

"Let them have it."

After lunch we drove to Viking Press. We were welcomed by Rich Barber, the publicist, dressed casually in a buttoned-down shirt, sweater, dark pants. He greeted Kesey, shook my hand, leaned against the desk and asked what brought us to town.

"Tail end of a speaking tour," Kesey said. "Had to get a bite out of the Big Apple, check the taste."

"What do you think, still tart or soft in the middle?"

"Hard to tell on the first nibble. How's it going here at Viking?"

"Your books are still on the shelves and selling and we always have something in the top ten. Come on, I'll show you around."

We peeked into offices where editors glanced up from manuscripts and waved pencils at us, composing rooms where book jackets were laid out and pinned to the walls, secretary dens with cluttered desks and ringing phones. We skipped the bigwigs' lairs and opted instead for dinner.

Rich took us to Elaine's, the literary hotspot. We ate in a back room and, when finished, walked into a larger room. Kurt Vonnegut stood inside the door leaning on the wall, a drink in his hand. Rich introduced us. Kurt, tall and mustachioed, gave us a grin and hello and shook our hands. He nodded toward the room. A long table ran its length, the table filled with men and women in animated conversation. A white-haired man sat at the head, his back to the window.

"Might want to meet the main man," Kurt said.

Rich led us around the table.

"I'd like you to meet my friends, the two Kens—Ken Kesey and Ken Babbs—from Oregon," Rich said.

Andy Warhol acknowledged us with a wave. He didn't say anything so we mumbled our glad-to-meetchas and left.

We said thanks and goodbye to Rich Barber, pointed the convertible west and drove through the night, a straight shot across the midsection of America, trading driving and sleeping, grabbing greasy-spoon, truck-driver specials at gas stops, jawing about our small press magazine fantasy while keeping a tally of roadkill on the dashboard by marking, with a sharpie, a series of four lines crossed by a slanted line: rabbits, skunks, deer, possums, cats, dogs, raccoons, sheep, cows, a horse, and, crossing the Rockies, an elk.

We arrived at Ed McClanahan's house in Palo Alto early one evening two days later. Ed opened the door with a surprised look on his face and a gin and tonic in hand.

After fortifying our road-weary selves with large, gin-laden drinks, we laid our latest small press plan on him and he reacted with total enthusiasm. Through working with the Midpeninsula Free U in Palo Alto and their publication, he was familiar with the literary magazine production process. When Kesey said his major contribution would be to write a novel and serialize it, chapter-by-chapter in issues of the magazine, Ed said, "Make it a seven-issue run. It can be like a seven-card poker game, like Spit in the Ocean, where the dealer throws one card face up in the middle of the table and that card is wild in everyone's hand."

"Seven cards, seven different editors," Kesey said, picking up on the notion.

"And there can be a joker in the deck," I said. "His name is Otis."

"Why Otis?" asked Kesey.

"S-I-T-O, Spit In The Ocean spelled backwards," I said.

"I like it," Ed said. "We can get my artist friend in Kentucky, Doug Simon, to do the covers."

The plan was a go.

The people who are insane are the people who cut themselves off from the future. What is human and sane is caring for people you don't even know. The truly great people—Gandhi, Jesus, Einstein— devoted their lives to caring about people and the future. Sanity is found in harmony.

— Ken Kesey

66

Singing Waiters
in a Dead Rat Cafe

We were feeling good. We had just knocked out the second issue of *Spit In The Ocean* and were downing Hill and Hill in beakers of ice and water. I tipped my glass: "Well, Chief, we're ready for the lead-in to the next edition. What will we do to titillate the readers' interest?"

The Chief furrowed his shaggy, John L. Lewis eyebrows and peered over the top of the specs he wore on the job but pretended he didn't need, even when he was giving a talk somewhere. He'd squint at the wriggly lines on the paper like a mole blinded by the sun.

"Since I was the editor of the first issue, and you the second," he told me, "I'm considering using a guest editor this time."

That drew Kathy—our lightning-fingered, Girl-Friday, earth-goddess, dark-tressed mistress of the keys and silk-sweet telephone voice—upright in her chair. A slightly drunken trill in her voice, she asked, "Someone else? It's all I can do to hold this floundering enterprise together working with you two nuts. And now you want to bring in someone else?"

She pursed her lips.

I asked the Chief, "Who'd you have in mind?"

"Tennessee Larry."

My eyes locked with Kathy's. A fleck of worry sparkled in her blue irises. I smiled reassuringly.

"Admirable choice," I said.

F ive-a.m. alarm-clock reveille woke me from my dream: *Tennessee Larry. Where'd the Chief come up with that one?* Outside, the crescent waning moon surrendered illumination rights to the beaming sun.

A solid breakfast of eggs, toast, and coffee, and I was ready to rumble. I fired up the old pickup and headed for Kesey's. While he got ready, I finished working on his new toilet. I bolted it to the floor, hooked up the water, and gave it a flush. Good to go.

So was Kesey. We threw our bags in the back seat of his black '66 Mercury convertible and, top down, drove south on I-5. Our destination: the Federal prison in San Diego where Tennessee Larry was incarcerated.

No clock in the car, no sense of time on the winding, forested road to Coos Bay, then the cold ocean air, heater on full blast, a long haul to the redwoods in California, where a giant statue of Paul Bunyan berated gawking tourists with amplified voice: "*If you don't take the walk through the Trees of Mystery, you won't see Babe the Blue Ox pulling a log big as a freight train.*"

Kesey sang in response:

"*Look at you, a real he-man,*
Not a ratchity flimflam geek,
But an honest-to-God woodsman,
Busts his ass the livelong week."

On to Bodega Bay where we stopped to buy oysters. I started to open one with my knife. Kesey shook his head.

"Watch it. Remember when you tried to do that in Portland?"

"Yeah, the knife stabbed me in the hand. I thought wrapping

the napkin around the cut until the bleeding stopped would be the end of it."

"Until your hand swole up like a Macy's Thanksgiving Day Parade balloon."

"I washed it out with cold water and that did the trick."

"So the moral to the story is, don't do it again."

"No sweat."

I opened the oysters with nary a scratch to my hand.

Afterwards, we swam in Mother Ocean, camped on the beach, rose in the morning, peed in the bushes, then hit the road for San Francisco, singing as we crossed the Golden Gate Bridge:

"Open up your golden thighs,

California here we come."

Down the Bayshore Freeway to Bryant Street in Palo Alto, where Ed McClanahan lived. There was no one home so we went inside, mixed orange juice and vodka and sat on the porch until Ed arrived with Jane Burton in tow. Since we'd finished off the vodka, Ed coughed up enough dough for Kesey and Jane to drive to Whiskey Gulch to buy beer. There was money left over, so they stopped at a store for hamburger and potatoes to cook an S.O.S. (Shit-On-Spuds) dinner.

After we ate, we hit Ed up for some more cash, telling him we were down to our last few dollars.

"I bought the grub," Ed said. "That'll cover my share of the dilly dallying you're up to."

"I owe Faye twenty dollars," Jane said. "I'll give you that."

"Saved again, thankee lawd," Kesey said.

We rolled a couple of joints from Ed's stash and, horn blaring, burned rubber around the block to the freeway. Then south for an all-night run, taking turns sleeping and driving, cassette player on low volume:

"The clock clicks slowly,

The hands drag 'round,

The tide washes in,
The river swells in flood.
I sit and stare
Out the cell all alone..."

We arrived in LA at dawn and woke up our old moviemaking pal, Redhead Bobby, long locks to his shoulders. His living room held a color TV, a phone, and an electric pencil sharpener. The kitchen had the requisite coffee maker. Bobby fired it up and we swilled its coffee down.

The three of us jumped into the convertible and, with Bobby at the wheel, Kesey threw the *I Ching*:

"Spying about with sharp eyes
like a tiger with insatiable craving.
Awareness of danger brings good fortune.
Thus in fear and trembling the superior man
sets his life in order and examines himself."

"That pretty much covers it," Kesey said, closing the book. "Now, let's execute it."

"Check that out," Bobby said, motioning behind us.

A brown Lincoln Continental with a scraped side and a flopping wheel was chasing a Ford pickup with a crushed fender.

"Whoa-eee," I chortled. "Keep your eyes on the road. I'll fill you in. The guy in the Continental is so intent, so what if he crashes in the attempt? Wife's hassling him, daughter's got a rash on her face and his son's in jail. *Revenge is mine,* he's thinking. *I'll crush that fucking Ford for side-swiping me."*

Bobby floored it and we left them smoking in the distance.

"There's the Nixon compound," Kesey said.

A plain adobe house behind a chain-link fence, an incinerator putting out black smoke.

"Still burning those tapes," I said. "Wonder if he's involved with the Vietnamese Refugee Adoption policy?"

"Maybe as a porno movie," Bobby said.

"Have mercy," Kesey said. "More likely a family that would

live on his place, do the cooking, cleaning, and yard work."

In San Diego we stopped at a bar for a beer and made a phone call to our contact, Mr. Hills, who told us that we had to get over to the Federal Courthouse before it closed at four.

"I'm clean," I said, checking my shirt pocket for roaches as we climbed the steps to the courthouse.

We went to Room 201 and met Mr. Hills, who told us he used to be an agent in Grants Pass, Oregon, and that his daughter went to the University of Oregon. He spoke English, Spanish, Italian, and Portuguese and used them all, talking to people he met as we walked out of the building and crossed the street to the correction center. He introduced us to the warden, a squat, bespectacled man. He looked at the paperwork Mr. Hills handed him.

"One thing," the warden told us. "Don't use his real name. Here he's known as Bruno."

The federal prison was a fifteen-story high-rise that, from the outside, looked like a hotel; inside it was institutional, bare concrete walls, steel desks and chairs, a metal detector walk-through, and a sign in front: *CAUTION. EXPLOSIVE DEVICES WILL DET-ONATE WHEN PLACED IN THIS MAGNETIC FIELD.*

A burly trustee wearing a blue jumpsuit came in and Hills talked to him in Spanish. A Black woman working behind the counter gave the trustee a bad time, goofing and jiving, aware of Kesey and me watching, playing to an audience.

"Arrest them," said the trustee, pointing to us, kidding—but who knows, this place played for keeps. We had to wait through a prisoner count.

"Usually it is over by now," Hills told us. "It has nothing to do with someone being missing, just making sure that the numbers are straight."

"Attention Institution," a voice announced over the loud-speaker. "The count is correct."

We stood waiting for Joanna, Bruno's wife, who was supposed to visit him with us.

"Want to go in without her?" asked Hills.

We agreed. He shook our hands and returned to his office. A guard looked through the stuff we brought: pages for the magazine, a cassette recorder.

"Just don't leave anything with him."

We passed through a metal detector, then took an elevator to Floor Seven. We stepped into a foyer. On the left a closed door, no window, on the right a door with a big window. A TV camera surveyed the room.

"Oh shit, the guy on the door isn't here," said the guard escorting us. "And the intercom is broken."

"Hey," he yelled at the half-glassed door. "Call 477 on your radio and tell Sid there's two here to visit Bruno."

A guard carrying keys and a walkie-talkie appeared at the window on the other side of the door.

"Shit," he said. "What is this?"

He picked up his walkie-talkie. "Desk, I thought you said Bruno's wife was here. There's two and neither one's his wife. What? She's coming up now? Okay, I'll let these two in."

He pointed the walkie-talkie at the door. An electronic beam, activated in Central, opened it. He motioned us into a visiting room: carpeted, metal tables, plastic chairs.

The guard let Joanna into the room at the same time Bruno came in through the other door. He pushed past the guard and embraced her. Then he turned to greet Kesey. Joanna stepped forward, oval face, dark eyes, long black hair parted in the middle. We shook hands and I gave her a slight kiss on the cheek. We separated: she to Kesey, Bruno to me. His brown hair was pulled back in a wave, exposing his high forehead. There was an Irish twinkle in his eye.

"Our code name for you has been Tennessee Larry," I told him. "Like agents clothed in mystery, our intentions unknown. I hear you're Bruno now."

"Yes, I picked the name from Giordano Bruno, an Italian philosopher in the late fifteen-hundreds, but shortened it to George Bruno because I was in a cell with some Mafioso stoolies who might not have gone for Giordano from an Irishman. The press said I used to wear robes. I never wore robes in my life. Like the priest they tried to unfrock, they couldn't do that to me; I was never frocked. Singing Waiters in a Dead Rat Cafe is what they call this place."

We sat down at the table. Bruno and Joanna pulled their chairs close together and sat with their arms interlocked. Bruno turned to Kesey.

"This is my twenty-ninth jail. One week before the filing deadline for the California gubernatorial race, I was slapped with two tenners, downed for two dimes running wild. The Weather Underground broke me out of jail. They cut the power during a movie and I went up on the roof where one of their men on the inside had tied a rope across to a telephone pole out on the road. I had to lower myself down the rope, hand over hand, my ankles crossed over the rope. From there they transported me to Algeria and turned me over to the Black Panthers, who didn't trust me and it was like jail all over again, until they got tired of me and let me go to Afghanistan, where I met Joanna. Two American agents were also there. They arrested me and brought Joanna with me back to the States.

"People vaguely remembered my face. 'Are you a movie actor?' they asked. 'Late twentieth-century,' I told them."

"They all wanted you for something, a guru or a fad," Kesey said.

"They wanted to know the answer beyond the 'turn on, tune in, drop out' thing. I have come to a very simple solution: All the technology has to go underground. Metal belongs underground. You take a hatchet out in the forest and drop it, it goes exactly where the Divine Process wants it to be: underground. I foresee where the tribal groups that drop out will be helping to get back in harmony with the land and will accomplish that by putting technology underground."

"That should flummox the authorities," I said.

Kesey grimaced. "It's all Earth Shoes. You haven't gone for any of it. You stayed with an original vision and they resent that. We had a plan once—for you to split."

Bruno laughed. "Yes, let's do it, split."

"First we'd go to Mexico, have you start all over again from the point where you were busted."

Bruno and his wife and children had been crossing into Texas from Mexico, and had his twenty-year-old daughter hide his pot in her underwear, when they were caught that time.

After Bruno and Joanna were brought back from Afghanistan, they were taken to San Francisco. The Feds were convinced Bruno was connected with LSD labs and two agents drove him around to suspected houses and asked him what he knew. They let Joanna ride along with Bruno in the back seat. One morning, Joanna opened her purse and showed Bruno a gun. Bruno shook his head. Then he saw another pistol lying on the floor. He picked it up and held it over the shoulder of the driver.

"Here, I think this dropped out of your holster."

"Oh, shit."

The feds, realizing Bruno wasn't involved in the drug lab thing, took him to San Diego, where he now awaited sentencing from the first arrest at the Mexican border.

"Your San Francisco lawyer, Michael Horowitz, wants me to come to the city for a press conference," Kesey said. "Since you met with him three weeks ago, he's been subpoenaed by the San Francisco grand jury."

"I can understand that. But why the press conference?"

"Probably to announce he won't cooperate with the authorities in any way."

"Horowitz used to call himself a hopeless paranoid," Bruno said. "Ever since he met me, he calls himself a hopeful paranoid. In India today, the people who get the most respect are those who went to jail for their principles during the independence fight. I see the people here being put in jail for possession of marijuana as being in a very similar position. Probably ninety percent of the people in jail for pot belong to three groups: they are either minorities, or young, or creative. There are very few white, middle-class Americans in jail for possession of marijuana."

He shook his head. "The seed-carrying soft body should not be embedded in steel. It does no one good. I had no intention of going to jail. I wasn't going to provide any kind of model for people to go to jail for spiritual purposes. And here I am for a pot bust almost a decade ago."

Kesey laid the cassette recorder on the table.

"We brought this because of the tapes Marge King made of some of your talks. She gave them to us wanting to know if you'd give her permission to distribute them."

Bruno shook his head. "That's a bad vibration trip. I don't want to mess with them. Just another instance of my words being taken over by someone else for their use and profit."

"I understand. But as long as the tape recorder is here, I thought maybe you'd like to make a statement I could take to the Horowitz press conference. You know, something like, 'The marlin are biting good today in Coronado Bay. Whoops, just dropped my gin and tonic.'"

"'Can't hardly see the ocean for those bikini-clad beauties lounging on the yacht,'" I added.

Bruno turned to Joanna. She made a sharp downward thrust with her hand and shook her head. Bruno laughed. He got it, and declined to make a statement.

Two rough-looking prisoners in sweat clothes came into the room. Bruno jumped up, went over and exchanged skin: the first prisoner, crew-cut, heavy, friendly; the other, a two-day beard, silent, wearing dark glasses. Both were young, in their twenties.

"These are my handball partners," Bruno told us.

"His patsies," said the friendly one.

"You mean this elderly gentleman can lick you?" I said.

"He cleans up the floor with us."

"We don't use the word 'lick' to outsiders," the other prisoner said.

The door was beamed open and they left.

"What did he mean by that?" I asked.

"I don't know," said Bruno.

"Probably something to do with affairs below the belt," Kesey said.

Bruno nodded. "I'll call Joanna tonight and make a statement and she can get it to Horowitz."

The prisoners had 24-hour phone privileges, but only collect calls, their keepers listening in so they could pick up any scraps of info that might come through from the singing waiters, like they were squeezing the last bit of juice out of a lemon.

"We have a new lawyer," Joanna told Bruno. "Milano, in San Francisco, is going to plead our case in Texas. The judge never said whether your two five-year sentences should run concurrently or consecutively, so Milano wants to take two US government agents there to agree that the sentences be run concurrently. Since you've already spent four years in different jails, it means you would be eligible for immediate parole."

"That's good news," Bruno said. "Let's hope it works out."

"There's one catch. Milano needs two thousand dollars. I'm going to give him all of my jewels."

"I'll throw in my watch and radio."

They smiled at one another.

"Before they kick us out, let's get down to the real reason Babbs and I are here," Kesey said.

He took out the *Spit In The Ocean* material and spread the

pages on the table. Bruno looked through them. Manuscripts sent in by scientists, swamis, spiritualists, spouses, space-nuts, spelunkers, star-builders, and other such prognosticators of the future. They had written theories and stories about higher intelligence based on scientific discoveries in neurologics, genetics, astronomy and physics, including responses from occultists, psychics, and spiritualists. Kesey and I had winnowed hundreds of entries down to nine.

"This is top-drawer stuff," Bruno said, "from relatively unknowns in the field, very refreshing. I'm not interested in so-called experts like Skinner and Sagan."

"The hard part is over," said Kesey. "You add something explaining what you were looking for, write a few intros to the selections, and we'll do the rest."

The door opened and trays of starchy food were wheeled in. Visiting hours were over.

Kesey handed Bruno a sheet of paper: A sketch of the cover of *Spit In The Ocean* number three. A small square in the upper right corner showed a spaceship shooting off into the sky with a word balloon coming out of it: *"I'm getting out of here."*

OTIS, the joker of the deck, was drawn in the middle of the page, his body rising from jail bars, hands clasped over his head, wrists manacled to stars, and below the picture, in large letters, the title:

COMMUNICATION
WITH HIGHER
INTELLIGENCE
EDITED BY DR. TIM LEARY

"I like it," Bruno said. "I'm aboard for sure. It will be nice to use my real name again."

I believe there are bad forces able to move people to do dumb shit. In the liquor store I've been going to for years, the counter is covered with scratch cards. I was buying a bottle of Southern Comfort and this woman says, "Which lottery ticket would you like?" and I say, "I'm not allowed to buy lottery tickets." The place was full of people my age scratching these things and they all turned outraged and looked at me like I should be banned from the store. The counter woman said, "What do you mean?" And I said, "My IQ isn't low enough to play the lottery." "What do you mean? Don't you like gambling?" And I told her, "Sure, I like gambling. I think poker is one of the greatest games in the world, but that's skill. It's not just chance, it's real gambling. I used to like to go duck hunting. But I don't consider going out and sitting in the fog just randomly shooting your gun in the air to be hunting. That's superstition. That's people believing if I wear a rabbit foot on my watch chain and I have my Mother Christopher medal and I pet them just right and I buy a lottery ticket... Buy lottery tickets? You don't need angels and saints; you're already up to your ears in bad forces."
— Ken Kesey

67

Harmless Act of Random Ridicule

The crowd was getting restless. Kesey and I had run out of things to say, wondering what was keeping Hunter S. Thompson. We were there to introduce him, not be his replacement. Mutterings from the floor, chairs scraping, bodies shifting. This could get ugly. I glanced at Kesey. He shrugged, no card tricks up his sleeve.

"Get off the stage," a voice shouted. "I didn't pay eight dollars to listen to you clowns."

Kesey jumped down, strode up the aisle to the guy and pulled out his wallet.

"Here's your eight dollars. Go spend it somewhere else."

He aimed the guy toward the door and went back to the stage, just as Hunter Thompson stumbled up the stairs and collapsed in a chair behind a table.

Hunter's sweaty shirt was open to his belt, his white skin blotched, hand shaking. He reached for water, splashed it across the table, gave up, pulled a crumpled pack of cigarettes out of his pocket, shook it, ripped at it, flung it on the floor.

"Goddammit," he said in a low-voiced mumble over the microphone, "what's a man have to do to get a cigarette, nothing working, the place fucked, sugar-cut coke, watered whiskey, steak tough as a bum's shoe leather. Don't you people understand, my best friend shot and killed his brother, my other best friend, last night. Hound me, ground me, bones in a pile, scrivened, beribboned, get me some whiskey, Kesey, dammit."

He continued his low mumble, veered from talking about shooting guns in his backyard at Woody Creek, Colorado, to the tragedy of the filmmaker Mitchell brothers in San Francisco, arguing, then fighting, and the final gunshot. One bereft, the other dead. Whiskey at last, gulping from a pint someone gave Kesey, the audience silent, enrapt, the gravelly, low voice drawing them forward in their seats as they strained to catch his words, an hourlong rambling, incoherent monologue, Hunter struggling to dredge stories he couldn't finish, the murder in San Francisco constantly intruding in his attempts to make sense out of something he couldn't yet believe—until in frustration he stood up, pint bottle in hand, and staggered to the stairs. I grabbed his hand to keep him from falling.

"Get me out of here, Babbs."

I helped him off the stage and said, "Get on this," boosting him onto a long serving table with wheels. I laid him flat, covered him with a white cloth, and pushed him through the crowd.

"Make way, make way, man with an emergency."

We went out the door to Kesey's bus, *Further.* I pulled Hunter off the cart.

"In you go."

I shoved him through the door and clambered inside, Kesey behind me.

Kit Kesey, Ken's nephew, sat in the driver's seat. He cranked up the engine and pulled out into the street.

The bus was packed to the gunnels: students, highbrows, lowbrows, long-haired, short-haired, men, women, even a couple of kids.

"We're taking this bus to San Francisco and we're not coming back," Kesey yelled at them. "It would behoove you all to get off now or it's going to be a long walk home. Pull over, Kit."

Kit found an empty spot at the curb. Kesey opened the door and the bus emptied, leaving the musician-Prankster John Swan and Kesey's son Zane sprawled on cushions in the back. I sat on the couch behind the driver's seat. Kesey plunked down alongside me. Hunter Thompson stood in front, staring out the windshield, looking over his shoulder, mumbling, words barely discernible over the engine roar, a running commentary on the passengers who had been riding in back: "...not a whisker on a chin nor a T-shirt with a word that makes head nor tail of which way the wind blows in a maelstrom of lust beheaded by a thrust nor any stray thought of malfeasance at the forefront..."

Suddenly, with a pull of the handle, he swung the door open and stepped out, heading for the pavement face-first, but Kit grabbed him by the shirt and yanked him back in. Kesey pulled him down on the couch and sat with his arm around Hunter's shoulder for the ride to the farm.

K it drove through the open door into the bus barn. Kesey got out first, grabbed one end of a poker table, I took the other, and we muscled it onto the bus. Kit brought in folding chairs. We took our places, Hunter, Kesey, Kit, Zane, me, John Swan. I put the container holding the poker chips in the middle of the table. A set of cards rested in a slot. Kesey held up the deck of cards to show the seal unbroken, slit the cellophane with his fingernail, fanned the cards across the table, and threw out the jokers.

"Nickel, dime and quarter," he said. "White, red, and blue chips. Buy as many as you like."

The money came out. I was the banker. I exchanged cash for chips, put the cash in a box by my feet.

"Ante a quarter," Kesey said. "Five-card stud, four cards down, one up."

"A quarter," Hunter Thompson bet, showing a king.

The game was on. Beer and whiskey, joints, and Hunter smoking tobacco, his cigarette in a holder, brandished like a concert conductor's baton.

"There's this cat," Hunter Thompson said, "started making Tricky Dicky talking dolls, sent them under assumed names and fake addresses to congressmen and journalists. Left them sitting on hotel check-in counters, bar tops, in truck stops. In cities, small towns, ski resorts, you name it."

"Call your quarter," I said, "and raise you a dime."

Everyone called, threw their dimes on the table.

"Chicken feed," Hunter said. "Raise fifty cents. They had this string sticking out the back. Pull the string and the doll talked in this squeaky whining voice: '*It is the responsibility of the media to look at the President with a microscope, but they go too far when they use a proctoscope.*'"

"I call your quarter and raise a dime," Swan said.

I called. Kit and Kesey folded.

"Call and raise twenty cents," Hunter said. "The dolls had different sayings. Another one was, '*I was under medication when I made the decision to burn the tapes.*'"

Swan and I called.

"Suckers," Hunter said. "Pull the string on another doll and you got, '*Goddamn it, get in and get those files. Blow the safe and get them.*'"

He showed his cards. Three sixes beat my pair of kings and Swan's two pair. Hunter scooped in the chips.

"They never did find out who was responsible for the dolls," Hunter said. "He pulled the plug ahead of the heat. The feds were fed up, wasting manpower on a piddly prank but word to squelch it came from the top."

"What's the point?" I asked.

"Harmless act of random ridicule. The sort of thing that drove Tricky Dicky crazy."

"Reminds me of some of the shows we've done," Kesey said. "My gauge of success is how much money I don't lose. They're not only free at the door, but we're having to pay to show them and bring them around to people. I wouldn't trade places with anyone. We're having a great time and it's creative; it's on the edge and sometimes we succeed and sometimes we don't and— look out Kit, you've got a horsefly on you, that's a horsefly take your head off, man, look at that booger. I'll try to catch him. Almost. What were we talking about?"

"Five-card draw," Hunter said.

"Yes, just like a poker game," Kesey said. "We stumble along and bumble along and pretty soon more and more stuff starts to stumble along and bumble along with us until we've got a great group stumbling and bumbling and people coming in we've never seen before and drummers—where are the drummers?"

"Out selling vacuum cleaners to housewives in aprons with their hair wrapped in bandanas," Hunter said.

B y dawn the poker table was strewn with empty containers, roach-filled ashtrays, cards scattered on the floor. Kesey went to bed in the house. The rest of us crashed in the bus.

Someone shook me awake. Swan stood over me.

"Hunter Thompson's gone."

We went outside. The morning fog was lifting off the ground. Kesey's Cadillac convertible sat in the hayfield, nosed up to a gate. Swan and I walked out, shoes and pant legs sopping the dew. Hunter sat in the driver's seat, head back, dark glasses covering his eyes, mouth open, a cigarette burning in the holder clutched between his fingers. The car was still running.

I touched his shoulder. His head snapped up.

"I had to get out of there. The bastards stole my winnings. They closed the gates. Locked me in. What are you after now, Babbs, my wallet?"

"No, the car."

I opened the door and shoved him into the passenger seat. Swan jumped in back. I turned the car around and drove to the house. We helped Hunter into the kitchen where I started making coffee. Kesey came out of the bedroom and took over. We drank coffee and when our bones were warm and our minds were working, Kesey drove Hunter to his room at the Hilton.

"I'm telling you," I heard Hunter say as they were leaving, "I cleaned everyone out and when I went to cash in my chips, the money was gone."

A fter that the faxes poured in from Woody Creek, where Hunter stayed up late at night, bottle of Wild Turkey on the table, cigarette holder clenched between his teeth—sending electronic missives flying through the air.

Ding ding the machine pinged in Kesey's upstairs office in the barn, then silence until morning when Kesey entered with coffee in hand and removed Hunter's fax from the machine.

"*I need LSD 25 at once. No kidding. I must have the acid. Tomorrow. Now. There are no jokes. Please. Yes. Thanks. HST note send word.*"

The fax was hand scrawled. Another came, late that night,

also written by hand.

"Time is a stock car race on the last lap, send post haste. HST."

Kesey answered with his own handwritten fax.

"I sent it days ago. 15 tabs. Small white envelope from Alice T. Crawley. Check your mail pile. The tabs are taped inside a folded valentine. No lie!"

Hunter faxed back:

"Thanx for the brain saving boost. $100 bill enroute to you tomorrow—and I implore you to send 100 more of those tabs ASAP. Thanx. HST."

And below his scrawl, the typed words: "STRANGE BIRTH TO WOODY CREEK COUPLE."

When Kesey received the hundred-dollar bill he faxed it back to Hunter and threw the money in his desk drawer.

Hunter answered:

"Keez. What? Is this (see enc.) from you? If so. Prepare to send the stuff—at once. Details TK. OK. Doc."

Kesey never answered and the faxes dried up.

*R*unning *Magazine,* based in Eugene, Oregon, sent Hunter Thompson to Honolulu to cover the Honolulu Marathon. They put him up in a four-star hotel, paid his expenses and waited for the story. And waited for the story. *And waited for the story.* Panicked because the deadline was near, they flew him to Eugene, put him up in a motel and told him they wouldn't let him out until the story was done.

The magazine people were dealing with a force of nature, not necessarily benign. The days passed, Hunter stared at the typewriter, paced the floor, tried to open the drapes and look out the window of the second-story room. Nothing doing. Paul Perry, the editor, ruled with an iron fist, no to everything until the story was done. Take-out containers littered the floor. Coffee cups, half drunk, left circles on the tables. Then the showdown.

With one day to go, Hunter locked himself in the bathroom

and wouldn't come out, no matter how hard Paul Perry pleaded, how much he extolled, offering bonuses.

"I need pot," Hunter yelled. "Get me some pot."

"How am I supposed to get you pot? I don't know where to buy pot."

"Get hold of Babbs, have him bring me some."

"And then you'll finish the story? Promise?"

"Sure."

Hunter cracked the door. Paul Perry leaned in. Hunter threw a lit string of firecrackers through the opening. Paul Perry yelped, skidded back and fell, firecrackers exploding around him. A loud cackle and the door slammed shut.

I laughed when I heard what happened but said I'd score some pot and bring it over.

"Fast as you can," Paul Perry said.

When I got to the motel, Paul Perry was frantic. "What took you so long? Never mind, give it here." He wouldn't let me in the room. I had to hand the lid through the crack in the door, the chain bolted.

"What about some money?" I started to say but the door shut in my face.

I shrugged and left. Hunter finished the story and when he was done Paul Perry turned him loose with a plane ticket home. Hunter had some time to kill so he called Kesey and said, "Get Babbs, and come down to the Vet's Club for drinks. I'm buying, I just got paid a bundle."

Hunter was sitting in a booth. Two young women gushed over him. He held a cigarette in his trademark long black holder with a solid gold tip, wore a snappy white hat on his head. When he jumped to his feet to greet us, his white polo shirt flashed atop white shorts, white athletic socks and white Nike trainers with a red swoosh.

We drank and shot the shit until Hunter looked at his watch and said, "All good things must come to an end and the end is near, for I have to go to the airport to catch my plane and these lovely ladies are taking me there."

We shook and Kesey and I went out to his Cadillac, sitting in the lot with the top down. Kesey started it up. Hunter was about to get into the car with the women when Kesey said to me, "Tell Hunter to come on over here."

Kesey leaned down toward the floor.

"Hey, Hunter," I yelled. "Tell us again what time your plane is leaving."

Hunter cupped his ear, *what's that?* I motioned him over. Long tanned legs glided across the asphalt. He reached the car on my side, Kesey reared up from the floor, and tossed a lit string of firecrackers at Hunter's feet. Hunter danced like a cowboy getting the floor shot up around him as Kesey peeled out, waving his arm in the air, Hunter screaming, "Damn you Kesey, I'll be seeing you again and then..." His words trailed and died behind us.

"Maybe when Paul Perry hears about this he'll pay you for that pot," Kesey said.

"Maybe."

No money and no more adventures with Hunter Thompson. He holed up in Woody Creek. His Honolulu Marathon story came out in *Running Magazine*. Later, Hunter expanded it into a book, *The Curse of Lono*, with drawings by his good friend and collaborator, Ralph Steadman.

A documentary on Hunter Thompson came out after his death. Kesey and I and our wives and older children and all the Pranksters we could muster went to see it at the Bijou Art Cinema in Eugene. At one point, in the middle of the film, Hunter picked up a bottle of Wild Turkey, raised it to his lips, missed. It slipped and fell to the floor just when I kicked over the bottle of Wild Turkey I had stashed under my seat and the glass bottle rolled, clinking and clanking down the concrete floor all the way to the foot of the stage while the audience cracked up laughing.

Afterwards, outside the theater, we heard some people talking. They thought the noise of the rolling bottle was on the soundtrack of the film.

*What it meant was that everybody had to consider
a new way for things to be. The real challenge for
superheroes was what to do between telephone booths.*
  — Ken Kesey

68

Little Too Rich
After a Long Nap

Kesey had decided to take the movie-making into his own
hands. He bought a professional Steenbeck 16 mm editing
table, set it up in his cabin on the coast and hired John Teton, a
filmmaker, to do the editing. While that was going on, Kesey
brought the original Pranksters to the farm, one at a time, and
recorded them on an Ampex tape recorder, asking them questions about Neal Cassady—Kesey had a screenplay in mind: Neal
Cassady was caught in no man's land in the spiritual world, not
in heaven, not in purgatory, not in hell. The judges on high
couldn't decide where he belonged so they decided to put the
spirit of Cassady on trial. The original Pranksters would be
called upon to testify.

Kesey planned to film it himself. He had a new structure built
at his farm: cement floor, concrete-block walls, cedar-shake
roof, floor-to-ceiling roll-up metal doors at each end, the interior an open space filled with church pews he bought at auc-
tion, an aisle down the middle and a raised judge's platform at
the end.

The whole plan got scuttled. John Teton quit and, with no
one to do the editing, Kesey decided to go another direction. He
sold the movie editing table, went through the tapes and, using

them for dialogue, wrote a screenplay which Sterling Lord, his agent, sold to Viking as a book: *The Further Inquiry.*

It was scheduled to come out in time for the American Bookseller Association's convention in Las Vegas. Viking was planning to throw a huge launch party for the *The Further Inquiry* at Caesar's Palace and Kesey would be the featured speaker. Searching for the ideal attraction that would make his appearance memorable, Kesey came upon a 1948 International Harvester school bus for sale. The original *Further* had been retired and parked under shady trees in a back plot on the farm where it would rust in peace.

Further would ride again, and if anyone asked Kesey which was the real bus he would tell them, "There is only one *Starship Enterprise*, no matter how many versions."

Kesey shoved the church pews to the side and parked the new bus in the new building. Everyone set to work, cleaning the interior, tuning the engine, checking the brakes and drive line and transmission. Lynda Lanker, the renowned Eugene artist, painted a rendition of Michelangelo's fresco on the Sistine Chapel: David reaching out with a finger to touch the outstretched finger of God. Her painting covered most of the right side of the bus.

The rest of the bus, from front to back, the roof and hood, were painted in dayglo colors, with a white swirl running from front fender to back platform. Kesey filled eggshells with different colored paints and had kids throw them at the bus, creating abstract lines.

A plywood platform was bolted to the top and metal railings installed along the sides. A truck windshield covered the front of the platform. Another platform was welded to the back of the bus with a ladder to the roof.

The Grateful Dead's Rex Foundation donated five thousand dollars to buy speakers on top and bottom, headsets with microphones, a sound mixer, CD player, an invertor to change the 12-

volt battery system to 110-volts AC, and a five-mile-radius FM transmitter so people driving in cars behind us and alongside us could listen to what was going on in the bus.

With Kit Kesey at the wheel, we headed for the Las Vegas Book Convention. On the freeway, cars passed on the left, then slowed down so they could read the sign in the window—TUNE IN TO 104.7 KBUZ—and dropped back, picking up our music and multi-miked rants: *They'll stone you...* "Duck in the alley, get hit with the finale..." *You're all alone...* "Hide your head, hide under your bed..." *Don't feel all alone...* "Not in a parade, on the promenade..." *Must get stoned...* "Boned, dethroned, overblown, microphonegrownstoned..."

We pulled over into a rest stop, a line of cars behind us. The drivers and passengers piled out and surrounded the bus. When we left, they zipped past, horns honking, arms waving while another line of cars followed.

In the late afternoon we pulled into a motel across the highway from an army base in Nevada. Parked the bus under the shade and went into the restaurant for grub. Outside in the cooling evening, Kesey broke out paints and, sitting on a stool, began working on the bus, adding faces, tails and animal bodies to the eggshell splatters.

Three young boys rode into the parking lot on Stingray bikes. They carried skateboards under their arms. Circling the bus, looking it over, they came to Kesey and one yelled, "Are you peacers or geezers?" The other two following behind yelled, "Peacers or geezers?"

They continued to circle the bus, yelling every time they passed Kesey. He finally lifted his paintbrush from the hull and turned around.

"Neither. We're the Merry Band of Pranksters."

The ice broken, they stopped to talk. Kesey explained what the bus was all about, then asked if they'd like to paint their skateboards. They were all for it. Kesey broke out paintbrushes and paint and turned the boys loose. They worked till dark, then rode off, carefully holding the skateboards by their edges.

A car pulled in and parked behind the bus. Timothy Leary, John Barlow, and Bill Walton emerged. We exchanged shakes and hugs. This was a planned meeting, the very reason we had stopped at this out-of-the-way motel. Leary also had a book coming out at the convention in Las Vegas and he and Walton were going to ride there with us on the bus. Barlow would drive their car back to California.

After dinner we climbed on top of the bus, above us the Nevada sky alight with stars and a crescent moon. Kesey waxed along with the moon. He talked about becoming enlightened, that it used to be done by going up in the hills or the desert, but now it's got to be done by community.

Leary nodded. He agreed up to a point, but added that you also have to talk about psychic energy and cosmic energy, and words hundreds of years old, the holy of holies.

"Like that," I said. "A holey in the sky."

A shooting star burned across the firmament, disappearing into a hole.

Bill Walton, a star basketball player in college and the NBA, had undergone numerous foot and back surgeries. He said his bike became his gym, church, and wheelchair all in one, a constant circling motion rolling over the curvature of the earth, and it overcame debilitating pain; he could think and he could dream.

"I ride the Internet," said John Perry Barlow, former Wyoming rancher and Grateful Dead lyricist. A pioneer in the formation of the Internet and a leader in the fight to keep it open, he said the Internet was going to do to monotheism what meat tenderizer does to meat. "But you have to remember," he added, "what comes at you out of that screen is not experience, it is information. It's got as much relationship to experience as beef jerky does to cows."

Leary didn't see that any of us were saying anything that had any relevance to the future. "We have a general agreement," he said, "that things are not going well, hundreds of negative solutions and regressive and restrictive possibilities, but I can't pick up on my radar screen any practical projection of the future."

At which point, two o'clock in the a.m., I decided to leave them to their intellectual ramblings and go to bed.

T he next morning we loaded our bags on the bus and hit the road for Vegas. In the late afternoon we parked in front of Caesar's Palace. We relaxed on the grass and saw a small parade stomping along the sidewalk. Don King, the flamboyant boxing promoter, strode in front, shouting, "The man beast, the giant killer, he believes in the unbelievable, snatches the possible out of the impossible, if you want to sell a steak, you can't just have the sizzle, you gotta have the sauce and behind me is the man with the juice, the giant killer."

Mike Tyson, muscled and glowering, shadowboxed ten steps behind Don King. People lining the sidewalk shouted and waved: "Mike. Mike Tyson. Yoo-hoo. Kill him, tiger."

Kesey's son Zane had given me a cab driver's hat that looked like a military officer's headgear, except it was bright yellow with a black brim and YELLOW CAB in big letters across the front.

I ran across the lawn and fell in step with Don King. He looked at me, *what the fuck?*

"Remember me, Don? I drove you in Cleveland. You liked it so much you kept me on for a couple of weeks."

"Oh yeah, good to see you, call me when I'm back in the Buckeye State."

"For sure."

I gave him a two-finger salute to the brim of my cap and returned to the lawn. Bill Walton, leaning on crutches, recovering from an operation on his foot, greeted me with a big grin. Leary patted my shoulder and laughed. Kesey shook his head, not a bit surprised. Don King's voice faded away as he strode into the main hall.

We went up to our rooms, frigid with air conditioning, carrying a funny smell with the cold air. Remembering Legionnaire's disease was said to be caused by something emanating from air conditioners, I put on my bathing suit and sat under an umbrella by the pool, reading a book and drinking gin and tonics until it was time for Kesey's talk and party.

Viking had paid for a big room on the ground floor of the casino. A stage and lectern stood at one end, rows of chairs filled the middle. Behind them, tables laden with food and drinks. The place was full and Kesey drew a resounding applause when he took the stage.

He welcomed everyone, told them about bringing the bus with Leary and Walton aboard, then did a short bit about how the book, *The Further Inquiry*, came about: the attempt to revive the '64 bus trip movie, how that didn't happen, and rather than abandon the work, he wrote a screenplay using taped interviews of the Pranksters. Viking published it and tonight they were gathered for the launch of the book.

"Prepare the court for the next inquiry," he read from the book. "The courtroom is vast and dim, starkly furnished, rows of old wooden church pews, threadbare carpet in the aisle, old four-bladed ceiling fan rotating lugubriously, the prosecutor picks up a dossier of the next case: Cassady, Neal; alias Moriarty, Dean; alias Pomeroy, Cody; alias Kennedy, Hart; alias Houlihan, Dean; alias Speed Limit."

Kesey turned to the end of the book where the spirit of Cassady climbs from the defendant's dock and moves toward the bus door. Cassady gets in and starts the engine.

"Let me smooth the old bitch out for you, little too rich after a long nap." His booted foot tromps down on the gas.

Kesey raised his hand and slapped the lectern.

A steel door in the back wall opened with a loud rumble and

Further roared into the room, Kit at the wheel. He went for the brake, his foot slipped and hit the gas. The bus careened into the food tables. Plates, glasses, chicken legs, salads, sandwich meats, Jell-o desserts, and bottles of wine and beer exploded across the floor. The bus slid to a stop, front end splattered in guck, windshield dripping with goo. Women shrieked, men knocked over chairs as everyone fled the room.

Sitting in his chair close to the stage, Peter Mayer, the CEO of Viking Penguin, calmly surveyed the mayhem. He turned to David Stanford, Kesey's editor, and said, "Now that's publishing."

When we were working on the musical play, Twister, the cast was there and ready but Ken hadn't written the last piece. I went to him and said, "Ken, we need that final scene." He looked at me with one of those funny little smiles and said, "I'm dancing as fast as I can." I realized he was doing all he could. I never tried to hurry him up again. Ken always said he promised more than he could deliver so he could do what he did get done.
— *Phil Dietz*

69

We Are, After All, Professionals

The early-morning ground fog lay on Kesey's pasture like a faded grey comforter. The bus sat in the driveway, door open. Kesey came out of the house, a cup of coffee in his hand. He looked at the sky, gauged the height of the sun rising over the pond, raised his right arm and grimaced, the old wrestling shoulder injury still grinding.

Dust swirled in the drive as I arrived in my station wagon. George Walker, Mike Hagen, and Phil Dietz pulled in within minutes of each other. The bus was packed with our *Twister* costumes. We were heading to San Francisco to do a gig at the Fillmore, bits from the musical we'd been performing: a stage production with dialogue, songs, a cast of eight and a four-piece band. It was a takeoff on *The Wizard of Oz*, foretelling the end times with famine, deadly viruses, and earthquakes.

Critics called the show everything from a "musical catastrophe" to a "technoidal travesty."

"If it must be labeled," Kesey said, "I prefer the *New York Times'* description: 'a ritual reality.' Hard times need strong rituals, and these are some hard times."

Dorothy was played by Frivol the Clown, a friend of ours from Seattle. She had the lead role, singing and dancing and talking throughout the show. Phil Dietz was the Scarecrow.

"Here in Oz we've got a name for each destructive power," he proclaimed. "Unlike the trees known by their fruits, they are known by what they devour."

Carol Provance played Glenda the Good Witch. Virus was her subject: "A slimy, liquid, poison, malodorous fluid. They are solitary, replicate in search of one another."

George Walker, the Tin Man, joined Glenda onstage. The Tin Man's limbs were creaking. Glenda picked up a can and squirted oil into his joints.

"Ah, you're an angel, an absolute angel," the Tin Man said.

They ran through a whole alphabet of bodily ills. There was a loud knock on the door.

"Hey in der," Arzinia Richardson, glasses on his nose, a small goatee on his chin, called from offstage. "Open dee door and let me in. I'm here with you in syncopation. You think rhythm come like instant pudding? I am dee African god Legba and Legba be more instant than any pudding."

My loud footsteps clomped heavily on the floor. I was playing the part of "The Restless Earth," in the form of Frankenstein's motherless monster.

"That's one pair of terrific shoes you're wearing," Dorothy said.

Frankenstein's monster looked at his shoes, large concrete blocks painted black. He lifted one and pounded the floor, then again with the other. The building shook.

"No wonder the earth is restless," Dorothy said. "Not much rhythm there, though."

Frankenstein's monster hated those shoes, so heavy they

exhausted him. He tried to smash them to pieces, clomping hard on each word.

"Not much rhythm but you gotta dance widdem."

He was interrupted by an image of Simon Babbs playing Elvis Presley, appearing on the big O-zone screen hanging from the ceiling.

"Whoa, Big Boss Man," Elvis said, "you're injuring my eardrums. You need a little rock-'n'-roll backbeat, son. Get that ungodly rear of yours in gear."

Elvis disappeared from the O-zone screen and danced onstage, singing and strumming 'bout a cryin' hound dog.

Frankenstein's monster roared and charged. Elvis stood aside and the monster lurched past. Dorothy jumped between them. Legba thumped his cane on the floor. Oz appeared and roared his disapproval. With the entire cast assembled, the musical rolled to a rollicking finish.

We played Eugene, Boise, LA, and Boulder, Colorado. On the way to Boulder, the bus broke down in a small town. We left the bus at a garage. Kesey rented a pickup to carry our gear. Before we were on our way, the owner of the pickup had us put our hands on the truck while he said a prayer for our safety— with the unsaid wish for his truck to make it back in one piece.

N ow in the bus, leaving Kesey's, we were headed for a short version of *Twister* at the Fillmore Auditorium in San Francisco.

Twenty miles down the road, Kesey sat up, nose twitching.

"Smells like we're in donut country."

Diabetic, Kesey wasn't supposed to eat sweets, but once we cleared the gravitational pull of home, he began slavering and quavering, savoring the thought of a friendly sweet taste.

George pulled off in Yreka, we went in the bakery, and stocked up. Outside, Kesey made a phone call from a booth.

There was no answer and the phone went to message.

"Paul, are you there? This is Kesey. We're headed your way. Should be there about dark."

Kesey was calling Paul Krassner to confer about their plan to do a new *Supplement of The Whole Earth Catalog* together. We'd spend the night at Paul's house and he'd go with us the next day to our San Fran gig.

We drove on, slurping our coffee and dunking donuts. We stopped for gas and Kesey called Paul again. Once more he got the message machine.

"We're three hours out," Kesey told the machine. "What's for supper?"

We stopped three more times before we got to the city, getting the answering machine every time.

It was dark when we pulled up in front of Paul's house. There were lights on in the windows, so we figured he was home. A phone booth stood on the corner.

Kesey dropped a quarter in the slot.

"Paul, we're standing right outside your house. Why don't you answer the phone? Turn off the damned machine."

Paul came bounding down the steps.

"What the hell are you guys doing here? Why didn't you call and let me know you were coming? I'd have had supper ready."

We looked at each other.

"We did call," Kesey said. "Three or four times. All we got was your machine."

"What the hell you talking about? The only reason I knew you were here is I saw you from the window. What number were you calling?"

Kesey showed him the scrap of paper.

"That's not my number."

"Then whose is it?"

"Damned if I know."

Paul went inside the phone booth. We followed to listen. He dialed the number we'd been calling from the road.

"Hello, this is Paul. Have I got any messages? Call me at home."

He hung up the phone and we went up to his house and settled in.

T he next morning, we drove along the bayfront, parked the bus on the side of the street to straighten it up and regroup before heading downtown. A group of kids came walking by. They were mentally and physically challenged. Differently-bodied: big bellies, short legs, swollen heads. They stood around the bus, touching it and exclaiming over it. Kesey came out and approached the kids. They swarmed around him, held his arms and patted his back and talked to him nonstop. After a while he got back on the bus, a big smile on his face.

"Those are our people," he said.

We drove to Broadway, near Grant Avenue, and found a place to park.

"Babbs and Paul and I have to meet some people," Kesey said. "The rest of you can get something to eat. We'll be back in a bit."

We walked to a sidewalk restaurant. Kesey pushed down the rope in front and stepped over. I looked at Paul. He shrugged, and we followed. The place was crowded, tables full, mostly men, dressed in suits. There was a podium in front and a woman was standing behind a lectern: Jan Kerouac, Jack Kerouac's daughter. Black wavy hair parted in the middle, falling to her shoulders. Full lips, dark eyes.

She was wan, pensive, defensive, seeking a donor for a kidney transplant but instead had been caught in the middle of a legal wrangle over who owned the rights to her father's estate.

On one side was a group arguing for Jan, on the other, a group arguing for the Sampas family, Jack Kerouac having been married to Stella Sampas. It was getting fierce, men standing and shouting and interrupting one another. A man wearing a pinstripe suit launched into a tirade against not only Jack's widow, but also Jack's mother, Jack's mother's cat, Jack's foul friends, Jack's biographer, Ann Charters, and Ann Charters's cat!

"*Lawyers*," Kesey muttered.

He strode into the middle of the room and said, "Stop it. Look at what you're doing."

He pointed to Jan, leaning on the lectern.

"This is what we're here for. For Jan, not to fight over the Kerouac estate. Jan needs a kidney transplant. Put your petty money fight aside and join in a worthwhile cause. Get her that transplant."

Everyone was quiet, stunned by the interruption. Some guy in the corner stood up.

"I've got an extra kidney; she can have mine."

He pulled his shirt up to show scars on both sides.

"I was born with four. I had the lower right removed a month ago, now they tell me I need to get the upper left out. For balance, they say. Trim. Here's my number at home. I would be honored to have my extra kidney traveling around in a daughter of Kerouac's."

It broke the tension. The lawyers sat down and picked up their drinks. Kesey gave Jan Kerouac a wave and led Paul and me out, over the rope onto the sidewalk, back to the bus.

On the way we looked for a store to buy patch cords we needed for the bus's sound system. While we were walking Kesey slumped against me. I propped him up.

"He okay?" Paul said.

"I need bread and a bed," Kesey said.

"He did it again," I told Paul. "Got up and headed out without eating and now his blood sugar is down to zilch."

"In here," Kesey said.

We stood in front of a restaurant. I looked for a place to sit but Kesey shrugged me off and headed into a back room that was set up for a meal. He sat down and helped himself to a piece of chicken while the seats filled up with people from a tour bus parked outside.

Soon he was eating and chatting with the ladies so, seeing an electronics store across the street, I left him, bought the patch cords, came back, retrieved him, and we drove to Paul's house for a nap before the gig.

A gate swung open behind the Fillmore Auditorium. We pulled the bus into the back lot and parked. We walked up a ramp and went inside the stage door to look the place over. A backdrop hanging from the rafters separated the front of the stage from the rear. A florid-faced, heavy guy in dark pants and grey flannel shirt told us we could bring in our props and store them backstage until it was time for our performance.

George and Phil and I went back to the bus and gathered up our costumes.

"Is that all you have?" the stage manager asked.

I nodded.

"Might as well take them up to the green room where you can change."

First I peeked around the backdrop. The stage was set for a concert: microphones and amps and musical instruments in place.

"Kesey, check this out," I said.

He took a look.

"More going on here than I thought," he said.

He thought we were the main draw but it turned out we had been demoted to one act out of six, and second from the end. That left us with time to kill; either lounge in the green room on the second floor or go into the auditorium and watch the other performers.

The green room—not because it was green but because the performer hangouts in venues going back to medieval times were called "the green room"—was a plain place with water pipes attached to yellow-painted walls, a bathroom at one end, no windows, bean bags scattered around the floor.

I went downstairs to watch the show. A man and a woman dressed in tights and black-and-white horizontal-striped shirts rode unicycles around the stage in circles and figure eights while juggling nine pins, flinging them back and forth to the beat of German oompah music, faster and faster. Then they jumped off the unicycles to land on one foot, jump over the top of the unicycle to the other foot, and back onto the seats.

They finished to loud cheering and applause. The curtains closed and everyone drank beers and pop while waiting for the next act.

There was a drum roll from behind the curtain. It opened and the band onstage began playing. The audience surged forward. The group It's a Beautiful Day, a San Francisco favorite, started their set:

"Yellow canary on my window sill
Fills the room with her plaintive trill
Open the window and let me fly
Up to the heavens where I will happily die."

David LaFlamme soared on violin, answered on piano by his wife, Linda. They drove the song to the end, then started another. Played for twenty minutes, then left the stage.

The next act was a magician, first doing coin tricks, rolling them around on his knuckles—they vanished—he found them on the top of his head and the toes of his shoes; then he did fancy maneuvers with cards, spreading the deck like a fan, throwing all the cards in the air and having them vanish, only to reappear behind his back; then the old rabbit pulled from a top hat trick, with an added flourish: tied to the bunny's tail was a long string of colored cloths, a clothes iron, a head of cabbage and, finally, an alligator which he swung around his head and threw into the audience at the same time the lights went out, leaving the auditorium filled with screams in the dark.

Kesey should have seen that, I thought, being a magician himself, but he was holed up in the bus with Krassner hashing out ideas for the magazine they were going to do together.

I went back to the green room and hung around until Kesey showed up with the stage manager who said we'd be on after the next act. We changed into our costumes and trooped downstairs just as the curtain closed on a dance troupe that scampered past us, marching in a row like soldiers dressed in flamboyant camouflage. We stood in line behind the curtain and, when it opened, Kesey stepped forward and bowed.

"Good evening, all. I have been asked to inform you that, by virtue of our exalted positions, I and others from the Land of Oz are privy to certain disturbing conditions which appear to be prevailing in our homeland. Fortunately, these world-class wise men can show the way to survive it."

Kesey stepped back and Phil Dietz took his place.

"The trouble is I have a brain instead of a mind. I'm worried about a menace nagging me. It's the wind, the hungry wind. Hungry for trailer houses and double-wides."

He broke into song:
"Empty bottles cry for drink
And hollow heads for filling.
But listen deep beneath these cries
You'll hear a thing more chilling.
It knows not race nor nation,
It only knows starvation."

He stepped back to scattered applause.

"Our second category is The Lonely Virus," Kesey said. "And here's the Tin Man to tell you about it."

George Walker clanked forward in his metallic outfit and talked through the mouth hole in his helmet.

"It's too late for any miracle solution. Enemies both ancient and new are coursing through the corridors unchecked."

He sang:

"*Mycosis, Myeloma*
And, my goodness, Mumps.
And lastly, as I warn-o
At the front door of your home-o,
Acquired Immune Deficiency Syndrome-o."

He clanked back into line.

"No more kid gloves," Kesey said. "It's time for the heavyweight."

My turn. As the ungodly monster Frankenstein, I clomped forward on the wooden stage.

"This is the ancient bootstep of the Stone Spirits Regulars. I learn it by the numbers in boot camp."

"Not much rhythm but you gotta dance widdem."

Oz and Scarecrow and Tin Man formed a line alongside and we danced and sang in formation, then shuffled off the stage, the audience wondering *what the fuck was that all about?*

We switched into our regular clothes in a hurry to leave, but before we got to the door, Kesey turned and grabbed a bean bag and took it with him. I looked at George and Phil and Hagen and we each grabbed one.

As soon as we were aboard, George fired up the engine and drove to the street, then paused, checking traffic.

A big burly guy, one of the Bill Graham Productions luggers, stepped in front of the bus and held up his hand. He walked to the door, George opened it, and the lugger stepped inside.

"You'll have to leave those bean bags here," he said.

Kesey rose from his seat and grabbed the guy around his neck. Zane grabbed him around the waist. There was nothing left for me to grab so I latched onto his leg, stiff as a tree.

"The worker is worthy of his hire," Kesey said, nose to nose.

The lugger held up his hands.

"You keep the bean bags."

We released our holds and he backed out of the bus.

"Walked away from another one, Chief," I said.

Kesey grimaced. "We are, after all, professionals. Take her away, George."

Until we were crossing the Bay Bridge, no one noticed that we'd left Krassner at the Fillmore.

We stopped at the Nut Tree at the junction of I-80 and 505 to gas up. Kesey went into the store and came back with a bag. He sat down on the seat and pulled a tube of super glue from the sack.

"What's that for?" I asked.

He pulled his lip back.

"Not again," I said.

He held out his other hand. The tooth.

"Fell out when we crossed the bridge. The final thrust, remnant of the Fillmore dust."

He handed me the tooth and super glue and leaned back. I squeezed a dollop of glue on the tooth and pushed it into the empty slot. I held it for a bit and let go. Kesey felt with his tongue, made a face and said, "That will do."

It did until we got home, when it came out again. The dentist, when he put Kesey's tooth back in, said, "Super glue won't work in the mouth. The juices dissolve the bond."

Back at the office, we opened the e-mail and found a message from Paul Krassner.

"Men. What happened?"

*We were moviemakers. Making a movie that had never
been done before. We would go out into America and
wherever we stopped—for gas, to swim, to grab a beer
in a bar, to camp out in a state park or a friend's yard—
we'd drag out our cameras and tape recorders and musical
instruments. Attired in our striped T-shirts, we mingled
with the people. Some kind of drama occurred and we joined
in, adding our LSD-laced creative juices to the mix. Our
movie then consisted of a series of episodes across the country,
a combination of real-life documentary and made-up
spontaneous action with music and dialog included.*
— Ken Babbs

70

What About Your Honor System?

"We can thank Steve Jobs for putting Apple computers in the classroom," Kesey said.

He was talking to Jeff Barnard, an Associated Press writer from southern Oregon who had come to the office to do an interview. After talking for a while, Jeff abandoned his notes and questions in order to find out exactly what we were doing in this room full of computer gear.

"Both Babbs's kids and my kids learned computers in high school," Kesey said, "and they bullied us into joining the digital world of storytelling. This brings us to *Twister, a Musical Catastrophe for the Millennium's End.* Set in the Land of Oz, it is peopled with a cast of archetypes ranging from the obvious, like the Tin Man and the Scarecrow, to the murky and mysterious, like Elvis and Frankenstein. Scramble them together in ever-bickering banter until they're all crazy at each other's throats, then snap them into sanity with a last-minute tearjerker twist guaranteed to touch everybody's heart."

"How did that go?" Jeff asked.

"Pretty well, considering. While doing the production live, we videotaped every performance, the goal being to publish *Twister* as a combination book and video. The book would be the script of the play with photos from performances. The video would be a two-hour lollapalooza. We were going to deal a limited number of *Twister* production packages over the Web.

"This kit would include the long-awaited video, some sharp-looking posters, classy tickets, free technical support, and a one-of-a-kind, hand-painted-by-yours-truly *Twister* T-shirt."

"We started our foray into digital mayhem with a basic desktop PC," I said. "Pat Mackey, a friend who worked at Symantec, helped us go online, dialup, where we snuck into chat sessions and were quickly recognized as total doofs—'Why are you shouting, Burly Ken?' someone asked. I had inadvertently hit caps lock. We gave up playing in the teenagers' room.

"One of my sons, Isaac, was working at Silicon Graphics in California. He got wind of what we were doing and talked his bosses into loaning us a video editing suite: a Silicon Graphics Indigo2 computer running Avid Media Suite Pro software hooked to four nine-gig Micropolis hard drives."

"Sounds impressive," Jeff said. "How did that work out for you?"

"Like a couple of cavemen trying to fly a jet plane," Kesey said.

When we heard the computer gear was coming, Kesey and I cleaned out the back room in the bus barn and put in tables and chairs and lights. A panel truck pulled up to the bus barn, two techs unloaded the gear and set it up. Two big monitors, the computer and keyboard and mouse.

"How do you turn this sucker on?" Kesey asked.

The tech pushed a button on the keyboard. The screen came to life with the Silicon Graphics logo. It faded and the Avid video editing program appeared. The other monitor glowed with an empty screen.

"That's the one where you'll see what you've edited," the tech said.

"Oh?" Kesey said.

The tech laughed.

"You'll get the hang of it. All the answers are in here."

He slapped a big book on the table. Kesey thumbed through it and handed it to me. I read a page, skipped to another, shook my head. Incomprehensible. I threw the book on a top shelf.

It was supposed to be a three-month deal but it took six weeks to get the hardware straightened out. We blew through four Cosmo 'boards. Kesey drove all the gear to Silicon Valley where he stayed until SGI had everything up and running. Then there was a six-week learning curve, getting to know the Avid editing system.

"I'd stay up all night breaking the machine," Kesey told Jeff Barnard, "and Babbs would spend all day fixing it."

"Thanks to Jacqui Perez at Avid Technology in Massachusetts, who knew the editing system inside out, upside down and backwards," I said. "She got a big kick out of our fuckups. She would laugh and then talk me through the cures, one keystroke at a time."

"So, what was the upshot?" Jeff Barnard asked.

"The upshot was that thanks to the contributing companies we had the gear long enough to finish *Twister*," Kesey said.

"Then they came and took everything away," I said.

We decided to keep going and work on the old 1964 bus movie. Kesey had our pal, Bob Laird, find a Macintosh video editing suite online: an Avid program on an 8100/100

Powermac with two nine-gig Avid hard drives. At the same time, we moved into a new office, up in the Pleasant Hill shopping center: two rooms in a one-time motel. With the post office in another room, the bank in front of our building, it was a perfect setting for our internet business.

We started doing straight online editing of the bus movie. The finished product would be a VHS cassette for an audience geared to six or eight people in the living room with a good TV using a stereo sound system. We'd make a master tape and from that make copies we would send straight to the viewer.

Kesey's son, Zane, and my son, Simon, set up in the other room with their computers and video gear. Kesey had his video editing station facing the wall at the back end of our room. I was at the other end with another video editing system, a blue and white Mac with Final Cut Pro. Phil Dietz, who did the bookkeeping and banking, had a desk facing the window. A couch sat against the wall just inside the door.

"What's that all about, those tie-dyed VHS covers hanging on the clothesline outside?" Jeff Barnard asked.

"Not tie-dye," Kesey said. "Dip-painting. Fill a tub with water, dribble different colored enamel paints on the top—Testor's model airplane paint works the best—dip the white cassette covers in and out and they're done, each one different."

"Are those the *Twister* videos?"

"No, we were done with that. Those are boxes for the bus movie VHS tapes. We had a problem with the bus movie. The sound was out of sync with the picture. But we learned we could speed up or slow down the sound to match the movie footage."

"The magic of video editing," I said. "Simon projected the 16 mm movie onto a screen and videotaped it onto a digital tape we then transferred into the computers. We transferred the sound off of the original reel-to-reel tapes and then, with both sound and picture in the timeline, could speed up or slow down the sound to match the moving picture. No more of that cutting and splicing movie film and audio tape by hand. We cyberhicks were blundering into new territory."

"You seem to have gotten it down, from the looks of things," Jeff Barnard said.

"We finished the first two parts of the bus movie," Kesey said. *"The Intrepid Traveler and His Merry Band of Pranksters Look for a Kool Place.* We made master VHS tapes and copied them on those decks in that rack against the back wall."

The rack held eight VHS recorder/players stacked vertically. The top player held the master tape, the other seven players held blank tapes. The way we worked it, two people bent over the rack, fingers poised on the buttons—GO! The motors whirred. Two hours later, seven tapes ejected. Labels printed from the computer were pasted on, the tapes slipped into their dip-painted sleeves, labels pasted on the sleeves, Kesey and I signed the boxes, and they were ready to go: mailed off to everyone who'd responded to the notice on our website, In-trepidTrips.com: *Gitcher Bus Movie tape by emailing us your address and sending twenty bucks when the movie arrives."*

"How's that working out?" Jeff Barnard asked.

"Pretty well," Kesey said. "We've got a nice little flow going. Phil packages them up, sends them out and puts the money in our bank account."

"What about your honor system on the paying? Any dead-beats?"

"No idea. We don't keep track."

Jeff got a kick out of that. He put his notebook away, shook hands and left. A few days later, his piece appeared in the newspaper. A slight intro about Kesey and life on the farm in Pleasant Hill, then the remainder of the article telling about our office: the video editing, the packaging, and the Internet marketing, ending with the information that for twenty bucks, interested parties could obtain the bus movie at www.intrepidtrips.com. The story went out on the AP all over the world. Orders poured in.

My son, Simon, realizing we couldn't keep up making seven copies of the tape at a time, sent a master tape to Portland. They were duped by the hundreds and, stuck in plain white sleeves, mailed to our office where we spent afternoons dip-painting and label-pasting. No more sitting and chatting with visitors. Anyone who showed up was put to work sticking labels on the tapes and sleeves. The bank account was swelling. Everyone was making a good salary as independent contractors.

We always looked forward to Kesey's arrival at the office, Phil and Simon and Zane and I already at our desks when he came through the door, his dog Happy at his heels, walking together to Kesey's station at the back of the room where he sank into his padded chair and Happy plopped down under the desk.

Kesey turned on the computer and, while it warmed up, swiveled in his chair and fed us our early morning morsel of scintillating news.

"Have you noticed how when men get older their ears get bigger? Due no doubt to the increasing role gravity is playing on the body. Could it be that it's part of the divine plan, that as we get older, we get deafer and, to compensate, our ears get larger so we pick up the sounds better?"

Not waiting for an answer, for he knew we weren't going to interrupt him before the climactic point, he continued: "Here it is, then. I'm going to give it away, free of charge, to anyone who wants it. You can take it and run with it, a million-dollar idea: The ear clip. A simple gizmo that clips on your ear around the point where the ear connects to your head, and behind the ear there's a soft piece that pushes the ear forward so it acts like an ear trumpet, funneling once-faint words into the earhole loud and clear."

His computer came to life, icons beaming, drawing him to

the keyboard. He hitched his chair forward, his eyes bored in, face set in the computer stare, time to get to work.

The next morning, Phil handed me a small box. Phil worked in metal—silver buckles and rings—and inside the box were two ear clips.

"*Perfecto majesto*," I said, and with his help, adjusted them on my ears. They stuck out like an alert goat's.

"How they working?" Phil asked.

"Won't know until the time comes," I said.

Kesey and Happy came through the door. Kesey sat at his chair, set the video editing pooter humming, then swiveled to face us. Phil and I waited, watching like eager schoolboys.

"Must be because it's football season I had this dream," Kesey said. "It was a long, drizzly, cold Saturday afternoon, and I was shivering in the car with my dad and brother Chuck, parked somewhere along the river with our shotguns between our knees, watching for ducks while we listened to the Ducks football game on the radio."

He paused and his eyes narrowed, staring at me.

"Go ahead," I said, "I'm all ears."

Kesey scowled, then continued. "'Yep,' Dad said. 'We're rootin' for 'em and shootin' for 'em.' You know, Babbs, you're too young for those ears. Give it another twenty or thirty years and you might grow into them."

"Thanks," I said. "By the way, happy birthday."

"Thank you. Who has a joint? I can't believe how much pot we're not smoking."

T he next day when he walked into the office, I could tell his duck feathers were ruffled. He plopped in his chair and didn't start telling us about the shows he had seen on TV the night before. He was definitely agitated.

"I've blown my stoic calm," he said. "Some jerk robbed our house yesterday and in broad daylight, too. When we got home from town we saw him running out and taking off in an old car. I was going to accept it, forgiveness nine-tenths of saintliness and all that."

He knew the old thing about getting fixated on something. Then you were obsessed and next thing you knew you were possessed. *Vengeance is mine,* saith the Lord. Okay, he'd let the Lord handle it. Then he discovered his dad's cufflinks were gone. That tore it. Particularly when some guy showed up later in the evening saying he'd been over to a friend's house and the friend was bragging about the burglary he'd pulled and it pissed this guy off when he found out whose house got robbed. He decided he'd go tell Kesey what he knew but he wouldn't say what the burglar's name was, just where he lived: in a trailer off Seavey Loop, on a dirt road, turn right at the first curve.

We headed out in my station wagon. My son, Simon, sat in the back seat with a wooden broom handle propped up between his legs. Someone might take it for a rifle. I grabbed the walk-around phone. It could be a walkie-talkie. Zane didn't bring a prop.

The trailer was there as described, a real speed-freak dump. Old cars and rusted auto parts scattered in a seedy lot. A sagged, mildewed singlewide. Kesey got out and I followed with the phone. The path was lined with canning jars filled with rocks. He banged on the screen door. No answer. He pulled it open.

"Wait a minute," I said. "You're not going in there? Speed and guns go together like milk and cookies."

"Not an apt comparison," he said and tried the door.

It was unlocked. He went inside. I put the phone to my ear and acted like I was reporting our situation. I could hear him banging around. Across the street there was movement in the curtains of an old farmhouse.

I was getting antsy and about to yell at him when he came outside.

"I found them."

He opened his hand, showing the cufflinks, round and golden with his dad's initials engraved: F.E.K.

A fierce old lady came striding across the street.

"What do you people want? There's no one home there. You shouldn't be snooping around."

"We're Mormons, ma'am," Kesey said, pushing past her. "You want to buy a subscription to *The Watchtower?*"

He didn't wait for an answer. We beat it out of there. He was thoughtful on the way back to the office.

"A real sad scene," he said. "All the windowsills were covered with Beanie Babies. There must have been hundreds of them."

He was quiet a minute.

"That Beanie Baby someone left at our house. It's not there anymore. I just realized it."

"We're not going back to look for it," I said.

D ogs use tire mail. They pee their message onto the tire and it goes all over town, all over the state, sometimes all over the country. Getting read everywhere with more messages being added.

One morning when I arrived at the office I was surprised to see Kesey outside, carrying a pail and a rag.

We went inside where his dog, Happy, was hiding under the table. Kesey put the bucket and rag in the bathroom. He came out and sat down.

"That man was so mad he was shaking," Kesey said. "I'd let Happy out and went looking for him and saw him down the line peeing on the tire of a new SUV. The man came out of his office and started yelling at Happy so I went down to cool the guy out. He was furious. 'Dogs are supposed to be on a leash,' the guy was yelling. 'Look at my wheel, all covered with dog piss.'"

Kesey said he took Happy back to the office, fetched the water and rag and washed the guy's wheel, the guy standing there ranting all the time: "Brand new car, just washed, just polished and look at it now," while Kesey swabbed with the rag.

A nother subject Kesey always expounded upon when he arrived in the office was the state of his various ills. A few years back he had an impediment in his nose removed and it left him without a sense of smell.

"It's starting to come back," he said one morning.

He didn't advise us to have our noses checked, not like when he found out he had type 2 diabetes and said we should all get tested. Happily, it wasn't catching. Then the time in England when we were doing a show, he gathered everyone together and told them he had the drizzly shits and for us all to be on the lookout for the same.

The downer was the morning he came in the office and said he had to have an operation. A black spot, the size of a quarter on his liver.

"Cancer," he said. "They're going to cut out a third of the liver, leave enough to do the job."

The day he went into the hospital I found a half pint of Tanqueray gin in the refrigerator in the office. I hefted a toast for success and finished the bottle.

All went well until a few days after the operation when I went to visit him. He was in bed, propped up, watching TV. He shut it off and that's when I noticed.

"What happened to your tooth?"

He grimaced.

"It came out when I bit down on a nut in my cereal. I put it on the tray and forgot about it when the nurse took the tray away. *Sayonara*, mofo."

I stayed and watched the Oregon football game with him. Next time I came to visit, he was in intensive care. An infection had set in. He couldn't fight it off and in a few days was comatose. I joined the family in the waiting room and we went in one at a time to say goodbye.

That night, I was awakened at three in the morning by the phone. Faye called to tell me Kesey had died. I dressed, rushed to the hospital and found his room empty, the bed made, no sign of anyone. I drove to the Kesey farm. As I approached, a flock of cowbirds, hundreds and hundreds, rose from the pasture, circled low and slowly spiraled upward into the first light of the oncoming dawn.

His spirit, I thought, being carried aloft by the birds. It takes that many of them.

I rode in the bus from the farm to the McDonald Theatre in Eugene for the packed-house memorial service. Afterwards, the coffin, coated with multi-swirled, dip-painted colors, was carried on the back platform of *Further* for the ride to the Kesey farm, where it was placed on a stand with the lid open for the line of people passing by to get a last look.

I paused and looked at Kesey, started to walk away, then turned back. His mouth wasn't right. It took me a minute. Then I got it. His lip had been pulled down on one side, covering the missing tooth. That damned tooth.

We lowered the coffin into the grave. The first shovelfuls hit with dull thumps. Then it was quiet as the hole was filled.

He rests alongside his son, Jed, who was killed on a University of Oregon wrestling trip to eastern Washington when the team van skidded off the road on an icy downhill curve.

The gravestone, a big Oregon rock, is inscribed:

KEN ELTON

KESEY

SEPT 17, 1935

NOV 10, 2001

"SPARKS FLY UPWARD"

The seasons roll on.
The years pass by.
The elders loosen the reins.
The youngsters take over.
The work continues.

Acknowledgments

First, my wife, Eileen, retired high school American Literature and Composition teacher who read and edited every version of the book, adding her insights and critique from the first draft to the last. Next, the renowned editor, David Stanford, brow furrowed, dictionary at hand, pencil clenched between his teeth, poring over every page and making perspicacious comments. My agent, Mary Krienke, of Sterling Lord Literistics, worked tirelessly, sending *Cronies* to every publishing house in America with no success, maybe because mainstream publishing wasn't ready for the kind of book she gravitates toward: "work that illuminates through humor or by playing with genre." Scott Landfield, owner and keeper of the books at Tsunami Books in Eugene, Oregon, for stepping up to the plate and hitting the ball out of the park when he decided to start Tsunami Press and make *Cronies* the first title out of the gate. Steve Gronert Ellerhoff, the computer maven and copy editor at Tsunami Press who went through the book top-to-bottom, to ensure against any typos or errors, plus prepared the book for the printer. Freddy Hahne, a professional preparer of books for printing, who assisted with type fonts and paper and layout. Charlie Winton, veteran retired publisher and once-owner of a book distribution company, who was invaluable with his wisdom and advice every step of the way.

About the Author

KEN BABBS, Ohio-bred and Ohio-born, is a graduate of Miami University in Oxford, Ohio, and a member of two NCAA tournament basketball teams. He was turned on to writing at Miami by Walter Havighurst, a fine scholar and scribe.

He attended graduate school at Stanford University, where he met Ken Kesey, Wendell Berry and other luminaries in the writing class. Five years in the Marine Corps followed, serving as a helicopter pilot, with his final tour of duty in Vietnam. He got off the chopper and onto the bus, *Further*, for the famous trip to Madhattan in 1964, chronicled in print by Tom Wolfe and filmed and taped by the Merry Pranksters.

He had forty-three years of collaborations and shenanigans with Kesey—doing shows, speaking engagements and musical catastrophes—plus, writing books, magazine articles, and co-editing six issues of *Spit In The Ocean*. Babbs co-wrote *Last Go Round* with Kesey, and went on to publish his novel, based on his experiences in Vietnam, *Who Shot the Water Buffalo?*

Married to a retired high school English teacher, he lives on a six-acre farm in the foothills of the Cascade Mountains.

He is reachable at www.skypilotclub.com.